The Qualities of a Citizen

D1292428

The Qualities of a Citizen

Women, Immigration, and Citizenship, 1870–1965

MARTHA GARDNER

PRINCETON UNIVERSITY PRESS   PRINCETON AND OXFORD

❧ Contents ❧

In the Shadow of the Law

Hoping to exchange the instability of 1918 revolutionary Mexico for the economic possibilities in New Mexico, Concepción de la Cruz and her family traveled from Sierra Mojada to the United States in search of work and peace. At the border, while her mother and her younger siblings had their clothing removed and disinfected, their scalps probed for lice, their bodies bathed and then inspected for disease and defect, and their intentions scrutinized during the arduous and demoralizing process of legal immigration, de la Cruz and her father were spared. "We all came together to the bridge, and they let my father and me pass and stopped my mother and the children and made them immigrate." "My father and I were never immigrated," she explained to United States immigration authorities.[1] How was that possible, officials queried? How had de la Cruz and her father managed to pass over the bridge that marked the border between the United States and Mexico without passing through the rigors of legal inspection?

Neither de la Cruz, nor the New Mexico immigration authorities, nor the records left behind offer an explanation for why de la Cruz crossed easily over a legal and geographic border her mother found daunting and prohibitive. Both women were subject to early twentieth-century immigration laws controlling the arrival of immigrants from Mexico, but in important ways their cases differed. De la Cruz sought work as a housekeeper, while her mother was responsible for the care of two young children. De la Cruz's work fit within a privileged space in the law reserved for women willing to work as domestic servants, while her mother ap-

---

[1] Concepción de la Cruz, casefile 54281/36C (1918); RINS, SCF, MI, reel 9. For details of immigration inspection process along U.S.–Mexico border, Irving McNeil, Acting Assistant Surgeon, to J. W. Tappan, Medical Officer in Charge, U.S. Public Health Service, El Paso, Texas, 22 December 1923, casefile 52903/29 (1923); RINS, SCF, MI, reel 3; Inspector in Charge, International Bride Foot Santa Fe Street, El Paso to Supervisor, Immigration Service, El Paso, Texas, 13 December 1923, casefile 52903/29 (1923); RINS, SCF, MI, reel 3; Inspector in Charge, Naco, Arizona to Supervisor, Immigration Service, El Paso, Texas 8 December 1923, casefile 52903/29 (1923); RINS, SCF, MI, reel 3; Jesse W. Thamos, Inspector in Charge, Ajo, Arizona to Inspector in Charge, Immigration Service, Tucson, Arizona 21 December 1923, casefile 52903/29 (1923); RINS, SCF, MI, reel 3. Abbreviations used throughout can be found in the section "A Brief Guide to Archival Sources" near the end of the book.

peared an unlikely candidate to immigration officials wary of new, economically dependent arrivals. Under United States immigration law, it has mattered whether a woman was a maid or a mother. "In the main, in the eyes of the law," a critical observer noted in 1922, "a man is a man, while a woman is a maid, wife, widow, or mother."[2]

Women immigrants endeavored to enter and to become citizens of the United States in the shadow of the law.[3] Immigrants like Concepción de la Cruz experienced arrival as a legal process, and many immigrants arrived at the border cognizant of the law and their place within it.[4] Just as it is a process of geographic, social, and economic mobility and cultural change, the process of leaving one nation and arriving in another is an experience of the law.[5] Mobility requires an intimate encounter of immi-

---

[2] "The Cable Act and the Foreign-Born Woman," *Foreign Born* 3, no. 8 (December 1922): 232.

[3] Although few historians have investigated immigrant women's historical relationship to the laws that governed their arrival, several important studies have explored immigrant women's interwoven roles in the economy, in the family, and in broader immigrant communities. On immigrant women as wage earners see, for example, Alice Kessler Harris, *Out to Work: A History of Wage-Earning Women in the United States* (New York: Oxford University Press, 1982); Elizabeth Ewen, *Immigrant Women in the Land of Dollars: Life and Culture on the Lower East Side, 1890–1925* (New York: Monthly Review Press, 1985); Vicki Ruiz, *Cannery Women, Cannery Lives: Mexican Women, Unionization and the California Food Processing Industry, 1930–1950* (Albuquerque: University of New Mexico Press, 1987). Work on immigrant women's roles in their families includes Virginia Yans-McLaughlin, *Family and Community: Italian Immigrants in Buffalo, 1880–1930* (Ithaca, N.Y.: Cornell University Press, 1977); Ewa Morawska, *For Bread with Butter: Life-Worlds of East Central Europeans in Johnstown, Pennsylvania, 1890–1940* (New York: Cambridge University Press, 1985); Susan A. Glenn, *Daughters of the Shtetl* (Ithaca, N.Y.: Cornell University Press, 1990). For work on immigrant women's roles in the community see, for example, Sarah Deutsch, *No Separate Refuge: Culture, Class, and Gender on an Anglo-Hispanic Frontier in the American Southwest, 1880–1940* (New York: Oxford University Press, 1987); Valerie J. Matsumoto, *Farming the Homeplace: A Japanese American Community in California, 1919–1982* (Ithaca, N.Y.: Cornell University Press, 1993); Judy Yung, *Unbound Feet: A Social History of Chinese Women in San Francisco* (Berkeley: University of California Press, 1995).

[4] As recent work exploring women's historical relationship to the law has suggested, the shadow of the law fell differently on women than it did on men. Linda Kerber has argued that the legal obligations of citizenship—to serve on juries, to work, to be taxed, or to take up arms in defense of the nation—precluded women's full and equal membership in the polity. Nancy Cott has argued that marriage law structured women's identity in the nation. She also suggests that by legitimating women's roles as wives and mothers, immigration and naturalization law sought to construct the body politic around specific and exclusionary understandings of race, gender, and citizen. Linda K. Kerber, *No Constitutional Right to Be Ladies: Women and the Obligations of Citizenship* (New York: Hill and Wang, 1998); Nancy Cott, *Public Vows: A History of Marriage and the Nation* (Cambridge: Harvard University Press, 2000).

[5] Historians have traditionally interpreted immigration as an experience of geographic, social, and economic mobility. Histories of arrival and exclusion, assimilation and cultural

grants and the state acted through legal procedures. In this encounter, some immigrants become residents, some aliens become citizens, some non-Americans become Americans, and some do not.

Helping to delineate the membership of a nation state, immigration and naturalization laws create a system of belonging and not belonging.[6] The place of immigrant women in this system has been judged by their work, their sexuality, their role in the family, and their race. By restricting how, why, when, and where women could enter, immigration law has protected a racially exclusive image of the American family, promoted a racially and sexually segmented labor force, and tied women's role in the nation to their domestic responsibilities in the American home. In defining the civic rights of aliens, immigrants, residents, and nationals, naturalization law tied race and gender to shifting understandings of the significance of moral character, family responsibility, and personal independence to citizenship. Historical debate over the law and its application make visible how Americans and would-be Americans, policy makers and immigrants, assessed the implications of women immigrants for the nation—their moral character, family status, race, poverty, marriage, citizenship, and alienage.

Over the twentieth century changing ideas of race difference were mapped onto those of gender to construct the walls and portals that governed immigrant women's arrival. In the late nineteenth and twentieth centuries, fluctuations in laws governing the arrival and citizenship of immigrant women were symptomatic of the major changes that punctuated this period—the growing concern about the nuclear family, the increased participation of women in wage labor, the shift from an industrial

resilience, or economic progress and stagnation are, for the most part, mobility stories. See, for example, John Bodnar, *The Transplanted: A History of Immigrants in Urban America* (Bloomington: Indiana University Press, 1985). Historians have debated the significance of cultural heritage, work skills, familial networks, wealth, race, and gender for the experience of mobility. Recent studies have suggested that mobility proved grudging for many immigrants facing tenacious racial discrimination and gender traditionalism. See, for example, Ronald Takaki, *Strangers from a Different Shore: A History of Asian Americans* (Boston: Little, Brown, 1989); George Sánchez, *Becoming Mexican American: Ethnicity, Culture, and Identity in Chicano Los Angeles, 1900–1945* (New York: Oxford University Press, 1993); Donna Gabaccia, *From the Other Side: Women, Gender, and Immigrant Life in the U.S., 1820–1990* (Bloomington: Indiana University Press, 1994). In addition to mobility, immigration history has become increasingly global in its frame of reference, increasingly interested in immigrant communities and social networks, and increasingly attentive to the ways in which notions of race and ethnicity structure immigrants' relationship to the polity and the economy. See essays collected by Virginia Yans-McLaughlin, *Immigration Reconsidered: History, Sociology, and Politics* (New York: Oxford University Press, 1990).

[6] For a discussion of women's relationship to law and to the nation see the essays collected by Gisela Bock and Susan James in *Beyond Equality and Difference: Citizenship, Feminist Politics and Female Subjectivity* (New York: Routledge, 1992).

to a service economy, the increase in migration to the United States of nonwhite, non-European peoples, and the growth of the United States as a global power. The perception of immigrant women and their citizen daughters either as assets or as threats to assimilation and nation building is linked to these important shifts in social, economic, and international power relationships.

This book is divided into three sections.[7] Part 1 explores the gendering of women immigrants and United States immigration policy from the first laws against Chinese prostitutes in the 1870s to the passage of the National Origins Act of 1924. In a period of derivative citizenship for women, the significance of race for the legal status of Americans and would-be Americans was gradually extended from naturalization law through immigration policy until it stood at its very center. In the context of massive movements of peoples to the United States, the combined racialization and sexualization of arriving immigrants allowed officials to carve out a definition of deviance that made marriage/morality and work/welfare the central tensions of immigration policy.

Part 2 begins with the formal recognition of women's independent citizenship in the 1920s and ends in 1965 with the formal renunciation of racial categories that structured the national origins system. Despite the erasure of sex and race differentials in the law, sex and race continued to be differences that mattered in the application of immigration and naturalization policy. Central to this effort to redefine the borders that separated insider and outsider was the symbol of "non-Americanism."[8] With fewer immigrants arriving at the nation's borders, an expanded definition and rhetoric of citizenship that included work and family challenged the status of nationals, long-term resident immigrants, and contract laborers living and working in the United States.

Part 3 suggests that post–World War II reforms laid the basis for a new gender system in immigration policy. With the advent of peace, women's traditional roles as wives and mothers reemerged as significant components of immigration law. Family reunification was embraced against a backdrop of exclusion for gay and lesbian immigrants and restriction for children born beyond the legal confines of marriage. The legal and moral

---

[7] I would like to thank Peggy Pascoe for her help in developing this three-part structure.

[8] For a discussion of current debates over the place of noncitizens in American law, see Peter H. Schuck, *Citizens, Strangers, and In-Betweens: Essays on Immigration and Citizenship* (Boulder, Colo.: Westview Press, 1998); Noah M. J. Pickus, ed., *Immigration and Citizenship in the Twenty-First Century* (New York: Rowman & Littlefield Publishers, 1998); Gerald L. Neuman, *Strangers to the Constitution: Immigrants, Borders, and Fundamental Law* (Princeton, N.J.: Princeton University Press, 1996); Bart van Steenbergen, ed., *The Condition of Citizenship* (London: Sage Publications, 1990); Peter H. Schuck and Rogers Smith, *Citizenship without Consent: Illegal Aliens in the American Polity* (New Haven, Conn.: Yale University Press, 1985).

legitimacy and illegitimacy of marriage and children became central concerns of immigration officials seeking to patrol of the borders of the postwar American family.

At the border, immigrants argued for the privilege of entry, while federal officials sought to interpret the law to protect national boundaries. The resulting conflict between immigrants and officials over how the law was understood and how it was applied, if it was flexible, and when it was broken is the central concern of this book. While the specifics of enforcement procedures have evolved over the twentieth century in response to increasing numbers of immigrants, along with the laws designed to regulate their arrival, the border has retained its significance as the site of assessment and judgment. Since the late nineteenth century, the power to regulate the nation's borders has rested entirely with Congress.[9] In practice, however, immigration law was interpreted, enforced, and adjudicated at the borders by federal officers of the Immigration Service. Law and bureaucracy met in the immigration experience as federal officials developed administrative policies with which to interpret immigrant racialized identities, and family and work histories within the letter of congressional law.[10] Detained in border facilities, immigrants and would-be citizens negotiated the administrative apparatus of the bureau.

Arriving at the nation's ports, immigrants were questioned by an immigration inspector and admitted only if they were clearly entitled to land. Doubtful cases were held for further review.[11] Appearance often became reality as inspectors evaluated which immigrants appeared morally re-

---

[9] Beginning in the late nineteenth century, the Supreme Court recognized the plenary power of Congress to define and exclude the unwelcome. The Constitution specifies that Congress shall establish a uniform rule of naturalization. The only reference to immigration lies in passages addressing the slave trade. The argument that Congress has almost unchecked power over immigration has been criticized by contemporary legal scholars. Louis Henkin, "The Constitution and United States Sovereignty: A Century of Chinese Exclusion and Its Progeny," 100 *Harvard Law Review* 853 (1987); Ibrahim J. Wani, "Truth, Strangers, and Fiction: The Illegitimate Uses of Legal Fiction in Immigration Law," 11A *Cardozo Law Review* 51 (1989).

[10] Immigration officials had the power to issue warrants, compel the appearance of witnesses, demand documentation, and conduct lengthy interrogations. Over the course of the twentieth century, elaborate and increasingly specific departmental procedures were developed to implement immigration laws. For example, in 1917, immigrants were granted the right to counsel but only during their appeal to the secretary of labor. For a discussion of departmental rules for Chinese immigrants, see Milton Konvitz, *The Alien and the Asiatic in American Law* (Ithaca, N.Y.: Cornell University Press, 1946), 37–45. For a discussion of bureau procedures up to the 1930s, see William C. Van Vleck, *The Administrative Control of Aliens: A Study in Administrative Law and Procedure* (New York: The Commonwealth Fund, 1932).

[11] The 1924 National Origins Act added an additional layer of administrative oversight by requiring immigrants to obtain a visa from a consular official. Van Vleck, *The Administrative Control of Aliens.*

spectable, racially eligible, or economically self-sufficient. Immigrants were also subject to medical examinations, which along the Mexican border included fumigation.[12] All immigrants who were not immediately admissible were held for a second hearing before a Board of Special Inquiry, a three-member panel that reviewed the case and voted to exclude or admit. Virtually all Chinese and Japanese immigrants had their cases heard before the Board of Special Inquiry, and an estimated twenty percent of Ellis Island arrivals were detained for further investigation.[13] Immigrants denied entry could appeal their cases to the commissioner-general of immigration, whose decisions were reviewed by the secretary of the department.[14] Immigrants who believed they were wrongly held by immigration authorities could petition the federal courts for relief and seek appeal through the judicial process.

During these appeals, immigrants faced detention, a grim and disheartening experience during which family members were separated and which could last weeks, months, and even years.[15] Husbands and wives had little and often no contact with one another, and family members were separated during questioning. Held at Ellis Island, New York for over two

[12] For a discussion of the arrival experience at Angel Island, see Him Mark Lai, Genny Lim, and Judy Yung, *Island: Poetry and History of Chinese Immigrants on Angle Island, 1910–1940* (Seattle: University of Washington Press, 1980). Jennifer Gee has richly documented the administrative procedures used at the Angel Island station; see Gee, "Sifting the Arrivals: Asian Immigrants and the Angel Island Immigration Station, San Francisco, 1910–1940" (Ph.D. diss., Stanford University, 1999). El Paso procedures are discussed in Jesse W. Thamos, Inspector in Charge El Paso, "Statement as to the Routine Examination of Arriving Aliens for the Immigration Service at This Port, 22 Dec. 1923," casefile 52903/29 (1923); RINS, SCF, MI, reel 3. A descriptive analysis of arrivals at Ellis Island is provided by Ann Novotny, in *Strangers at the Door: Ellis Island, Castle Garden, and the Great Migration to America* (Riverside, Conn.: The Chatham Press, 1971). In addition, see M. Mark Stolarik, ed., *Forgotten Doors: The Other Ports of Entry to the United States* (Philadelphia: The Balch Institute Press, 1988).

[13] Novotny, *Strangers at the Door*, 22. Unfortunately, the Immigration Bureau did not publish data on the number of immigrants held for questioning. Officially, Chinese cases were not heard before Boards of Special Inquiry until 1919; up until that time immigrants testified before one or more immigration inspectors with the Chinese Division. Enforcement of the Chinese exclusion laws was vested with customs officers at individual ports until 1903 when the Chinese Division was relocated within the Bureau of Immigration under the Department of Commerce and Labor.

[14] Sharon D. Masanz, *History of the Immigration and Naturalization Service: A Report Prepared at the Request of Senator Edward M. Kennedy, Chairman, Committee on the Judiciary of the United States Senate* (Washington: U.S. Government Printing Office, 1980).

[15] INS records contain evidence of suicides at Caste Garden, Angel Island, and Honolulu. Casefile 52706/4 (1889); RINS, SCF, EI, reel 5; INS file 4384/245 (1932); Chinese Wives of Native-Born American Citizens, box 4; INS, HDO, RG85; NA-PSR; INS files 1300–78976 and 1300–78977 (1948); Unprocessed; INS, SFD, RG85; NA-PSR; INS files 1300–78970, 1300–78976, and 1300–82828 (1952); Unprocessed; INS, SFD, RG85; NA-PSR.

months in 1921 while awaiting the board's decision in her case, Alexia Puskas wrote to the secretary of labor to request relief. "Two full months have passed since my case was appealed and I still wait,—wait until I am practically at my wits' ends," Puskas explained, "and it hardly seems to matter what will happen to me."[16]

The meticulous case files kept by the INS during these detention periods often include an extended interview with the woman seeking admission, as well as memos and reports from immigration investigators looking into immigrant women's behavior through interviews with family, friends, neighbors, and even employers.[17] In their interviews with INS officials, immigrant women strategized to achieve immigration or citizenship through calculated misrepresentations.[18] Often, when women immigrants altered their testimony under cross examination, they explained that their original answers had conformed to what they thought the law read, how they thought policy was applied, or what they had been advised to say by other immigrants. Indeed, in the case of Chinese applicants, INS officials maintained complete case files on immigrant families over multiple generations in order to check one family member's story against another's.[19]

[16] Alexia Puskas arrived from Czechoslovakia in 1921 with her daughter, intending to work as a domestic servant for her brother-in-law. Suspicious that her employment in a man's home lacked both moral propriety and fiscal certainty, immigration officials excluded Puskas as a likely public charge. Puskas [pseud.], INS file 54999–324 (1921); DJA-INS, acc. 60 A 600, box 1420; INS, DC, RG85; NA, DC.

[17] All interviews and supporting materials were transcribed and preserved in English. The bureau both employed official translators and made use of immigrant aid society service providers who were often fluent in the languages of those they sought to assist. Little is known about how translators were selected or evaluated, and no written record remains of a translation process. Arriving immigrants were asked if they understood the translator, and when they answered affirmatively the interrogation proceeded. Undoubtedly, translators could dramatically influence the outcome of women's appeals by helping them respond appropriately to examiners' questions or by frustrating women's efforts to articulate their claims to membership. INS officials were aware of this potential abuse of power, and investigations of fraud were periodically conducted in which evidence of extortion and bribery was uncovered. Because the hearings are available only in their English translation, it is difficult to evaluate the quality and honesty of specific translators and the effect this may have had on individual women's cases. Him Lai notes in the case of Chinese applicants that interpreters, along with immigration inspectors, could be easily bribed to reach a satisfactory decision. Lai, "The Chinese Experience at Angel Island," East/West 10 (1976): 7–9; Lucie Chen Hirata, "Free, Indentured, Enslaved: Chinese Prostitutes in Nineteenth-Century America," Signs 5 (1979): 11.

[18] For example, Faith Hopkins confessed to International Institute staffers that she had hidden her marriage from immigration officials for fear it would jeopardize her application for naturalization. Faith Hopkins [pseud.] casefile 12–13 (1952) box 190; International Institutes of Minnesota.

[19] Detailed maps of Chinese villages and diagrams of extended kin networks were continually referenced and revised as new immigrants told their stories.

At the border, women citizens returning from abroad could find themselves detained and deported as inadmissible "immigrants." Women who did not fit within the racial dyad of American citizenship, and thus did not appear to be citizens, were at particular risk. Faced with deportation, would-be citizens were asked to provide immigration and naturalization officials suspicious of their claims to membership with birth certificates, evidence of residence, proof of racial status, and documentation of their marriages and family histories.

Along with those women seeking naturalization and women citizens attempting to prove their citizenship, immigrant women who could find no relief before immigration authorities or social service providers sought legal redress before the federal courts. Court officers reviewed women's testimony and the opinions of immigration officials and decided the law's application.[20] The federal courts thus functioned as a second border wherein women, immigration officials, naturalization examiners, and their lawyers debated to whom the law should be applied. The judiciary has possessed only limited oversight over the process of exclusion and deportation.[21] Despite this, would-be immigrants and would-be citizens continued to challenge their exclusions at the border before the courts, and at times the federal courts could prove more lenient and offer women immigrants some relief. The power of judicial review, however, was limited.[22]

What follows is a history of the effort to belong; a belonging that was shaped by both legal definitions of membership produced by the state and personal meanings expressed by immigrants, residents, and citizens. State-defined membership in the nation was categorical in procedure but fluid in practice. Shifting constructions of race, marital legitimacy, moral conduct, work skills, varying interpretations of citizenship law, and inconsistent enforcement of statutes constantly changed the terms and requirements of state-defined membership. On this unstable ground, immigrants, residents, citizens, noncitizens, and their children created their own self-defined issues of belonging, conceptions of membership that often directly

---

[20] The federal courts could not, and did not, seek to judge the constitutionality of expulsion provisions but only whether the law as written was fairly applied.

[21] Arriving immigrants held in the United States during the late nineteenth century could and did appeal their detention to the courts through writs of habeas corpus. By 1894, Congress legislated that the decisions of immigration officials and the secretary of the treasury were to be "final." Eleven years later, the Supreme Court interpreted the 1894 legislation to apply to those arriving "immigrants" who claimed to be "citizens." *United States v. Ju Toy* 198 U.S. 253 (1905).

[22] Beginning in 1903 with the Japanese immigration case, judicial review was widened in deportation cases as courts demanded greater evidence of due process. William B. Ball, "Judicial Review in Deportation and Exclusion Cases," *Interpreter Releases* 34, no. 20 (10 June 1957), RACNS, reel 11.

challenged the law and its application. Americans, would-be Americans, and permanent immigrants flexed the law where they could, broke it when they felt they must, as they carefully constructed stories of work skills, family relationships, and moral behavior to prove their admissibility.

Immigration and naturalization law has endeavored to create race and gender categories; so too have women inhabited, challenged, transgressed, and violated these categories in their efforts to become members of the nation. As immigration officials endeavored to fit the law onto arriving immigrants, immigrants sought to mold their testimony to fit within the law. As a result, arrival interviews with immigration officials and naturalization petitions before officers of the court are structured by multiple, often unstated, historically contingent understandings of the law. What is left behind from the efforts of women immigrants to gain admission and the efforts of administrators and policy makers to adjudicate borders is a set of legal stories, stories which are as much about citizens as they are about immigrants, as much about those inside the nation as those who remained outside.

∞ Part I ∞

WIVES, MOTHERS, AND MAIDS

CHAPTER ONE

Immigrants, Citizens, and Marriage

Testifying in 1930 before the House Committee on Immigration and Naturalization, Kenneth Y. Fung, executive secretary of the Chinese American Citizens' Alliance of San Francisco, argued for the primacy of moral law over the dictates of immigration policy. The threat to the nation, Fung suggested, lay not in the inclusion of more racial others, but in the exclusion and separation of increasing numbers of families. "The home is the basis of the life of the Nation," Fung warned, "and without a wife and mother a home can hardly exist." Fung cautioned committee members against allowing the appearance of racial difference to cloud what united all Americans: a belief in the moral sanctity of the family.[1] A wife's place was with her husband, Fung argued, as a mother to future citizens and as a bulwark against moral decay.[2]

At the heart of Fung's testimony was a debate over the place of wives in United States immigration and naturalization law. For many Americans and would-be Americans, family unity was a civic right. Immigrant wives circumvented racial, geographic, and medical exclusions through their privileged position in the law. When she married a citizen or a resident immigrant, an alien woman became an alien wife, and her new marital status could make all the difference in determining her rights and privileges under the law. Immigration and naturalization laws dictating racial exclusion collided with those encouraging family reunification. As a result, while loyal wives would continue to find favor in the law for much of the nineteenth and twentieth centuries, suspect marriages were held

---

[1] According to Fung, "A law permanently separating a husband from his wife is an unnatural law," a law "contrary to common humanity" and contrary to "the institutions of civilized society." Testimony of Kenneth Y. Fung, *Wives of American Citizens of the Oriental Race: Hearings before the Committee on Immigration and Naturalization*, 1930, HR 2404, HR a5654, HR 10524; House of Representatives, 71st Cong., 2nd sess., Washington, D.C., 548.

[2] Fung testified before the House Committee as an advocate for legislation that would allow Chinese wives of American citizens to join their husbands in the United States despite severe race-based exclusion laws that prohibited the immigration of people from Asia. As committee members questioned Fung, concerns about miscegenation and racial heterogeneity weighed heavily against arguments for gender traditionalism and the right of a male citizen to the company of his alien wife. Ibid., 548, 554.

responsible for the vulnerability of the nation's geographic borders and the deterioration of its uniquely racialized national identity. Powerful traditions of class, race, and ethnic difference brought these women and their marriages under investigation as immigrant women arrived at the border and claimed a special status as wives.

The principle of coverture, which linked husband and wife into one legal identity in marriage, was an important strategy for immigrant women in the late nineteenth and early twentieth centuries. Beginning in 1855, any alien woman who wed an American citizen became a citizen by virtue of her marriage, and until the 1920s and 1930s a woman's citizenship status was derivative, through her father as a child and through her husband as a married woman. The law remained mute on the status of American women who married alien men until 1907. That year, Congress legislated that any American woman who married an alien would herself become an alien.

Ideals of domesticity remained a fixture of immigration law and immigrant women's tactics long after American women had won the rights to independent suffrage and citizenship in the 1920s and 1930s. Family status gave immigrant wives an entrée into the United States that for many women would have been otherwise impossible in the face of racial, medical, economic, moral, or geographic exclusions. While marriage presented a weakness in the law to some officials, it presented a strategic strength to many women immigrants who drew on their status as wives to achieve entry into the nation.

Yet entering as family members necessarily tied these women more closely to their roles as wives and mothers. Domesticity became the price of admission.[3] Traditional notions of domesticity governed immigration and judicial officials' evaluations of women's conduct by insisting that admissible wives remain loyal to their husbands and to their work in the home.

Throughout the period from 1880s through the 1930s, race proved a constant refrain in the efforts by legislators, immigration, and judicial authorities to articulate the qualities of a loyal wife and to adjudicate the boundaries of a legal marriage. Upon marriage to a citizen, women who were nonwhite, nonblack, or Native Americans living on reservations became the *alien* wives of American citizens.[4] Ideals of domesticity granted

---

[3] Donna Gabaccia notes that the emphasis on domesticity in American immigration law paralleled colonial policies in Zimbabwe. Gabaccia, *From the Other Side*, 40; Teresa A. Barnes, "The Fight for Control of African Women's Mobility in Colonial Zimbabwe, 1900–1939," *Signs* 17, no. 3 (spring 1992): 586–608.

[4] Similarly, as a result of United States imperialism overseas, nonwhite women from Hawaii, the Philippines, and Puerto Rico became incorporated into the body politic as "nationals," neither citizens nor aliens.

these women some privileges while anxieties about race worked to curtail their civic rights. The result was a legal limbo between full citizenship and alien status within which immigration officials, the courts, and immigrants themselves debated the consequences of citizenship, the importance of family, and the significance of race.

LOOKING LIKE A WIFE: RACE AND MARRIAGE

Family-based exemptions proved critical for Asian immigrant communities living in the United States. As "wives," Asian women occupied a privileged place in immigration and naturalization law that enabled them to circumvent the law's racial exclusions. Treaties negotiated with China and Japan regulated the numbers of Asian immigrant men who could migrate to the mainland as laborers through severe race-based exclusion laws, while at the same time recognizing the right of Chinese merchants and Japanese workers to the company of their wives. Although family status offered Asian women possible entry, their status as members of an unwanted and vilified racial minority guaranteed them scrutiny when they arrived at the border.

Even before the Chinese exclusion movement of the 1880s, race provided a significant tool for defining both the borders of citizenship and the status of wives under immigration and naturalization law. Beginning in 1855, and continuing until the early decades of the twentieth century, any woman who married a citizen was considered a citizen by virtue of that marriage. The act of 1855 stipulated, however, that only those women who might themselves be naturalized were eligible for derivative naturalization through their husbands. Courts interpreted the phrase "might herself be naturalized" to refer to the strict racial requirements under naturalization law.[5] As a result, the 1855 law allowing derivative naturalization for wives of citizens was limited to white women. Through racially exclusive derivative naturalization policies, Congress sought to expedite the Americanization process of foreign-born mothers of American-born children in a way that emphasized the specific color coding of American nationalism.

Reconstruction opened citizenship to some while denying it to others. Following the Civil War, the act of July 14, 1870 provided for the citizenship of "aliens of African nativity and to persons of African descent," extending derivative naturalization to African American women.[6] How-

---

[5] *Kelly v. Owen* 7 Wall 496 (1868).

[6] The act was held to apply to African Americans in *Broadis v. Broadis* 86 F. 951 (N.D.Cal. 1898); in this case the wife had been a British subject before marriage.

ever, faced with insistent and violent denials of their civil rights, citizenship for black women was little more than a chimera. The Dawes Act of 1887 offered citizenship to Native American men willing to forsake their claims to reservation lands and sever their relations with tribal communities and native governments. Native American women's derivative citizenship required a similar Faustian bargain.[7] In 1888, Congress broadened the list of eligible women by including Native American women who married citizens and lived off tribal lands among white society.[8] Thus, by the end of the nineteenth century, citizenship was possible only for white, black, and Native American women living off the reservation who married American citizens. Nonwhite and nonblack could become citizens only through birth, never through marriage.

Chinese immigrants, and by racial association all other Asian peoples, were deliberately excluded from Reconstruction era policies that had expanded naturalization to African Americans and Native Americans under certain conditions.[9] Until 1952, access to the privileges of citizenship would be possible only for second-generation, American-born children of Asian ancestry who were guaranteed citizenship under the Fourteenth Amendment.[10] Over the course of the late nineteenth and twentieth centu-

---

[7] In *Hatch v. Ferguson* 57 F. 959 (N.D.Wash. 1893) a Native American woman born in the United States and widow of an American citizen was found entitled to bring suit in a federal court against another citizen. Bringing suit, historically, has been a right preserved for citizens (*Dred Scott v. Sandford* 60 U.S. 19 How. 393 [1857]).

[8] 25 Stat. at. l. 392 (ch. 818, sec. 2); W. E. Waltz, *The Nationality of Married Women: A Study of Domestic Policies and International Legislation* (Urbana: The University of Illinois Press, 1937), 24. A 1906 report by the secretary of state outlining citizenship and expatriation laws for the House of Representatives explained that Native American women could be citizens only if they chose to live off the reservation, among white society. *Letter from the Secretary of States submitting Report on the Subject of Citizenship, Expatriation, and Protection Abroad*, 1906, H Doc., 326; House of Representatives, 59th Cong., 2nd sess, Doc No. 326, Washington, D.C., 59. Also see Wendy Wall, "Gender and the Citizen Indian," *Writing the Range: Race, Class, and Culture in the Women's West*, ed. Elizabeth Jameson and Susan Armitage (Norman: University of Oklahoma Press, 1997), 202–229.

[9] 1878, in *In re Ah Yup*, the California Circuit Court ruled that Chinese applicants were racially classified as Mongolians and thus ineligible for naturalization. 1922, *Ozawa v. United States*, the Supreme Court held that Japanese applicants were not white and could not be naturalized. 1922, *United States v. Bhagat Singh Thind*, the Supreme Court held that Asian Indians were also not white and were racially ineligible for citizenship. Not until 1952 were all racial restrictions on naturalization eliminated. For additional cases, Ian F. Haney L„pez, *White by Law: The Legal Construction of Race* (New York: New York University Press, 1996).

[10] In *Wong Kim Ark* 169 U.S. 649 (1898), the Supreme Court found that, although the United States had a right to determine which classes of people would be entitled to citizenship, a child born in the United States of Chinese parents acquired citizenship by virtue of the Fourteenth Amendment. The logic was repeated in 1925 when the State Supreme Court of Washington found children born in the United States of Japanese parents were citizens under the Fourteenth Amendment; see *State v. Kosai* 234 Pac. 5 (1925).

ries, the Fourteenth Amendment's insistence on the irrelevance of race to birthright citizenship came into direct conflict with persistent fears surrounding immigrant women's reproduction, fears that inscribed race difference into the very fabric of American naturalization law.

The series of laws passed between 1862 and 1917 made immigration from Asia an increasing impossibility.[11] Despite growing racial animosity and legislative prohibitions, within the network of race-based exclusions a few "exempted" categories remained, most significantly for Chinese and Japanese women married to admissible Asian and Asian American men. The 1882 Chinese Exclusion Act, which had brought a virtual halt to Chinese immigration and categorically prevented Chinese immigrants from becoming naturalized citizens, did recognize the rights of Chinese merchants to be accompanied to the United States by their wives, children, and domestic servants as members of their household.[12] The 1907 Gentleman's Agreement negotiated with Japan recognized the right of the United States to prohibit the arrival of new Japanese laborers but also acknowledged its responsibility to allow those Japanese immigrants already in the United States to send for their wives.[13] The third group of women able to permeate the net of race-based exclusions were the wives of native-born Chinese and Japanese American citizens. For Asian immigrant women, entering as wives (and daughters) provided one of the only means of access.[14] Negotiating within the shadow of the law, Chinese and Japanese immigrant women saw access in marriage and family status.

[11] By 1917, Congress had established the Asian barred zone, defined by longitude and latitude, prohibiting all immigration from Asia. With the Immigration Act of 1924, Congress would finalize its systematic exclusion of Asian immigrants by prohibiting the immigration of all immigrants ineligible to citizenship. See E. P. Hutchinson, *Legislative History of American Immigration Policy, 1789–1965* (Philadelphia: University of Philadelphia Press, 1981), 65–66; Bill Ong Hing, *Making and Remaking Asian America through Immigration Policy, 1850–1990* (Stanford, Calif.: Stanford University Press, 1993), 19–38; Sucheng Chan, ed., *Entry Denied: Exclusion and the Chinese Community in America, 1882–1943* (Philadelphia: Temple University Press, 1991).

[12] The Burlingame Treaty, negotiated with China in 1880, allowed Chinese merchants to immigrate to the United States, and to bring their body and household servants with them as well. Courts interpreted "body and household servants" to include Chinese wives. This treaty right guaranteeing merchants the ability to work in the United States and to have their wives with them continued to be recognized and respected despite ever-increasing racial restrictions.

[13] Concerned with the status of its citizens in foreign counties, Japanese government regulations allowed only farmers and businessmen to send for their wives. By 1920, the Japanese Government agreed to stop issuing visas to Japanese wives, bringing the "picture bride" period to an abrupt end. Yuji Ichioka, *The Issei: The World of the First Generation Japanese Immigrants, 1885–1924* (New York: The Free Press, 1988).

[14] For example, in 1921, well over half (sixty-one percent) of all Japanese women admitted to the mainland were wives of residents, eighty-four percent of Chinese women arrived in the United States as wives of either merchants or citizens. *Annual Report of the Commissioner General of Immigration to the Secretary of Labor* (1921), 34–35, 144–152.

Immigration officials suspected, however, that most of the Asian women who arrived at the nation's ports were neither virtuous nor married women, as they claimed to be. Wary of the relationship between restrictive law and exemptions for wives, immigration authorities sought to evaluate women applicants as Asian women, thus targets of racial restriction laws, rather than as wives and beneficiaries of family reunification policies.

The issue for the federal courts, however, was not a woman's admissibility as an immigrant but the rights of her husband. Importantly, the courts found in favor of men's rights to their wives, but not necessarily women's rights to join their husbands. In hearing women's appeals for entry, the federal courts emphasized the significance of women's roles as "wives" to understanding their status as Chinese women.[15] Treaty rights permitting Chinese merchants to bring their household servants with them implied a related right to bring their wives and children. "It is impossible to believe," one court insisted, "that parties to this treaty which permits the servants of a merchant to enter the country with him, ever contemplated the exclusion of his wife and children." Courts reasoned that the treaty neglected to mention wives within its provisions not because it intended to exclude these women, but because it assumed a wife belonged with her husband.[16]

Marriage in immigration and naturalization law embraced traditional gender roles while still insisting on the significance of racial difference by withholding the privileges of citizenship. Theories of common law coverture linked a wife's legal identity to that of her husband. Importantly, however, for Asian women, racial and political status remained their own. Asian women who married native-born citizens took on their husbands' class status, such as merchant under the provisions of the treaty negotiated with China, but not his political status as an American citizen.

Theories of shared domicile foundered on racial difference; Asian women were racially ineligible for citizenship and thus could not become citizens upon marriage to a citizen. Tsoi Sim, wife of a native-born citizen, was

[15] Beginning in the 1890s, in evaluating the application of immigration laws to the wives of Chinese merchants, the federal courts confirmed a husband's right to the company of his wife by treaty (in the case of merchants) and by citizenship (for native-born men). Moreover, the courts ruled that a woman's economic status was determined and contingent upon her husband's; if he was a merchant then she too had merchant status. *In re Chung Toy Ho and Wong Choy Sin*, 42 F. 398 (D. Or. 1890); Chan, "Exclusion of Chinese Women," 114.

[16] *In re Chung Toy Ho* 42 F. 398 (D.Or. 1890). Ten years later, the U.S. Supreme Court confirmed the lower court's ruling. Mrs. Gue Lim, wife of a merchant working in Washington, was arrested under charges that she was in fact a laborer. In finding in favor of Mrs. Gue Lim, the Supreme Court reiterated the reasoning of the lower court—husbands, by right, were entitled to the company and service of their wives. *United States v. Mrs. Gue Lim* 176 U.S. 459 (1900).

arrested in 1901 and held for deportation.[17] Both the United States commissioner of immigration and the U.S. District Court of California ruled that Tsoi Sim was deportable as a manual laborer. The Ninth Circuit Appeals Court, however, disagreed. Significantly, the case hinged not on her status, but on his citizenship. The appeals court emphasized that not only were her rights as a wife at stake, "but his rights, as well as hers, are involved." The sanctity of marriage should overrule the dictates of immigration law, the court argued, "her husband's domicile became her domicile," and while an Asian woman was not entitled to derivative citizenship, she was entitled to live with her husband in the United States.[18] As a result, Asian women like Tsoi Sim entered a kind of legal limbo, entitled to join their husbands but not entitled to the rights of derivative citizenship.[19]

As wives of merchants or financially independent workers, Asian women were expected to appear "respectable." Respectability was marked by race, gender, and class codes that immigration authorities believed could be relied on to authenticate wives or expose women as frauds, and immigration officials evaluated women's demeanor and appearances accordingly. Ideals of white middle-class domesticity, when viewed through race-colored glasses and articulated in immigration law, challenged Chinese and Japanese women to prove their status as "wives" loyal to their husbands, and as "housewives" economically dependent on their bread-winning spouses. When Leong Shee arrived with her son in 1881 to join her husband, the San Francisco official linked Leong She's bound feet, "a mark of respectability," to the veracity of her claim to be the wife of a merchant.[20] Women who *appeared* as respectable wives and mothers

[17] By 1893, Chinese laborers were required to identify themselves to immigration officials and receive in turn certificates verifying their legal residency in the United States. Tsoi Sim was charged with failing to register for a laborer's certificate; this of course was a technicality and the essence of the charge was the suspicion that she was in the United States illegally. There is no record in the extant documents detailing why Tsoi Sim came to the attention of immigration authorities. She had immigrated as a child to the United States with her parents in 1882. When she was twenty-one years old, she married Yee Yuk Lum, a native-born citizen.

[18] *Tsoi Sim v. United States* 116 F. 920 (9th Cir. 1902).

[19] In evaluating the 1900 appeal of Li Ham Shi, a Chinese woman and wife of a native-born citizen, the solicitor for the Treasury Department ruled, "There is no question of citizenship as to the wife involved. She does not apply to be landed because of any supposed right to be lawfully 'naturalized,' but because she is the wife of a native-born citizen of the United States." As long as she made no pretense to citizenship, Li Ham Shi's right to live with her husband superseded immigration exclusions based on race. "Letter by the Assistant Secretary to the Collector of Customs, San Francisco," case number 22,551, *Treasury Decisions* (Jan.–Dec., 1900), vol. 3; as cited in *Tsoi Sim v. United States* 116 F. 920, 925 (9th Cir. 1902).

[20] Leong Shee, INS file 10–3–1885/336; AICF, box 7 3240H; INS, SFD, RG85; NA-PSR; also see Chan Shee, INS casefile 14851/9–3 (1915), AICF; INS, SFD, RG85; NA-PSR.

were often assumed to *be* respectable wives and mothers. Despite discrepancies in Chan Shee's testimony, the immigration inspector concluded in favor of apparent respectability: "The applicant Chan Shee, has the appearance of being a family woman and undoubtedly the child she has with her at present time, namely, San Gim Way is her child."[21]

Appearances, however, could be deceiving. In the eyes of immigration officials, women were "alleged" wives before they were legal wives. Immigration officials suspected that Wong Lai's marriage was a fraud, and as evidence they pointed out that Wong appeared much older that the traditional Chinese bride, "Will you explain to me how it is that this woman was 35 years old before she was ever married. I have been taking Chinese cases here for the past nine years and this is the first time in that nine years that I have ever seen a man marry a Chinese woman 35 years old."[22]

Assessing the veracity and legitimacy of marital relationships, immigration officials became the self-appointed gatekeepers of the American family. Chinese women immigrants, in particular, were subjected to long and detailed questioning during which they were expected to demonstrate an intimate knowledge of the specifics of their marriage ceremony, familial relations of their husband's distant kin, and village geography. Women were often required to provide witnesses who could corroborate their status as wives.[23] Immigration officials waited to interview Chinese wives until they had gathered testimony from their husbands, relatives, and even neighbors living in the United States. The practice of having husbands and wives testify against one another in violation of common law spousal immunity traditions underscored official policy that these women were single until proven wives.

As a result, women's narratives of marriage and family life in China were compared with a prerecorded script to which women had limited access. Moreover, questions about a husband's distant family or the layout of his home village necessarily privileged the husband, while asking the wife to recall familial details she had never known or places she had never seen. Couples often rehearsed elaborate family histories before their arrival into American ports, a practice endlessly frustrating to immigration inspectors who demanded increasing levels of exactness from would-be wives.[24] Women were often accused of lying when their story did not

[21] Chan Shee, INS file 15287/4–11 (1916), AICF; INS, SFD, RG85; NA-PSR.

[22] Wong Lai, INS file 4383/17 (1916); Chinese Wives of Merchants, box 1; INS, HDO, RG85; NA-PSR.

[23] See, for example, Wong Shee, INS file 4383/2 (1916); Chinese Wives of Merchants, box 1; INS, HDO, RG85; NA-PSR.

[24] Jennifer Gee, "Housewives, Men's Villages, and Sexual Respectability: Gender and the Interrogation of Asian women at Angle Island Immigration Station," in *Asian/Pacific Is-*

compare well with those of their husbands, relatives, or neighbors. Unsatisfied with her responses to questions about her husband's children, Chung Shee was shown a picture of her husband and asked to identify it. Inspectors noted that she hesitated before offering final confirmation:

Q: Do you know that man (alleged husband)?
A: (After several minutes hesitation) That is my husband.
Q: Why did it take you several minutes to recognize that picture?
A: I was afraid that I would be mistaken.

In concluding in favor of exclusion, the immigration officer raised serious doubts about Chung Shee's marriage and her claim to be a wife. Faced with his wife's deportation, Chung Shee's husband confessed that he had in the past identified another woman as his wife. He had hoped to have this woman join him in the United States, but when that became impossible he sent for Chung Shee.[25] Immigration inspectors once highly critical of Chung Shee now reassessed her appearance, making particular note of her "bound feet," as that of a respectable Chinese wife. However, lingering doubts remained in the minds of immigration inspectors, "It is barely possible that applicant may be the wife of some laborer and is being brought here to join him, and in order to prevent the possibility of such a slip, I shall require that the applicant and her alleged husband be married according to the laws of this State before she is permitted to land."[26]

Women faced a barrage of questions, many of which they were not in a position to answer, and yet they were under immense pressure to provide responses that exactly matched those offered by their husbands. "Discrepancies" in the testimony between husband and wife were taken as evidence of fraud. Pak Mi She arrived in San Francisco in 1923 with her husband, a native-born citizen, and marriage certificate in hand. At sixteen years old, Pak Mi She's testimony was tentative and halting. Carried in a sedan chair from her village to the railroad station and then on to Hong Kong, Pak Mi She was unable to answer the questions put to her about the trip from her village to Hong Kong, where the couple embarked for the United States. "I don't know," she explained to officials, "I couldn't see."[27] Lum She arrived in Honolulu as the wife of a native-

---

lander American Women: A Historical Anthology, ed. Shirley Hune and Gail Nomura (New York: New York University Press, 2003).

[25] His mother was opposed to the first wife immigrating, so the husband had given information about the second with hopes she could join him in the United States.

[26] Chung Shee, INS file 10015/3530, 101 (1904); AICF; INS, SFD, RG85; NA-PSR.

[27] After reviewing her testimony, along with her husband's, the inspector concluded: "Both the applicant and her husband are of a low order of intelligence and of poor memory. Their statements agree in some things but do not agree in others, as to matters which you would think they both ought to know very well." Despite apparent doubts, they were admit-

born Hawaiian in 1918. She too was rigorously questioned, and she too faltered under such intense scrutiny:

Q: What did your husband do in China before he came to Hawaii?
A: Nothing.
Q: He said he had something to do himself when he came, and told what he had been doing?
A: He was planting rice.
Q: That is not what he said.
A: He was farming and planting rice.[28]

"Discrepancies" and "inconsistent statements" led immigration officials to find for Lum She's exclusion, offering as evidence the fact that "Lum She says there is one bed room in her house in China, while Sin Lin gives two bed rooms, and four rooms all told, Lum She giving three all told. This may not amount to much, but nevertheless it is a matter of which she should have knowledge."[29]

By definition, women who entered as wives were economically dependent on their husbands. Women suspected of working outside the home were condemned as laborers and held subject to laws prohibiting the arrival of Chinese and Japanese unskilled laborers. To confess any interest in or intention of working outside the home would bring the hapless wife out from under the cover of her exempted status and into the excludable category of laborer or even prostitute. Women denied that they had independent work skills that could be applied to work outside the home. Japanese picture brides presented themselves as "housewives" with intentions to work in the home and for their husband. When Yoshida Kinu arrived in Seattle in 1906 authorities refused to recognize the validity of her marriage to a first cousin; without the support of a breadwinner, a wife without a husband, authorities ruled she be excluded as "likely to become a public charge."[30] Yoshida assured authorities she would seek work as a

---

ted, she as the wife of a citizen. Pak Mi She [pseud.], INS file 4384/279 (1923); Chinese Wives of Native-Born American Citizens, box 4; INS, HDO, RG85; NA-PSR.

[28] Lum She, INS file 4384/63 (1918); Chinese Wives of Native-Born American Citizens, box 2; INS, HDO, RG85; NA-PSR.

[29] In his final ruling, the immigration inspector sited the significant role observation played in his decision, "After careful consideration of this case, and my personal knowledge and observation of the applicant—LUM SHE—while in the detention quarters, I am of the opinion that she is a dull and ignorant woman. She has a peculiar look and stare on her face, and keeps herself apart somewhat from the other Chinese in detention, and has the child with her constantly." Lum She, INS file 4384/63 (1918); Chinese Wives of Native-Born American Citizens, box 2; INS, HDO, RG85; NA-PSR.

[30] At the time, Seattle authorities did not recognize picture marriages as legally binding and regularly remarried Japanese women arriving as picture brides. In this case, authorities

domestic servant and would not become a public burden. Unfortunately, by admitting her intention to seek work outside the home Yoshida was no longer an inadmissible wife and became instead an excludable laborer.[31] By contrast, when May Shee arrived in San Francisco in 1928 as a merchant's wife, she denied any intention of working outside the home while living in the United States:

Q: What pursuits have you been following in China since your marriage?
A: I was housekeeper, with the exception of two years when I taught school—that was in CR 14 and CR 15 inclusive (1925 and 1926).
Q: What is your purpose in coming to the US?
A: To keep house for my husband. . . .
Q: Do you intend to live with Lee Shou as man and wife, if you are admitted?
A: Yes.[32]

Theories of political coverture as wives and derivative economic status as housewives protected Asian women from racial exclusion but also made them legally vulnerable. To enter as a wife necessarily placed women's immigration status within that of their husbands, and wives remained at risk if their husbands lacked necessary racial, social, political, or economic qualifications.[33] Women attempting to arrive as wives waited anxiously while immigration officials investigated their husbands' economic or citizenship status. Under the terms of the Gentleman's Agreement with Japan, only men who had proven fiscal means to support a family were qualified to summon their wives.[34] Would-be Japanese immigrant husbands were required to show substantial savings, along with proof of

---

could not remarry Yoshida under state laws prohibiting marriage between first cousins. Yoshida and her husband agreed not to consummate the marriage.

[31] Commissioner-General to the Secretary, memorandum, 10 April 1906 in Katsuru Iki, INS file 52424/13 (1905–); RCO, box 107; 53434/1–52424/13-C; INS, D.C., RG85; NA, DC.

[32] In evaluating her testimony, the immigration inspector noted, "She gave her testimony in a free and convincing manner and her demeanor was good." May Shee [pseud.] and Yip Ngan [pseud.], INS file 27326/5-3 (1928); Unprocessed, box 336743; INS, SFD, RG85; NA-PSR.

[33] See, for example, Au Yip, INS file 4383/11 (1915); Chinese Wives of Merchants, box 1; INS, HDO, RG85; NA-PSR. For a case in which an investigation produced proof of bona fide merchant status, see Lee Yuit, INS file 4383/1 (1916); Chinese Wives of Merchants, box 1; INS, HDO, RG85; NA-PSR; Lee Yuit, INS file 4383/1 (1916); Chinese Wives of Merchants, box 1; INS, HDO, RG85; NA-PSR; Chan Shee, INS file 14851/9-3 (1915), AICF; INS, SFD, RG85; NA-PSR.

[34] Yuji Ichioka notes that picture bride visas were closely monitored by the Japanese consulates, and until 1915 laborers were ineligible to send for their wives living in Japan. After 1915 laborers became eligible assuming they could demonstrate $800 in savings. Ichioka, The Issei, 71–72.

steady employment, and husbands who failed to demonstrate adequately their fiduciary fitness placed their wives in jeopardy. When Hisa Midzuno, an experienced farm laborer and seamstress, arrived in San Francisco in 1919 as a picture bride, her husband was unable to meet her. She was found to be without means of financial support and denied entry as a public charge, since regulations required that picture brides be received by their husbands in port. Employed in Colorado, it was unlikely that Hisa's husband could afford the trip.[35]

CITIZEN WIVES: MARRIAGE, IMMIGRATION LAW, AND DERIVATIVE CITIZENSHIP

While Asian women used their husband's economic position to gain entry, European women drew on their husband's political status. European immigrant women who could meet the race requirements for naturalization became citizens upon marriage to an American citizen. Thus, when a white immigrant woman arrived as the wife of an American citizen she was not subject to immigration laws but was herself a naturalized citizen. As a result, white women immigrants were able to immigrate on the strength of their marital and racial status, even when medical, educational, or geographic exclusions would determine otherwise.

Derivative citizenship laws, however, did not place these women's arrival above suspicion. Immigration and congressional authorities worried that morally unworthy European women immigrants might have access to American citizenship, and that derivative citizenship allowed physically and mentally unfit women to circumvent the nation's eugenic safeguards.[36] While the racial and civil status of their husbands often trumped other concerns, it was not always effective and white women were still subject to heavy scrutiny by officials.

Residency requirements, stipulated in naturalization law, structured migration patterns as white male immigrants arrived first, established residency, and then sent for their wives and children after filing their declarations of intention.[37] Tessie Argianas immigrated from Greece in 1914

---

[35] Hisa Midzuno, INS file 18629/20–23 (1919); AICF, box 1387; INS, SFD, RG85; NA-PSR.

[36] In 1917, Congress passed legislation to prevent women held for deportation on grounds of immoral behavior from acquiring citizenship by marriage to a citizen. Hutchinson, *Legislative History of American Immigration Policy*, 421.

[37] Naturalization law required five years of residency before immigrants could file their first papers (or declaration of intention). With residency established, immigrants were in a better position to supply affidavits of financial support for family members. For example, see Ann Vida, interview by E. Applebome, 1986, in *Voices from Ellis Island*, reel 7, oral history no. 148.

when she was nine years old. Her father had left for the United States in 1904, saved his money, and acquired citizenship in order to send for the rest of the family. Asked to relate her arrival story, Arigianas described the relative ease of the family's arrival compared to those without citizenship status:

> We had papers. Because see, those years, when my father was in here, when he was here for nine years before we, we came. When my father came in here, he became American citizen. And then, those years, if the husband is an American citizen, including the whole family, okay.[38]

Rose Siegle was not as fortunate. Siegle and her mother, sister and her sister's three children fled Russia in 1918. Her father, uncle, and grandfather had all been killed. The women escaped to Poland where they attempted to make contact with Siegle's sister's husband, who lived and worked in the United States. Her sister obtained a visa and passage to the United States for herself and her children in 1921 as the wife of a citizen. Siegle and her mother were left in Warsaw.[39]

Years of waiting for a husband to establish citizenship took its toll. European women immigrants, like their Chinese and Japanese counterparts, often had to provide for the day-to-day needs of their families still in Europe, sometimes with limited financial support from their expatriated husbands. These women then faced the prospect of immigrating with children in tow, increasing the risk that they could be denied admittance if any of their children were found to be inadmissible for moral, educational, or physical reasons.[40]

European immigrant women were well aware of the risks—as the wife of a citizen they were admissible but as the mother of a sick child they

[38] Tessie Argianas, interview by D. Dane, 1985, in *Voices from Ellis Island*, reel 5, oral history no. 106. Also see Millie Cranford, interview by N. Dallett, 1985, in *Voices from Ellis Island*, reel 4, oral history no. 081; Rose Breci, interview by W. Appel, 1985, in *Voices from Ellis Island*, reel 3, oral history no. 051; Fannie Shoock, interview by D. Dane, 1985, in *Voices from Ellis Island*, reel 4, oral history no. 072.

[39] Her brother-in-law had been drafted into the army and had received citizenship as a reward for his service. Rose Siegle and her mother emigrated the following year. Her sister, now a citizen, was able to obtain preference visas for her immediate family members, and along with assistance from HIAS, the two arrived in the United States in 1922. Rose Siegle, interview by D. Dane, 1985, in *Voices from Ellis Island*, reel 3, oral history no. 066.

[40] Edith Abott, in her analysis of the case records of the Immigrants Protective League in Chicago, cites the example of Mrs. Kapolo. Kapolo's husband had emigrated ahead of his family, and Kapolo and her three children followed eight years later. En route, her daughter Mary's measles developed into nephritis (an inflammation of the kidneys), and the four were detained at Ellis Island. Mary was held for treatment at the Ellis Island hospital for four months, and after multiple hearings by the Board of Special Inquiry, Kapolo and her two sons were allowed to proceed to Chicago. Edith Abott, *Immigration: Select Documents and Case Records* (Chicago: The University of Chicago Press, 1924), 303–307.

could be returned. If found to have curable diseases, family members could be paroled for treatment rather than being summarily deported for their medical conditions.[41] However, parole was in no way guaranteed, but was instead subject to the discretion of immigration authorities. Anglea Esposito intended to join her husband in New Haven when she arrived from Italy with her son in 1911. When her son was diagnosed with "idiocy" and denied admittance, Esposito was deported along with her son. According to immigration authorities, "we thought he required his mother's care and attention, and so sent her back with him, though she was willing to be separated from him."[42]

Ideals of domesticity pulled immigrant women in two directions, as wives and as mothers. During the trip from Lithuania to New York in 1914, Julia Mack's mother prepared her children to respond appropriately to the examiner's question "What is your name?"; she herself had trouble with this question when she first emigrated in 1903.[43] Mack's mother was concerned that one small mistake, one sign of ill health and the family would be returned to Europe.

> And she was aware of the eye examination, and so she would tell us about that. She would examine, she'd pull our eyelids down, you know, lower lids just to make sure that they looked allright to her. Now what she understood about them or not, but anyway. And she would examine our heads. And she'd say "Don't catch cold."[44]

Kate Simon's father sent money to Poland in 1918 for her mother, her brother, and herself to purchase passage to the United States. Simon's brother had rickets and her mother was advised by doctors to leave him behind with relatives and to take only her daughter. Simon's mother re-

---

[41] Hutchinson, *Legislative History of American Immigration Policy*, 507.

[42] Danl. J. Keefe, Annual Report of the Commissioner-General of Immigration, in *Reports of the Department of Commerce and Labor* (1911), 302. Keefe also refers to the case of the Wulfovich family. The mother arrived from Russia with her four children, and each was found to be suffering "from a loathsome disease." The mother was deported along with her children "because the children required her care." Women were not always returned with their inadmissible children. Sure Ross arrived in 1911 with her three children. One of her children, Mirel, aged eleven, was found to be an "imbecile." Ross was willing to be separated from her daughter, and immigration officials determined "as there were other children already here and Mirel was no longer of tender years she was sent back with an attendant and the mother landed." See *Annual Report* (1911), 302.

[43] Julia Mack's mother had emigrated to the United States from Lithuania once before in 1903. In 1914 she made the trip again, this time accompanied by her three daughters and a clanswoman.

[44] Julia Mack, interview by D. Dane, 1986, in *Voices from Ellis Island*, reel 8, oral history no. 172.

fused, choosing to take her chances at Ellis Island. "Then came the terror," Simon remembered, "would we be excluded? Because of my brother's rickets."[45]

The possibility of families like the Macks or Simons using derivative naturalization to circumvent immigration restrictions raised red caution flags for immigration and judicial officials. In a 1903 notice to immigration inspectors and boards of inquiry, the commissioner-general cautioned his staff to be on guard against misuse of family reunification provisions. "It frequently happens that a woman and several children reach Ellis Island practically without funds and helpless unless there be some one in the United States legally bound to care for them," the commissioner-general warned: "The fact that the husband and father may be in the United States and that they intend joining him does not in itself entitle them to admission."[46] In his 1911 annual report, the commissioner-general defended the bureau's policy of not allowing family reunification policies to undermine immigration exclusions. The commissioner-general insisted it was not the law that separated immigrant families but the families themselves, who sent able members ahead first "to secure a footing in this country and later plead for the admission of diseased members on the ground that the family should be together."[47]

As immigration officials feared, the citizenship status of husbands was employed by European immigrants to ease the arrival of more vulnerable family members in ways that suggest a strategy of "family naturalization." When Thakla Nicola arrived from Syria in 1908, and was diagnosed with trachoma, she was denied admission by immigration authorities.[48] Yet Nicola was married to a citizen. In hearing her petition, the court ruled that Nicola was not an alien upon arrival, but a citizen, and thus not subject to immigration laws. According to the court, Nicola met the race requirements for naturalization, and the law did not require she

[45] Kate Simon, interview by N. Dallett, 1986, in *Voices from Ellis Island*, reel 8, oral history no. 180.

[46] Wm. Williams, Commissioner, Notice to Primary Inspectors and Boards of Special Inquiry, 20 June 1903, casefile 52727/2; RINS, SCF, EI, reel 8.

[47] Danl. J. Keefe, Annual Report of the Commissioner-General of Immigration, in *Reports of the Department of Commerce and Labor* (1911), 301.

[48] Trachoma, a chronic inflammatory eye disease considered by early twentieth-century public health officials to be a "loathsome" and "dangerous contagious disease," provided one of the most common grounds for medical exclusion. Exacerbated by poor sanitation and spread by contact, trachoma was a disease of the poor. Untreated, trachoma could lead to blindness, a disability which often precluded immigrants from finding sustainable work. Effective vaccines became available in 1957. Up until then, little effective treatment was available. "Trachoma," *Britannica Online*; <http://www.eb.com:180/cgi-bin/g?DocF =micro/601/3.html> (accessed 13 January 1999).

meet any medical standards for derivative citizenship.[49] Not all women had access to marital exemptions. Lee Shee, wife of a native-born Chinese American citizen, was denied admission when she was diagnosed with "clonorchiasis" upon arrival. The court ruled that, although Lee Shee was the wife of a citizen, as a Chinese women she was ineligible for citizenship and "remained an alien not withstanding her marriage to a citizen of the United States." Consequently, race placed her outside legal exceptions for medical exclusion, and according to the court, Lee Shee "still remains an alien."[50]

"Family naturalization" strategies on the part of European families were not always successful. Immigration and court officials were well aware of the possible loophole citizenship provided for those who could meet the racial requirements. Evidence suggests officials denied naturalization to husbands whose wives were unable to meet medical requirements or whose families were living in Europe. Egsha Rustigian, a Turkish woman, was diagnosed with trachoma upon arrival in 1908. Her husband's effort to petition for his naturalization to guarantee her release was thwarted by a judge who saw derivative naturalization as a threat to immigration restrictions and "the welfare and happiness of the citizens of the United States." Given derivative citizenship laws, the court argued, the citizenship application of one was "in substance for the naturalization of two persons." As a result, the court maintained, the "the incapacity of one may well be regarded as sufficient cause for refusing naturalization to both."[51] In 1927, the Immigrants' Protective League in Chicago reported to the National Conference on Social Work that for the previous two years the commissioner of naturalization had directed its naturalization officers to "oppose the granting of all petitions where the family is not residing in this country."[52] According to representatives from the Immigrants' Protective League, naturalization examiners in Chicago required each applicant to obtain three affidavits, one from his wife testifying to her willingness to join her husband in the United States, one from

---

[49] Nicola was released from custody. *United States v. Williams* 173 F. 626 (S.D.N.Y. 1909). On appeal, the decision of the district court was confirmed: *In re Nicola* 184 F. 322 (2nd Cir. 1911).

[50] *Chung Fook v. White* 287 F. 532 (9th Cir. 1923).

[51] *In re Rustigian* 165 F. 980 (D.R.I. 1908).

[52] Bureau policy reflected the opinion of Acting Secretary of Labor Henning, "an alien whose family is in Europe has never lived in the United States, no matter how many years he may have been here." Mr. Henning, acting secretary of labor, and Raymond Christ, commissioner of naturalization, memo to district directors and naturalization examiners, communication, 14 February 1925, as quoted in Mrs. Kenneth F. Rich, Director Immigrants' Protective League, Chicago, "Separated Families," in *Proceedings of the National Conference of Social Work*, 54th Annual Session, Des Moines, 1927 (Chicago: University of Chicago Press, 1927), 536.

a reputable physician testifying to the mental and physical condition of his wife and children, and one demonstrating his ability to financially support his family upon their arrival.[53] Five years later, in 1930, Mary McDowell, head resident of the University of Chicago Settlement, reported that the practice of denying naturalization petitions to husbands separated from their wives continued.[54]

While the total number of European women admitted under family reunification policies as nonquota immigrants remained low in the years before 1930, reflecting historically lower levels of women's migration to the United States, women as wives were the primary and intended beneficiaries of special, exempted status under the law. The particular importance of being a wife for a woman's ability to emigrate to the United States is strikingly evident in the case of literacy requirements. Wives were exempt from the provisions of the 1917 literacy test.[55] Only a small number of women arrivals were illiterate (approximately seven percent). Yet the vast majority of immigrants arriving who could not pass the literacy test were women (eighty-eight percent), and women were the majority of those exempted from deportation under family reunification policies (eighty-eight percent).[56]

As wives, immigrant women had access to a privileged space in the law. Theories of coverture incorporated a wife's legal, political, and economic status within that of her husbands. As a result, Chinese and Japanese women were able to circumvent race-based immigration exclusion mea-

[53] Some judicial officials disagreed with the bureau's position, finding absurd a policy that denied naturalization because a petitioner's family was in Europe but would not allow that person to bring his family to the United States. According to Mrs. Kenneth Rich, Director of the Immigrants' Protective League in Chicago, Judge P. J. Stern, of Philadelphia, granted certificates of citizenship to men whose wives were still in Europe (11 May 1925). Rich, "Separated Families," 536–537.

[54] Mary McDowell, "The Quota Law and the Family," in *Proceedings of the National Conference of Social Work*, 57th Annual Session, Boston, 1930 (Chicago: University of Chicago Press, 1930), 484.

[55] The 1917 law establishing the literacy test allowed any admissible alien to send for "his father or grandfather over fifty-five years of age, his wife, his mother, his grandmother, or his unmarried or widowed daughter, if otherwise admissible, whether such relative can read or not." (First proviso, sect. 3 of the 1917 act; continued by sec. 212b of the 1952 act), Hutchinson, *Legislative History of American Immigration Policy*, 506.

[56] *Annual Report of the Commissioner General of Immigration to the Secretary of Labor* (1921), 34–36. In her analysis of women's historical immigration patterns, Donna Gabaccia suggests that, while historically family reunification has been an important theme in immigration policy, few women before the post–World War II period benefited from laws allowing immigrant wives to circumvent restrictive immigration laws. Gabaccia notes that, while almost ninety percent of illiterates admitted under the law exempting immediate family members from the rigors of the literacy test were women, their total number was small. Gabaccia, *From the Other Side*, 38.

sures though their marriage to merchants, farmers, and native-born citizens. European women who could not pass increasingly strict physical, mental, educational, or even geographic restrictions, often became admissible as wives. Indeed, Asian immigrant families used treaty and citizenship rights, while white immigrant families used naturalization as a strategy to expedite the arrival of more vulnerable members. For many women, marriage meant access.

CHAPTER TWO

The Limits of Derivative Citizenship

In the years before women achieved independent citizenship, marriage did not mean access for all women. Marriage was at center of the conflict between laws allowing family reunification and those preventing the arrival of unwanted laborers, prostitutes, and racial "others." As a result, marriage and wives came under intense scrutiny. Derivative citizenship had its limits.

In the process of identifying a loyal and valid wife, authorities found themselves having to define the boundaries of legal marriage. The merits of correspondence marriages, religious marriages, common-law marriages, and intended marriages were all debated in terms that reflected a growing concern over the sanctity of marriage and its misuse as a vehicle to gain admission or citizenship. At stake in the debates over the legal status of Chinese marriage customs, Mexican and Jewish religious ceremonies, and Japanese picture brides was the legal conflict between the right of a husband to the company of his wife and the right of a nation to prohibit the inclusion of those deemed morally or racially unfit.

Women charged with prostitution also remained beyond the bounds of derivative citizenship. Their suspected moral transgressions outweighed their marriages to American citizens, and it was as if they had never been married. Immigrants were prohibited from engaging in immoral behavior, and applicants for citizenship were required to demonstrate good moral character. Women found guilty of the first could not seek refuge in the second, neither through marriage, nor, later in the century, through independent application. Prevented from acquiring derivative citizenship, women suspected of prostitution could not use their marriage to American citizens to prevent their deportation.[1] Women judged guilty of immoral behavior lived in a legal limbo in which deportation was a possibility and citizenship was often an impossibility.

LEGAL WIVES: DEFINING THE LIMITS OF MARRIAGE

As women claiming to be wives arrived at the nation's borders, not only their behavior as respectable wives, but also the legality of their marriage

---

[1] See case of Bessie Stein, *Ex parte Bigney* 285 F. 669 (D.Or. 1923).

was subject to scrutiny. Chan Shee arrived from China in 1914 and sought admission as the wife of a Chinese merchant. She presented immigration officials with a marriage certificate (in Latin) drafted by a Catholic missionary at Canton. Immigration officials suspected that Chan Shee's marriage was a fraud, a ruse used to avoid exclusion and deportation. While on bail, Chan Shee and her husband were remarried with the hope that this would substantiate their claim of marriage with immigration authorities. It did not. The bureau concluded that the couple's "remarriage" provided only further evidence that Chan Shee was not a legal wife upon her arrival. On hearing her case, however, the federal court disagreed and found that, since being paroled to her husband, Chan Shee had lived with him as his wife, thus removing all doubt about her right to remain.[2]

The law allowed for the immigration of wives, but immigration and judicial officials were left to determine what constituted a legal marriage. In Shee's case, immigration officials sought written documentation while judicial officials scrutinized behavior to discern evidence of a legal marriage. Immigrant women brought with them a host of unique legal traditions that defined marriage in culturally specific ways, ways that quite often posed significant challenges to American legal customs. Ah Yip had lived with her husband for thirteen years by 1915, but that did not make her a legal wife in the eyes of American immigration authorities and under the dictates of U.S. law:

Q: Have you a marriage certificate?
A: Only a Chinese marriage certificate.
Q: Did your husband ever have any other wife except you?
A: No.
Q: Were you married according to Chinese custom?
A: Yes.
Q: Not according to American custom?
A: No.
Q: Did you get a marriage license, as required by the law?
A: No.
Q: Have you been living with Lau Sing as his wife ever since you were married
   13 years ago?
A: Yes.[3]

---

[2] *Ex parte Chan Shee* 236 F. 579 (N.D.Cal. 1916). In Sucheng Chan's discussion of this case, she notes that on the advise of attorneys, Chan Shee was remarried twice on American soil—once before a justice of the peace and once before a Catholic priest. Chan, "Exclusion of Chinese Women," in *Entry Denied: Exclusion and the Chinese Community in America, 1882–1943*, ed. Sucheng Chan (Philadelphia: Temple University Press, 1991), 117.

[3] Au Yip, INS file 4383/11 (1915); Chinese Wives of Merchants, box 1; INS, HDO, RG85; NA-PSR.

Au Yip's case, and others like hers, posed a problem of translation as differing legal understandings of marriage confronted one another. Polygamous marriages, explicitly and quickly condemned by immigration and judicial officials, still raised difficult questions about which wife should be considered the first and legal wife under the law. Common-law and religious marriages were viewed with equal suspicion because they took place outside the confines of the civil state. Proxy marriages, picture brides, and fiancées posed the most sustained challenge to immigration law, extending the reach of derivative status and the privileges of being a wife to women who barely knew their American husbands or were not yet wives.

Polygamous marriages were never recognized as legal marriages by immigration authorities. However, the problem remained as to which of the marriages would be considered polygamous and which would be found original and authentic. Polygamy, immigration officials suspected, was often disguised by applicants claiming that prior wives had died. Lee Wong She arrived with her husband in Honolulu in 1916, along with their daughter Au Moy. Officials were immediately suspicious, noting "There have been quite a number of Chinese of the exempt classes, citizens and others, who have recently gone to China and brought back young wives in lieu of former wives who, it is claimed have died." According to the official, "There are getting to be so many of them that it seems improbable that the same circumstances should surround so many cases. The fact that many Chinese practice polygamy tends to strengthen the suspicion." Officials searched Lee Wong She and her daughter's luggage looking for evidence of multiple wives but could find nothing to substantiate their suspicions. The family was released.[4]

Accusations of polygamy subjected arriving women immigrants to interrogation and possible deportation for their husbands' conduct. When she arrived in Honolulu in 1922, Li Shee's husband asked her to lie about her age and the date of their marriage in order to conceal his other, polygamous marriages. Under repeated questioning, Li Shee confessed to immigration officials that they had attempted to hide the date of their marriage:

Q: Did you change your age and date of your marriage on account of this other woman that was in Hawaii here?

A: Yes—he said because the law in the United States a man is not allowed to marry two wives so he told me to change the age and date of marriage.[5]

[4] Lee Wong She [pseud.], INS file 4384/223 (1922); Chinese Wives of Native-Born American Citizens, box 4; INS, HDO, RG85; NA-PSR.

[5] It appears from the extant evidence that Li She was eventually admitted. Included in her file is a 1945 application for old-age and survivors insurance listing her address in Honolulu. Li She [pseud.], INS file 4384/213 (1922); Chinese Wives of Native-Born American Citizens, box 4; INS, HDO, RG85; NA-PSR.

Marriages performed outside the confines of the state were viewed with equal suspicion. Catholic and Jewish religious marriages posed a legal problem for their lack of official state sanction. Immigration officials were wary of relationships that persisted without official paperwork certifying a legal marriage. Husband and wife were required to prove they had been united in a religious ceremony by retrieving precise details about the service.[6] The process of questioning bride and groom separately about the specifics of their marriage ceremony was an investigative tool developed in Chinese exclusion cases. Francisca Cardona arrived in El Paso in 1919 with her husband Apolonio Vasquez and their son Anastasio Cardona. Questioned separately, husband and wife were asked to substantiate their marriage by providing key facts about the marriage ceremony, including the name of the church, priest, and godparents present. When interviewed, Francisa Cardona responded as best she could:

Q: What was the name of the priest who married you?
A: I do not remember.

In evaluating the record, the supervising inspector for El Paso cautioned his staff to be more rigorous in future. Reminding inspectors that a civil ceremony was required by Mexican authorities, the supervising inspector argued that immigrants like Vasquez and Cardona who could only provide evidence of a church ceremony should not be admitted as a legally married couple.[7] Immigration officials in Presidio, Texas, required that immigrant wives arriving along the southern border provide proof of legal marriages, evidence that they had been sent for by their husbands, and documentation of their husbands' legal right to remain in the United States.[8] These requirements bear a striking resemblance to those required of arriving Japanese picture brides in the early twentieth century.

Common-law marriages and religious ceremonies lacked the necessary legal proof immigration authorities used to evaluate marital validity. The courts, however, looked for evidence of a nuclear family rather than proof

[6] Ambrosio Jiminez and Emiliana Gonzalez testified before immigration officials in El Paso in 1918 that they had been married by "both church and civil." El Paso officials were particularly condemning of Emiliana Gonzalez, noting in the record that "the alien is so densely [sic] ignorant that it is practically impossible to obtain intelligent answers to the questions propounded [sic] to her in her own language." Ambrosio Jiminez, Emiliana Gonzalez, Eustacio Jiminez, Geronima Jiminez, Crecencia Gonzalez, BSI no. 5449/manifest no. 13115, casefile 54281/36C (1918); RINS, SCF, MI.

[7] Apolonio Vasquez, Francisca Cardona, Anatasio Cardona, BSI no. 7141/manfiest no. 12164–66, casefile 54281/36D (1919); RINS, SCF, MI, reel 9.

[8] Leo B. Smith, Immigrant Inspector, Presidio, Texas to Supervisor, Immigration Service, El Paso, Texas, 10 December 1923, casefile 52903/29; RINS, SCF, MI, reel 3.

of a legal ceremony in their evaluations of these marriages. Relationships that were buttressed by children and solemnized by community recognition were often found by the courts to be valid civil marriages despite their common-law origins.[9] Rebecca Bloom was held for deportation in 1909 when immigration officials refused to recognize the legitimacy of her marriage. Bloom had been married nine years before in London in a Jewish ceremony. She and her husband moved to the United States, all the while being recognized as man and wife. In reviewing her case, the court emphasized that evidence that Bloom and her husband had "held themselves out to the public" as man and wife, as well as the fact that "two children have in the meantime been born unto them," were "sufficient to constitute a valid common-law marriage." In concluding in favor of Bloom, the court emphasized her role as wife and mother as further evidence of an authentic common-law marriage: "She is living with her husband, lawfully and quietly, taking care of and raising her offspring, and to break up this family, and leave the children motherless, either by the continued confinement or deportation of their mother, would seem to be cruel in the extreme."[10]

In one particularly complicated case, Honolulu immigration officials weighed the merits of a common-law marriage against those of a second, polygamous marriage. At stake was the question of which woman was entitled to come and go freely, immigrating as the wife of a citizen. Ho Ah Keau (Ho She) and Hung She both claimed to be the wife of Lau Ah Leong, a citizen. As evidence, Ho Ah Keau (Ho She) offered a marriage certificate, while Hung She testified to a long-term relationship. Although Hung She had never legally married, the two had been living together as man and wife since her arrival in 1883. Hung Shee and Lau Ah Leong had a number of children, as did Ho Ah Keau and Lau Ah Leong. In her testimony before immigration officials, Hung Shee insisted that, although she lacked a legal marriage certificate, she was the legitimate "wife":

> Q: How many children did you have born before Ho She [Ho Ah Keau] came to Hawaii?
> A: Four children.

---

[9] Sadie M. Sprung, a young Jewish immigrant and wife of an American citizen, was held for deportation in 1909, charged with prostitution after immigration authorities determined she had, in fact, never been legally married to her husband. The couple had obtained a civil marriage license, but while visiting family in Europe they learned their marriage lacked a necessary formality. Upon return to the United States, they were re-married by a rabbi in New York in pursuance of the original license. *Sprung v. Morton, Immigrant Inspector, Bloom v. Same* 182 F. 330 (E.D.Va. 1909).

[10] Ibid.

Q: And you were living with Ah Leong and regarded by him as his wife in all respects?

A: Yes.

Hung She's claim to marriage lay in motherhood, loyalty, and commitment to husband and family; Ho Ah Keau's (or Ho She)'s status as wife was based in law and procedure, represented by her marriage certificate. In ruling on this case, the board debated the merits of a common-law marriage against those of a legal, though possibly polygamous, marriage. According to one inspector, Hung She's position had moral weight but Ho Ah Keau's (Ho She) had the weight of law. The inspector acknowledged that Hung She had been living with Lau Ah Leong as his wife, had given birth to a large number of children, and had helped to develop the family business. However, despite her status as a loyal wife, Hung She was not a legal wife. She lacked the necessary marriage license that Ho She had secured.[11] In this clash between civil and common law, validity hung on a marriage certificate. Both the Honolulu District Court and the Ninth Circuit Court of Appeals in San Francisco agreed. In reviewing the testimony, both courts recognized the relationship between Hung Shee and Lau Ah Leong as a common-law marriage, one without benefit of state approval or certification. Yet while acknowledging the validity of their relationship, the courts did not recognize its legality—a marriage without a marriage license was a not a legal marriage.[12]

Within immigration law, marriage was a significant legal category, and one that was closely guarded. Couples who planned on solemnizing their relationship after arrival in the United States met resistance from immigration officials who demanded proof of legitimacy before entry. Lida Stribei and her daughter Marie arrived at Ellis Island in 1923 from Romania to join Stribei's common-law husband, Geroge Strurdza, who worked as a laborer in Chicago. Immigration officials, however, did not recognize their marriage as valid and found Stribei and her daughter to be without the support of a male breadwinner and thus likely to become public charges.[13] George Strurdza sought assistance from the Immigrants' Protective League in Chicago. He explained that he had wanted to marry Stribei

---

[11] Ho Ah Keau, INS file 4393/1 (1921); CICF, box 1; INS, SFD, RG85; NA-PSR.

[12] Sucheng Chan notes that Hung Shee subsequently sued for her share of their common property. Married without a license, Hung Shee faced "insurmountable" legal obstacles, according to the presiding judge; *Fung Dai Kim Ah Leong. v. Lau Ah Leong* 27 F.2d 582 (9th Cir. 1928). Chan, "Exclusion of Chinese Women," 121–122.

[13] Additionally, Stribei was illiterate, and because immigration officials did not recognize Stribei as a legal wife, she was not exempt from laws excluding illiterates and was subject to deportation.

legally before leaving for the United States, but had not been old enough according to Austria-Hungarian law. He insisted that he had supported his wife and child up until the time he came to the United States in 1914, and had intended to bring them over soon after arriving, but the war had made that impossible. In their letter to the secretary of labor, representatives of the Immigrants' Protective League explained the family's situation and pleaded their case, noting that George Strurdza "impresses us very favorably." Subsequently, the league was notified that wife and daughter had been released on bond and that immigration authorities would consider concealing the bonds if husband and wife were legally married.[14]

Remarriage in accordance with United States law was often proposed as an alternative to deportation, but it was not one with which immigration authorities were altogether comfortable. Before being officially landed, single immigrant women arriving at United States ports destined for fiancées were frequently married on the dock before watchful immigration authorities and Travelers Aid Society volunteers to ensure their moral purity and marital legitimacy. Immigration officials, however, remained concerned that such ship-side marriages thwarted their efforts to expose marital fraud. In his 1914 annual report, the commissioner-general encouraged legislators to outlaw marriages at immigration stations, "once and for all." No woman, the commissioner-general argued, "should be admitted as the wife of a resident who has not consummated marriage with such resident entirely and completely in the country in which marriage is alleged or claimed to have taken place."[15]

JAPANESE PICTURE BRIDES: RACE, MARRIAGE, AND LAW

While many different groups of women found themselves subject to remarriage upon arrival in order to substantiate their status as wives, the most infamous by far were Japanese picture brides. Japanese picture brides became a lightning rod for early twentieth-century legal and policy debates over sexuality, race, lawful brides and unlawful aliens. Labeled as either prostitutes or clandestine laborers, Japanese wives were charged with working outside the home in ways that threatened the morality of a community or the job security of its workforce.

[14] Abott, "Lida and Marie Stribei (A 'Common-Law' Wife and Illegitimate Child)," *Immigration*, 384–386.
[15] A. Caminetti, *Annual Report of the Commissioner-General of Immigration to the Secretary of Labor* (1914), 23.

As a result of increased restrictions on the arrival of Japanese laborers over the first decade of the twentieth century, Japanese women constituted an ever larger percentage of arriving Japanese immigrants. The 1907 Gentleman's Agreement prevented further immigration of Japanese laborers but allowed those men already in the United States to send for their wives, formalizing what had already become an effective immigration strategy for Japanese men seeking wives.[16] The women who arrived to marry these men would become known as "picture" or "photo" brides. Japanese men living in the United States were married to their brides in absentia. Upon arrival in the United States, young Japanese women, armed with a picture of their intended husband and a certificate from Japanese authorities attesting to their marriage, navigated their way through immigration procedures as wives of resident immigrants or citizens. As a result, the proportion of women among Japanese immigrants soared. In 1911, for instance, Japanese women were almost seventy percent (69.2%) of all arriving Japanese immigrants to the continental United States. Most of these women (86%), identified themselves as married, and most were between the ages of fourteen and forty-four.[17]

The advent of the picture bride era corresponded with the height of the panic over the arrival of immigrant women as prostitutes and the use of naturalization law to circumvent racial and medical immigration exclusions.[18] The Dillingham Commission, an early twentieth-century Congressional committee charged with investigating the "immigration problem," expressed grave reservations about the validity of picture bride marriages and the morality of its adherents. The commission recognized that "some Japanese women doubtless come to this country to meet their proxy husbands when their purposes are entirely legal and proper." Experience and the opinion of immigration inspectors, however, suggested this was the

[16] San Francisco office to Washington, D.C. office, 8 February 1905, memorandum, "Re 'photographic' or 'proxy marriages'," in Katsuru Iki, INS file 52424/13 (1905–); RCO, entry 9, box 107, 53434/1–52424/13-C; INS, DC, RG85; NA, DC.

[17] While women comprised a larger percentage of Japanese immigrants, their numbers remained small. In 1911, Japanese women were 0.25% of all arriving women immigrants. *Annual Report of the Commissioner-General of Immigration* (1911), 174, 178–179; see also 218.

[18] Increased moral scrutiny by immigration officials of Japanese women arriving as brides, resulted in a relatively high percentage of Japanese women debarred or deported for suspected prostitution. However, Japanese women accused of prostitution remained a minority of the total number of immigrant women debarred or deported as prostitutes. *Annual Report of the Commissioner-General of Immigration* (1902), 7; *Annual Report of the Commissioner-General of Immigration* (1905), 8–9; *Annual Report of the Commissioner-General of Immigration* (1911), 231–32, 236–37; *Annual Report of the Commissioner-General of Immigration* (1914), 104–105.

exception, not the rule. According to the commission, "a large majority of the women coming in this way are intended for purposes of prostitution."[19]

The arrival in 1905 of a young Japanese woman, Kanjiro Iki, prompted the first procedural crisis around the issue of "picture brides." Immigration officials had responded to the arrival of "picture brides" by remarrying these women to their intended husbands before they were released. Kanjiro, however, was too young to be remarried without the consent of a guardian, and she was paroled to the Japanese Methodist Mission, whose officers began a campaign of protest against the picture bride practice. In a letter to the secretary of commerce and labor, Margaret Lake, director of a missionary home for Japanese women in San Francisco, linked the experiences of Japanese picture brides to those of Chinese "slave girls." The successful enforcement of the 1882 Chinese exclusion law, Lake argued, had made it "almost impossible for the Chinese slave girl to enter" through San Francisco; consequently, "Japanese women and girls are taking their place." No good could come to San Francisco or to the nation, Lake insisted, from the arrival of Japanese picture brides.[20] In his response, the secretary emphasized that immigration officials were concerned with two things when interrogating the picture brides—were they lawful brides or fraudulent aliens and were they virtuous women or were they prostitutes.[21] If a Japanese woman was neither an alien nor an immoral woman, then she was a virtuous wife of a resident or citizen and could be remarried to her intended husband and allowed to enter the United States.

Kanjiro's case created a firestorm of publicity about the bureau's policy toward "picture" and proxy marriages generally, and Japanese "picture brides" specifically.[22] In a directive to San Francisco authorities from the Commissioner of Immigration, a memo which was subsequently re-

[19] Immigration Commission, *Importation and Harboring of Women for Immoral Purposes*, Reports of the Immigration Commission presented by Mr. Dillingham, 1911, vol. 19; United States Senate, 61st Cong., 3rd sess., Washington, D.C., 69.

[20] Lake's home for Japanese girls was affiliated with the Woman's Home Missionary Society. Katsuru Iki, INS file 52424/13 (1905–), RCO, entry 9, box 107, 53434/1–52424/13-C; INS, DC, RG85; NA, DC. Also see M. E. Lake to Honorable Victor H. Metcalf, Secretary of Commerce and Labor, 9 March 1905, in Katsuru Iki, INS file 52424/13 (1905–); RCO, entry 9, box 107, 53434/1–52424/13-C; INS, DC, RG85; NA, DC.

[21] V. H. Metcalf, Secretary Department of Commerce and Labor, to Miss Margarita Lake, 17 March 1905, in Katsuru Iki, INS file 52424/13 (1905–); RCO, entry 9, box 107, 53434/1–52424/13-C; INS, DC, RG85; NA, DC.

[22] In its reporting on Kanjiro's case, the *San Francisco Bulletin* painted a sympathetic picture of divided love, and of a young bride's fears and apprehensions. This article appeared in the *San Francisco Bulletin* of 23 March 1905; see Katsuru Iki, INS files 52424/13 (1905–); RCO, entry 9, box 107: 53434/1–52424/13-C; INS, DC, RG85; NA, DC.

printed in the *San Francisco Bulletin*, the commissioner-general questioned the legality of a marriage contracted through correspondence.[23] According to the commissioner-general, proxy marriages, like polygamous marriages, while legal elsewhere, were not recognized in the United States. The commissioner-general concluded, "in cases of this kind which may arise at your port hereafter, if the alien be clearly a member of the excluded classes the better course would be to deny her admission."[24]

As the number of picture brides arriving in the United States increased, so too did local opposition, and with it governmental concern over the legality of these marriages and the moral quality of Japanese immigrant women.[25] Seattle immigration officials reported that officials there did not recognize proxy marriages, and that they required Japanese immigrants to comply with local marriage laws before they could be admitted.[26] Women should be remarried, a San Francisco inspector explained, to ensure that, when they inevitably turned to prostitution, their "husbands" could be held legally liable for their conduct.[27]

On the one hand, the policy of "remarrying" picture brides in port served to reinforce their case for admission as legal wives, and few were denied.[28] On the other hand, remarriage served to reinforce the idea of these women as a threat to the very sanctity of marriage. "Fifty percent of such women," San Francisco officials claimed, "lead immoral lives in

[23] After having consulted with Mr. K. Uyeno, consul of Japan in San Francisco, the San Francisco commissioner recognized the legality of such a marriage in Japan. However, he remained opposed to the immigration service recognizing these marriages. F. P. Sargent, Commissioner-General to Commissioner of Immigration, an Francisco, 16 February 1905, in Katsuru Iki, INS file 52424/13 (1905–); RCO, entry 9, box 107, 53434/1–52424/13-C; INS, DC, RG85; NA, DC.

[24] F. P. Sargent, Commissioner-General to Commissioner of Immigration, San Francisco, 16 February 1905, in Katsuru Iki, INS file 52424/13 (1905–); RCO, entry 9, box 107, 53434/1–52424/13-C; INS, DC, RG85; NA, DC.

[25] Immigration officials would receive occasional anonymous reports on the nefarious goings on of Japanese women. For example, an anonymous "American citizen" sent a clipping from the *Philadelphia Evening Ledger* that referred to the arrival of Japanese picture brides. The "American citizen" appended a letter which read, "I think the US Govt. should look into this matter, it looks very much like a white slave scheme to prepare for the Panama Exposition." INS file 52424/13A (1917–); RCO, entry 9, box 107, 53434/1–52424/13-C; INS, DC, RG85; NA, DC.

[26] Seattle officials reminded Washington, D.C. officials that its procedures were a result of central authority directives. Katsuru Iki, INS file 52424/13 (1905–); RCO, entry 9, box 107, 53434/1–52424/13-C; INS, DC, RG85; NA, DC.

[27] Commissioner of San Francisco to Commissioner-General of Immigration, Washington, D.C., 24 June 1908 in Katsuru Iki, INS file 52424/13 (1905–); RCO, entry 9, box 107, 53434/1–52424/13-C; INS, DC, RG85; NA, DC.

[28] Each picture bride was held for special inquiry which demanded a considerable amount of staff time. Many offices reported that they were overwhelmed. INS file 52424/13A (1917–); RCO, entry 9, box 107, 53434/1–52424/13-C; INS, DC, RG85; NA, DC.

this country."[29] In addition, San Francisco officials warned that they would soon be inundated with requests for citizenship by the children of these marriages.[30]

Japanese women attempted to defend their respectability against charges of prostitution and fraudulent marriage. Sawa Kikuchi, arriving in San Francisco in 1908, testified that she owned a toy store in Japan. While working as a housekeeper in Hong Kong, Sawa married a United States citizen. Officials in San Francisco received a telegram from Hong Kong police charging Sawa with prostitution. Under further questioning from San Francisco immigration inspectors, Sawa admitted that she had lived with another man and also with her husband, both before she was married, but she denied she worked as a prostitute. She was denied admission as a prostitute.[31] Sawa's past indiscretions were taken as evidence of her future immoral intentions, and while she was not guilty of prostitution, neither was she a respectable wife in the eyes of immigration officials.

By 1915, reports from San Francisco had shifted from a concern that proxy marriages were used to cover prostitution to concerns that picture brides were in fact workers, not wives. Unlike other wives, the San Francisco commissioner observed, picture brides did not confine their work to inside the house but worked outside the home as well, "in what are ordinarily considered the occupations of common laborers."[32] Japanese wives who worked in the kitchens or dining rooms of family-owned restaurants raised the hackles of San Francisco authorities, who questioned "whether we were not really admitting Japanese laborers in the guise of wives."[33]

The San Francisco Woman's Home Missionary Society disagreed. The threat posed by the arrival of picture brides, according to the society, was not economic but moral. Members of the society condemned the plight of Japanese picture brides in a language of female victimhood. In a letter

---

[29] Commissioner of San Francisco to Commissioner-General of Immigration, Washington, D.C., 24 June 1908 in Katsuru Iki, INS file 52424/13 (1905–); RCO, entry 9, box 107, 53434/1–52424/13-C; INS, DC, RG85; NA, DC.

[30] INS file 52424/13A (1917–); RCO, entry 9, box 107, 53434/1–52424/13-C; INS, DC, RG85; NA, DC.

[31] Sawa Kikuchi [pseud.], INS file 51952/4 (1908); DJA-INS acc. 58 A 2038, box 46; INS, DC, RG85; NA, DC.

[32] Central authorities eventually asked San Francisco officials to look into the matter of picture brides as laborers. In a 1915 letter of 31 December, Washington offices asked San Francisco to determine if indeed women did go on to live with husbands and what their occupations were. Washington, D.C., office to San Francisco office, 31 December 1915, INS file 52424/13A (1917–); RCO, entry 9, box 107, 53434/1–52424/13-C; INS, DC, RG85; NA, DC.

[33] Samuel W. Backus, Commissioner of San Francisco to Commissioner-General of Immigration, Washington, D.C., report, 6 January 1914, INS file 52424/13C; RCO, entry 9, box 107, 53434/1–52424/13-C; INS, DC, RG85; NA, DC.

to the commissioner-general, Mrs. D. B. Street, field secretary for the Missionary Society, attempted to refocus the immigration agency on the significance of the moral threat: "The one thing that is a disgrace to our Nation is the coming of the 'Picture Brides,' who are claimed by men who never intend to marry them. So these poor girls become the victims of man's inhumanity."[34] In response, the commissioner-general asked Street her opinion on whether these women were in fact "laborers" as San Francisco officials suspected. Street informed the commissioner-general that San Francisco officials were in fact wrong; the women arriving as picture brides, according to Street, were clearly housewives deserving protective treatment as women, not punitive treatment as laborers: "I carefully noted the appearance of the Japanese women when I visited this Island and a number impressed me as *not* belonging to the working class."[35]

In their report to Washington, D.C., Sacramento authorities linked Japanese wives' work outside the home to their supposed immoral conduct. Sacramento inspectors reported that Japanese picture brides were not wives in the traditional sense of the word, but combined domestic work outside the home with paid sexual labor. "Japanese women," one inspector argued, "travel about in groups, from ranch to ranch, where Japanese men are employed, for the ostensible purpose of visiting relatives, their real mission being the practice of prostitution." Similarly, Sacramento inspectors insinuated that Japanese prostitutes used restaurant work as a "cloak to hide their commercialized immorality."[36]

Concerns that picture brides were in fact more workers, whether sexual or manual laborers, than wives exposed Japanese picture brides to possible exclusion as Japanese laborers. Immigration authorities carefully questioned Japanese wives, attempting to ascertain whether these women planned on working after they were admitted. Natsu Tujoyashi arrived in San Francisco in 1919 to join her husband. Natsu had worked on her father's farm in Japan, but when asked about her future means of support she insisted that her husband would be the family's sole provider.[37]

---

[34] Mrs. D. B. Street to Hon. A. Caminetti, Commissioner-General of Immigration, 9 July 1914, INS file 52424/13C; RCO, entry 9, box 107, 53434/1–52424/13-C; INS, DC, RG85; NA, DC.

[35] A. Caminetti to Mrs. D. B. Street, 16 July 1914, INS file 52424/13C; RCO, entry 9, box 107, 53434/1–52424/13-C; INS, DC, RG85; NA, D.C; Mrs. D.B. Street to Hon A. Camminetti [*sic*], 14 September 1914, INS file 52424/13C; RCO, entry 9, box 107, 53434/1–52424/13-C; INS, DC, RG85; NA, DC. Emphasis in original.

[36] San Francisco office to Washington, D.C., office, memorandum, 14 December 1915, INS file 52424/13A (1917–); RCO, entry 9, box 107, 53434/1–52424/13-C; INS, DC, RG85; NA, DC.

[37] "Q: Are you absolutely dependent upon your husband for support?" "A: Yes." Natsu Tujinayashi, INS file 18778/3–17 (1919); AICF, box n/a; INS, SFD, RG85; NA-PSR.

The Labor Council of San Francisco, a powerful federation of local unions, insisted that Japanese women like Natsu Tujoyashi did in fact work as laborers upon arrival. In a letter to President Woodrow Wilson, the Labor Council argued that these women undermined American labor by circumventing immigration restrictions through the guise of marriage. "The majority of such women," the Labor Council insisted, "become the servants and wives of Japanese farmers and horticulturists of this State, thereby displacing white persons or entering into competition with them in various industries and eventually contributing to the increase at a rapid rate of the native born Asiatic population." The council offered the specter of Hawaii as the example of what California might become, "the menace of political domination by Japanese in the Islands that is certain to follow their economic control."[38]

With the passage of the literary test in 1917, the issue of exactly what Japanese "photo brides" were came to a head. Were Japanese picture brides indeed wives as understood by immigration law, devoting their labors to domestic work in the home for the exclusive benefit of their husbands, or were they laborers, plying their domestic or sexual labor for pay? If they were "wives," then Japanese picture brides, like other immigrant wives, were exempt from the literacy test. If they were not, then Japanese women were subject to educational exclusions, as they were to general race-based prohibitions against Japanese laborers. As the assistant secretary of labor explained in a letter to the secretary of state, the government had to remain vigilant against fraud and not allow the exemption for wives to be used to admit women who were not legally married. The Department of State must decide if these women were in fact married and if these women were legally wives.[39]

The status of picture brides became tinder in the strained relationship between the United States and Japan. While Japanese officials insisted that such proxy marriages were recognized by the Japanese government, U.S. immigration officials argued in response that Japanese insistence on the legality of proxy marriages was insufficient to overcome the weight of American custom and common law.[40] The brewing controversy over the picture brides and the literacy test law was covered in the San Francisco Japanese press. Both the New World and the Japanese American News tried to calm community fears that Japanese picture marriages

---

[38] Danile C. Murphy, President, and James O'Conner, Secretary, San Francisco Labor Council, to the President, Hon. Woodrow Wilson, 28 April 1916, INS file 52424/13A (1917); RCO, entry 9, box 107, 53434/1–52424/13-C; INS, DC, RG85; NA, DC.

[39] Assistant Secretary of Labor to Secretary of State, 24 April 1917, INS file 52424/13A (1917); RCO, entry 9, box 107, 53434/1–52424/13-C; INS, DC, RG85; NA, DC.

[40] INS Commissioner, report, INS file 52424/13A (1917–); RCO, entry 9, box 107, 53434/1–52424/13-C; INS, DC, RG85; NA, DC.

would not be recognized as they protested against the injustice of applying literacy laws to lawful wives.[41] In resolving the dispute, the secretary of commerce and labor sided with international law over local custom. The United States government, he concluded, could not question the Japanese ambassador and therefore must recognize the validity of picture bride marriages.[42] The secretary issued instructions that brides must henceforth present a certified copy of notification of marriage made out by the husband in the United States. Brides would no longer be remarried in United States ports, and they would be required to meet all other physical, moral, and economic requirements of the law.[43]

The Japanese government's agreement in February 1920 to discontinue issuing passports to picture brides brought the matter to a close but not to a resolution.[44] The debate over Japanese picture brides dictated the

[41] The *New World* reported that the practice of remarrying picture brides was adopted in Seattle in response to the arrival of a number of prostitutes disguised as brides, not because American immigration authorities did not recognize the legality of Japanese marriages, "Photography Marriages Recognized as Legal. Opinion of Consul-General Hanihara," The *New World*, 28 April 1917, San Francisco, INS file 52424/13A (1917–); RCO, entry 9, box 107, 53434/1–52424/13-C; INS, DC, RG85; NA, DC. The *Japanese American News* assured readers that if Japanese brides were subjected to the literacy test the text they would be required to use was the Japanese Fourth Reader, which was easily read and "hence we may expect that Japanese women will not fail in the test." The paper, however, adamantly defended the practice of photo marriages and denied they posed any threat to the sanctity of marriage or American mores: "Educational Test for Wives. Likely to be Strongly Opposed," *Japanese American News*, 26 April 1917, San Francisco, translated by B.C.H, Office of Naval Intelligence, INS file 52424/13A (1917–); RCO, entry 9, box 107, 53434/1–52424/13-C; INS, DC, RG85; NA, DC. Also, "Legal Precedent against Recognition of Japanese Marriage. Positive Opinion of Immigration Official in Hawaii. Japanese Association will Insist to the End on Recognition of Validity of Marriages," *The Japanese American News*, 19 April 1917, San Francisco, translation by B. C. Haworth, INS file 52424/13A (1917–); RCO, entry 9, box 107, 53434/1–52424/13-C; INS, DC, RG85; NA, DC.

[42] When responsibility for immigration was shifted to the new Department of Labor, the policy of admitting women as picture wives under specified conditions was reluctantly continued. In a report to the State Department, the Department of Labor explained that current policy was untenable: "In other words, a woman, no matter whence she might come, arriving at one of our ports without the qualifications required by laws for entry might qualify by being permitted to do *after* arrival that which, as one of the necessary elements for admission, should have been a fact *before* arrival." In deciding in favor of compromise, the Department of Labor noted that Japan was not the only country that permitted proxy marriages, both Spain and Portugal allowing their citizens to marry in absentia. INS file 52424/13C (1917–); RCO, entry 9, box 107, 53434/1–52424/13-C; INS, DC, RG85; NA, DC.

[43] As a critic of the policy explained, "This, in effect, allowed a 'picture bride' while in an immigration station at a United States port to qualify as the wife of a resident of the United States in order to become admissible under the immigration law—something not contemplated by its provisions." INS file 52424/13A (1917–); RCO, entry 9, box 107, 53434/1–52424/13-C; INS, DC, RG85; NA, DC.

[44] United States immigration authorities agreed to stop contesting the arrival of the remaining picture brides for a period of six months. Assistant Commissioner-General to Com-

terms in which other women, married in absentia, were evaluated as wives, and correspondence marriages from other countries continued to be viewed with suspicion as a means of evading immigration law. Indeed, there were cases of European proxy marriages. When Sabina Suzanna arrived in 1924, immigration authorities determined she was illiterate; moreover, authorities ruled that her marriage to a citizen was not a legal marriage. Suzanna had been married by proxy to Manual Gomes while she was in Portugal and he was in Philadelphia.[45] Similarly, when Elodia Gisbert Lledo arrived in 1923 from Spain, she was excluded upon arrival, according to authorities, on numerical, economic, and marital grounds, "in view of the fact that the department does not recognize proxy marriages." They had been engaged to be married before he departed, but Lledo had refused to finalize the commitment for fear of being left behind. In defending her marriage to immigration authorities, Lledo emphasized her legal and emotional commitment to her husband:

Q: Why didn't your husband come to Spain to marry you?
A: Because we are poor, and it would entail great expense to us.
Q: You are advised that for immigration purposes proxy marriages are not recognized by our department. Now, in the event that they should want you to remarry this man, would you be willing to do that?
A: Yes; I want to comply with the marriage laws of the United States.

Lledo's husband testified that the two had been married by proxy out of fear that if he left the country he would be unable to return given the new, stricter quota provisions. Immigration authorities found the marriage illegal, and held Lledo for deportation.[46] By 1924, all dispute would be removed. In the 1924 National Origins Act, Congress specified, "the terms 'wife' and 'husband' do not include a wife or a husband by reason of a proxy or picture marriage."[47]

---

missioner of Immigration, San Francisco, California, 2 July 1920, INS files 18589/15–6 and 7, AICF; INS, SFD, RG85; NA-PSR.

[45] Upon hearing her case, the court disagreed and recognized Suzanna's marriage as legal. *Ex parte Suzanna* 295 F. 713 (D.Mass. 1924).

[46] The court disagreed and ruled in favor of the couple and their marriage. Proxy marriages, the court ruled, were legal in Spain. According to the court, marriages should be evaluated based upon the laws of the state within which they were conducted. *United States ex rel. Aznar v. Commissioner of Immigration at Port of New York* 298 F. 103 (S.D.N.Y. 1924). In a similar case, Maria de Jusus Lopes Baptista arrived in 1923. Illiterate, Lopes Baptista had hoped to enter as the wife of a resident alien. Immigration authorities refused to recognize the validity of her marriage and excluded her upon arrival. Released on bond in 1923, Lopes Baptista's case was heard three years later. *Kane v. Johnson* 13 F.2d 432 (D.Mass. 1926).

[47] Section 28(n) of the Immigration Act of 1924; see Frank L. Auerbach, ed., " 'GI Brides Act' and 'GI Fiancees Act': Some Questions Concerning Their Interpretation and Administration," *Interpreter Releases* 24, no. 10 (24 February 1947), RACNS.

CONDUCT UNBECOMING A CITIZEN: PROSTITUTION, MARRIAGE, AND "MORAL CHARACTER"

If proxy or picture marriages risked the legal sanctity of marriage, then the marriages of suspected immoral women jeopardized its moral core. By the early twentieth century, immigration authorities began to suspect that marriages between citizens and immigrant women charged with prostitution were also efforts to evade immigration law.[48] Inspectors reported conspiracies by pimps and other sordid men to marry prostitutes threatened with deportation.[49] In theory, an immigrant woman unable to prove her status as a legal wife or charged with immoral conduct could avoid the perils of immigration law only by becoming a citizen. Yet laws providing women derivative citizenship status intersected with laws regulating prostitution, morality, and immigrant women's sexual behavior in ways that served to reinforce the dictates of heterosexual marriage. Laws against prostitutes acquiring derivative citizenship through marriage in the years before 1922 worked to exclude women suspected of immoral conduct from the privileges of citizenship and the protected status of a wife.

Many prostitutes may indeed have used the law to avoid deportation, as one woman supposedly commented to a New York police officer, "Of course you know, John, that if I married that fellow Roe [pseudonym] it was only to beat deportation and be safe forever, as I am now an American citizen."[50] The 1910–1911 Dillingham Commission report criticized immigration authorities who allowed women subject to deportation to remain if they married American citizens. "There is every reason to believe," the report claimed "that this device is followed by professional prostitutes who have no intention whatever of giving up their practices or of making a home for the men whom they marry."[51] The theory behind derivative citizenship had been to link the home within one national identity, one civic loyalty. As the loyal wife of a citizen and the loving mother of future American citizens, an immigrant woman's role in the family and in the nation was clear. Professional prostitutes, according to the Dillingham Commission, mocked the image of the American home and the legitimacy of derivative marital citizenship, and therefore should be excluded from its privileges.

[48] "Report to Commissioner-General of Immigration, Washington, D.C.," 24 March 1911, casefile 52241/5; RINS, SCF, PWS, reel 1. See also Marcus Bruan, Special Immigrant Inspector, "Report to Commission-General," 29 September 1908, casefile 52484/1-A; RINS, SCF, PWS, reel 3.

[49] Office of Inspector in Charge, Galveston Texas, "Report to Commissioner-General of Immigration, Washington DC," 22 July 1909, casefile 52484/8-B; RINS, SCF, PWS, reel 4.

[50] *Importation and Harboring of Women for Immoral Purposes*, 112.

[51] Ibid., 70.

The Immigration Bureau held to a policy that citizenship could not be conferred upon an alien woman who demonstrated immoral conduct at the time of her marriage to an American citizen, reasoning that derivative citizenship passed only to those persons who themselves might be naturalized.[52] In May 1909, the bureau instructed its officers that "whenever it comes to your notice that a woman of alien birth who is shown to be here less than three years is engaged in the practice of prostitution at the time of her marriage to an American citizen, you may take up her case as if such marriage had not taken place."[53] The attorney general confirmed the legality of the bureau's policy and emphasized the significance of moral legitimacy for marital validity.[54]

Suspicion of Asian marriages, a long-time practice, reemerged in the context of deportation proceedings against prostitutes married to American citizens. Looe Shee came to the United States in 1906 from Mexico as the lawful wife of Lew Chow, a citizen. Three years later she was arrested in a house of prostitution, charged with being a prostitute for the last year. In issuing the warrant for deportation, the secretary of commerce and labor ruled that their marriage was not "for the purpose of creating the relation of husband and wife," but a "mere sham," and "a means for evading the laws of the United States."[55] The Ninth Circuit Court of Appeals agreed, finding that despite her technical status as wife of a citizen, at the time of her arrest she was not a wife in the true meaning of the law. Legal traditions of coverture providing that wives could not testify against their husbands did not extend to prostitutes. Beginning in 1910, in cases involving alien prostitutes, husband and wife were allowed to testify against one another in a court of law.[56]

Li A. Sim, also the wife of a citizen, was held for deportation in San Francisco as an inmate of a house of prostitution.[57] In its 1912 decision on her appeal, the Supreme Court upheld Immigration Bureau policy by ruling that women could not acquire derivative citizenship through mar-

---

[52] The INS based this on the circuit court's ruling in *In re Rustigian* 165 F. 980 (D.R.I. 1908), Daniel J. Keefe, Commissioner-General, "Memo to Daniel J. Leonard, Immigrant Inspector, Boston, MA," 21 May 1909, casefile 52484/11; RINS, SCF, PWS, reel 4.

[53] Daniel J. Keefe, Commission-General, "Memo to Daniel J. Leonard, Immigrant Inspector, Boston, MA," 21 May 1909, casefile 52484/11; RINS, SCF, PWS, reel 4.

[54] Commissioner-General, "Memorandum for the Acting Secretary, In re adoption of a definite policy with respect to the decision of cases in which alien women, after deportation proceedings are instituted, contract marriages with American citizens," 7 October 1915, casefile 52241/5; RINS, SCF, PWS, reel 1.

[55] *Looe Shee v. North, Immigration Com'r et al.* 170 F. 566 (9th Cir. 1909).

[56] Connelly, *The Response to Prostitution in the Progressive Era*, 56.

[57] "Decision of the Supreme Court of the United States approving deportation of departmental warrant of an immoral Chinese woman," memorandum, 25 June 1912, casefile 52241/5; RINS, SCF, PWS, reel 1.

riage if they themselves were not eligible for citizenship. According to the Court, Li A. Sim failed to meet both the racial and moral character requirements for naturalization. "Good moral character" and whiteness had been requirements of citizenship since the first naturalization statutes passed in the late eighteenth century. Li A. Sim was not a citizen, although she was married to one, because she was neither white nor of good moral character. Consequently, she remained an alien and subject to the laws against alien prostitutes.[58]

Administrative practice and judicial review were eventually incorporated into the Immigration Act of 1917; women who fell within the laws against prostitutes and were married to citizens would not acquire United States citizenship.[59] Its impact is clear in the case of Bessie Stein, who arrived from Poland in 1902 or 1903. Stein drifted westward from New York to Portland, where she worked as a prostitute from 1912 to 1919. She was arrested ten times on charges of vagrancy and solicitation. At her hearing, Stein testified that she had quit the "rooming house business" and had begun living with Harry Fisher, although the two were not married. Six months later, in 1922, she married H. Bigney, a naturalized citizen. The court found that she did not become a citizen though marriage under the act of 1917 and was liable to deportation.[60] Similarly, Guadalupe Flores first emigrated to the United States from Mexico when she was fourteen. Before her marriage to Columbus Smith, she traveled back and forth between Nogales, Arizona and Nogales, Sonora, working as a prostitute while in Mexico. Flores married Smith, a citizen, at age twenty and attempted to return to the United States for permanent residence. She was excluded under the terms of the 1917 statue.[61] Prostitution precluded derivative citizenship; immigrant prostitutes married to citizens remained aliens.

Marriage provided the linchpin between policies of family reunification and those of immigration restriction. If there was no legal marriage, there could be no legal family and thus no claims to entry or access. As long as "wife" remained a privileged category under the law, immigration and judicial officials were forced to contend with the question of marriage—what exactly constituted a legal, state solemnized relationship. Religious

---

[58] *Low Wah Suey v. Buckus, Commissioner of Immigration* 255 U.S. 460 (1912); see the decision of Justice Day, 476.

[59] The proviso was introduced twice before, once in 1913 and again in 1915, before finally being passed in 1917; see *Ex parte Bigney* 285 F. 669 (D.Or. 1923). The policy of excluding prostitutes from citizenship continued under the Cable Act with the 1930 amendment excluding prostitutes from the provisions of the 1922 act. Hutchinson, *Legislative History of American Immigration Policy*, 162.

[60] *Ex parte Bigney* 285 F. 669 (D.Or. 1923).

[61] *Ex parte Flores* 272 F. 783 (D.Ariz. 1921); also see case of Anna Sage, *United States ex rel. Sage v. District Director of Immigration* 82 F. 630 (7th Cir. 1936).

marriages, common-law marriages, and even polygamous marriages had brought the problem into legal relief. However, picture brides, correspondence marriages, and the marriages of women charged with prostitution brought the problem of marriage into legal crisis. The debate over the parameters of lawful marriage would be revisited twenty years later in the context of a second war and a second incarnation of domesticity in immigration policy.

CHAPTER THREE

Seeing Difference

Perhaps the greatest challenge to the legal image of women immigrants as wives lay in the threat of women's sexual labor outside the home. In his December, 1874 message to Congress, President Ulysses S. Grant called upon the legislature to shore up the nation's borders against the arrival of Chinese women "brought for shameful purposes, to the disgrace of the communities where settled and to the great demoralization of the youth of these localities."[1] Anti-Chinese sentiment had been building on the West Coast; although primarily aimed at laboring men, racialized hostility was also directed at Chinese women. Grant's message to Congress called the nation's attention to the permeability of its borders to lewd and dishonorable sexual labor. A year later, Congress acted on Grant's call for the selective exclusion of this immoral class of immigrants and passed the Immigration Act of 1875. The law designated two excludable classes of aliens, those who had been convicted and were serving a sentence for committing a felony, and women imported for the purposes of prostitution.[2]

First evident in the development and application of laws against Asian prostitutes, gender and racial hierarchies merged in the process of evaluating immigrant women. Marriage and morality became a central tension in immigration law dividing citizens and immigrants from undesirables. The 1875 act was the nation's first selective exclusion law and ushered in an era of restrictive legislation that would, by the early decades of the twentieth century, proscribe a long list of immoral behaviors, physical defects, mental deficiencies, and racial characteristics.

Legislating against undesirable classes of immigrants was one thing—detecting and differentiating undesirable from desirable immigrants at the moment of their arrival or their application for citizenship proved far more difficult. Laws implicating immigrant women upon their arrival relied on the visibility of immorality to determine which women were immoral women. The problem of detection became a problem of seeing difference, one which linked abhorrent sexual behavior to race, emphasizing the visibility of immorality on the nonwhite female body. As a practical

---

[1] Hutchinson, *Legislative History of American Immigration Policy*, 65.
[2] Ibid., 65–66.

measure, immigration officials at the nation's borders defined moral deviance as a visible procedure long before the federal courts would confirm the visible common sense of racialized and sexualized identities.

Through the early decades of the twentieth century, more and more American women sought work and leisure outside the home, and concerns over prostitution expanded to include a growing number of white ethnic women. Although the strong perceptual link established in the late nineteenth century between race, sex, and prostitution would prove enduring well into the twentieth century, race would become an increasingly troublesome marker for immorality. Detecting "white" women's moral and sexual intentions proved difficult. Increasingly, immigration inspectors and court officials relied on a process of disclosure that interrogated the testimony of women themselves to reveal their past indiscretions and future intentions.

SEEING RESPECTABILITY: ASIAN WOMEN AND LAWS AGAINST PROSTITUTION

The 1875 law excluding prostitutes was in many ways a response to anti-Chinese agitation on the West Coast that had painted all Chinese women immigrants with the broad brush of moral and physical contagion.[3] During the 1870s and 1880s, the height of agitation against Chinese immigrants in California, Chinese women working as prostitutes were never more than six percent of the total immigrant population.[4] The number of Chinese women who worked as prostitutes, however, remained high, the tragic result of race, gender, and class discrimination both in the United States and in China, which left these women vulnerable to an exploitative labor system.[5] Despite their overall small numbers, the very presence of

[3] Beginning in 1870, California itself had passed a series of laws attempting to prevent the arrival of Chinese prostitutes. These laws were eventually held to be unconstitutional, a violation of both Chinese treaty rights and the rights of any person to equal protection, as well as an infringement on federal jurisdiction over commerce and trade. Sucheng Chan, "The Exclusion of Chinese Women, 1870–1943," 99–105; Charles J. McClain, *In Search of Equality: The Chinese Struggle against Discrimination in Nineteenth-Century America* (Berkeley: University of California Press, 1994), 56.

[4] The enactment of the 1875 immigration law against prostitutes and the 1882 Chinese Exclusion Act frustrated the organized traffic in Chinese women that had characterized the period between 1849 and 1870, making the importation of Chinese prostitutes prohibitively expensive. Lucie Cheng Hirata, "Free, Indentured, Enslaved," 27.

[5] Estimates of the incidence of Chinese prostitution in San Francisco have varied, but historians agree that heavy proportions of Chinese women worked in the sex trade during the 1860s and 1870s, with smaller percentages during the 1880s. Judy Yung summarizes the calculations offered by Lucie Cheng Hirata and Sucheng Chan as follows: eighty-five to

Chinese prostitutes inspired weighty fears over the permeability of the nation's borders to race, sex, and moral contamination.

Women being imported for "lewd or immoral purposes" or as prostitutes would hardly admit to their illegal activities. Particularly after consulting with a lawyer, women attempted to craft their stories for immigration officials in a more moral and respectable light; others simply chose not to speak at all. Chow Gum Ying and Yet Sue, charged with practicing prostitution in Los Angeles in 1898, refused to speak with immigration officers after talking with their attorney.[6] Thus, enforcing the law against prostitutes required that immigration officials, in essence, know one when they see one. Immorality, however, proved difficult to see. For example, in August, 1874, twenty-two out of eighty-nine Chinese women on a ship arriving in San Francisco were detained under California law for suspicion of coming for immoral purposes. They had been singled out for their unsavory demeanor and immodest dress.[7] The captain of the ship disagreed, and appearing on the women's behalf he insisted their conduct while aboard ship was nothing less than honorable and respectable. Neither court officials nor expert witnesses could manage to agree on how to differentiate moral Chinese women from their immoral and degenerate sisters.[8]

Faced with the responsibility for enforcement, immigration officials attempted to discern immoral from moral women through careful observation of women's appearance and their behavior and repeated interrogation of their testimony.[9] If race and gender status raised suspicions, then investigation provided proof.[10] Unaccompanied young women were ques-

---

ninety-seven percent of Chinese women worked as prostitutes in San Francisco in 1860; seventy-one to seventy-two percent in 1870; and twenty-one to fifty percent in 1880. Yung, *Unbound Feet*, 29.

[6] Lee Yow Kam, INS files 9560/725–728 (1896); AICF, box 34; INS, SFD, RG85; NA-PSR.

[7] Reverend Otis Gibson, director of the Methodist mission in Chinatown, claimed that the handkerchiefs the women wore on their heads along with their brightly colored embroidered dresses were similar to those worn by courtesans in China. McClain, *In Search of Equality*, 57.

[8] Fifty to sixty of the eighty-nine women arriving were held for questioning with twenty-two eventually detained. The captain's testimony may have been less than reliable. Shipping companies were often required to return inadmissible immigrants to their original destination free of charge. See Chan, "The Exclusion of Chinese Women," 99–100; McClain, *In Search of Equality*, 55–61.

[9] Drawing on U.S. government reports, Lucie Hirata suggests that some Chinese prostitutes were coached to respond to probable questions from immigration authorities. One such coaching paper that circulated in Canton and Hong Kong, Hirata notes, included some eighty-one questions, including questions about San Francisco geography. Hirata, "Free, Indentured, Enslaved," 11.

[10] Young Choy Ling, INS files 9582/ 795 and 796/797 (1890); AICF, box 36; INS, SFD, RG85; NA-PSR.

tioned about how they had paid for their steamer tickets, whether anyone from the United States had visited them in China (presumably to arrange to purchase their sexual labor), and if they had spoken to anyone while awaiting their hearings.[11] Chong Kwai arrived with her sister en route to join their father, who lived in San Francisco. Born in San Francisco but raised in China, Chong was suspected of being a prostitute. The investigator's line of questioning was typical:

Q: Has anyone, man or woman, from San Francisco been to see you in China?
A: Yes. Somebody has been to China but I do not know who it was.
Q: When?
A: 1890.
Q: Did you see him often?
A: Only once.
Q: Was it a man or a woman?
A: A woman.
Q: Did she come from San Francisco?
A: She lived in Canton City. No. She did not come from San Francisco.
Q: Did anyone from San Francisco come to see you in China?
A: No.
Q: No one at all?
A: No.[12]

Born within a few years of the passage of the 1875 act prohibiting the importation of women to work as prostitutes, Chong had left the United States a few months before the passage of the 1882 Immigration Act prohibiting the immigration of all Chinese except for merchants and their families. She returned to California to face the combined weight of race- and sexuality-based exclusion laws.

As the enforcement of laws excluding prostitutes was layered onto the enforcement of more general race-based exclusion laws, Chinese women's moral and familial status became the subject of intense scrutiny. Wives and daughters of merchants, along with returning native-born Chinese Americans, constituted the limits of permissible immigration. Those who were not permissible were excludable, and those who were excludable were often dismissed through the language of immorality and sex labor. The Dillingham Commission expressed grave suspicions about those few Chinese women who were able to emigrate under the exempt familial status. "Doubtless," the commissioner warned, "in many instances women are brought in as wives of members of these exempt classes and are then sold to keepers of houses."[13] In defending themselves,

[11] Ho Kum Nuey, INS file 9541/155 (1896); AICF, box 33; INS, SFD, RG85; NA-PSR.
[12] Chong Kwai, INS file 9532/108 (1896); AICF, box 32; INS, SFD, RG85; NA-PSR.
[13] *Importation and Harboring of Women for Immoral Purposes*, 69.

Chinese women attempted to prove their moral character by laying claim to respectability as the wives and daughters of merchants and citizens. Visibility, the ability to discern respectable women, took on a new valence as the arrival hearing became a more formalized process of revealing and exposing, on the one hand, and legitimating and defending on the other.[14]

If immorality was marked primarily by race, respectability came to be marked by a series of gender and class codes. In the eyes of immigration officials, respectable women did not travel unaccompanied by male family members.[15] Gook Chun arrived from China in 1936 to join her father and brothers in San Francisco. All were interviewed by immigration officials. Minor discrepancies were apparent in their testimony, having mostly to do with the families of their neighbors in China. More damning, however, was a letter and telegram received by immigration authorities that insisted two girls who had arrived on Gook Chun's steamer were coming for immoral purposes. Gook's luggage was searched by immigration officials. Authorities concluded her baggage contained more clothing than thought proper for a girl of her age and station in life, as well as a few articles authorities deemed strange.[16] Gook Chun, a single girl with too many clothes, found herself outside the confines of respectability.

Immigration officials were guided by a uniquely western understanding of respectability in their evaluation of women immigrants. The "strange" and incriminating things found in Gook Chun's luggage were reflective of racial, class, and gender codes developed within the American context and applied to non-American women. Immigration officials attempted to see respectability in the unfamiliar by layering what they knew of Chinese cultural customs onto American understandings of class and gender. For example, respectable middle- and upper-class Chinese women, immigra-

---

[14] Leon Shee, INS file 10111/10 (1906); AICF, box n/a; INS, SFD, RG85; NA-PSR. At times, the courts severely criticized the Immigration and Naturalization Service's use of hostile interviewing techniques in which they attempted to confound the witness by pointing out discrepancies in the testimony. In *Wong Hai Sing v. Nagle* 47 F.2d 1021 (9th Cir. 1931) the Ninth Circuit Court of Appeals held "in long and involved cross-examination of several persons covering the minutiae of daily life, discrepancies are bound to develop and are inconclusive with regard to the testimony as a whole when they are on minor points." In *Hom Chung v. Nagle* 41 F.2d 126 (9th Cir. 1930), the court ruled similarly, "The discrepancies which existed between them are fairly attributable to the frailties of human memory, the method of the examination and the difficulties of language; and do not fairly indicate a deliberate conspiracy to obtain a fraudulent entry into the United States. . . ." In *Gung You v. Nagle* 34 F.2d 848 (9th Cir. 1929), the court suggested, "The difficulty in these cases of 'discrepancy' is that there is no standard of comparison. The immigration authorities know nothing of the actual facts, but match witness against witness and thus develop inconsistencies." See also *Go Lun v. Nagle* 22 F.2d 246 (9th Cir. 1927); *Ex parte Jew You On* 16 F.2d 153 (N.D.Cal. 1926); *Wong Gook Chun v. Proctor* 84 F.2d 763 (9th Cir. 1936).

[15] Wong Sing How, INS file 10002–32 (1904); AICF, box 98; INS, SFD, RG85; NA-PSR.

[16] *Wong Gook Chun v. Proctor* 84 F.2d 763 (9th Cir. 1936).

tion authorities maintained, had bound feet. Lum Ah Ging arrived in 1896, claimed to have been born in San Francisco, and was engaged to be married. Despite disagreements with her uncle about whether her mother had died in China or in San Francisco, or whether her father had a younger brother, the appearance of respectability proved convincing. The immigration inspector concluded the case was meritorious, remarking, "This case bears a badge of respectability. The elder girl is a small footed woman, and the witnesses, with the exception, are of a superior class to those who generally appear in these women cases."[17] Prostitution was assumed to be the province of the lower classes. Lum Ah Ging's bound feet signaled a "superior" class status and provided a "badge of respectability," that, according to San Francisco immigration officials, placed her character beyond the pale of moral indictment. Words disguised what the body disclosed. While women's stories and autobiographies came under increasing suspicion, visible clues to a woman's moral worth, like bound feet, remained an important tool for immigration officials.

Immigration officials assumed that respectable married women lived with their husbands, providing household and reproductive labor. Thus when Ho Shee arrived in San Francisco in 1911, immigration officials sought guarantees from her husband that the couple intended to live together as man and wife:

Q: And are you bringing this woman to be your wife?
A: Yes, my legal wife.
Q: If any of the Immigration officials should call at your rooms would they be able to find your wife there?
A: Yes.

In questioning Ho Shee's mother-in-law, officials challenged the validity of the marriage with the presumed likelihood of prostitution:

Q: Do you believe your son truly married this woman and that she is his lawful wife?
A: He wrote to me all about his engagement.
Q: (Alleged wife brought in) Are you positive that your son married this woman to be his wife?
A: Yes, I am positive that this is my son's wife.
Q: And that he is bringing her for no other purpose than to be his wife?
A: This is my only son and I wouldn't have him do anything like that for any amount of money.

[17] Lum Ah Ging and Lam Ah Kue, INS files 9555/590 and 591 (1896); AICF, box 33; INS, SFD, RG85: NA-PSR; also see Chung Shee, casefile 10015/3530, 101 (1904); AICF, box n/a; INS, SFD, RG85; NA-PSR.

Immigration inspectors drew on the unequal power relationship between Ho Shee and her mother-in-law in monitoring Ho Shee's status as a wife. If Ho Shee should leave her husband, she could be turned in by his mother as a prostitute:

> Q: If this girl is inclined to be wayward and runs away from home and becomes a prostitute will you notify this office?
> A: Yes, I will watch her.
> Q: If your son gets rid of her will you notify this office, do you promise that?
> A: Yes, I promise.[18]

Striking in this interchange between the immigration inspector and the mother-in-law was the suggestion that Asian women who became prostitutes were not victims of male sexual debauchery or economic destitution, but "wayward" girls who spurned the protection of the home and sought unwarranted independence from their families. This depiction of Asian women as voluntary prostitutes remained an insistent theme in public discussions of Asian women's immigration, and stood in marked contrast to the sympathetic images of naive ethnic European women tricked or seduced into prostitution that perforated the literature of the white slave panic of the 1900s and 1910s. The language of slavery when applied to Chinese immigrant women served only to deepen their sexual degeneracy and moral inadequacy as members of the nation.

Chinese women temporarily paroled to alleged husbands were often investigated in the months following their arrival. Investigators sought to determine whether in fact the couple representing themselves as husband and wife actually cohabited and consummated the marriage. Chan Ching was visited by an immigration inspector ten separate times between 20 April and 24 September 1917, four months after her arrival. In his reports, the inspector noted apparent evidence of prostitution—"her general appearance indicated that she had dressed hurriedly and she had a very dissipated look." On another occasion, he remarked the presence of a male visitor, "There was a Chinaman sitting on the bed in this room, who said his name was Louie Shew," and the suspicious nature of Chan Ching's apartment, "The general appearance of the room was such as is generally found in Chinese houses of prostitution." According to Chan, her husband was working in Bakersfield, California, but his continued absence served as further proof of their fraudulent marriage.[19] Segregated

---

[18] Ho Shee [pseud.], INS file 1300/108183 (1911–1932); Unprocessed, box 336186; INS, SFD, RG85; NA-PSR.

[19] Chan Ching, aka Chan Shee, INS file 15834/5–4 (1917); AICF, box n/a; INS, SFD, RG85; NA-PSR. In October 1918, Chan Ching was arrested and detained for deportation

housing and job discrimination made it all but impossible for Chan to maintain the marital relationship and home life immigration officials expected of respectable women. As Chan Ching's experience demonstrates, women's respectability remained on trial long after they had passed through Angel Island.

When women like Chan Ching attempted to defend their respectability and stave off deportation, however, they were at a decided disadvantage in immigration hearings, where they faced circumstantial evidence, insinuation, and inspector's judgments. Rarely were women given an opportunity to confront their accusers. For example, a letter from the matron at the detention center condemning Chan Ching's unladylike and indecent behavior, and a photograph of Chan Ching in street attire (a shorter dress falling to mid-calf), were all referenced in the Commissioner's final letter recommending dismissal.[20]

Reliance on testimonials from often estranged family members or judgmental community members reveal the fragility of respectability and women's vulnerability to rumor and insinuation.[21] Drawing on witnesses' testimony in the case of Honolulu arrival Lum Mew Lan "that her character is not very good" and they had "only seen her on the street," the Honolulu inspector was "well satisfied that she does not bear a good name" and her "reputation for moral character is not of the best." Importantly, witnesses had corroborated what the inspector believed could be easily seen: Lum Mew Lan's son was "evidently half white and half Chinese" and therefore could not be the legitimate son of Lum and her husband, both Chinese. The visibility of immorality on the nonwhite body provided conclusive evidence. Lum was accused of adultery as well as prostitution, and even marriage could not rescue her from moral incrimination.[22]

Nineteenth-century sexualized images of Chinese women threw long shadows over Japanese women arriving decades later. William Gates, secretary of the California State Board of Charities and Corrections, argued in his 1907 national address that "the Japanese are but little better than the Chinese," and it was "safe to say that far more than a majority of these females were prostitutes."[23] In a 1907 investigation of Japanese

---

proceedings by immigration officials. She presented letters from her husband as proof of their relationship. Also see *Looe Shee v. North* 170 F. 566 (9th Cir. 1909).

[20] Chan Ching, aka Chan Shee, INS file 15834/5–4 (1917); AICF box n/a; INS, SFD, RG85; NA-PSR.

[21] For relevant cases see INS file 13406/13–8 (n.d.); AICF, box n/a; INS, SFD, RG85; NA-PSR; and Wong Sing How, INS file 10002–32 (1904); AICF, box 98; INS, SFD, RG85; NA-PSR.

[22] Lum Mew Lan, INS file C-2378 (1912–); CICF, box n/a; INS, SFD, RG85; NA-PSR.

[23] W. Almont Gates, *Oriental Immigration on the Pacific Coast: An Address Delivered at the National Conference of Charities and Correction at Buffalo, New York, June 10,*

prostitution rings in Washington, a local witness testified to the prevalence of syphilitic Japanese girls in local restaurants and brothels.[24] Local perceptions inflated the actual incidence of Japanese prostitution, and reports of large numbers of Japanese prostitutes testified to the visibility of nonwhite prostitutes and the fear of moral and racial contamination this visibility engendered in the collective white imagination.[25]

The arrival of a troupe of Japanese dancers to perform at the Panama-Pacific International Exposition held in San Francisco in 1915 gained public notoriety when these women were detained under suspicion of prostitution.[26] An anonymous letter from a fellow passenger claimed the "faithful and sincere" members of the Japanese community in San Francisco found these women to be disreputable. "Among the many delicate stories during the trip," the letter detailed, "Miss Yoshida was known to have had a quaint intercourse with one of the high officers named Kobayashi." The conduct of one woman was enough to raise grave suspicions of all the single women abroad. "Therefore," the letter concluded dramatically, "the rest of them can easily be surmised."[27] Articles in local Japanese newspapers scorned the efforts of Japanese officials to obtain the women's release when "passports are issued so grudgingly to the wives and daughters of men who have prospered in honest enterprise in America."[28] Katherine R. Maurer, deaconess with the Methodist Episcopal Church, testified that she had visited two of the girls, Hana Watanabe and Yoshida Tsuyake, after they had been paroled:

Q: Do you recall whether or not these two particular girls appeared confused or embarrassed at the time you first entered the room?

1909 (San Francisco, 1909), 10, collected in *Japanese Immigration Pamphlets*, Stanford University Green Library, Stanford University.

[24] C. A. Turner, "In the Matter of the Investigation Conducted by Immigrant Inspector Charles L. Babcock, of Washington, DC," report, 27 October 1907, casefile 51701/2A; RINS, SCF, PWS.

[25] Ruth Rosen notes that Chinese and Japanese women were at greater risk for prostitution given anti-Asian activism on the Pacific Coast, along with economic and social conditions in China and Japan that made the prostitution of daughters a viable alternative for families. Rosen, *The Lost Sisterhood: Prostitution in America, 1900–1918* (Baltimore: The Johns Hopkins University Press, 1982), 112–135, esp. 121–122.

[26] For "Cherry Dancing Troupe" see the following files: Kiyoko Kanimatsu, INS file 14571/11–13 (1915); AICF, box 955; INS, SFD, RG85; NA-PSR; Gin Seikiguchi, INS file 14571/11–14 (1915); AICF, box 955; INS, SFD, RG85; NA-PSR; and Hana Watanabe, INS file 14571/11–13 (1915); AICF, box 955; INS, SFD, RG85; NA-PSR.

[27] Hana Watanabe, INS file 14571/11–13 (1915); AICF, box 955; INS, SFD, RG85; NA-PSR. The file includes other similarly damaging letters from anonymous fellow passengers.

[28] Leader in the *Japanese-American News*, 3 August 1915, in Hana Watanabe, INS file 14571/11–13 (1915); AICF, box 955; INS, SFD, RG85; NA-PSR. The file contains other translations of local coverage in the foreign language press.

A: Very much! Everybody seemed confused. I was even embarrassed because I did not expect to find anything of that sort. I told them I would call on them when they were here.

Q: Did you notice anything in the shape of cigar ashes or cigar stumps around the room?

A: Yes, I remember seeing some ash trays and cigarettes. It almost looked to me that the men made a regular business of visiting there. It surprised me so; I did not know whether it was customary or not.

Q: What was the condition of the two girls with reference to being clothed at that time?

A: Well, they had very plain kimonos on, just little kimonos. I suppose they sleep in them, I don't know how Japanese people do. They just had plain little kimonos.[29]

In relating her encounter, Maurer's embarrassment upon confronting the women, and even her seeming discomfort retelling the story to immigration inspectors, contrasted with the confusion and lack of shame demonstrated on the part of Hana and Yoshida. Maurer was ignorant of the scene before her, "It surprised me so," and "I don't know how Japanese people do," while insinuating that Hana and Yoshida were all too familiar with ash trays, cigarettes, and very plain little kimonos. In Maurer's telling, modesty became linked to morality; her embarrassment at things unsightly or unseemly was a sign of her own respectability and served as a foil to the disreputable character of the Japanese women.

Kiyoko Kanimatsu, a third member of the dancing troupe, testifying at her deportation hearing held nearly a year after she was first paroled, denied that she had been working as a prostitute. She was questioned repeatedly about whether she ever entertained men in her room during the evenings, whether she ever received late night telephone calls at her hotel room, and whether she ever met men in the parlor of the hotel:

Q: Are you married?

A: No, I am not married.

Q: Were you ever married?

A: No.

Q: Are you a virtuous girl?

A: Yes, I am believed to be a woman of such character.

Q: I am asking you the question direct. Are you a virtuous girl? I do not want to know the opinion of others. I want to know direct from you what the situation is.

Q: Would you submit to a medical examination to prove that?

[29] Statement of Miss Katherine R. Maurer, 16 March 1916, in Hana Watanabe, INS file 14571/11–13 (1915); AICF, box 955; INS, SFD, RG85; NA-PSR.

A: Certainly (Questions apparently have no embarrassing effect on the witness).[30]

Kiyoko's lack of embarrassment served to confirm the inspector's conclusions that she was not a respectable woman. Her forthright defense of her moral character, and willingness to submit to a humiliating and intrusive medical examination to prove herself, starkly contrast with the notes of surprise, embarrassment, and uncertainty that had rung through deaconess Maurer's testimony. Embarrassment provided a measure of virtue, revealing what lay behind a woman's testimony.

The link between race and sex established in the early laws against Chinese prostitutes endured through the twentieth century to taint the arrival of both Chinese and Japanese women coming as wives and daughters. A woman's sexual history, improper clothing, or even lack of modesty was taken as evidence of disreputable character, sometimes to such an extent that not even marriage could save her from the charge of immorality. An early emphasis on the visibility of immorality on the body of nonwhite, Asian women gave way to an emphasis on disclosure through interrogation. As race-based exclusions increased and the number of Asian women decreased to include only those who were the wives and daughters of merchants or citizens, respectability was put on trial as women attempted to substantiate their moral worth through claims to class and marital status.

THE "WHITE SLAVERY" PROBLEM: WHITENESS AND LAWS AGAINST PROSTITUTION

"Slavery" was a familiar term in debates over controlling the immigration of women working as prostitutes. Both Chinese and Japanese women immigrants had been depicted as sex "slaves." The use of "slavery" to characterize the arrival of "white" women, however, was something new. In the early twentieth century, changing conceptions of racial otherness and anxieties about the white American family intersected with long-held concerns over the moral conduct of immigrants to produce the "white slavery" panic. The group of laws that came under the rubric of white slavery began from an assumption that prostitution could be linked to racialized ethnic categories.

The first immigration law directed at prostitutes in 1875 had been a response to the arrival of Chinese women suspected of prostitution, but

[30] Kiyoko Kanimatsu, INS file 14571/11–13 (1915); AICF, box 955; INS, SFD, RG85; NA-PSR.

it had also established broad prohibitions against the importation of women "for the purposes of prostitution." When the Immigration Acts of 1903, 1907, and 1910 reiterated general restrictions against prostitutes, the application of the policy was redirected toward new European arrivals. Techniques of inquiry and observation developed by immigration officials to test the moral worth of Chinese women arriving at the nation's borders in the last decades of the nineteenth century were being used by the twentieth century to evaluate the moral and sexual respectability of women arriving from Europe and Mexico. Throughout, race remained central to how gender and class ideals of respectability and modesty were applied to white ethnic women immigrants.

Between 1900 and 1910, women made up approximately thirty percent of all new arrivals. The number of new women arrivals as a percentage of all new immigrants would steadily increase over the next decades to forty-three percent in 1915 and forty-six percent in 1925. Women immigrants comprised the majority of new arrivals beginning in 1930. By the turn of the century, white immigrant women were more likely to be southern Italians or Russian Jews than the earlier German or Irish emigrants. In 1885, German and Irish women comprised 48.9% of all arriving female immigrants. Italian and Russian immigrants comprised only six percent. By contrast in 1915, German and Irish immigrants women comprised only fourteen percent of new women arrivals, while Russian and Italian women made up 29.2 percent.[31]

The "new" immigrants from southern and eastern Europe, Mexico, and Japan heightened fears about race difference and biological purity in ways that echoed earlier periods of antagonism against Irish, German, and Chinese immigrants.[32] Immigrants arriving in the decades before 1880 who did not speak English and were not Protestant, who worked for low wages and lived in ethnic enclaves, and who were not white—in the case of the Chinese—or whose racial status was in doubt—in the case of Irish immigrants—were perceived as a threat to a way of life that for many Americans was rooted in specific religious, class, and race experiences. Jewish, Polish, southern Italian, Mexican, and Japanese immi-

[31] *Annual Report of the Superintendent of Immigration to the Secretary of the Treasury* (1892), 7; *Annual Report of the Commissioner-General of Immigration* (1900), 6–7, 14; *Annual Report of the Commissioner-General of Immigration* (1905), 6–7; *Reports of the Department of Commerce and Labor* (1911); *Report to the Secretary of Commerce and Labor and Reports of Bureaus* (1912), 216; *Historical Statistics of the United States*, 112.

[32] John Higham traces the development of nativism in post–Civil War American society; in *Strangers in the Land: Patterns in American Nativism, 1860–1925* (New Brunswick, N.J.: Rutgers University Press, 1955, 1992); Matthew Frye Jacobson, *Whiteness of a Different Color: European Immigrants and the Alchemy of Race* (Cambridge, Mass.: Harvard University Press, 1998).

grants who entered in the years between 1880 and 1910 confronted the legacies of an earlier era which linked the racial status of new arrivals to an evaluation of their moral worth as potential citizens. New arrivals were perceived as a source of moral decay, a sexual threat from outside the nation's borders. Yet, unlike their predecessors, immigrants arriving at the turn of the century met an industrialized, increasingly urban, and newly commodified American society dependent on large numbers of low-wage immigrant workers.

The decades between the so-called closing of the frontier in 1890 and the end of World War I were anxious times for both immigrants and native-born citizens. Change was revealing new social fissures, new economic forces, new population pressures, new gender roles, and a new sexual order. Rising levels of immigration from new areas of Europe, Mexico, and Asia, and greater internal mobility leading to historic migrations out of the South and toward expanding urban metropolises transformed the United States from a nation of distinct ethnic and race regions to a multiethnic, multiracial state. The increased presence of women at work and in public space, and a developing consumer economy with sites of urban, commercialized leisure pulled homosocial words into new heterosocial configurations. Immigrant women entering into this shifting landscape became the focus of reforms intended to reestablish an earlier moral, sexual, and race order. Over time, the effort to control the arrival of immigrant women working as prostitutes, and the ensuing panic over white slavery, raised significant questions about a progressive project invested in the validity of distinct racial categories and the viability of a singular moral order.

Charged with defending the nation's borders, imbued with a confidence that social problems could be diagnosed and treated effectively, and armed with the new social science techniques developed during the Progressive period, Congress studied the twin problems of immigration and prostitution.[33] Over the first decade of the twentieth century, Congress produced two substantive evaluations of immigration law, including a critical appraisal of laws directed at enforcing the moral order. In its 1901 report to Congress, the Industrial Commission, chaired by Albert Clarke, reiterated traditional moral codes as an important component of effective immigration policy. The Commission recommended the exclusion of "prostitutes and persons who procure or attempt to bring in prostitutes or women for

---

[33] Mark Connelly has suggested that the Progressive Era crusade against prostitutes reflected many of the tensions of this conflicted period. Insisting on race, ethnic, and moral distinctions among immigrants was part and parcel of the process of reinventing a social order that would fortify the moral nation against the tides of change. Connelly, *The Response to Prostitution in the Progressive Era* (Chapel Hill: University of North Carolina Press, 1980), 7–8.

the purpose of prostitution," a proposal that became part of the Immigration Act of 1903.[34] The Immigration Act of 1907 reaffirmed the nation's intolerance for the immoral classes and appointed the Immigration Commission, chaired by Senator William Dillingham, to study the immigration problem. Released in 1910 and 1911, the Dillingham Commission issued a forty-two-volume report to Congress on the immigration problem. It included both a meticulous explanation of the racial characteristics that distinguished immigrant groups (those differences that were visible and those that were not) and a detailed evaluation of the so-called "white slavery" problem, a practice the report condemned as "the most pitiful and the most revolting phase of the immigration question."[35]

The Dillingham Commission warned Congress of the moral and physical degeneracy that accompanied the importation and immigration of prostitutes. The threat to the nation's physical and moral health from its borders was real and urgent, the commission concluded, and it called for increasingly strict laws controlling the immigration of women and their procurers.[36] The commission made a number of final recommendations to Congress, including detaining "doubtful cases of young alien women" until their cases had been fully investigated, arresting women found practicing prostitution on site and without warrant, extending the time within which a prostitute could be deported after arrival, imprisoning prostitutes attempting to re-enter after deportation, and shifting the burden of proof in excluding hearings to the alien.[37] All of these recommendations would

---

[34] The 1903 act was a large piece of legislation that served to codify the series of immigration laws passed up until this point. The act reaffirmed existing legislation, such as the contract labor law and Chinese exclusion, while adding to the list of excludable classes, and setting the two-year period of deportability and terms for the exclusion and deportation of prostitutes and their pimps or madams. See Hutchinson, *Legislative History of American Immigration Policy*, 128–131; quote appears on p. 129.

[35] Immigration Commission, *Importation and Harboring of Women for Immoral Purposes*, 57; Immigration Commission, *Dictionary of Races or Peoples*, Reports of the Immigration Commission presented by Mr. Dillingham, 1911, vol. 9; United States Senate, 61st Cong., 3rd sess., Washington, D.C.

[36] The Commission also made brief mention of a growing traffic in male prostitution. (*Importation and Harboring of Women for Immoral Purposes*, 86.) I have found no cases of INS officials investigating male prostitutes. Timothy Gilfoyle documents early concern with male prostitution, noting that several antebellum New York district attorneys prosecuted brothels for "harboring" young boys. Later social surveys conducted during the 1900s also eluded to the presence of male prostitutes, "who talk and acted like women." Gilfoyle, *City of Eros: New York City, Prostitution, and the Commercialization of Sex, 1790–1920* (New York: W.W. Norton & Company, 1992), 137–138, 200, 369–370 fn. 42. Also see George Chauncey, *Gay New York: Gender, Urban Culture, and the Makings of a Gay Male World, 1890–1940* (New York: Basic Books, 1994). Immigrant male sexuality would become the focus of legislative restriction in the post–World War II period.

[37] *Importation and Harboring of Women for Immoral Purposes*, 57, 89–93.

have a significant impact on the law and its application, and many would be incorporated into the Immigration Act of 1910.[38]

The Dillingham Commission produced a *Dictionary of Races or Peoples* which served as an authoritative guide to subsequent volumes in the study. The *Dictionary* grouped peoples within five major classifications— the Caucasian, Ethiopian, Mongolian, Malay, and American, or, as they were termed colloquially, the white, black, yellow, brown, and red races.[39] The *Dictionary* supplemented earlier classification systems and reflected an increasingly schematic and pseudoscientific understanding of race. As first evident in 1899, immigration authorities shifted from categorizing immigrants according to country of birth to a more complex system of racial classification that recognized some forty-five different races (with thirty-six of these indigenous to Europe).[40] Building on this transition from nation as geography to nation as race, the *Dictionary of Races or Peoples* rooted race primarily in phenotype, language, and culture. It suggested that race be understood as a hierarchical form of ethnicity that encompassed historical migration and settlement patterns, contemporary linguistic and religious practices, and an assessment of social development along a continuum of societies, with Anglo Saxon at the pinnacle.[41] The growing complexity of race in immigration law contrasted sharply with its simplicity in naturalization law, which awarded citizenship only to people who were white or who were of African descent. As a result, naturalization examiners and federal court officials were faced with adjudicating the relationship between forty-five "races" of immigrants and two "races" of citizens.[42]

[38] Hutchinson, *Legislative History of American Immigration Policy*, 147–148.

[39] The *Dictionary of Races or Peoples* attempted to sort through rather contentious debates among ethnologists and anthropologists about the role of geography, language, history, and phenotype in classifying the worlds' peoples, eventually settling on the five-part schema developed by Blumenbach. Other writers had proposed three, four, fifteen, twenty-nine, or even sixty-three "great" races. See *Dictionary of Races or Peoples*, especially 1–12.

[40] There was little change in the original classification system developed in 1899 and in use until 1952. Some categories were combined, while others were modified or added, but the essential list stayed much the same. By 1943 the list reflected the separation of race from ethnicity, and distinct white European groups were dropped from use and replaced with a generic category of "White." The 1943 list also replaced African (black) with "Negro"; Central American, Mexican, and South American were replaced by "Latin American." Arabian, Eskimo, and Hawaiian were also eliminated in 1943. Nathan Goldberg, Jacob Lestchinsky, and Max Weinreich, *The Classification of Jewish Immigrants and Its Implications: A Survey of Opinion* (New York: Yiddish Scientific Institute–Yivo, 1945), 104–105.

[41] The commission commented that the difficulty of correctly identifying racial classifications for immigration inspectors made a reliance on phenotype and language a practical necessity. *Dictionary of Races or Peoples*, 3–4.

[42] The result was a series of court cases disputing the contours of "whiteness": López, *White by Law*; Jacobson, *Whiteness of a Different Color*, 223–245. In my own research I

Race, as delineated in the *Dictionary*, was central to the effort to enforce laws against "white slavery." Volume nineteen of the Dillingham Commission report, *Importation and Harboring of Women for Immoral Purposes*, addressed the recruitment of women in Europe, their importation to the United States, and their exploitation as prostitutes. The report attempted to discern which "races or peoples," as defined by the *Dictionary of Races or Peoples*, were most often associated with foreign prostitution. With statistics compiled from the 1908 and 1909 reports of the United States commissioner-general of immigration, the commission concluded that, while French women presented the largest threat at the border, Hebrew women posed an internal threat and were easily seduced into the life once they had been admitted as residents.[43]

By contrast, in its study of New York City arrest records, the commission found that of 2,093 women arrested for prostitution in four months between November 1908 and March 1909, the vast majority were American born. Of the smaller number of immigrant women arrested over this period, 225 (eleven percent) were Jewish, 154 (seven percent) were French, and 31 (one percent) were Italian.[44] Despite the fact that the data seemed to point to a domestic problem rather than an international conspiracy to traffic in women, the commission concluded that congressional and moral authority pointed in only one direction, toward stricter regulatory safeguards at the borders. "Of far greater significance" than the apparent prevalence of domestic prostitution, the commission maintained, was "the inadequacy of the law itself to protect our country against such importation."[45]

A large perceptual disparity separated the commission's report and the experiences of immigrant women. Small numbers of immigrant women deported or arrested for prostitution may attest to women's success in evading detection at the nation's borders and on its city streets. Undoubt-

---

have found evidence that suggests "African descent" may have been contested as well. Before the district court of New York, Bernedito Cruz argued that because his mother was "half African," he was of African descent and therefore entitled to naturalization under law. *In re Cruz* 23 F.Supp. 774 (E.D.N.Y. 1938).

[43] Significantly, the Commission did not contextualize incidents of prostitution in overall annual numbers of women immigrants who entered United States ports. *Importation and Harboring of Women for Immoral Purposes*, 62–65.

[44] Ibid., 62–63. A predominance of native-born women in the sex trade is confirmed by similar contemporary surveys of prostitutes. Gilfoyle notes that a 1912 study of 1,000 streetwalkers in New York City found sixty-nine percent to be native born. Katharine Bement Davis's study of 647 prostitutes argued sixty-three percent of the women were native born. Finally, Gilfoyle's own sampling of 1,106 women who passed through the Women's Court in New York City from 1914 to 1917 confirmed that the vast majority of prostitutes were native born women. Gilfoyle, *City of Eros*, 292.

[45] *Importation and Harboring of Women for Immoral Purposes*, 65.

edly, some women immigrants intended to work as full- or part-time prostitutes upon arrival; many more found sex work more lucrative than factory labor or domestic service and may have chosen to work as prostitutes after having settled in American cities. Hilma Baardsen arrived in New York in 1907 from Finland. She was temporarily detained and then discharged to an employer as a servant. Two years later, Baardsen was arrested in New York for loitering and accosting men on the street for prostitution. In her file, immigration authorities noted that Baardsen was now a resident and not an immigrant; thus it was too late to deport her.[46] Through carefully calculated appearances, immigrant women could blur the assumed visible distinction between immorality and morality. For these reasons, while the actual number of immigrant women deported or arrested for prostitution remained low, fear of immigrant women's sexuality was high.

The Dillingham Commission's report argued for a link between sexual deviance and visible ethnic-racial otherness, in essence, "foreignness."[47] Immigration agents in the field attempting to enforce laws against "white slavery," however, wrote central administrators for greater clarification. Should "white slavery" enforcement be directed at all those ethnically and racially foreign, as the commission seemed to suggest, or all those "white?" In his 1909 report to the INS, a San Antonio district inspector questioned whether "white slavery" laws should be used against Mexican prostitutes:

> Another feature in connection with the work along the Mexican border is the handling of the so-called White Slave cases. In the majority of these cases the women are not such as are termed "White Slaves," by any means. They are merely prostitutes who cross the Border from Mexico for the purpose of practicing prostitution in the adjacent cities, and do so of their own volition, merely for the purpose of increasing their revenues.[48]

For the inspector, racial identity, sexual identity, and consent were linked. The San Antonio inspector argued that Mexican prostitutes should not be included under "white slavery" policies because they were neither "white" nor "slaves" and thus they did not deserve the protection from procurement the San Antonio inspector believed the law afforded.

---

[46] Hilma Baardsen [pseud.], casefile 52241/129 (1909); DJA-INS acc. 60 A 600, box 125; INS, DC, RG85; NA, DC.

[47] Mark Connelly notes that anti-Semitism provided an important theme in white slavery tracts. Procurers were often scripted as dark, lecherous, foreign men. Connelly, *The Response to Prostitution*, 61, 118.

[48] Immigrant Inspector Richard H. Taylor, "Report on Inspection of San Antonio District," casefile 52541/44, 11–12 (1909); RINS, SCF, MI, reel 2.

Reports from San Francisco also pointed out the irrelevancy of "white" slavery laws to Asian prostitution, drawing similar distinctions based on skin color and the assumed willingness of Chinese and Japanese women to participate in prostitution. The Dillingham Commission had condemned the severity and degradation of Chinese prostitution: "Under the conditions ruling in the Chinese quarters of our cities, such women become really slaves; doubtless in many cases they have been slaves at home."[49] Yet it had offered little sympathy for the women forced to work in the sex trade. Similarly, in a 1910 report to Washington, D.C., the immigration commissioner for San Francisco noted in reference to the "so-called White Slave Traffic" that "when Chinese women arrested in connection with this traffic are released upon bail, almost invariably they immediately return to the practice of their nefarious occupation." The San Francisco commissioner questioned whether resources were well spent enforcing "white slavery" laws on nonwhite prostitutes:

> Early next month we shall be ready to proceed to enforce the new Act [Immigration Act of 1910] and wish instructions as to how vigorously you desire us to take action, inasmuch as with a sufficient number of officers we can of course arrest every Japanese woman in this district engaged in this pursuit and the number is multitudinous, and likewise almost every Chinese woman, as well as a very number of European aliens.[50]

If new regulations governing the arrival of immoral women were an effort to control alien prostitutes, San Francisco authorities alerted Washington officials that much of their time and energy would be directed toward arresting Asian women.

Despite the Dillingham Commission's condemnation of the slavelike condition of Chinese prostitution, by 1911 the commissioner-general advised San Francisco that new laws against "white slaves" should be applied to "immoral aliens of other than the Chinese race." In response, the San Francisco office submitted examples of informant letters which testified to the presence of Chinese "slave girls" and asked the central office once again "whether Chinese prostitutes shall be included in the same policy."[51] For officials working on the Pacific Coast, the moral crisis remained decidedly nonwhite in origin, and laws directed at abolishing "white slavery" had little to offer immigration officials in San Francisco concerned with the arrival of Asian slave girls.

---

[49] *Importation and Harboring of Women for Immoral Purposes*, 69.

[50] H. H. North, "Letter to Commissioner-General of Immigration, Washington, D.C.," 27 April 1910, casefile 52809/7; RINS, SCF, PWS, reel 6.

[51] Samuel W. Backus, "Letter to Commissioner-General of Immigration, Washington, D.C.," 14 March 1913, casefile 52809/7-E; RINS, SCF, PWS, reel 6.

The incriminating and even dismissive treatment of Asian and Mexican prostitutes contrasted rather sharply with the sweeping intent of immigration laws and policies directed at eradicating prostitution by European immigrant women. As the reports from San Antonio and San Francisco suggest, "white slavery" had complicated the process of relying on race as a code for sexual deviance. Mexican women were broadly classified by the *Dictionary of Races and Peoples* as "Caucasian" or of mixed "Caucasian" and "Indian" blood, but their seemingly voluntary participation in prostitution denoted sexual degeneracy.[52] They were white but not slaves. Chinese women who were forced into prostitution against their will were described as "slaves," but they were clearly not white.

The group of laws that came under the rubric of "white slavery" attempted to link prostitution to certain racialized ethnic categories and hence relied on the ability to see immorality, along with race difference, on the female body. However, in their application, these same laws served to undermine a singular reliance on race as a visible code for sexual deviance. "White slavery" policies were confounded by the seeming invisibility of immorality and the growing complexity of race as new ethnic groups became players on the American scene. Immigration authorities were continually criticized for being unable to curb "white slavery" as they seemed unable to detect prostitutes at the borders.

In a series of investigative reports conducted in 1907, Hellen Bullis, herself an immigration inspector, informed the commissioner of immigration at Ellis Island and the commissioner-general in Washington of a pattern of lax surveillance and weak enforcement. According to Bullis, "several women were openly manifested to houses of ill-fame and unknown disreputable persons." Moreover, "a woman (passenger) was followed from the pier to an address on 42nd St., and has since been seen on the street in the company of a known prostitute."[53] A second report to the commissioner-general prepared by inspector Frank L. Garbarino expressed frustration at the poor handing of these prostitution cases: "while I am morally certain these girls have been imported for immoral purposes, their suspicion of all visitors leads them to give fictitious names and also indefinite information as to their landing."[54] As had been true for Asian

---

[52] *Dictionary of Races or Peoples*, 5, 96.

[53] Letter to Hon. Robert Watchorn, U.S. Commissioner of Immigration, 28 October 1907, casefile 51652/41-B; RINS, SCF, PWS, reel 1. Bullis's reports were forwarded on to the inspector-in-charge of the boarding division with instructions for tighter scrutiny. Also see Bullis's letters dated 8 October 1907 to the Hon. F. P. Sargent, Commissioner-General Immigration and Naturalization, and 5 October 1907 to the Hon. Robert Watcharn, U.S. Commissioner of Immigration; RINS, SCF, PWS, reel 1.

[54] Letter to Commissioner of Immigration, Philadelphia, PA, 2 September 1907, casefile 51652/46-B; RINS, SCF, PWS, reel 1. The commissioner of the New York Harbor denied

women working as prostitutes, white immigrant women arriving as prostitutes were not going to inform inspectors of their intentions.

In contrast to calls for greater supervision, sociologist and activist Frances A. Kellor suggested alternatives to punitive policies and government intervention. General director of the Inter-Municipal Research Committee of New York, Kellor submitted her 1908 report on the conditions of white women's immigration directly to President Roosevelt. In it she argued that (white) women were arriving in increasing numbers and that more attention must be focused on their protection in two ways: first, ensuring that immigrant women reach their destination in moral safety; and second, providing immigrant women with the opportunity for fair living conditions after arrival. Kellor recommended that women immigration officials be posted at all ports with specific responsibilities to care for arriving women, including assurance they reach their inland destinations safely.[55] Kellor was insistent that the focus of laws against white slavery should be protective rather than punitive. In her more general framework for reform, Kellor suggested that immigration authorities devote time and resources to assuring all arriving women safe and secure passage, rather than attempting to discern prostitutes from respectable women.

New York officials denied that prostitutes were evading border detection procedures or that immigration officials looked the other way as vulnerable white women immigrants were seduced into prostitution. In a memo to the U.S. commissioner-general, the commissioner of New York Harbor was at a loss to explain public fervor over white slavery other than as a result of "radical" statements made in the press, comments he attributed to Frances Kellor. According to the New York commissioner, there was no reason to panic: "The total number of immoral women arrested and deported under authority of the Secretary of Commerce and Labor since I became Commissioner of Immigration is 33; the total number of aliens excluded at the time of arrival on the ground of immorality

---

charges of negligence and in his own letter to the commissioner-general asserted, "No unmarried women are ever permitted to land on primary inspection, who are destined to points in or adjacent to New York City, and not to remote places unless upon the most satisfactory showing." See Letter to Hon. F. P. Sargent, Commissioner-General of Immigration, Washington, DC, 9 November 1907, casefile 51652/46-B; RINS, SCF, PWS, reel 1.

[55] Kellor was particularly critical of the INS's failure to realize that addresses listed on manifests were fraudulent or represented, according to her, the well-known addresses of houses of prostitution. Kellor's emphasis on protection of women immigrants is consistent with her work on protective labor legislation. In her report Kellor argued, "The moral protection of the workers of this country is the business of our government, and the moral progress of the great body of working women in this country seems to us to depend upon the answer to this question. 'What will our Government do about organized vice.' " See Letter to Mr. Sargent, Department of Commerce and Labor, Bureau of Immigration and Naturalization, Washington, 28 May 1908, casefile 51777/164; RINS, SCF, PWS, reel 1.

is 19; the total number of convictions under Section 3 of the Immigration Act of March 3, 1903 is 6."[56]

As had been true in the effort to exclude Asian prostitutes, officials became wary of the hidden truth prostitutes sought to conceal behind respectable appearances. In assessing the low numbers of prostitutes detected upon arrival, the Dillingham Commission pointed not to their low number in fact but to the difficulties in determining which of the white women were indeed prostitutes. As one official noted in his report to Washington, "much lying occurs before the Board by immigrants."[57] Investigators for the Dillingham Commission reported a number of cases in which prostitutes were able to slip past immigration authorities disguised by seemingly respectable facades. In its report, the commission noted,

> It is often extremely difficult to prove the illegal entrance of either women or procurers. The inspector has to judge mainly by their appearance and the stories they tell. . . . The possibility of such mistakes permits almost any reasonable, well-behaved women, with some ingenuity in framing skillful answers to the usual inquiries, to enter the United States, whatever her character.[58]

This image of a wily and savvy immigrant woman fooling the practiced gaze of immigration inspectors belied the story of white female victimhood at the hands of unscrupulous foreign procurers recounted in much of the white slavery literature, including the Dillingham Commission's report.

Despite increasingly rigorous deportation statues directed at curbing the traffic in "white slavery," prostitutes were neither being detected nor detained at the border in substantial numbers. At the height of the movement to restrict the arrival of foreign-born prostitutes in 1911, only 253 women were debarred as prostitutes out of a total of over 300,000 female immigrants.[59] Three years later, in 1914, less than one percent of all female immigrants arriving in U.S. ports were found to be prostitutes.[60] Whether the cause was in fact the reality of low numbers of women actually arriv-

---

[56] "Memorandum, Ellis Island, New York," 25 January 1907, casefile 51777/164; RINS, SCF, PWS, reel 1. Drawing from the annual reports of the commissioner-general of immigration, the Dillingham Commission confirmed these low numbers of deportations: *Importation and Harboring of Women for Immoral Purposes*, 60.

[57] Wm. Williams, Letter to Commissioner-General of Immigration, Washington DC, 4 September 1903, casefile 52727/2; RINS, SCF, EI, reel 8.

[58] *Importation and Harboring of Women for Immoral Purposes*, 60, 71.

[59] *Annual Report of the Commissioner-General of Immigration* (1911), 216, 231.

[60] Total number of prostitutes debarred in 1914 was 380, total number of female immigrants was 419,733. *Annual Report of the Commissioner-General of Immigration*, 1914, 42, 104–5.

ing as prostitutes, as the commissioner of New York suggested, or a result of a lack of vigilance and commitment, as Kellor argued, or because of the difficulty of sorting immoral women out from respectable immigrants, as the Dillingham Commission observed, seeing abhorrent sexual behavior as women disembarked proved elusive. Perhaps through the appearance of respectability, perhaps through calculated misrepresentation, immigrant women managed to avoid detection. The borders had not proved to be an effective battleground against immorality.

Was there an international traffic in white women? Certainly many Americans seemed to think so. In truth, they may have had good reason to fear for the safety of many immigrant women arriving at the nation's borders.[61] Sylvia Wexler remembered that when she arrived from Paris in 1910 at age sixteen, a man operating the ferry between her ship and Ellis Island attempted to prevent her from disembarking:

> A: And the man who was on the ferry kept on keeping them in back so I felt that I had to go by turn. Then I realized that they wanted to keep me for good.
>
> Q: This is on the ferry boat from . . .
>
> A: From the ship to Ellis Island.
>
> Q: You mean that he was trying to . . .
>
> A: Hold me back.
>
> Q: Hold you back because he would have liked to have molested you or something?
>
> A: I don't know. You see, in those years there was a lot of white slavery going on, you see? We heard about it, we knew about it and, of course, in my mind I let the idea that I had that and finally I had said, "No" and he cussed me out and let me off.[62]

The white slave traffic, however, offers more insight into domestic anxieties than it does into international migrations. While it is likely that some immigrant women were forced into prostitution against their will, and while it is even more likely that some immigrant woman arrived as working prostitutes and were able to slip past immigration stations, their numbers were small.[63] However, their very presence, and an even greater fear

---

[61] Ruth Rosen suggests that while there may not have been an organized, international traffic in women, a domestic white slavery was a reality. Rosen, *The Lost Sisterhood*, 118.

[62] Sylvia Wexler, interview by D. Gumb, 1986, in *Voices from Ellis Island*, reel 8, oral history no. 160. Arriving in 1925, Dr. Karen Christie remembered being propositioned on the dock by a man who offered to take her to Kentucky. She notes, "And of course, I had read about white slavery, you know." Dr. Karen Christie, interview by N. Dallett, 1986, in *Voices from Ellis Island*, reel 6, oral history no. 122.

[63] Ruth Rosen has estimated that white slavery, both domestic and international, was experienced by less than ten percent of working prostitutes in the United States during the Progressive Era. Rosen, *The Lost Sisterhood*, 133–134.

of their impending arrival, served as a lightning rod for anxieties about the moral quality of women immigrants, the significance of race difference, the advent of increased immigration, and the responsibilities of law. As the movement to eradicate prostitution turned from the borders to the nation's cities and towns, these tensions over gender, morality, race, immigrants, and law would have a lasting impact on defining the rights of citizens and the responsibilities of a moral citizenry.

CHAPTER FOUR

Constructing a Moral Border

Morally acceptable and racially permissible, Aurelie Darlet arrived in New York on February 14, 1905. Five years later, in 1910, she was arrested in Oakland, California, for practicing prostitution and was subsequently deported. In a series of statutes beginning in 1907, the law excluding prostitutes was amended to include women or girls coming to the United States "for any other immoral purposes" and to increase the period after arrival within which immigrant woman could be deported for immoral conduct. Laws directed at prohibiting "other immoral purposes," however, offered little guidance in adjudicating what conduct should be considered immoral. The process of evaluating moral standards became a process of defining sexuality.

Definitions of "prostitution" or "lewd or immoral behavior" and even of "good moral conduct" proved nebulous and malleable. Was a woman who had received gifts of cash after having sex with men, men to whom she was attracted, guilty of prostitution?[1] Were women who played cards, drank, or socialized with crew members aboard ship guilty of immoral behavior?[2] Over the twentieth century, a growing list of nonmoral behaviors were interpreted as grounds for exclusion in federal legislation. While the exclusion of prostitutes attempted to regulate public morality, broad language directed at immoral behavior shifted the focus of exclusion law to private sexuality. In its application, immigration and naturalization law policed the borders of domesticity, marriage, and heterosexuality by listing fornication, premarital sex, adultery, and homosexuality under the rubric of immoral behavior.

By reinforcing the dictates of heterosexual marriage, immigration and naturalization law sought to protect the nation from immorality and racial hybridity. Charges of prostitution and other sex offenses excluded

---

[1] See *Ernestine Greene v. Immigration and Naturalization Service, Los Angeles, California* 313 F.2d 148 (9th Cir. 1963). Kathy Peiss traces turn-of-the-century public debates over the moral status of "charity girls," who traded sexual favors for affection and access to urban leisure activities. Peiss, *Cheap Amusements: Working Women and Leisure in Turn-of-the-Century New York* (Philadelphia: Temple University Press, 1986).

[2] See Martha Ash, INS file 17556/3–1 (1918); AICF, box 1322; INS, SFD, RG85; NA-PSR.

women immigrants from the familial privileges structured into immigration law. Immigrants suspected of prostitution remained vulnerable to deportation long after they had passed through the nation's borders. In practice this meant that a woman could to be identified as a prostitute upon her arrival as an immigrant or identified as an immigrant upon later arrest as a prostitute. As immigration law expanded over the twentieth century to allow for the deportation of long-term residents and naturalization law continued to emphasize the links between morality, race, and citizenship, women who remained beyond the confines of derivative citizenship faced an uncertain future as permanent noncitizens. As the court noted in discussing Darlet's case, the implication of the 1910 law was to legislate that an immigrant woman "remain publicly chaste during the rest of her life."[3]

At what point did an immigrant woman cease to arrive and begin to reside? If a woman, like Darlet, arrived as a seamstress, but five years later found work as a prostitute, could she be deported as an alien prostitute?[4] In the question of time, immigration and naturalization law met and reinforced one another. How long after a woman stopped practicing prostitution did she stop being a prostitute and become respectable, and how long after a woman arrived did she stop being an immigrant and become a resident? Could immoral women become moral citizens? Whereas convicted felons were excluded based on past illegal conduct, and medical patients for their present condition, prostitutes were excluded for their past, present, and potential future conduct. Time mattered, and it mattered in two important ways through the issues of residency and reform. Residency requirements highlighted the distinction between the rights of citizens and those of immigrants; and the question of reform linked the future to the past in evaluating credentials for membership.

---

[3] *United States v. Northern German Lloyd Steamship Co, The Same v. International Mercantile Marine Co, United States Circuit Court, Southern District of New York*, casefile 52809/7-C; RINS, SCF, PWS, reel 6. Importantly, under the law steamship companies were fined the cost of returning ineligible immigrants. For other cases interpreting the 1910 law and whether it could be applied retroactively, see decisions by U.S. District Judge Carpenter, Northern District of Illinois, *United States ex rel. Martha Brio v. Prentis*; Judge Rose, District of Maryland, *United States ex rel. Mango v. Weis*; Judge Hollister, Southern District of Ohio, *Margaret Braun*; Judge Hanford, Western District of Washington, *Oynkio Ishizaki*; and Judge Lewis, District of Colorado, *Lilly Weiner, Anna Schwarz*, and *Helena Bugajewitz*—cases referenced in Geo. W. Wickersham, Attorney-General, "Instructions as to the Enforcement of the White-Slave Traffic Act," Department Circular No 174 to all United States Attorneys, 31 October 1910, casefile 52809/7-B; RINS, SCF, PWS, reel 6.

[4] See case of Lina Marino, *United States ex rel. Mango v. Weis* 181 F. 860 (D.Md. 1910).

HOW LONG AN IMMIGRANT, HOW LONG A PROSTITUTE?
TIME, CHANGE, AND RESIDENCY

Seeing immorality at the moment of arrival proved elusive. The focus of immigration laws regulating morality was increasingly directed toward immigrant prostitutes living and working in the United States and not those arriving at the border. The Dillingham Commission presented these resident women as a continuing threat to a moral nation. Once a prostitute always a prostitute. Prostitutes, according to the commission,

> enter upon a life of such physical ills and moral degradation that relatively few find it possible to regain any status of respectability or comfortable living. Here and there the agents of the Commission have found one and another who have been rescued from the slavery, others who have gladly abandoned the life, and a few who have married, but these cases are rare. The usual history is one of increased degradation until death.[5]

This distinctly modern construction of a prostitute differed from older ideas of the charity girl who participated in casual or temporary sex to gain access to leisure activities or to supplement her meager income. Modern prostitutes employed sex for profit, while charity girls practiced more casual sex in the context of dating.[6] Modern prostitutes could not be saved, according to the commission, but they could be deported. As the movement against prostitution gained momentum, the emphasis in immigration law shifted from detection to expulsion. Prostitutes, along with felons, were the first deportable "class" of aliens.[7]

Passed in 1907, the new immigration law reiterated traditional restrictions against prostitutes, but it also expanded the purview of immigration law to resident immigrant women. According to the new law, any immigrant woman found living in a brothel or practicing prostitution within three years of entry "shall be deemed to be unlawfully within the United States" and would be deported.[8] Present sexual indiscretion would be taken as evidence of past prostitution. Prostitution had become a permanent status, with the capacity to taint an immigrant woman's past just as it was believed to blacken her future. In guidelines issued in the wake of

---

[5] *Importation and Harboring of Women for Immoral Purposes*, 86.

[6] Kathy Peiss, *Cheap Amusements*.

[7] Beginning in 1891, an immigrant woman living in the United States found to have been a prostitute upon arrival could be deported within one year of her arrival. Hutchinson, *Legislative History of American Immigration Policy*, 452.

[8] Where formerly immigration officials had to prove that a woman had entered illegally (that she was a prostitute upon arrival), after 1907 current prostitution would be taken as evidence of former prostitution. Ibid., 128–133.

the 1907 law, immigration inspectors were directed to investigate any alien women in their district whom they believed to be engaged in prostitution and to ascertain the date they arrived. If an immigrant woman was found practicing prostitution, it was to be taken as a strong indication that she had been a prostitute when she entered and thus had entered in violation of the law.[9] If a woman refused to give inspectors the date of her landing, it would be assumed she fell within the three-year statutory limitation. She would have to prove otherwise.[10]

By March 1908, the bureau had adopted an even more rigorous policy enforcing laws against the arrival of immoral women. The bureau developed its own prostitution task force, hiring immigration inspectors specifically for the purpose of rooting out resident alien women practicing prostitution within three years of entry.[11] Surveillance policies were radically expanded from arrival to residency and from the nation's borders to its interior.

The new policy against prostitutes harnessed the convictions of a moral crusade to the weight of law. In a memo to new immigrant inspectors, Commissioner-General Daniel J. Keefe issued a call to arms, as he outlined the importance of the new initiative and the parameters of the inspectors' new duties. The battle against immorality, Keefe warned, would prove a "delicate and arduous task." "Zealous, unflagging efforts," Keefe insisted, "must be exerted to insure anything like success." Yet in the shift from the border to the interior, from arriving aliens to resident immigrants, the bureau found itself on uneven legal ground in which policing the social evil could mean ignoring the civic rights of immigrant women.[12]

The greatest effect of the bureau's more rigorous enforcement of the 1907 law did not lie in larger numbers of arrests and deportations, but in the extension of immigration law to resident aliens like Dolores Torres and Louise Reaux. Dolores Torres was arrested by immigration officials in Metcalf, Arizona on March 17, 1909 and confessed that she had been "dancing and drinking there in the saloon, and I also did business with

[9] "Memorandum by Office of the Solicitor, Department of Commerce and Labor," 19 July 1907, casefile 51777/164; RINS, SCF, PWS, reel 1.

[10] "Arrest and Deportation of Prostitutes and Procurers of Prostitutes," Department Circular No. 156, 26 September 1907, Bureau of Immigration and Naturalization, casefile 51777/30; RINS, SCF, PWS, reel 1.

[11] This special immigration enforcement division mimicked the Chinese Division of the Immigration Bureau with officers designated to monitor immigrants who came within a specific provision of the law.

[12] "Letter to Anthony de la Torre, Jr., Immigrant Inspector, San Francisco, Cal. from Department of Commerce and Labor, Bureau of Immigration and Naturalization, Washington," 10 March 1900, casefile 52484/9; RINS, SCF, PWS, reel 4.

men in my room." Torres was deported to Mexico.[13] Louise Reaux, alias Flora Durand, arrived in January 1906 and was arrested in 1908 and subsequently deported for prostitution.[14] Rigorous application of the law worked to control a broader group of women's sexual behavior. More and more women were forced to defend their citizenship, their legal residency, and their moral conduct before immigration officials. Immigration law had turned inward, raising serious questions about the rights of resident immigrants and the responsibilities of the nation.

Despite increased surveillance, inspectors reported, not without frustration, that few of the women they found were in fact deportable under the 1907 law.[15] Evidence suggests that immigrant women were well aware of the law and its limitations, often claiming long-term residence status which placed them beyond the province of immigration law. Boston inspectors concluded with what would become a widely held suspicion that awareness of the limitations of the law was allowing many prostitutes to avoid deportation:

> One peculiar feature I desire to call the Bureau's attention to is as follows: Interviews by Acting Inspector Hartland and myself with a number of girls of foreign birth, speaking broken English, and whose appearance and actions would ordinarily note a short residence in this country, has led us to believe that in some manner these girls are tipped off to state they are in America for more than 3 years, as invariably girls of this type have claimed to be here from 5 to 10 years.[16]

---

[13] "Report to Inspector in Charge, Immigration Service, Touson, Arizona," 14 June 1909, casefile 52484/23; RINS, SCF, PWS, reel 5.

[14] Durand had argued that her arrival predated the 1907 law. The court argued that her arrest fell within the deportability period encompassed by the 1903 law. *Ex parte Durand* 160 F. 558 (D.Or. 1908). Also see *Ex parte Petterson* 166 F. 536 (D.Minn. 1908).

[15] The inspector in Norfolk, Virginia, wrote that he had made an "extensive and strict investigation" of resident immigrant prostitutes in his district, and "No women were found who would have been in the United States less than three years since their last entry." "Report to Commissioner-General of Immigration and Naturalization, Washington, DC, from the Office of Inspector in Charge, Norfolk, VA," 12 May 1909, casefile 52484/13; RINS, SCF, PWS, reel 5. Baltimore added "African American" to the list of applicable racial categories, concluding that some prostitutes were possibly West Indian women. As had been true in Norfolk, no immigrant women found practicing prostitution in Baltimore were deportable under the 1907 law. "Report to Commissioner-General of Immigration and Naturalization, Washington, DC, from the Office of the Commissioner, Baltimore, MD," 22 April 1909, casefile 52484/13; RINS, SCF, PWS, reel 5. Also see "Report to Commissioner-General of Immigration and Naturalization, Washington, DC, from Office of the Commissioner, Boston, Mass.," 24 April 1909, casefile 52484/11; RINS, SCF, PWS, reel 4.

[16] "Report to Commissioner-General of Immigration and Naturalization, Washington, DC, from Office of the Commissioner, Boston, Mass.," 24 April 1909, casefile 52484/11; RINS, SCF, PWS, reel 4. Based on immigration statistics, many immigrant women would

The Dillingham Commission echoed these suspicions: "It will be noted that very few of those convicted acknowledge that they have arrived in this country within a period of three years. Such acknowledgment would of course subject them to deportation. Most of them apparently find it safer to name a period of from five to ten years."[17]

By 1910, Congress strengthened the deportation laws by striking out the three-year limitation, leaving the words "after she shall have entered the United States."[18] In the wake of the 1910 law, as one inspector put it, "we could arrest and deport every foreign born prostitute found practicing prostitution, who has not become a citizen of the United States, without regard to the length of time she has resided in the United States."[19]

By shifting the focus of exclusion from an alien threat to a domestic problem, the 1910 law raised into sharp relief the growing gap between two political statuses—resident alien and naturalized citizen. The impact can be seen in the case of Lina Marino, who arrived from Italy in 1906 at the age of eighteen as a domestic servant but after leaving her employer found herself forced to rely on prostitution.[20] Women like Marino maintained they had emigrated in search of honest work, and that they had been in full compliance with the law upon arrival; their prostitution was a result of financial and moral crises experienced as residents, not as immigrants. Marino testified "that she was a pure girl when she came to this country, that she does not like the life she is living, and that if she could get honest work she would take it."[21]

---

have arrived between 1880 and 1900 when the largest numbers of European immigrants migrated to the United States. Thus these women would have had at least five years of residency. This is especially true given that the interest in "white" slavery focused inspectors' attentions on European immigrants rather than those from Asia or Latin America.

[17] Importation and Harboring of Women for Immoral Purposes, 64.

[18] Also passed in 1910, the White Slave Traffic Act, or the Mann Act, prohibited the importation or interstate transportation of women for immoral purposes. The Mann Act focused on importers, procurers, and managers, while the Immigration Act of 1910 focused on the prostitutes themselves. Connelly, The Response to Prostitution in the Progressive Era, 59.

[19] "Letter to Commissioner-General of Immigration, Washington, DC from Inspector in Charge," 17 May 1910, casefile 52809/7-A; RINS, SCF, PWS, reel 6. In this letter, the inspector also notes the difficulty in getting women to admit their arrival dates: "The majority of the alien prostitutes here are Russian and Polish Jews, who claim to have come to the United States many years ago, but who are unable, or will not, give the date of their arrival or the port at which they landed."

[20] Marino lived in a brothel for six months, but became ill and subsequently spent some time in a charity hospital. Upon release she rejoined a man she had met in Boston and traveled with him, working as a prostitute. When she found he had another woman, she left him.

[21] United States ex rel. Mango v. Weis. Com'r of Immigration, et al. 181 F. 860 (D.Md. 1910).

The district court of Maryland, however, found Marino deportable under the new 1910 law. In concluding that Congress had the right to deport immigrants for an unlimited period after arrival, the court argued for the necessity of exclusion law based on race and sexuality.[22] The 1910 law, it stated, did not

> seek to punish any one for any offense any more than the provisions excluding Chinese are intended as a punishment for being born of the Mongolian race. One class of considerations has led Congress to believe that the presence of Chinese laborers in this country was contrary to the best interests of the nation; another and different class of considerations has convinced it that the continued residence in this country of alien prostitutes should be prevented.[23]

Significantly, the court found precedent in the laws mandating Chinese exclusion which had established immigration regulation as a matter of national sovereignty. Race order and moral order were linked; in the right to exclude racialized minorities, the court found a similar right to evict immoral women.

Moral dictates were given the force of law, and without access to citizenship women, especially those women classed as racial outsiders, were left without legal recourse. Immigrant women accused or suspected of prostitution could not become citizens through marriage to a citizen. Nor in the years after women achieved independent citizenship could women charged with immoral behavior demonstrate the "good moral character" necessary for citizenship. The result was a class of permanent noncitizens. Japanese women living in Hawaii, for example, were "born alien," unable to meet the sex and race requirements for naturalization in 1913, which limited citizenship to white and black men. As a result, Japanese prostitutes living and working in Hawaii were deported despite the fact that they had emigrated before U.S. annexation of Hawaii in 1898. Or, as the Ninth Circuit Court explained, they were "born alien within the United States."[24]

The legal position of women like the Japanese women born in Hawaii raised a difficult question about the responsibility a host society bore for

---

[22] In 1913 the Supreme Court affirmed the 1910 law, ruling that Congress had the power to order the deportation of immigrants whose presence was deemed harmful, and the ruling applied to prostitutes regardless of how long they had lived in the United States. *Bugajewitz v. Adams, United States Immigration Inspector* 228 U.S. 585 (1913). For other Supreme Court decisions see *Zakonaite v. Wolf, Jailor of the City of St. Louis* 226 U.S. 272 (1912); and *Lapina v. Williams, Commissioner of Immigration* 232 U.S. 78 (1914).

[23] *United States ex rel. Mango v. Weis. Com'r of Immigration, et al.* 181 F. 860 (D.Md. 1910). Also see cases of Rose Dickman and Margaret Braun, casefile 52809/7-B; RINS, SCF, PWS, reel 6; and *Ex parte Cardonnel* 197 F. 774 (N.D.Cal. 1912); *Choy Gun v. Backus* 223 F. 487 (9th Cir. 1915).

[24] *United States v. Kimi Yamamoto* 240 F. 390 (9th Cir. 1917); also see *Tama Miyake v. United States et al.* 257 F. 732 (9th Cir. 1919).

the prostitution of the women who lived within it. Low wages and under-employment led many immigrant women to supplement their meager incomes with the proceeds from occasional prostitution. The 1910 legislation left immigrant women to weigh the risks of poverty against those of deportation. With the deportation of long-term resident immigrant women, the legal distance between citizens and resident aliens expanded, and immigrant women who practiced prostitution remained vulnerable. Vilma Megyi arrived with her father from Budapest in 1913. She briefly returned to Hungary in 1922 to visit her mother. After returning, Megyi found work as a telephone operator at eighteen dollars per week; by 1924 her salary had been increased to twenty-two dollars per week. One year later, however, Megyi was arrested for prostitution and committed to the Bedford Hills Reformatory in New York. Deportation orders followed and she was returned to Hungary in December 1925.[25] Hélène Mousseau's story was similar. She had worked as a dressmaker in New York after she first arrived in 1921, but by 1929 Mousseau was arrested for prostitution in San Francisco, and one year later she was deported to France.[26]

The deportation of resident immigrant prostitutes was not without its critics. Justice Holmes argued in 1909, that "If a woman were found living in a house of prostitution within a week after her arrival, no one, I suppose, would doubt that it tended to show that she was in the business when she arrived." "But," he continued, "how far back such an inference shall reach is a question of degree, like most of the questions of life."[27] Nevertheless, immigration law, together with naturalization law, presented a catch 22. On the one hand, resident immigrants living in the United States could be deported for prostitution at arrival and at any time thereafter. On the other hand, women suspected of prostitution could not acquire citizenship, either derivative or independent, and thus avoid deportation, if they were suspected of lacking proof of "good moral character." The concept of once a prostitute always a prostitute now extended to once an alien always an alien.

UNDESIRABLE RESIDENTS: DEFINING "OTHER IMMORAL PURPOSES"

With the 1910 legislation, immigration law expanded the scope of exclusion beyond prostitutes to include women and girls coming "for any other immoral purpose." Adjudicating the boundaries of "other immoral pur-

---

[25] As reported in Jane Perry Clark, *Deportation of Aliens from the United States to Europe* (New York: Columbia University Press, 1931), 241.

[26] As reported in Ibid., 242–243.

[27] *Keller v. United States* 213 U.S. 138 (1909), dissenting opinion.

poses" would prove equally troublesome for both immigration officers and court officials. Yet while the definition of immoral behavior remained fuzzy, the threat was clear. As the Supreme Court explained, immoral women were "in hostility to family," and to "the holy estate of matrimony." Marriage and family provided "the sure foundation of all that is stable and noble" in American society, and "reverent morality" was the "source of all beneficent progress in social and political improvement."[28]

Sara Petersen and her three children applied for admission at Philadelphia in 1911. Petersen had been found by immigration authorities to be "cohabitating with a man other than her husband." In deciding this case, authorities were forced to consider what practices would be included within the broad framework of other immoral purposes. In evaluating the merits of Petersen's appeal, the bureau instructed its officers to judge "all the crimes against morality"—including abortion, adultery, fornication, keeping a bawdy house, and concubinage—as crimes that involved moral turpitude. The Immigration Service acknowledged, however, that administrative discretion should be used in evaluating the longevity and legitimacy of adulterous relationships and the general character of the immigrant.[29] The resulting discretionary latitude offered immigration officers administrative leeway in evaluating conduct.

Unmarried immigrant women's sexual liaisons with men were carefully scrutinized for evidence of immorality.[30] The distinction between "other immoral purposes" and prostitution was often blurred, and extramarital sexual relations were often labeled prostitution by immigration authorities.[31] For example, Anne Wilke had been living with a man named Cole

[28] *United States v. Bitty* 208 U.S. 393, 401 (1908).

[29] Bureau memorandum 53148/19, 6 February 1911, INS file 53371/25 (1911–1937); DJA-INS acc. 600 A 60, box 403; INS, DC, RG85; NA, DC. I have found one case of a woman deported under charges of abortion. A native of Jamaica, she entered the United States in 1898 and was arrested in 1944 at age seventy for providing abortion services. Under New York law, abortion involved a crime of moral turpitude and thus was a deportable offense. See, *In re M———*, 2 I&N Dec. 525 (BIA 1946). Maurice Roberts notes that in more recent decisions the BIA followed the Supreme Court distinction between first-, second-, and third-trimester abortions. In the case of a woman who had been convicted in Mexico of having an abortion, the court found that because the abortion took place in the first trimester it was not a crime in the United States and thus she could not be deported for moral turpitude. *In re Morales & Salinas*, files A-10721162 and A-1304267 (BIA 1973, 1974); Dorothy E. Roberts, "Sex and the Immigration Laws," 14 *San Diego Law Review* 16 (1976–1977).

[30] In *Athanasaw and Sampson v. United States* 227 U.S. 308 (1913) the Court ruled "debauchery" was not limited to actual sexual intercourse but included actions or advances that might lead to sex.

[31] As Mark Connelly notes, this was also true in the case of the Mann Act forbidding interstate traffic in women. Connelly, *The Response to Prostitution in the Progressive Era*, 129.

who had promised to marry her. Her lover owned a saloon, and Wilke was charged with living in a house of ill repute. Wilke explained that she had met Cole while working in his hotel as a housekeeper in upstate New York. Cole had promised to marry her and the two had lived together as man and wife. Wilke denied that she ever worked as a prostitute or had sex with any other man. At her hearing, Wilke's lawyer argued in her defense, "It cannot be claimed that a girl of former good repute, who makes her abode with a man under solemn promise of marriage, living with him under the belief that he will fulfill that promise is thereby rendered an undesirable citizen."[32] Nonetheless, deportation orders were issued in 1908 against Wilke for practicing prostitution.

Immigrant women like Wilke found their sexuality under the lens of immigration law. Sara Cervantes and her daughters, Margarita and Refugia Vela, were held at the United States–Mexico border as they attempted to return to El Paso in 1908. Cervantes was charged with being imported for immoral purposes. Cervantes had been involved with and supported by Simon Chavez, who paid her living expenses when she visited him in El Paso.[33] Mary Matsumoto, a fifteen-year-old Japanese girl working as a domestic servant, was charged with prostitution and held for deportation in 1936. Given her youth, authorities decided to parole Matsumoto to social service workers who promised to find her employment and provide her with schooling. Three years later Matsumoto was arrested again, this time for associating with "persons of questionable character." She was deported.[34]

Immigrant women like Wilke, Cervantes, and Matsumoto, accused of "other immoral purposes," were, in effect, guilty of status offenses, charged with crimes against family, marriage, and womanhood rather than crimes against law.[35] None of these women had stood trial for statutory crimes, prostitution or adultery for example. Instead, each woman was classed within the vagaries of "otherness," a sexual and legal space between marital monogamy and prostitution. In discussing the 1908 case of a woman who arrived as the "concubine" of a married man, the Su-

[32] Anne Wilke [pseud.], INS file 51, 777–265 (1908); DJA-INS acc. 58 A 2038, box 46; INS, DC, RG85; NA, DC.

[33] Luther C. Steward, acting supervising inspector San Antonio, Texas, "Letter to Hom. Commissioner-General of Immigration, Washington, DC," casefile 522241/20; RINS, SCF, PWS, reel 1.

[34] "Reports to Central Authorities for Calendar Year 1939," INS file 55965/8 (1939); DJA-INS accession 58 A 734, box 1288; INS, DC, RG85; NA, DC.

[35] The difference between status offenses and statute (civil and criminal) offenses is most clear in juvenile law. A young person under age eighteen can be charged with "delinquency" in ways that a legal adult cannot. (I would like to thank Joby Gardner for bringing this point to my attention.)

preme Court argued that "illicit intercourse, not under the sanction of a valid or legal marriage," was immoral. The Court went on to define prostitution in broad and sweeping language, "women who hire or *without hire* offer their bodies to indiscriminate intercourse with men," that could include many different types of sexual encounters. In arguing the case for deportation, the attorney general insisted that the 1907 immigration law was intended by Congress "to exclude various undesirable classes of persons, among others women of loose moral character." The Court agreed, adding that the statute prohibiting the arrival of prostitutes and women coming for "other immoral purposes," was meant to protect American society from women like those mentioned in the case, and thus women like Wilke, Cervantes, and Matsumoto: "Congress no doubt proceeded on the ground that contact with society on the part of alien women leading such lives," whether prostitutes or women having illicit sex outside of marriage, "would be hurtful to the cause of sound private and public morality and to the general well-being of the people."[36]

Even before a woman reached American shores, she could be judged a threat to American family, marriage, and moral order, and her conduct aboard ship could be used as evidence of immoral character.[37] Martha Ash was detained upon her arrival in San Francisco in 1918 under suspicions of improper behavior aboard ship. A twenty-three-year-old seamstress from New Zealand, Ash was on her way to meet her fiancé. Upon arrival, Ash was asked if she had become friendly with any of the other passengers on the boat, whether she had entertained any of them in her cabin, taken part in any games in the evening with them, or spent any part of the day or night in the cabin of anyone else:

Q: To what extend [*sic*] was your association with any of the officers?
A: Just to meet them.
Q: Well, were you entertained by them at any time or did you entertain them at any time?
A: No.
Q: Did any of these passengers you have named or these officers you have named visit you in your stateroom?
A: No.

---

[36] Emphasis added. *United States v. Bitty* 208 U.S. 393 (1908); this case is discussed in Connelly, *The Response to Prostitution in the Progressive Era*, 51–52.

[37] Bertha Kuppies (alias Goldstein, alias Glick, alias Gluck) was excluded when she arrived in New York in 1911 for crimes involving moral turpitude. Kuppies had traveled from Austria with a man who was not her husband, and the two had occupied the same state room. Although under subsequent examination Kuppies revealed she had previously worked as a prostitute in Pittsburgh, it was her conduct on ship that drew the attention of the authorities. *Sibray v. United States* 185 F. 401 (3rd Cir. 1911).

Q: Did you visit in the stateroom of any of them?
A: No.
Q: Where did you spend you evenings on the vessel?
A: On deck in my own cabin.
Q: Did you ever spend any part of the day or night in the cabin of anybody elses[*sic*] except your own?
A: No.
Q: Take any part in any games of cards while on the vessel?
A: No.

Finally, Ash was asked pointblank:

Q: Were your actions on the vessel those of a strictly moral woman?[38]
A: Yes.

Fellow passengers disagreed and testified that Ash's behavior was "not proper for young single women." Ash's fiancé's brother was one of the ship's officers and had testified that Ash had gone to officers' rooms. Despite these accusations, Ash and her fiancé were married six days later, escorted to city hall by volunteers with the Travelers' Aid Society. The willingness of her fiancé to marry her despite recriminations against her character was enough to convince authorities to allow Ash to land.[38]

Charges of immoral conduct were often levied against sexual relationships that challenged marriage as an institution of moral and social order. By far, the most common deportation charge encompassed within the "other immoral purposes" clause was adultery.[39] In evaluating women's conduct, immigration authorities were guided by state law. In states where adultery was considered a felony, immigrant women were charged with moral turpitude and deported.[40] Mary F. Olsen was held for questioning upon her arrival in San Francisco in 1919. Olsen was destined to meet her lover, G. N. Lamb, an American citizen, with whom she had one child. Olsen was estranged from her husband, who was in the Australian military stationed in France. She testified that her husband refused to support her and that she believed he was having affairs with other women while stationed abroad. Confronted with charges of her own immoral conduct, Olsen responded "No, because this man I married—You could find out he was no good and he drove me to everything I have done—and I feel I should have Mr. Lamb." Lamb had received a separation from his

---

[38] Martha Ash, INS file 17556/3-1 (1918); AICF, box 1322; INS, SFD, RG85; NA-PSR.
[39] *United States ex rel. Tourney v. Reimer* 8 F.Supp. 91 (S.D.N.Y. 1934).
[40] Solicitor General, "In re definition of the terms 'adultery,' 'fornication,' and 'concubinage,' " memorandum, 1922, INS file 53371/25 (1911–1937); DJA-INS acc. 600 A 60, box 403; INS, DC, RG85; NA, DC. Also see *Victoria Marquez Talavera v. Thomas M. Pederson, District Director, Immigration and Naturalization Service* 224 F.2d 52 (1964).

wife in Australia, but not a legal divorce. Lamb's wife and Olsen's mother-in-law notified immigration officials in San Francisco of Olsen's arrival and her affair with Lamb, information that resulted in Olsen's detention. Olsen and her daughter were paroled for six months and advised that resumption of sexual relations before formal divorce proceedings had been finalized on both sides would result in immediate deportation (she eventually received an extension so that she could file for divorce). Immigration authorities went to great lengths to ensure the continued moral conduct of parolees. Seven months later the couple was secretly investigated by immigration officials, but they were unable to determine if Lamb and Olsen had resumed sexual relations.[41]

In reviewing immigrant women's cases, however, the courts could prove tolerant in their interpretation of immoral conduct. Class distinctions and the appearance of moral respectability led judicial officials to reevaluate illicit sexual relationships as private wrongs rather than public offenses. For example, Therese Statlichnitzer left Austria in 1907 to follow her lover, a married man, to the United States. Statlichnitzer found work as a confectioner and baker in Pittsburgh but was forced to quit as her pregnancy advanced and she left to live with the father of the child, Hans Huber. The two continued to live together as man and wife and had two children when they were both arrested by immigration authorities in 1909. During questioning, the couple would only admit to having sex once before returning together to the United States. Fornication and bastardy, according to the court was "little more than a private wrong." In evaluating Statlichnitzer's appeal, the court quoted the findings of the immigration inspector, "I was impressed with the modest bearing and appearance of the woman," as it emphasized her role as a mother to American citizens, to find for Statlichnitzer's release. "There is a tendency to disregard the rights both of the mother and the children," the court insisted, "who are entitled to remain in this country and who need their mother's care and protection." Both Huber and Statlichnitzer were released.[42]

Laws excluding prostitutes and women accused of a variety of "other immoral purposes" constructed a moral border around the nation. Laws linking good moral character to naturalization tied moral citizenship to political citizenship. Dictating the moral border proved far easier than defending it, and patrolling the boundaries of this moral nation and its moral citizenship proved treacherous. Which women were immoral women? What conduct should be considered immoral conduct? How

[41] There is no notation of final resolution in this file. Mary F. Olsen and Mary E. Olsen, INS files 18220/3–10 and 3–11 (1919); AICF, box 1351; INS, SFD, RG85; NA-PSR.
[42] *United States ex rel. Huber v. Sibrary* 178 F. 150 (W.D.Penn. 1910).

long before immigrants stopped arriving and began residing? Could immoral immigrants become moral citizens?

In defending themselves—their respectability, their sexuality, their marriages—before immigration inspectors, judicial officials, and the court of public opinion, immigrant women accused of conduct unbecoming a citizen challenged traditional ideas of women's sexual passivity and contested marital monogamy. Laws extending the purview and power of exclusion based on immoral behavior brought increasing numbers of women within the law's jurisdiction. The nation, these women argued, bore some responsibility for their economic and moral predicament.

CHAPTER FIVE

Likely to Become

When Etta Horowitz arrived in the United States in 1910, immigration officials expressed concern that she had neither enough money nor the necessary earning potential to support herself and her two youngest children. A thirty-five-year-old Jewish widow from Romania, Horowitz insisted her skills as a tailoress had always proved sufficient to keep body, soul, and family together. "Since your husband died," officials at Ellis Island queried, "how had you made your living?" "I work as a tailoress," Horowitz responded. Unconvinced, officials probed further for evidence of poverty, "Did you ever receive any assistance from any charitable organizations." "No, I received no assistance," Horowitz maintained, and "I have been working as a tailoress and always supported myself and my family."[1]

A mother, a widow, and a tailoress, Horowitz presented an unlikely candidate to officials wary of arriving immigrants becoming economic burdens on American communities. In evaluating her application, officials noted that while Horowitz was apparently "healthy," she did not "appear" "physically strong" and as a result it would be difficult to "secure and retain employment." "Encumbered as she is with two children," officials argued, she would be unable to devote sufficient time and energy to work outside the home. Horowitz was excluded as "likely to become a public charge."[2]

"Likely to become a public charge," or "LPC" in the parlance of immigration officials, denoted not only *current* poverty but *potential* poverty. "Likely" required that immigration officials weigh an immigrant's work skills against the deficiencies of the domestic labor market, her earning potential against the proclivities of the going wage, her work history against the realities of her domestic burdens, even her appearance, as in

---

[1] Etta Horowitz [pseud.], INS file 52743/21 (1910); DJA-INS, acc. 60 A 600, box 214; INS, DC, RG85; NA, DC. Horowitz was accompanied by her two youngest children, ages two and three and a half. She left her three older children (sixteen or seventeen, thirteen, and ten) in Romania in the care of her sister and brother, and planned on financing their passage with money she earned working as a tailoress in the United States. Her husband had been dead for over a year.

[2] Ibid.

the case of Etta Horowitz, against the appearance of want. While laws against potential public charges were mandatory in theory, they proved discretionary in practice. Flexible by design, the law evaluated each immigrant as an economic entity and often as a financial burden.

Historically, laws against poverty were directed at both men and women arriving at the nation's borders. However, "likely to become a public charge" was uniquely gendered in ways that reflected a constrained and diminished evaluation of women's role in the economy. During the early twentieth century, immorality was linked to indigence, and laws against poverty were layered onto those directed at patrolling women's morality and their roles within a family economy. Regardless of their work skills, women arriving during the early twentieth century who were alone, pregnant or with children, or with a checkered moral past were routinely found to be LPC. LPC stigmatized women's work outside the home by dismissing the ability of single women, divorced women, or widows to support themselves and their families. Poverty, in essence, was a gendered disease.[3]

The contrast between how the law valued work done by seamstresses and the labor of domestic servants reveals the significance of gender for concepts of work, skill, and worth. Compare the experience of Etta Horowitz with that of Augustina Alonso. Both were single women, both were accompanied by children, both offered a history of paid work, yet Horowitz was a tailoress while Alonso claimed to be a domestic servant. When Augustina Alonso arrived in San Francisco with her niece Cristina in 1918, she informed immigration officials that she had come seeking work. With seventy-five dollars in cash and without property or savings to speak of in Mexico, Alonso, like Horowitz, was an unlikely candidate for admission. Yet unlike Horowitz, Alonso explained that she planned to find work as a domestic servant. According to immigration officials, Horowitz, a tailoress with two children, had the appearance of want, while Alonso, a single woman with charge of her niece, had "every appearance of being a woman able to make a living for herself and child." Etta Horowitz was excluded while Augustina Alonso was admitted.[4] The proximity

---

[3] In his 1892 annual report, the superintendent of immigration argued that skilled artisans (blacksmiths, bakers, butchers, architects, carpenters, cigar-makers, tailors, shoemakers, painters, musicians, and masons) added "social value" approximated at "one thousand five hundred dollars," while laborers, farmers, servants, and peddlers constituted a drain on American society. Importantly, many occupations traditionally worked by men were defined as fiscally and socially valuable. *Annual Report of the Superintendent of Immigration* (1892), 15.

[4] Importantly, as Mark Reisler has suggested, the Immigration Bureau did not regularly apply the 1917 law regulating contract laborers to Mexican immigrants until the post–World War I period. By the late 1920s and 1930s, the arrival of increasing numbers of

of Mexico suggested to immigration officials that Alonso was a temporary laborer, available to work when work was available and ready to return when it was not.[5] In striking contrast to Horowitz's work as a tailoress, Alonso's work as a domestic servant was valued under immigration law.

Women immigrants oscillated between two points of legal contact—work and want. While separate and distinct, ideals of skilled wage labor and conceptions of poverty were linked across space, creating a field of meanings within which self-sufficiency, personal autonomy, and republican citizenship took shape. In dividing those likely to become a burden from those likely to contribute, immigration law sought to evaluate women's contribution to the nation.

LPC: POVERTY AND IMMIGRATION LAW

As women arrived at the border, they confronted the shadows of an artisanal republican ideal, in which the independent worker capable of financial self-sufficiency, moral responsibility, and familial authority remained white and male. A woman's marital status, her race designation, her moral reputation, her physical condition, even her unpaid responsibilities in the home were as important as her work history in an economic assessment of her earning potential. As Linda Kerber has argued, "If Americans have had a civic obligation to *appear* to be self-supporting, what counts as appearance of self-support has varied by race as well as by gender."[6] Between 1880 and 1924, "likely to become a public charge" (LPC) provided a catchall category of exclusion within which vast numbers of women found themselves deported as potential paupers for moral, marital, physical, and economic deficiencies.

---

nonwhite immigrants across the southern border had become an issue of public concern and, as a result, administrative regulation. Reisler, "Always the Laborer, Never the Citizen: Anglo Perceptions of the Mexican Immigrant during the 1920s," *Pacific Historical Review* 45, no. 2 (May 1976): 231–254.

[5] Cristina Alonso, INS file 17411/14–5 (1918); AICF, box 1304; INS, SFD, RG85; NA-PSR. Originally from Sinaola, Alonso explained that she could not find work in Mexico. She had lived in the United States previously from 1911 to 1917 and had worked as a domestic servant but she had returned to Sinalo to visit her mother. She had no plans to remain permanently in the United States, but intended to return to Sinola after two or three years of work. Cristia Alonso's father had died in the war three years before, her mother five years before that.

[6] Kerber, *No Constitutional Right to Be Ladies*, 55, emphasis in original. Kerber argues that laws against vagrancy emphasized the appearance of idleness. This emphasis on appearance mingled ideas of poverty with those of race. As a result, women of color in the United States bore the brunt of legislation directed at controlling vagrancy.

Domestic poverty and foreign immigration have been strongly yoked in the minds of immigration officials, policy makers, and the American public. Colonial governments and state legislators alike attempted with mixed success to control the arrival of indigent immigrants.[7] Congress studied, debated, and decried the arrival of needy foreigners many times both before and after the Civil War.[8] In 1882, the first federal legislation excluded "any persons unable to take care of himself or herself without becoming a public charge."[9] "*Likely* to become a public charge," added to the law in 1891, introduced a new language of interpretation and discretion, shifting the law's focus from the probable present to the possible future.

Foreign-born poverty was not solely a problem of border control but also one of internal surveillance. Poverty could not always be detected effectively at the border, and over thirty percent of women and over forty percent of men living in almshouses in the United States in 1890 were foreign born.[10] By 1891, Congress expanded the provisions of the 1882 act by legislating that any immigrant found to be a public charge within one year of arrival could be deported. By 1903, this provision was expanded to two years after entry. By 1907, immigrants found to be public charges for reasons existing prior to their arrival could be still be deported within three years of arrival, and by 1917, the probationary time was extended to five years. Like charges of immorality, the burden of poverty was placed outside the United States. Poverty and immorality, the law hinted, were something immigrants brought with them. The link between time and need would have a severe impact on immigrants arriving in the late 1920s on the eve of an economic disaster beyond their control and one they could never have predicted.

Reports from immigration officials reveal that laws against want did in many ways prove an effective deterrence to the arrival of would-be

---

[7] For example, the Massachusetts legislature called for protective legislation in 1835–1836; Hutchinson, *Legislative History of American Immigration Policy*, 410.

[8] The issue of foreign paupers was debated nine times in the years between 1835 and 1855. The destruction wrought by the Civil War and the resulting need for labor briefly subdued the calls for immigration restrictions until the 1870s, when the issue of indigent immigrants again took center stage. Ibid., 410–412.

[9] Hutchinson notes that this legislation followed closely on the heels of a Supreme Court decision which invalidated the states' efforts to control the immigration of alien paupers. As a result, a number of states, especially New York, actively petitioned Congress for federal protection. Ibid., 411–412.

[10] The total number of people living in almshouses remained small in 1890 (0.1 percent of the population). However, while foreign-born immigrants represented only 16.5 percent of the population, they were 38.9 percent of almshouse residents. Frederick H. Wines, *Report on Crime, Pauperism, and Benevolence in the United States at the Eleventh Census: 1890, Part I, Analysis*, Department of the Interior, Census Office (Washington, D.C.: Government Printing Office, 1896), 7–120, 267–314.

immigrants. By far, LPC provided the most common reason for exclusion. Between 1895 and 1915, immigrants excluded as LPC upon arrival accounted for approximately two-thirds of all exclusions nationally. By World War I, the overall number of immigrants arriving in the United States declined. LPC, however, remained a significant deterrent during the war, comprising just under half of all exclusions. Thus, during the period of greatest immigration to the United States, most immigrants who were refused entry were denied as "likely to become a public charge."[11]

Immigrants arriving at the nation's borders during the late nineteenth and early twentieth century were hardly akin to the stricken rural peasants of popular mythology. Indeed, many immigrants arriving between 1821 and 1924 were skilled industrial workers who left the cities and towns of Europe and Asia to seek higher-paying work in the United States.[12] While poverty certainly was a lived reality for many arriving immigrants, in many ways the frequency of LPC was more a reflection of its inherent flexibility than of the economic scarcities of those who bore the label. As the case files of immigrant women reveal, poverty could be used to reinforce immigration laws regulating traditional gender roles and historic race and ethnic prejudices.

Single women, women who had left their family behind, or unmarried women who were visibly pregnant upon arrival were often labeled LPC. Reformers and immigration officials alike believed strongly that poverty bred immorality as surely as immorality wrought both moral and financial destitution. In its 1910 report to Congress, for example, the Dillingham Commission maintained that immigrant girls arriving with little money and less work skills were prey for corrupt and opportunistic labor contractors working under the cover of immigrant aid societies and seeking to place these women as servants, or worse as prostitutes, in local brothels, bars, and unsavory hotels.[13] Laws against poverty and those regulating morality wove easily through one another.

According to immigration officials, women who seemed to flout traditional strictures against premarital sex, or who appeared to have forsaken

---

[11] *Annual Report of the Commissioner-General of Immigration* (1895), 4; *Annual Report of the Commissioner-General of Immigration* (1900), 8–10; *Annual Report of the Commissioner-General of Immigration* (1905), 8–10; *Annual Report of the Commissioner-General of Immigration* (1920), 196–198; *Annual Report of the Commissioner-General of Immigration* (1915), 124–125; *Annual Report of the Commissioner-General of Immigration* (1920), 192–195.

[12] Thislewaite, "Migration from Europe Overseas in the Nineteenth and Twentieth Centuries," in *A Century of European Migrations, 1830–1930*, eds. Rudolph J. Vecoli and Suzanne M. Sinke (Urbana: University of Illinois Press, 1991), 17–49. Also see Herbert Gutman, *Work, Culture, and Society in Industrializing America* (New York: Knopf, 1976).

[13] Immigration Commission, *Immigrant Homes and Aid Societies*, Reports of the Immigration Commission presented by Mr. Dillingham, 1911, vol. 19; United States Senate, 61st Cong., 2nd sess., Washington, D.C.

their domestic responsibilities, were not only morally questionable but economically at risk as well. When Rosa Olivia Jensen arrived from Denmark in 1902, immigration officials voted to exclude her as LPC and noted in their report that Jensen was pregnant and had left her parents and the father of her child in Denmark. Although her sister was living and working in the United States as an actress and had pledged to support Jensen, her appeal was denied. In a letter from the commissioner, Jensen's unwed pregnancy loomed large: "I am opposed to the admission to this country of all such persons as come here to hide their shame."[14] Similarly, when Johanna Ambli attempted to enter the United States, her pregnancy was taken as evidence of immorality and thus certain poverty. "This is the usual method of dealing with such cases, and for very good reasons," the commissioner explained.[15]

Women who left their children behind were as suspect as those who transported theirs in utero. When Rosino Ferlaino, a forty-year-old Italian widow, arrived in 1902, she was excluded as LPC when officials noted she had left two children in Italy.[16] In a similar case, Maria Antonia Lastorina was held as LPC when she arrived from Italy in 1899 without her husband. According to the commissioner-general's report, "She states that it is the intention of her husband to come later on, but she shows no evidence of ability to support herself in the interim." "She should," according to the bureau, "be sent back to her husband and child."[17]

Laws against immigrants considered LPC reinforced traditional gendered divisions between male breadwinners and female homemakers. Immigration officials denied that a woman could provide the primary or

---

[14] Commissioner Williams to Bureau, 13 October 1902, casefile 52707; RINS, SCF, EI, reel 6. Similarly, Elka Bergman and her eleven-month-old child were denied admission as LPC in 1912. Bergman, a twenty-three-year-old Jewish woman from Austria, was pregnant when she arrived and it appears from the record that she attempted to disguise her pregnancy from authorities. Elka Bergman, casefile 53620/84; RINS, SCF, EI, reel 13.

[15] Although Ambli insisted that a rogue man was responsible for her unenviable position, the Commissioner concluded that pregnancy out of wedlock was "the result of a loose conception of morality"—hers. This was Ambli's second attempt to enter the United States. There is no explanation provided for why she was denied the first time. Commissioner Williams to Bureau, 13 October 1902, in Johanna Ambli, casefile 52707; RINS, SCF, EI, reel 6.

[16] Commissioner Williams to Bureau, 13 October 1902, in Rosino Ferlaino, casefile 52707; RINS, SCF, EI, reel 6.

[17] Fortunately, her husband did indeed arrive a month later and she was admitted. T. V. Powderly, Commissioner-General to Commissioner of Immigration, New York, 17 October 1899, "In re appeal of Maria Antonia Lastorina," casefile 52706/4; RINS, SCF, EI, reel 5. Caterina Graffeo was not as lucky. When she arrived in New York in 1898 five months pregnant and accompanied by her five other children she was "excluded from landing on account of having left her husband in Italy." While awaiting her husband's delayed arrival, Graffeo became ill and was taken from the Barge Office, where she had been detained, to the hospital where she subsequently died. Caterina Graffeo, casefile 52706/4; RINS, SCF, EI, reel 5.

only financial support for herself or her family. In many ways their constricted assessment of women's earning power reflected real inequities in the workplace. The industrializing economy drew single, young women into the wage labor force in part because they earned less than male heads of household. Traditional conceptions of women's domestic role segregated women into a limited number of paid positions outside the home and left them vulnerable to unemployment and low wages. Racial intolerance compounded gender inequity, and women of color found themselves employed in the dirtiest, meanest, lowest-paying work available. LPC was not just a theoretical possibility but a practical risk for many women arriving in the years before World War I. The Dillingham Commission reported that fully one-third of all foreign-born women seeking local financial relief between December 1908 and May 1909 were deserted, separated, or divorced.[18]

However, in their evaluation of women's work and wage, immigration officials stressed women's moral propriety or domestic responsibilities over their weekly earnings and employment history, and found large numbers of women LPC despite evidence of sustainable work skills. Women immigrants actively disputed the assumption that they were not economically viable, and they offered life histories of gainful employment and self-sufficiency. According to immigration authorities, however, a daughter's work was not that of a son, and a woman's wage not that of a man.

Women outside the assumptions of a "family wage" system—neither daughters in their father's house nor wives in their husband's—often found themselves excluded as LPC. Marriage and family were as much economic institutions under immigration law as they were moral, civic, or religious entities. Rebecca Hercovici, twenty-two, and her mother Chaia Hercovici, fifty-five, arrived from Romania in 1902 and were denied entrance as LPC. The "only support appellants would have" the commissioner explained in his report, "would be the earnings of the daughter as a tailoress, even assuming that she can at once secure and hold employment."[19] Similarly, when Marianna Tabit arrived with her two children but without her husband they were denied admission as LPC. According to the inspector's report, Tabit and her children "left their natural guardian and protector in Europe and have no one here legally bound to care for them should they fall into distress from any cause."[20]

---

[18] Immigration Commission, *Immigrants as Charity Seekers, Vol. 1*, Reports of the Immigration Commission presented by Mr. Dillingham, 1911, vol. 10; United States Senate, 61st Cong. 3rd sess., Washington, D.C.

[19] Hercovici's father had died and the two were intending to join relatives in New York. Department to Commissioner Williams, 11 October 1902, in Chaia Hercovici and Rebecca Hercovici, casefile 52707; RINS, SCF, EI, reel 6.

[20] Marianna Tabit, casefile 52707; RINS, SCF, EI, reel 6. Tabit's husband had intended to immigrate with his family but had been "rejected on account of his eyes." In addition to

Many woman who left as wives could find themselves alone, deserted, or widowed upon arrival. A woman's economic identity derived from her husband's or her father's. As a wife or daughter, an immigrant woman was a member of a viable, cooperative economic unit; alone she was more than likely LPC.[21] Giovanna Buttafuoco's husband was diagnosed with an eye disease and denied entry when the couple arrived from Italy with their children in 1902. With two small children and "without means of securing employment," according to immigration authorities, "the appellants are paupers in their present condition."[22] After a year's separation, Jenny Teitelbaum and her infant daughter followed her husband to the United States from Hungary in 1902. According to immigration officials, Teitelbaum's husband had neither communicated with his family nor invited them to join him. A "woman of very ordinary appearance," and "burdened with the care of an infant," "practically without means," and "showing no ability to secure employment," Teitelbaum was excluded as LPC.[23]

Women immigrants who were neither wives nor daughters required affidavits of support from male relatives living in the United States. Female family members were perceived by immigration officials as unreliable sources of economic support; the testimonial of a male family member was essential. Renee Berkoff, born in Hungary, immigrated in 1922 to join her sisters already working in the United States. Recalling her experience, Berkoff remembered that her sisters were unable to provide adequate financial reassurances and an uncle was called in to act as the legal guarantor. Berkoff explained that while her sisters "worked very hard and saved every penny," her uncle had to supply the fiscal assurance "so that nobody has to support me, he would take care of me."[24] When Vera Zimmerman arrived from Austria in 1912 to join her sister, Yana Zimmer-

---

charges of LPC, the inspector noted that if Tabit were to be admitted her husband might have better grounds to enter despite a medical condition that warranted exclusion.

[21] A Turkish woman, Sultana Cohen arrived with her two-year-old son in 1902 only to find that her husband had left the United States three weeks earlier. Pregnant upon arrival, Cohen was taken to the hospital and subsequently deported. There is no discussion in this case as to the status of her American-born child. The technicalities of children born "on the island" did eventually become a problem for immigration officials. Sultana Cohen, casefile 52707; RINS, SCF, EI, reel 6.

[22] Giovanna Buttafuoco, casefile 52707; RINS, SCF, EI, reel 6.

[23] Jenny Teitelbaum, casefile 52707; RINS, SCF, EI, reel 6. In a memo to primary inspectors and Boards of Special Inquiry, the commission explained that women could be landed only if their husbands were "able and willing" to support them. Wm. Williams, commissioner, "Notice to Primary Inspectors and Boards of Special Inquiry," 20 June 1903, casefile 52727/2; RINS, SCF, EI, reel 8.

[24] Renee Berkoff, interview by D. Gumb, 1985, in Voices from Ellis Island, reel 1, oral history no. 016.

man, she was held as LPC. Although Yana Zimmerman testified that she had saved sixty dollars working as a domestic servant for twenty-two dollars a month, immigration officials doubted Yana could mange the financial burden her sister Vera represented. In her appeal, Vera Zimmerman insisted that "I have enough relatives here besides my sister," that her brother-in-law worked as a hog carrier "earning union wages at three dollars a day," and she was "healthy and able to perform any housework." Despite possible assistance from other family members, Vera's sister remained her primary and legal financial backer. Wages earned in domestic service were not enough. In a final report to the commissioner, the inspector dismissed Vera Zimmerman's claims to self-sufficiency, "she is frail and undersized." Zimmerman was deported as LPC.[25]

THE APPEARANCE OF WANT: RACE, POVERTY, AND IMMIGRATION LAW

Poverty looked different. Racialist thinking provided an important conceptual grid for the complex maze of poverty exclusions and labor exemptions in immigration law. Poverty was identified, qualified, and substantiated by community expectations and intolerances. Eugenicts writing in the early twentieth century argued that less sophisticated, less entrepreneurial, less European, less white races from Africa, Asia, South America, and eastern and southern Europe had evolved in ways that allowed them to respond effectively to the demands of menial labor. While such natural section processes made them ideal candidates for America's industrial and agricultural work forces, it also left them at greater risk for indigence.

As was true in the efforts of Asian women to deflect attacks on their moral character through the appearance of respectability, the *appearance* of poverty was often taken as *evidence* of poverty. Race and ethnicity were important visual cues in the process of discerning evidence of LPC. When a Romanian woman arrived with her husband and five children in 1902, for example, the Commissioner noted that the family was "forlorn and frail looking persons," "typical of the class of Roumanians" who were "in effect paupers." Moreover, the Romanian family stood in marked contrast to the recent arrival of fourteen hundred immigrants "consisting of fine looking, healthy lot of people chiefly from the Scandinavian countries and well provided with funds."[26] In an address before

<hr />

[25] Vera Zimmerman [pseud.], INS file 53452/455 (1912); DJA-INS, acc. 60 A 600, box 448; INS, DC, RG85; NA, DC.

[26] Meschiler Langer, Wife and 5 children, casefile 52727/2; RINS, SCF, EI, reel 8. The commissioner noted that the State Department had recently warned the immigration bureau against the arrival of Romanian paupers.

the Union of American Hebrew Congregations in 1911, Max Kohler explained that LPC laws "work[ed] particular hardship upon the Russian Jew, with his deceptive appearance of slight physique, particularly at the end of abnormal conditions attending living in the badly conducted steerage, after being deprived of appropriate food, because of observance of the Jewish dietary laws."[27]

The Dillingham Commission's 1911 report to Congress attempted to evaluate and schematize poverty in ways that postulated a relationship between race and want. The two-volume report detailed the nativity and race of all those receiving relief or living in almshouses between December 1908 and May 1909, as well as compiling information supplied by the Immigration Bureau on the number and race of immigrants paroled to immigrant aid societies along with those deported outright as public charges.[28] Despite the fact that the data the commission collected revealed little evidence to support a conclusion that poverty and race were linked, the commission concluded that the two were mutually constitutive and equally destructive to the nation. The report commended recent efforts to stymie the arrival of racially marked, indigent immigrants, and suggested poverty and want were more common among the new, less white immigrants from southern and central Europe and Asia than among the old, acculturated immigrants from England, Ireland, France, and Germany.[29]

[27] Max J. Kohler, "The Immigration Question: with Particular Reference to the Jews of America," an address delivered at the Twenty-Second Council of the Union of American Hebrew Congregations, on January 18, 1911, at New York, in *Collection of Pamphlets and Articles Chiefly on Jewish Immigration to the United States*, Green Library, Stanford University. For example, a letter from the commissioner of immigration for Ellis Island dismissed the appeal of a Jewish woman and her six children by noting "None of them presents a robust appearance, and several of them are distinctly frail in appearance." INS file 53390/146 (1912); DJA-INS, acc. 60 A 600, box 406; INS, DC, RG85; NA, DC.

[28] The commission sent forms to charity organizations asking aid workers to list the number of family members, native or foreign born, that received assistance from 1 December 1908 to 31 May 1909. (Boston included only new cases during this period.) Data were compiled from forty-three cities, including many locations that figured prominently on migration routes. However, the report did not include information from New York City, a significant omission. Moreover, the commission made no effort to contextualize foreign-born poverty within more general population statistics for immigrant communities. 31,685 total cases were reported to the commission. *Immigrants as Charity Seekers, Vol. 1*; Immigration Commission, *Immigrants as Charity Seekers, Vol. 2*, Reports of the Immigration Commission presented by Mr. Dillingham, 1911, vol. 11; United States Senate, 61st Cong., 3rd sess., Washington, D.C.

[29] This despite the fact that in its analysis the commission had noted, "In only a small proportion of cases were those receiving charitable assistance recent immigrants to the United States," *Immigrants as Charity Seekers, Vol. 1*, 70. Immigration Commission, *Brief Statement of the Conclusions and Recommendations of the Immigration Commission, with Views of the Minority*, Reports of the Immigration Commission presented by Mr. Dillingham, 1911, United States Senate, 61st Cong., 2nd sess., Washington, D.C, 18, 27.

Indeed, the data do not suggest that nonwhite, new, or even racially different immigrants made up a disproportionate number of the immigrants deported as public chargers, especially given that these "other" immigrants comprised the majority of new arrivals to the United States in the early twentieth century. What the data do reveal, however, is that the law against poverty was applied with disproportionate severity to nonwhite, non–Western European immigrants. In 1904, Asian and southern and eastern European immigrants made up over half of all immigrants deported as paupers or likely paupers. As significant, two-thirds of all Chinese, Greek, "Hebrew," Mexican, and Southern Italian immigrants arriving in 1904 were deported as LPC. In 1908 the combined totals of southern Italians, Jews, Greeks, Poles, and Mexicans continued to represent over a third of all poverty exclusions.[30]

The experiences of two women in particular reveal the complex interplay between race, work, and poverty at stake in the application of immigrant law to nonwhite women workers.[31] Aurea Infante, a domestic servant, attempted to return to El Paso in 1918, and Ogawa Sekiyo, a washerwoman and farmer, arrived in San Francisco in 1919 to assist her daughter in the final months of her pregnancy. Both women fit within the few exempted categories available to working women at the time—those from the Western Hemisphere, those willing to work as domestic servants, and those contracted to work on Hawaiian sugar plantations. Even exempted immigrants, however, had to meet LPC requirements. As single women, a daughter without a father and a wife without a husband, arriving into a labor market truncated by race and gender, Infante and Ogawa appeared likely paupers.

In Infante's case, charges of poverty and prostitution were infused with a regional politics of race specific to the Southwest. For El Paso officials, Mexican women were both a ready supply of inexpensive labor and a

[30] Table 44, "Number of aliens debarred and number deported, by race or people, fiscal years 1904 and 1908," *Immigrants as Charity Seekers, Vol. 1*, 320.

[31] Ironically, legal challenges brought by two Japanese women confirmed the nation's right to exclude those deemed likely to become public charges and solidified the legal precedent that would govern future challenges to economic exclusion policies. In 1891, in a case that hinged on the right of a young Japanese woman to join her husband living and working in San Francisco, Justice Gray, writing for the U.S. Supreme Court, affirmed Congress's unconditional right to "forbid the entrance of foreigners within its dominion." Race and economic status, if deemed by Congress to be threats to the nation's security, could provide just grounds for exclusion. Eleven years later, the Supreme Court reiterated its 1891 decision—LPC was a matter of police and public security. In this case, Kaoru Yamataya had been arrested a year after her arrival and held for deportation as LPC. Writing for the Court, Justice Harlan argued that "Congress did not intend that the mere admission of an alien" would place her "beyond the control or authority" of the government. *Nishimura Ekiu v. United States* 142 U.S. 651 (1891); *The Japanese Immigrant Case* 189 U.S. 86 (1903).

constant drain on local social services. Immigration records revealed that Infante and her mother, Victoria Chavez, had been deported once before in 1914 as "professional beggars." The family denied that they had been begging on the streets of El Paso and argued that they had only asked for an apple. Unfortunately, the family never attempted to appeal their case and the record of indigence remained uncontested. In 1916, Infante and Chavez recrossed the southern border and secured work as domestic servants until Chavez was forced to quit because she did not speak English. Chavez subsequently found work washing clothes for hotels at a dollar a bundle, and, in addition to her work as a laundress for a private family, earned about six dollars a week. Immigration inspectors suspected that the family supplemented their small income with what Infante could earn as a part-time prostitute. In her interview with immigration inspectors, however, Infante insisted that the two dollars a week she earned came from moral work and honest effort:

A: I help her whenever I have work. Sometimes I help her wash.
Q: Have you ever lived with boys or men without being married to them?
A: I never lived with anybody and never stayed with anybody; and I am willing for the doctor to examine me.[32]

Ogawa Sekiyo's case highlights the legal knot of laws against laborers, on the one hand, and needy immigrants, on the other, that wound around Asian woman immigrants and tied them to both work and poverty. Immigration officials expressed grave reservations about Ogawa's ability to support herself, despite the fact that she arrived in 1919 on a first-class ticket into San Francisco. Ogawa responded that the officials' suspicions were unfounded, and that she was well able to earn a living wage, often supplementing the family's income from their Hawaiian cocoa farm through her weekly earnings of five to six dollars washing clothes. Evidence of work, however, brought Ogawa out from under the charges of poverty and into a second excludable category—Japanese laborer. Ogawa was forced to deny her work experience in order to fit within the narrow understanding of Japanese wife admittable under immigration law. "No, but I am not of the laboring class now," Ogawa insisted, and in an affida-

---

[32] Aurea Infante, casefile 54281/36C (1918); RINS, SCF, MI. In a similar case, Maria Chávez was held for deportation in 1920. A widow, Chávez had immigrated to San Antonio some time after her husband's death in 1918. Chávez worked a chili stand in San Antonio for one dollar a day and occasionally crossed the border through Nueva Laredo to visit friends and relatives in Mexico. Officials were suspicious of Chávez's ability to support herself and questioned her repeatedly about her work, her expenses, and her living arrangements. Officials suspected Chávez supplemented her limited earnings through occasional prostitution. She was deported as a public charge in 1920. Maria Chávez [pseud.], INS file 54919/32 (1920); DJA-INS, acc. 60 A 600, box 1360; INS, DC, RG85; NA, DC.

vit supplied on her behalf by the Japanese Association of America, she testified that her work for the past four years had been confined to the house and her domestic duties within. Appealing on her behalf, her son-in-law insisted that Ogawa would neither become a public charge nor ever seek work while in the United States. Immigration officials, however, remained unconvinced, and maintained that Ogawa belonged with her husband.[33]

At the border, "likely to become" provided a malleable phrase within which appearance, time, cause, and effect influenced how poverty and its impact on the nation was understood. Self-sufficiency remained a male prerogative while dependency continued to delineate what was feminine. LPC worked to distinguish "others" who lay outside the social community and beyond the bounds of charity from those who were members and entitled to work and welfare. Visual clues marked by race assisted immigration officials in this process of differentiation.

---

[33] On appeal, Ogawa was admitted. Okawa Sekiyo, INS file 18504/19–6 (1920); AICF, box 1371; INS, SFD, RG85; NA-PSR.

CHAPTER SIX

Toil and Trouble

Laws against indigence and laws controlling where and how immigrants were employed, were two sides of the same coin. How poverty was understood was intimately linked to ideas of work and wage. "Likely to become" not only served to regulate the relationship between individual need and community responsibility, but also valued and schematized work along a double helix of gender and race. In the early twentieth century, immigration laws favored the arrival of women whose primary work lay in the home, theirs or someone else's, while frustrating the arrival of women with work skills that took them into the factories and shop floors of the industrializing American economy. These laws denied women's abilities to support themselves independently of male breadwinners, perceiving immigrant women without husbands or fathers as financial risks and likely drains on the nation's resources.

Laws against so-called "contract laborers," or those immigrants solicited abroad for employment in the United States, provide the backbone for legislative efforts to control the arrival of unskilled or low-skilled immigrants. Laws regulating work and those prohibiting want went hand in hand—immigrants labeled LPC could not defend themselves with claims of secure employment upon arrival without violating laws against contract laborers. The earliest contract labor law, passed in 1862, was a response to labor agitation protesting the arrival of increasing numbers of Chinese men hired to work in the mine shafts and railroad camps of the American West. The so-called "coolie trade" was denounced by labor leaders and politicians alike as a threat to white man's wages and thus to the fiscal success and moral stability of a white nation.[1] The principle of labor exclusion was quickly expanded, first to Japanese laborers in 1869, and then in 1885 to all immigrants arriving with the promise of work. Laws against contract laborers remained a fixture of immigration law

---

[1] Alexander Saxton, *The Indispensable Enemy: Labor and the Anti-Chinese Movement in California* (Berkeley: University of California Press, 1995); Martha Mabie Gardner "Working on White Womanhood: White Working Women in the San Francisco Anti-Chinese Movement, 1877–1890," *Journal of Social History* 33, No 1 (fall 1999).

until they were supplanted by laws allocating visas according to work skills passed in the 1950s and 1960s.[2]

While contract labor laws were primarily directed at men hired to lay the track, dig the shafts, and harvest the trees in the nation's railroad, mining, and timber industries, laws regulating labor also had an impact on women immigrants. From the beginning, immigration law exempted women's work in domestic service, agriculture, and eventually nursing from the provisions of the contract labor law. While not classified as skilled work, immigration law recognized domestic work in particular as providing a worthy, remunerative service to the nation. Beginning in 1885 and continuing through the 1920s and 1930s, contract labor laws specifically exempted women working as nurses or domestic servants from the blanket prohibitions against the arrival of immigrant labors.[3] Women's paid work outside the domestic sphere, however, whether as factory operatives, seamstresses, or retail clerks, was classified as low-skilled labor, neither essential to economic development nor valuable for the nation. By privileging women's paid work in professions that mirrored their traditional responsibilities in the home, immigration law valued women immigrants' domestic skills while it undervalued their potential contributions to an industrializing economy.

Immigration policy also allowed for the temporary admission of agricultural laborers into the South and Southwest, Pacific Northwest, and Hawaiian Islands to harvest the cotton, hops, fruits, vegetables, and sugar crops of an expanding American agricultural empire. As members of farming families, women immigrants from Mexico, Canada, the Philippines, China, and Japan were pickers for hire, comprising both a ready reserve of necessary hands and a temporary labor force empowered to work but not to stay. Women's work in agricultural labor was often hidden behind immigration statistics that enumerated these women as wives rather than workers. However, when immigration restrictionists lobbied for tighter control over the arrival of foreign labor, the issue of women and paid agricultural work emerged as a powerful rhetorical tool with which to raise the specters of racial mixing, economic competition, and poverty.

[2] Laws against contract laborers were passed in 1885, 1907, 1917, 1921, and 1924. Hutchinson, *Legislative History of American Immigration Policy*, 429, 494–496.

[3] Passed in 1885, the first contract labor law exempted domestic servants, servants, and private secretaries. The language was slightly amended in 1907 to read "persons employed strictly as personal or domestic servants." In 1917, nurses were added to the exempted categories, and the category of servant was even more narrowly limited to "persons employed as domestic servants." Finally, the 1921 quota law allowed nurses and domestic servants, along with actors, artists, lecturers, singers, ministers, college or seminary professors, and those in the learned professions, to arrive in excess of quota. Hutchinson, *Legislative History of American Immigration Policy*, 429, 494–496.

WORK AND DOMESTICITY: WOMEN'S WORK
AND IMMIGRATION LAW

Arriving at the border, women were quick to identify themselves as domestic servants and thus harness the weight of gender stereotype to their application for admission.[4] When Gerda Serrano arrived in El Paso with her niece Dolores she assured immigration authorities that she intended to work as a domestic servant although she admitted she preferred the higher paying wages offered by the cannery factories around Los Angeles. Serrano explained that she had previously been admitted as a domestic servant and had "quit working about two years ago to work with the Ortega Canning Company." Inspectors queried Serrano about her employment intentions given that, as one inspector noted, "there are no canning factories here in El Paso." Serrano replied that she planned to return to domestic service in El Paso, earning five dollars a week, although she might save her money and return to Los Angeles and the canning factories when she could. Despite her guarded response, Serrano was admitted as a domestic servant.[5] Similarly, when Anna Arps arrived in San Francisco with her German-born parents from missionary work in Manila in 1918, she too assured immigration authorities that she intended to find work as a domestic servant although she had never worked for a wage before.[6]

[4] Labor exemptions, however, offered no absolute guaranties. When Alexia Puskas arrived from Czechoslovakia in 1921, she testified that she planned on working as a housekeeper for her brother-in-law while his wife was ill. A widow, officials were concerned about the moral propriety of her intended employment and thus suspicious of Puskas's ability to support herself and remained unmoved by evidence of a history of domestic service: "Q: How have you been supporting and maintaining yourself and child since the death of your husband? A: I worked as a servant for a rich family; I had my child with me." The board voted to exclude Puskas as a public charge. Puskas's appeal was bolstered by a supportive letter from the YWCA Committee on Immigrant Aid promising they could find work for Puskas and offering to post bond. Alexia Puskas [pseud.], INS file 54999–324 (1921); DJA-INS, acc. 60 A 600, box 1420; INS, DC, RG85; NA, DC.

[5] Serrano was born in Leon, Mexico, and had lived in Los Angeles from 1912 to 1918. She told immigration authorities that El Paso was her final destination, but it seems likely that if she could get better-paying work in a canning factory in California she would take it. In its final ruling, the board emphasized that Serrano was "above the average Mexican working woman, both in intelligence and appearance," that she appeared to be "a good, capable business woman who is able to take care of herself under any circumstances," and that she was both "strong and healthy." Gearda Serrano, casefile 54281/36E (1918); RINS, SCF, MI, reel 10.

[6] The family was German and came within the confines of wartime restrictions against enemy aliens. They were paroled and subsequently allowed permanent entry. Anna Arps, INS file 17452/1–12 (1918); AICF, box 1307; INS, SFD, RG85; NA-PSR.

Young women working as domestic servants were allowed to emigrate with their employers despite immigration laws requiring that children travel with their parent or be on route to their legal guardians.[7] The violence and chaos of the Mexican Revolution left many Mexican women to care for the children of family members who had been lost or killed in the turmoil. Between 1918 and 1920, many of these women sought to immigrate, or often to return, to the United States in search of higher wages and the support of family members unscarred by revolution.[8] Arriving with cousins, nieces, nephews, and orphans in tow brought these women under the purview of immigration law regulating children, specifically ensuring that children allowed to enter the United States would abide by child labor laws and education requirements.[9] Arriving without husbands, brothers, or fathers also brought these women under the glare of laws regulating want.

As they arrived at the southern border, Mexican women were questioned about their capacity to support themselves and their extended families. A skilled woman with experience as a stenographer and as a saleswoman, demonstrator, and instructor for the Singer Sewing Machine Company, Adela Cardova was detained at Nogales, Arizona, in 1917 with her nieces to answer questions about her ability to support herself and her two young charges. What work did she intend to do? Did she think she was competent enough to find employment in Los Angeles?[10] Similarly, when Eloisa Lopez arrived in Nogales, Arizona, in 1918 with her niece, she assured immigration officials that with the wages she earned as a dressmaker she was able to support herself and her young charge. Officials, however, remained unconvinced, "And her father does not help you support her at all?" "Some," Lopez qualified, "he is going to send me money." "How do you know?" officials retorted. Eventually immigration

---

[7] The 1907 act excluded "all children under sixteen years of age, unaccompanied by one or both of their parents." These children could be admitted only by discretionary authority. The exclusion remained until 1952. Hutchinson, *Legislative History of American Immigration Policy*, 438.

[8] This was also true of Jewish families escaping the chaos of Russia during World War I. See, for example, Feiga Bayefsky, INS file 16778/25-3-4-5 (1917); AICF, box 1276; INS, SFD, RG85; NA-PSR.

[9] For example, Tomasa Cuevas, INS file 1886/16 (1920); AICF, box 1411; INS, SFD, RG85; NA-PSR; Candelaria Ramos, casefile 54281/36H (1919); RINS, SCF, MI, reel 10.

[10] She explained that she planned on learning English so that she could apply her stenography skills in the United States. Until then, she offered, "I know enough about sewing to get work." Cordova and her nieces were admitted only after her brother provided assurances of adequate financial support. Adela Cordova, casefile 54281/36B (1917); RINS, SCF, MI, reel 9. Similarly, immigration officials were concerned that Juana Gil, a seamstress, would be unable to support her young niece. En route to Los Angeles, Gil was detained at the Nogales border in 1917. Juana Gil, casefile 54281/36B (1917); RINS, SCF, MI, reel 9.

officials sought assurances from Lopez's brother living in the United States that he would be willing to support an additional child.[11]

While many of these Mexican women and their charges were eventually admitted by local inspectors after testifying to their readiness to work and the children's eagerness to attend school, central authorities continually warned that these women were more burden than asset, and insisted that suspect women be investigated after arrival to verify their employment and the children's enrollment in school.[12] After officials at Calexico admitted Julia Fierrors and her niece, their decision was roundly criticized by district headquarters in El Paso. Fierrors, a widow, testified that she "worked in factories, as a house servant, cigar factories, and so on" to support herself and her young niece. While she only had nine dollars, Fierrors planned on working in Calexico before moving on to Los Angeles. "Are you in a position," Calexico officials queried "to take her to a place that would not prove injurious to her morals, health, and condition in general?" Yes, Fierrors confirmed, adding that she had always found regular work for one and a half to two dollars a day. "Have you ever received any charity while in the United States?" the questions continued, "Did you ever apply for any?" No, Fierrors insisted, when she had needed it she sought aid from family members. Upon reviewing this case, El Paso officials demanded further investigation.[13]

Policy makers sought to prevent the importation of child laborers by requiring officers to question accompanying adult immigrants about their intentions for their young charges. Domestic service, however, was rarely seen as a possible violation of child labor laws. With assurances that young women would be offered some schooling and that their paid work would be limited to the home, employers were permitted to immigrate with their young employees in tow. For young women, domestic service was presented as a component of their education, excellent training for their future responsibilities as wives and mothers. Enfronsina Nesbbertt had been hired in Panama in 1919 to work for an American family at five dollars a month. Her employer insisted that female help was scarce in the United States and thus Nesbbertt should be permitted entry under the exemption for domestic servants. Immigration officials disagreed and retorted that help was available at the prevailing wage but not at the sub-

[11] The child, Librada Lopez, had been orphaned and left in the care of her aunt. Eloisa Lopez was also bringing two additional children, a niece and nephew, to join their father living in Jerome, Arizona. Eloisa Lopez, casefile 54281/36F (1918); RINS, SCF, MI, reel 10.

[12] In a memo from the district headquarters in El Paso, the supervising inspector criticized the Nogales officers for their lax investigation and warned that greater care should be taken to insure that arriving immigrants would not become public charges when they reached their final destination. Manueal Morales, casefile 54281/36G (1918); RINS, SCF, MI, reel 10.

[13] Nestora Franco, casefile 54281/36G (1919); RINS, SCF, MI, reel 10.

standard income Nesbbertt received. While held in detention awaiting the board's decision in her case, the matron at Angle Island immigration station petitioned to have Nesbbertt released into her custody as her own domestic employee. Mrs. Green confirmed the shortage of good help available for hire and offered to pay Nesbbertt the same wage as her original employer. Whereas previously such a low wage had garnered suspicions of abuse, new emphasis was placed on Nesbbertt's "promise of developing into a good household servant." A "healthy" and "robust" girl, the San Francisco commissioner argued, Nesbbertt would be "well cared for and given every opportunity to improve her station in life" with Mrs. Green.[14] Other girls also arrived with their employers and were admitted as domestic servants. Rosa Quijada, a fourteen-year-old Mexican girl, was admitted into Naco, Arizona, as a part-time maid for her employer in 1918. The board voted to admit Quijada noting that she was "strong and healthy" and that her work would be after school hours.[15]

While domestic servants were required to show little more than a willingness to work for a private employer, nurses were held to higher standards of professionalization. In the midst of World War I and with a growing domestic movement for public health services, nurses were added to the list of exemptions in 1917. Like domestic servants, proponents argued that nurses were in chronic short supply and that foreign nurses were essential to meet the needs of American hospitals, clinics, and private employers. In enforcing the law, immigration officials maintained that the exception in the contract labor laws offered to nurses was limited to those who had received training and whose duties went beyond those of a personal servant.[16] When Henrika W. Loveriks arrived with her employer from Java in 1919, she lacked any evidence that she had been professionally trained or employed by a doctor or clinic. Without professional credentials, Loveriks could not offer proof of her status as a nurse and thus

---

[14] Included in this file was a handwritten note from Nesbbertt asking to be paroled into Green's custody: "I here by respectfully ask to be paroled to Mrs. Green who is willing to take me. I promise to go to school until sixteen and to be good girl. I also understand that if I do not behave myself and do right I will be returned to Panama." It seems likely, given the attention to diction, spelling, and behavior, that Green oversaw the letter's drafting. Eufronsina Nesbbertt, INS file 18609/1-1 (1919); AICF, box 1384; INS, SFD, RG85; NA-PSR.

[15] Rosa Quijada, casefile 54281/36B (1918); RINS, SCF, MI, reel 9; also see Maria Ortiz, casefile 54281/36B (1917); RINS, SCF, MI, reel 9.

[16] By 1917, the service distinguished between "domestic servants" who were included under the exempted categories, and "personal servants" who were not. In a 25 June 1917 memo for the assistant secretary, the assistant-commissioner general explained that "personal servants are commonly understood to be valets, lady's maids, etc." INS file 54261/196 (1917–); RCO, entry 9, box 271, 54261/181–54261/202; INS, DC, RG85; NA, DC.

avoid race-based exclusion policies prohibiting the arrival of all Asian immigrants.[17]

Despite this professional distinction, nursing and domestic service were linked through their significant contribution to the middle- and upper-class American home. While personal servants were dismissed by the bureau as those "menials engaged to wait hand and foot upon persons who are old enough and physically able to attend to their own personal wants," trained nurses and those employed on behalf of the needs of the entire household were perceived as providing a valued service to the middle- and upper-class family.[18] Nurses for young children and midwives often failed to meet the professional criterion established for nurses, but were nevertheless grouped with cooks, butlers, waiters, and waitresses as a "necessary part of the domestic force."[19] For example, a Japanese woman with three years training as a midwife but without evidence of formal training as a nurse arriving with her employer in 1917 was admitted as a domestic servant rather than a nurse.[20] Similarly, Gladys Taylor's work as child's nurse was found to be "essential to the welfare" of the household despite the fact that she had no professional nursing credentials.[21]

In addition to specific exempted categories of domestic service and nursing, women working as temporary, low-wage, primarily agricultural laborers were permitted to accompany their husbands and families to the Pacific Northwest, South and Southwest, and Hawaii during peak season to harvest the hops, cotton, fruits, vegetables, and sugar cane crops. According to white union organizers and other immigration restrictionists, women entering as wives were able to evade laws excluding Asian laborers by claiming a purely domestic role as housewife and masking their

---

[17] Eventually she was admitted on temporary bond and departed for Europe a year later with her employers. Henrika W. Loveriks, INS file 18431/1–6 (1919); AICF, box 1365; INS, SFD, RG85; NA-PSR. Also, Marie Anna Berg, INS file 17549/2–8 (1918); AICF, box 1319; INS, SFD, RG85; NA-PSR.

[18] A. Warner Parker, Law Officer for the Commissioner-General, "Supplemental Memorandum for the Assistant Secretary," 9 October 1917, INS file 54261/196 (1917–); RCO, entry 9, box 271; 54261/181–54261/202; INS, DC, RG85; NA, DC.

[19] Assistant-Commissioner General to Assistant Secretary, 25 June 1917, INS file 54261/196 (1917–); RCO, entry 9, box 271, 54261/181–54261/202; INS, DC, RG85; NA, DC.

[20] Assistant-Commissioner General to Assistant Secretary, 25 June 1917, INS file 54261/196 (1917–); RCO, entry 9, box 271, 54261/181–54261/202; INS, DC, RG85; NA, DC.

[21] A. Warner Parker, Law Officer for the Commissioner-General, "Supplemental Memorandum for the Assistant Secretary," 9 October 1917, INS file 54261/196, 1917–); RCO, entry 9, box 271, 54261/181–54261/202; INS, DC, RG85; NA, DC. Governesses, however, were not included in the discretionary space created for children's nurses and midwives. Memo for the Commissioner General, 6 July 1922, INS file 54261/196 (1917–); RCO, entry 9, box 271, 54261/181–54261/202; INS, DC, RG85; NA, DC.

intention to work alongside their husband in the fields or in family-owned business. In addition, and much to the frustration of organized labor in the United States, until the 1920s immigrants from the Western Hemisphere were exempt from many immigration regulations, including laws against contract laborers.[22]

Legal prohibitions against foreign labor did allow employers to contract for immigrant workers when no other suitable supply of labor could be found.[23] Agricultural employers encouraged immigrants to migrate with their families. According to employers, immigrant families promised a more stable, as well as a geometric expansion, of their workforce. Labor-intensive sugar plantations in Hawaii relied on poorly paid Asian labors from China, Japan, Korea, and the Philippines to generate profit and fuel growth.[24] When labor laws were extended to the Hawaiian Territory in 1903, "men with families" became increasingly important to create a stable, self-generating labor force.[25] Mexican immigrant women comprised an equally important source of labor for farmers in the South and Southwest. Indeed, American farmers in Texas and California utilized the labor of entire Mexican families to make quick work of the cotton, sugar beet, and lemon crops.[26] When Virginia Olvera arrived in El Paso

[22] As early as 1897, trade unions, labor societies, and individual workingmen filed urgent protests with Congress and the INS against the immigration of skilled laborers from Canada and Mexico. *Annual Report of the Commissioner-General of Immigration* (1897), 7. By the late 1920s, the Immigration Bureau and the State Department began to apply the provisions of the contract labor law to Mexican immigrants. See Reisler, "Always the Laborer, Never the Citizen."

[23] McNeff Brothers, Pacific Coast Hops Dealers to U.S. Senator C.C. Dill, 22 June 1925, INS file 55466/182 (1925–); RCO, entry 9, box 384, 55466/51–55466/444; INS, DC, RG85; NA, DC; Seattle to Central Offices, memorandum, 13 May 1926, INS file 55466/182 (1925–); RCO, entry 9, box 384, 55466/51–55466/444; INS, DC, RG85; NA, DC.

[24] Takaki notes that the Japanese government had originally stipulated that forty percent of all labor émigrés should be women. In practice, however, between 1885 and 1894 Japanese women were twenty percent of the Japanese immigrant labor pool. From the beginning these women were workers; seventy-two percent of arriving Japanese women were assigned to field labor. Takaki, *In a Different Mirror: A History of Multicultural America* (Boston: Little, Brown & Co., 1993), 250.

[25] Manager of the Hutchinson Sugar Company to W. G. Irwin and Company, 25 January 1905, as quoted in ibid., 250–251. Takaki argues that the increasing emphasis on families came as a response to annexation in 1900. Planters may have anticipated that immigration laws would be extended to the new territory, but this legislative link was not established until 1903. Within decades, the significance of immigrant women for the production of sugar, the reproduction of the labor force, and the development of the Japanese American community was evident. By 1920, fourteen percent of the plantation workforce in Hawaii were women, and most of these women were Japanese; forty-five percent of Japanese living in Hawaii were less than nineteen years old; and, plantation owners began razing single-sex barracks and replacing them with cottages for families. Ibid., 255, 262, 264.

[26] Ibid., 320–326.

in 1918 with her three-year-old sister, she explained to immigration authorities that she planned on joining her aunt in Sinton, Texas picking cotton. "I can pick four hundred pounds per day," Olvera offered, "and we are usually paid from forty to seventy-five cents per hundred pounds."[27]

As Virginia Olvera's testimony reveals, immigrants were aware of the legal exemptions provided for agricultural workers and many presented themselves and their work skills in ways that conformed to legal conventions. The 1924 National Origins Act specifically provided that up to half of each national quota be allocated for the admittance of agricultural laborers and their families as preference immigrants.[28] Importantly, this occupational preference was granted only to those nations within the quota system and those nations with a quota of three hundred or more, thus emphasizing exclusions against Asian and Southeast Asian immigrants. Maria Schulhoff attempted to use the exemption for agricultural families to gain admission to the United States along with her three-year-old son in 1926. A widow, Schulhoff testified that she was to join her brother-in-law, a farmer in Oregon. Immigration officials grew suspicious when relatives living in Brooklyn posted a bond in support of Schulhoff and her son. Under further investigation, authorities ascertained that the visas had been forged. In hearing Scholhoff's appeal, the Circuit Court of Appeals, Second Circuit, noted that it was "doubtful if the preference granted to a quota immigrant who is skilled in agriculture applies to a female."[29]

OF LIMITED WORTH: OTHER WOMEN'S WORK

Working outside the confines of domesticity placed women at a decided disadvantage. In contrast to domestic servants, nurses, or agricultural workers, women who arrived with other marketable skills confronted a wall of doubt as immigration officials expressed uncertainty about women's ability to support themselves without relying on public relief or private charity. Women who arrived at the border with intentions to work in occupations other than domestic service or nursing were often labeled LPC not only because work, independence, and self-sufficiency were gendered male but also because of the material reality of a gender-segregated

---

[27] Virginia Olvera, casefile 54281/36c (1918); RINS, SCF, MI, reel 9.

[28] Hutchinson, *Legislative History of American Immigration Policy*, 496.

[29] There was no question, however, about the fake documents or Schulhoff's misrepresentation before the board; she and her son were returned to Germany. *United States ex rel. Smith v. Curran, Commissioner of Immigration* 12 F.2d 636 (2nd Cir. 1926).

labor market and sex-specific wage scales which left women at greater risk for poverty.[30]

Women who worked as seamstresses, dressmakers, waitresses, store clerks, or factory operatives were questioned extensively about their estimated income, asked to provide proof of former employment, and often requested to disclose the financial details of their day-to-day lives. How much rent did they pay? Whom did they support? Had they ever been out of work? Did they rely on private relief to supplement their weekly incomes? How were the male members of their family employed and could they be relied upon for financial assistance? These questions probed the gendered subtext of work and poverty—women's underpaid work outside the home both fueled newly emerging sectors of the service and industrial economy and yet reinforced women financial dependence on the family.

In passing laws to regulate the arrival of indigent immigrants, Congress was careful to distinguish between the nation's need for inexpensive labor and its desire to be insulated from foreign poverty.[31] Because it relied on subjective evaluation, LPC permitted a more flexible response to cyclical downturns in the market economy than prohibitions against contract laborers. In general, LPC exclusions were applied more vigorously during periods of economic contraction and high unemployment.[32] Despite deep-seated anxieties about race difference, moral laxity, and economic dependency, immigrants remained an essential and necessary source of surplus labor for the American economy. Exemptions for women willing to work as domestic servants and nurses or as temporary agricultural laborers reflected an astute awareness of current labor market deficiencies and employer demands.

[30] This is not to say that women arriving as domestic servants did not also confront questions about their financial wherewithal. For example, Dolores Garcia, a domestic servant, arrived with her granddaughter in Nogales, Arizona in 1918 and was questioned about her wages, her financial obligations, her savings, and any history of public or private assistance. As was often true in the case of immigrant women working as domestic servants, Garcia received room and board along with her wage. Boarding-in incorporated working women within a family, guaranteeing, as far as immigration officials were concerned, that they were under the financial care and of their employer and thus would not become a burden on local communities. Dolores Garcia, casefile 54281/36C (1918); RINS, SCF, MI, reel 10.

[31] Kitty Calavita notes that congressional discussion of the act of 1903 revealed the uneasy balance in immigration policy between excluding excess laborers while encouraging a surplus labor supply. Shattuc, the bill's sponsor in the House of Representatives, explained that new legislation "must avoid measures so drastic as to cripple American industry, agriculture, and the great shipping and transportation interests." Calavita, "A Sociological Analysis of U.S. Immigration Policy, 1820–1924" (Ph.D. diss., University of Delaware, 1980), 285, 286.

[32] According to Kitty Calavita, contract labor laws were politically palatable only when they excluded a minority of arriving immigrant laborers. Ibid., 305–317.

Sophie Cadogan, a dressmaker with aspirations to nursing, arrived with her husband Samuel in San Francisco from Panama in 1919. Although Cadogan was literate and insisted her dressmaking skills could support them both, husband and wife were denied admission on the grounds that he was both illiterate and unable to provide sufficiently for himself and his wife.[33] In questioning Cadogan about her work history, immigration officials raised serious doubts about her claims to occupational skill and financial independence:

> Q: Did you ever make a living at dressmaking?
> A: All the time.
> Q: How long have you made a living as a dressmaker?
> A: Ever since I was 20.
> Q: Are you a dressmaker, or merely a sewing woman?
> A: I cut and fit and do everything.

As the questioning continued, officials remained unconvinced of Cadogan's earning potential as a skilled seamstress:

> Q: About what have you been earning a day?
> A: Sometimes I make three or four dresses a day.
> Q: How much do you earn for that?
> A: Sometimes I make $21, sometimes $18.
> Q: How long does it take you to make 3 dresses?
> A: About 2 days.
> Q: You get $21 for three dresses?
> A: Yes.[34]

When immigration inspectors voted to refuse the couple admission as LPC, Cadogan appealed their case. Drawing on her occupational and educational skills, Cadogan argued that her own strengths more than compensated for her husband's weakness as an illiterate common laborer. In response to questions posed by her attorney, Cadogan alerted officials to her proven ability to support herself and to her future plans to pursue training as a nurse:[35]

---

[33] Samuel Cadogan was born in Barbados and had attended school for five to six months. Sophie Cadogan was born in Jamaica and had a cousin living in West Oakland. The two had met and married in Panama. In his interview, Samuel Cadogan testified that his wife was dependent on him for support.

[34] Cadogan clarified subsequently that she received twenty-one dollars in Panamanian currency, amounting to about $10.50 in American dollars. Cadogan testified that in general her work garnered approximately three dollars a day.

[35] Cadogan changed her mind at least once on the question of being separated from her husband. Originally, she testified she wanted her case to be considered independently of his. Samuel Cadogan was reluctant to file an appeal, fearing that the couple would be faced with

Q: [I]n the matter of desiring to remain in the U.S. even without your husband, have you any trade or occupation?

A: Yes, I am a dressmaker by trade, and a manicurist, and a cook too.

Q: And you are capable of working at any or all of these trades?

A: Yes, and healthy and able bodied.

Q: You can live independently of your husband?

A: Yes.

Q: You can earn your own livelihood?

A: Yes.

Despite Cadogan's insistence that she was neither a public charge nor a likely recipient of public relief, her appeal was denied and the couple was deported, Samuel Cadogan for illiteracy and LPC and Sophie Cadogan as LPC.[36]

Immigration officials questioned whether working women's wages could stretch much beyond their own needs. In the eyes of immigration officials, women who were neither domestic servants, nor nurses, nor agricultural workers, were likely public charges. Beyond the assumptions of the family wage and the male breadwinner, women seamstresses, laundresses, factory operatives, and retail clerks were beyond the limits of viability and self-sufficiency. By their exclusion, immigration officials reinforced the conceptual and legal links between home, work, wage, and worth for women immigrants. Work that was in, of, and for the home was valuable, admittable labor, work that was not, was not.

POSSIBILITY AND PLAUSIBILITY: CHALLENGES AND CRITICISMS OF LPC

Gender bias did not go unnoticed, and by the late 1920s and early 1930s judicial officials and social activists became increasingly critical of how laws against poverty and those regulating work were applied to women immigrants. Writing for the liberal magazine *Survey* in 1927, Emma Wold, a lawyer and active member of the National Woman's Party, argued

---

long delay and detention awaiting a final decision. A few days later, Sophie Cadogan changed her mind and asked that their case be jointly appealed and used evidence of her own educational and occupational skills to weigh against her husband's deficiencies.

[36] The couple had a difficult time securing transport back to Panama, for many ships did not include women passengers. They arrived in February and were not able to leave until April; the couple was held in detention the entire time. A few months after returning to Panama, Sophie Cadogan wrote to the Immigration Bureau requesting that the cost of their original tickets be refunded. The Commissioner responded that seventy-six dollars, the amount covering Samuel's ticket, had been sent to the British Consul in Panama in his name. There was no explanation of why her ticket was not refunded as well. Sophie Cadogan, INS casefile 17913/4–1 and 4–2 (1919); AICF, box 1340; INS, SFD, RG85; NA-PSR.

that charges of LPC were applied unevenly by the INS and with greater severity to women: "Agonies unguessed lie in that phrase, 'likely to become a public charge.' " LPC, according to Wold, provided "fruitful ground" for the exclusion of women charged with "lapses from virtue" or "immoral character," women abandoned by their husbands or women raising children out of wedlock. Women who appealed their deportation cases, Wold argued, found relief from the federal courts. "What I learned" Wold concluded "was that it pays to go to the court if one would be delivered out of the hands of the immigration officials."[37]

In general, the courts proved far more tolerant in their understandings of work and poverty than immigration officials. Moreover, most courts were unwilling to assume that economic deficiency always followed moral lapse. Women with the financial and social resources who took their cases to court, as Wold suggested, often found relief. The flexible language of possibility that allowed immigration officials to apply the law in response to local need troubled federal court officials concerned with adjudicating standards of evidence, proof, and interpretation. As William Van Vleck, dean of George Washington University Law School, noted in his 1932 study of immigration law, LPC was used by immigration officials "as a kind of miscellaneous file into which are placed cases where the officers think the alien ought not to enter, but the facts do not come within any specific requirements of the statutes."[38]

In a number of cases, the judiciary dismissed charges of LPC out of hand. Women who demonstrated work skills, who appeared in good health, or who had no record of receiving private or public relief were released by court officials who found these women economically viable. Whereas immigration officials often assumed women were economically dependent until they proved themselves otherwise, court officials insisted that LPC be substantiated through evidence of past or present poverty. When Enriquita Paxos arrived from Cuba in 1910 to join her husband in New Orleans, immigration officials excluded her as LPC. On appeal the district court found charges of LPC without merit, noting that her husband was employed and "earning daily wages sufficient to prevent himself and his wife becoming public charges." Both husband and wife, according to the court, were "strong," "healthy," and "intelligent." Paxos was released.[39]

[37] Emma Wold, "Alien Women vs. the Immigration Bureau," *Survey* 59, no. 4 (15 November 1927): 217–219.

[38] Van Vleck observed that "In some cases this category is stretched to include situations where the issue is disobedience to law, disrespect for and lack of cooperation with the immigration officers, moral unfitness, general undesirability in the minds of the immigration officer, or even the question of whether the aliens in question would not be better off at home." Van Vleck, *The Administrative Control of Aliens*, 54.

[39] *United States ex rel. Paxos v. Redfern* 180 F. 500 (E.D.L.A. 1910). Similarly, when Karola Klein and her husband Isidor Klein were denied admittance as LPC by New York

Immigration and judicial officials disagreed over cause and effect. The bureau maintained that "likely to become a public charge" authorized officials with the service to evaluate whether an immigrant was likely to find work, likely to be paid sufficiently, or likely to be able to remain free of public or private relief. According to immigration authorities, LPC was fundamentally a charge of inference rather than fact, and officials often referenced local employment conditions or wage scales and even an applicant's physique in their findings of LPC. Court officials disagreed. LPC, the courts argued, appeared in the law among a list of personal, individual deficiencies, alongside "paupers," "professional beggars," "idiots," "persons dangerously diseased," "prostitutes," and even "convicted felons." Thus LPC was not a quality of national economic indicators or even of future personal crisis, but was instead a quality of the individual and her present, immediate, and verifiable limitations. LPC was of the person not her circumstances. Ruling in 1915, the Supreme Court dismissed social, structural arguments presented by the immigration service, and argued instead that immigrants excluded as LPC must be found, in the words of Justice Holmes, to have "permanent personal objections" akin to mental deficiencies or physical maladies.[40]

Following the Supreme Court's decision, Congress shifted the language of LPC in 1917 from the section in the law addressing individual limitations to the section that addressed issues of work and contract labor.[41] This positional maneuvering reassociated poverty with work and the demands or contractions of the national economy. Rulings following in the wake of the 1917 law, however, argued that the change in location did not change the meaning of the words. The courts continued to interpret "LPC" as akin to disease or deformity, a physical condition which would lead an immigrant to become a charge on the public.[42]

In addition to associating laws against LPCs with laws against contract laborers, the 1917 law also emphasized that if poverty was to be understood within a grammar of disease, as the courts had suggested, then it

---

immigration officials, they found a sympathetic hearing from the federal courts. The Second Circuit Court of Appeals was quick to dismiss the appeal against Klein: "She has been in this country for two years and there is not a particle of proof that she has been supported by charity or at the expense of the public." *United States ex rel. Klein et al. v. Williams* 189 F. 915 (S.D.N.Y. 1911); *Williams v. United States ex rel. Klein* 206 F. 460 (2nd Cir. 1913).

[40] *Gregiow v. Uhl, Acting Commissioner of Immigration at the Port of New York* 239 U.S. 3 (1915).

[41] Calavita, "A Sociological Analysis of U.S. Immigration Policy," 288.

[42] *Ex parte Mitchell* 256 F. 229 (N.D.N.Y. 1919); *Ex parte Hosaye Sakaguchi* 277 F. 913 (9th Cir. 1922). For a case in which a young woman trained as a dressmaker was found "physically defective," afflicted with "grave valvular disease, chronic and cardiac, which may affect [her] ability to earn a living," *Wallis, Immigration Com'r v. United States ex rel. Mannara et al.*, 273 F. 509 (2nd Cir. 1921).

was an individual failing from which there was little hope of recovery. As Congress recast the language of LPC within the context of work, so too it extended the time period within which an alien could be charged with LPC to five years after entry and shifted the burden of proof to rebut these charges to the alien. Technically, immigrants deported as LPC within five years of arrival were argued to be public charges for reasons predating their arrival in the United States. Physical defects, mental deficiencies, or moral failings, though perhaps hidden from view upon arrival, were inherent and thus inevitably visible. Informed by eugenic conceptions of genetic inheritance, Congress understood physical, mental, and moral disorder as a generational quality which multiplied over time, growing increasingly invidious and pervasive. Immigrants diagnosed as "mental defects" or found to have "immoral character" needed to be excluded to prevent the pauperization of future generations irrespective of their professed capacity for work and wage.[43]

Time became a central element in debates over cause and effect. If poverty was vested in the individual and born of generational inheritance, than afflicted immigrants were always already likely to become public charges. To immigration officials, LPC was both a response to market fluctuations driven by conditions of work and a result of inherently personal flaws. Court officials, however, were reluctant to entertain arguments that read the genetic past and the possible economic future into the legal present. In general, the courts proved more restrained in their interpretation of "likely to become." Anita Brungnoli was held for deportation in 1923 as LPC. Brungnoli had arrived twenty-two years earlier from Italy to live with her brother, a naturalized citizen. After returning from a brief visit to Italy, and at age fifty-six, Brungnoli was diagnosed with a mental disorder and held for treatment at the Manhattan State Hospital. An inmate of a state-funded institution, Brungnoli's case was brought to the attention of immigration authorities who charged her with being a public charge for reasons predating her recent arrival in the United States, namely, insanity. The secretary of labor confirmed the decision and Brungnoli was ordered returned to Italy as a public charge. On hearing her appeal, the district court of New York disagreed and ruled that there was no evidence to demonstrate that Brungnoli had been either mentally or economically deficient upon her arrival.[44]

---

[43] Senate Report 352, 64th Cong., 1st sess., as cited in *United States ex rel. Brugnoli v. Tod* 300 F 913 (1923).

[44] *United States ex rel. Brugnoli v. Tod* 300 F. 913 (S.D.N.Y. 1923). Ironically, Brungnoli had been sent to the state hospital on the recommendation of her private physician who believed she would receive better care there. When the INS began deportation proceedings her brother offered to move Brungnoli to a private facility to avoid accusations that Brungnoli was a recipient of public assistance.

The courts were also hesitant to blur suspicions of immorality into actual charges of poverty.[45] Immigration officials frequently combined charges of "immoral character" and "LPC" in their findings to exclude women accused of crimes against marriage or morality.[46] Hilda Rose Cavanaugh, an actress, singer, dancer, and typist engaged to a wealthy New Yorker, was excluded as LPC when she arrived from Ireland in 1916. Immigration officials had received an anonymous letter disclosing that Cavanaugh had intimate relations with her American fiancé during an earlier visit. While the charge of immorality could not be proven, immigration officials suggested that evidence of lax morals raised serious doubts about her ability to support herself through honest work. On hearing her case, the court dismissed the charges of LPC as mere speculation, pointing out that either she would marry and enjoy a life of quiet comfort or she would use her evident skills as a singer, dancer, and typist to gain lucrative employment. Either way, the court concluded, she was not likely to become a public charge.[47] Similarly, Josefa Rukerova was found likely to become a public charge in 1920 "because of her loose moral standards and character, as evidenced by her conduct subsequent to entry." Rukerova had arrived four years earlier in 1920 and had worked in a brass factory and later as a domestic servant. By the time of her arrest, Rukerova had saved four hundred dollars. While employed as a domestic servant, Rukerova began an affair with her employer, who was then separated from his wife. The appeals court dismissed the charge that Rukerova was LPC when she arrived because of her actions four years later. Noting that she was gainfully employed, "in good physical condition," that she had "by industry and frugality" saved much of her earnings, and was "living a moral and useful life," the court found no evidence to support accusations of indigence.[48]

While the immigration bureau was increasingly reluctant to admit women arriving without evidence of male financial support, the courts expressed greater confidence in women's independent earning potential and were more likely to admit women who demonstrated marketable

---

[45] See, for example, *Ex parte Mitchell* 256 F. 229 (N.D.N.Y. 1919).

[46] The use of LPC in morality cases reveals an important relationship between the process of evaluating immigrant women's sexuality and a similar evaluation of their perceived financial independence. *United States ex rel. Mantler v. Commissioner of Immigration* 3 F.2d 234 (2nd Cir. 1924); Emma Wold, "Alien Women v. the Immigration Bureau," *Survey* 29, no. 4 (November 15, 1927): 217–218.

[47] The court argued that "Innuendo, surmise, or guess of immorality will not suffice." Poverty must be proven in the present. *United States ex rel. Cavanaugh v. Howe, Commissioner of Immigration* 235 F. 990 (S.D.N.Y. 1916). This case is discussed in Wold, "Alien Women vs. the Immigration Bureau," 218.

[48] *United States ex rel. Mantler v. Commission of Immigration* 3 F.2d 234 (2nd Cir. 1924).

skills.[49] Hosaye Sakaguchi arrived in Seattle in 1919 as a picture bride, married in absentia to Sakaguchi Kuinobuemon. Hosaye's husband refused to receive her, arguing that she had been married once before, and insisted that she be returned to Japan. With a sister and brother-in-law living in Seattle, and as a skilled seamstress and artificial flower maker in her own right, Hosaye argued she was able to support herself without her husband's assistance or consent. The special board of inquiry, however, argued that it was improbable Hosaye could find work, given her limited understanding of English and American customs. The Ninth Circuit Court of Appeals disagreed. An "able-bodied woman," with "a fair education," "no mental or physical disability," and "a disposition to work and support herself" was not likely to become a public charge.[50] Similarly, a woman who arrived with her three children was held likely to become a public charge when her husband was denied admittance in 1924. On hearing her appeal, a New York district court dismissed the charges of LPC ruling, "I find there is no foundation for the claim that the mother and three children are likely to become public charges, merely because they will be separated from husband and father."[51]

Over the first two decades of the twentieth century, the courts held to a more narrow understanding of "likely to become a public charge." Despite congressional efforts to allow immigration officials greater discretion in applying LPC to control the arrival of immigrants, the judiciary insisted that charges of LPC be substantiated with proof of current physical, mental, or economic deficiencies. The two-pronged debate between judicial and immigration officials over the significance of structural changes in the economy and individual work skills or limitations, and the importance of time, cause, and effect in assessing whether an immigrant was LPC upon arrival or after five years of residency, would become crucial in the decades to follow as the nation fell into a well of economic depression and stagnation neither immigrants nor policy makers could have anticipated. Importantly, while the courts presented perhaps a more sympathetic tribunal, only a small percentage of women were able to muster the financial reserves and social resources necessary to mount a de-

---

[49] This was also true for girls. Ruling in 1926, both the Third Circuit Court of Appeals and the Second Circuit Court of Appeals dismissed claims that young girls arriving to relatives in the United States were likely public charges. *United States ex rel. Azizian et al. v. Curran* 12 F.2d 502 (2nd Cir. 1926); *United States ex rel. Berman et al. v. Curran, Commissioner of Immigration* 13 F.2d 96 (3rd Cir. 1926).

[50] The Ninth Circuit noted that despite her husband's rejection Hosaye remained his legal wife and thus entitled to entry under the terms of the Gentlemen's Agreement. It is likely that charges of LPC were levied to provide justification for her exclusion. *Ex parte Hosaye Sakaguchi* 277 F. 913 (9th Cir. 1922).

[51] *In re Keshishian et al.* 299 F. 804 (S.D.N.Y. 1924).

fense. As Emma Wold noted in the conclusion to her analysis of the antagonistic relationship between immigrant women and the immigration bureau, of the thousands of women who "mutely accepted the orders of the immigration boards," and did not appeal their case to the judiciary, "how many have lacked not a good cause, but good friends and ample funds?"[52]

[52] Wold, "Alien Women v. the Immigration Bureau," 219.

∞ Part II ∞

CITIZENS, RESIDENTS, AND NON-AMERICANS

CHAPTER SEVEN

When Americans Are Not Citizens

In a 1932 letter to the immigration authorities in Washington, D.C., Mary Ann Montoya inquired about the state of her citizenship. "Would you please tell me if I can take out my first naturalization papers," Montoya wrote, "I was born in Austria in 1907 came to Canada in 1914 and in August 1914 came to the US. In 1926 I was married to a Filipino, although there is a law in Oregon forbidding marriage between whites and orientals, a marriage license was issue to us at the Court House."[1]

While Mary Ann Montoya, a European immigrant, sought help from INS authorities in securing naturalization, Fung Sing, a native-born American, appealed to the federal courts to restore her citizenship rights. Fung Sing was born in the United States in 1898 of immigrant Chinese parents. She went to China in 1903, married a Chinese subject in 1920, and was widowed soon thereafter in 1924. In 1925 Fung Sing tried to return to the United States to resume her American citizenship, but she was held as an alien and not allowed to reenter.[2] Fung Sing took her case to court and sued for her citizenship.

Neither Mary Ann Montoya nor Fung Sing was a citizen, nor could either woman become one in the years between 1907 and 1931. Both women lost the privilege of citizenship by virtue of their marriages to men who were neither white nor black—men who were racially ineligible to citizenship. Continued anxieties over immigration and deep-seated fears of racial heterogeneity were central to the advent of independent women's citizenship and its implementation. The next two chapters will explore the legal shift from derivative citizenship to married women's independent citizenship over the first three decades of the twentieth century. What was the impact of independent citizenship on the lives of immigrant women and native born women of color?

The transition to women's independent legal status was marked by anxieties about race and gender similar to those that had dominated in the earlier period of derivative citizenship. Women's roles as mothers of future citizens, and the significance of race in the task of socializing Ameri-

---

[1] INS file 20/2 (1922–); RCO, entry 26, box 399, 20/1–20/21; INS, DC, RG85; NA, DC.
[2] *Ex parte Fung Sing* 6 F.2d 670 (W.D.Wash. 1925).

can citizens, continued to inform debates on immigration restriction and women's citizenship throughout the 1920s and 1930s and even into the World War II period. The 1922 Cable Act and the series of amendments that followed it had three implications for women like Mary Ann Montoya and Fung Sing. First, immigrant women who had used derivative naturalization policies to circumvent restrictive immigration policies in the years before 1922 became legally separate from their families and vulnerable to deportation. Second, native-born women of Asian ancestry like Fung Sing, along with Native American, Hawaiian, Filipina, and other women nationals, navigated a labyrinth of immigration and naturalization law. Expatriated and excluded, Asian American and nonwhite (or nonblack) women who married men ineligible to citizenship were unable to avoid race-based exclusion policies; after 1922 they could not return to the United States as citizens. Finally, by making subtle distinctions between women who had been born Americans and those who had become Americans through acts of Congress, the Cable Act partitioned the civic rights of nationals from those of the native born.

CITIZEN WIVES: PRELUDE TO THE 1922 CABLE ACT

It comes as little surprise that Mary Ann Montoya and Fung Sing were confused about their citizenship status. Up until even the 1950s, citizenship law remained a mass of inclusions and exclusions, creating a web of law that few women could see their way out of. Separating out the different legal strands uncovers important historical shifts in the relationship between marriage, race, and citizenship. For the moment, let us look at the set of laws that governed women's citizenship in the years before 1922.

While often dismayed at their religious proclivities and dismissive of their cultural traditions, the new republic was a nation hungry for immigrants. Yet as a slave society as well as a developing industrial power, ideas about race, citizenship, and economic growth grew alongside one another, providing the central core of an enduring belief in white America's manifest destiny. While Federalist and Republican Congresses debated who should be assumed to be a citizen with the founding of the new republic, all agreed on who should be allowed to be a citizen in the building of the nation's future.[3] The earliest nationalization statute limited naturalization to "free white persons." Children's civic status followed their fathers.

[3] Rogers M. Smith, *Civic Ideals: Conflicting Visions of Citizenship in U.S. History* (New Haven, Conn.: Yale University Press, 1997), 159.

What of women? In general, under common law, women were neither expatriated nor naturalized upon marriage. Rather, a wife's citizenship went into a kind of legal limbo, momentarily suspended for the duration of her marriage.[4] Yet, by the mid-nineteenth century, older ideas of coverture were infused with newer ideas about consent, resulting in the act of 1855. Any alien woman who consented to marriage also acquiesced to having her citizenship status follow that of her husband. Any immigrant woman who married a citizen and could meet the racial requirements of citizenship (whiteness, and, after the Civil War, blackness), was considered a citizen.

If marriage for immigrant women linked consent with citizenship, the 1855 law said nothing about the status of American-born women. With the arrival of ever-greater numbers of immigrants whose presence was seen to challenge the racial and moral parameters of citizenship in the later decades of the nineteenth century, the civic status of American women who married these foreign elements became an important matter of public policy. Beginning in 1907, not only did white or black immigrant women who married citizens become citizens, but American women who married noncitizens became noncitizens.[5] Private became public as citizenship law created a nation of families with male citizens as their political expression.[6]

For many immigrant women, the 1907 law facilitated their passage through immigration stations, offering them privledged positions under the law. However, passed in the midst of increased immigration to the United States and growing opposition to the presence of so many others who looked so different, the 1907 law also stripped white and black American-born women of their citizenship when they married, and permanently expatriated native-born Asian ancestry women who married men who were neither white nor black. By the end of the nineteenth century, the federal courts had narrowly interpreted the spectrum of "whiteness" to exclude Chinese applicants to citizenship, and by the early twenti-

---

[4] Both expatriation and naturalization required positive acts of consent. The major exception to this principle of consent was *Dred Scott* 60 U.S. 393 (1856).

[5] Derivative citizenship placed American-born women on a par with children as married women's civic identity was incorporated within the household. Nancy Cott notes that the 1907 law followed the lead of most European nations: *Public Vows*, p. 143.

[6] The Supreme Court confirmed the legality of marital expatriation in 1915. In agreeing to marriage, the court ruled, a woman had simultaneously given her consent to expatriation. In its decision, the court drew on what it perceived as a commonsense interpretation of marriage and women's role as wives. "The identity of the husband and wife is an ancient principle of our jurisprudence," the Court argued. Although gender roles were undergoing transformation, the Court insisted that "by their intimate relations and unity of interests, and this relation and unity may make it of public concern in many instances to merge their identity." *Mackenzie v. Hare* 239 U.S. 299 (1915).

eth, to exclude Japanese and Asian Indians as well. Fung Sing married an alien and a man "ineligible for citizenship," and as a result she was no longer a citizen. Once stripped of her citizenship, Fung Sing could never meet the racial requirements for naturalization necessary to regain her civic rights.

With the passage of the Nineteenth Amendment in 1920, American women won the right to vote. Women's citizenship now came with a new and powerful political tool. Immigrant wives married to white and black American men, who in 1907 became citizen wives, now in 1920 were women voters. However, while their vote was their own, their citizenship was not. A woman derived her citizenship from her father or (under the 1855 and 1907 laws) her husband. Following the success of the Nineteenth Amendment, women's activists mobilized to eliminate the vestiges of sex discrimination in the law, including nationality law. Passed in 1922, the Cable Act, or Married Women's Independent Nationality Act, provided some women with independent citizenship.

The 1922 Cable Act signaled a departure from a tradition of derivative citizenship status for married women and established the principle that marriage and citizenship could be separate and unique civic identities. Yet for immigrant women it had been the linking of these two identities— wife and citizen—which had provided an opening in immigration law. For these women, the Cable Act meant that the process of entering the United States was potentially more difficult and potentially more uncertain. The 1922 act also reinforced ideas of race difference that were equally important to the way Americans understood both citizenship and marriage. The Cable Act applied only to women who had lost their citizenship because of their marriage to an alien "eligible for citizenship." Both Fung Sing and Mary Ann Montoya had married men racially ineligible to citizenship. National identity had been separated from marriage, but racial identity had not, and race status remained a marital quality long after citizenship had become an independent one.

ONE NATION, INDIVISIBLE: EUROPEAN WOMEN AND THE 1921 QUOTA ACT

The movement to recognize sexual equality under the law and the movement to define the racial and ethnic parameters of the nation were at once contradictory and mutually reinforcing. While one called for inclusion and the other exclusion, arguments for sexual equality were rooted in racial hierarchy and arguments for racial determinism often had sexual fears at their root. Questions of gender equality, marriage, miscegenation, reproduction, and race were intimately bound up in one another. Debates over the 1921 and 1924 quota laws, laws that dramatically limited the number of new immigrants admitted into the United States by establishing a quota system based on first the 1910 and finally the 1890 census, reveal the ties that bound race, family, gender, and nation.

The 1922 Cable Act theoretically transformed many women from wives and daughters into independent citizens; marriage to a citizen or to a resident immigrant after 1922 was no longer enough to guarantee entrée to the United States. Immigration and naturalization laws now required that women have independent status as admissible aliens or as permissible citizens. In many ways, this presented a real departure from a historic commitment to family reunification policies. Immigration law had traditionally considered the family as a unit, and policies had been built on a legal tradition of derivative citizenship for wives and children of citizens. Debates over the implications of ethnic and racial difference among arriving immigrants and the consequence of women's independent legal status collided with those arguing for the significance of women's role in immigrant families. As a result policy shifted back and forth between allowing families of citizens to remain together, even if emigrating in excess of quota, and holding all immigrants to the strict confines of numerical quota limits.[7]

The efforts to immigrate to the United States of two women in particular, Gittel Gottlieb and Henazante Markarian, brought the conflict between women's independent citizenship and the needs of immigrant families into stark relief and onto court dockets. Each case arose because the first quota law, passed in 1921, departed from past immigration policy by making no provision for wives of citizens or residents to be admitted as nonquota immigrants.[8] When women's independent naturalization was layered onto the 1921 law, the immigration bureau faced the unsavory task of balancing a historic belief in the importance of families to American national identity with laws requiring drastic restrictions on new racialized arrivals and the separation of husband and wife as a legal identity.

Gittel Gottlieb and her son Israel arrived in New York from Jerusalem in 1922 to join her husband, Solomon Gottlieb, working as a rabbi in

---

[7] Candice Bredbenner traces the efforts of the Immigration Bureau to assess the impact of the Cable Act for immigration regulation: Bredbenner, *A Nationality of Her Own: Women, Marriage, and the Law of Citizenship* (Berkeley: University of California Press, 1998), 117–119.

[8] Under the 1921 law, only the children of citizens who were under eighteen years of age were entitled to nonquota status. Other immediate family members, including wives, parents, brothers, sisters, and fiancées, were given preference in visa selection but no guarantee. Thus the select few excused from the quota provisions all together—temporary visitors, native-born or naturalized citizens of Western Hemisphere countries, members of certain learned or professional classes, domestic servants, and the minor children of citizens—did not include wives of residents and citizens as had been true in decades past. Hutchinson, *Legislative History of American Immigration Policy*, 175.

New York City. The Gottliebs could not afford to immigrate as a family, and Solomon Gottlieb had gone ahead fourteen months earlier, found work, and filed his declaration of intention to become a citizen. This pattern was traditional for immigrant families, building off laws that encouraged the immigration of skilled male laborers and professionals along with the wives of residents and natives. When Gittel Gottlieb and Israel arrived in 1922, they were denied admittance because the quota for Palestine had been filled. Their appeal to the secretary of labor was denied and mother and son were held for deportation.

Henazante Markarian also arrived in 1922, accompanied by her husband, a merchant living and working in the United States who had filed his declaration of intention and returned to Turkey in 1921 to marry. When Markarian arrived with her new husband, however, the Turkish quota was filled and she was denied admission. Her husband insisted he would not abandon his wife, and both were subsequently excluded.

Gottlieb and Markarian turned to the courts for relief. At stake in their appeals was a conflict between two opposing conceptions of the status of wives as immigrants, and two differing interpretations of women's place in the law. Before 1921, and built on the precedent experience of Chinese women arriving as wives of merchants, courts had held and Congress had confirmed that policies allowing husbands to enter but excluding their wives were "absurd."[9] After the 1921 Quota Act and in the wake of the 1922 Cable Act, no such guarantee based on women's status as wives could be assumed.[10] The parallels to the experience of Chinese women entering as wives of merchants was clear: immigration law offered their husband special, exempted status but made no provision for either Gottlieb or Markarian. Together, immigration and naturalization law required that families be separated, and each member considered independently of the others. In the success of the Gottlieb and Markarian appeals lay the possibility to circumvent the severe restrictions of the 1921 quota law and the consequences of the 1922 Cable Act by rejoining family members within a single immigration status.[11]

---

[9] *U.S. v. Gue Lim* 176 U.S. 459 (1900) continued to provide the precedent case for the linking of a wife's arrival status with that of her husband.

[10] Important in Gittel Gottlieb's appeal, the 1917 Immigration Act had specifically exempted ministers, their wives, and their minor children from the excluding provisions of immigration law. The 1921 law, however, offered no such guarantee. It mentioned "ministers of any religious denomination" but was silent on the status of their families. Markarian's husband, an alien returning from a temporary visit abroad, was among the few exempted categories in the 1921 law. Although the new regulations did not specifically provide for the wives and children of returning resident aliens, precedent and common sense might.

[11] *New York Law Journal*, 26 February 1924.

In finding in favor of the Gottlieb family, the appeals court invoked the reasoning offered by the Supreme Court in 1900 in the case of Mrs. Gue Lim, the wife of a Chinese merchant: to permit the arrival of a husband under special, privileged legislation, but to exclude the arrival of his family was "absurd." The court argued that Congress could not have intended such an outcome as that which would divide a family.[12] As had been true for Gittel Gottlieb, on appeal the court ruled that to find Henazante Markarian excludable was an overzealous interpretation of the new 1921 restrictions. The Markarians were released.[13]

Following these two decisions by the New York Circuit Court of Appeals, steamship companies advertised widely in the foreign language press, informing foreign-born residents of the court's support for men returning from Europe with their alien wives and children, even though the quota for most countries was exhausted. According to the Foreign Language Information Service, news of the favorable decisions circulated rapidly among resident immigrants. "Many men whose wives and families are still abroad have sailed with the hope that they can get back with their families before any adverse decision in reached by the Supreme Court," the service explained, and "Many other men are doubtless considering taking this step."[14] Months later, the Foreign Language Information Service reported that ocean liners began arriving in New York with several thousand immigrants, most of them Italian women and children. Although the Italian quota had been exhausted, most of these women and children were admitted under the authority of the Gottlieb and Markarian decisions.[15]

Following the New York court's decisions, the Bureau of Immigration acquiesced and issued instructions to its officers in December, 1923, to consider the wives and minor children of exempted categories—actors, artists, lecturers, singers, nurses, ministers, professors, domestic servants, learned professions, and returning aliens—as members of households incorporated within their husbands' and fathers' privileged immigration status. As had been true in the years before Cable, alien women would be treated as wives and accorded the same exempt status as their husbands. The commissioner-general added that wives of citizens would be considered exempt from quota restrictions altogether. However, should the Gottlieb and Markarian decisions be overturned, the commissioner-general

---

[12] *United States ex rel. Gottlieb et al. v. Commissioner of Immigration of Port of New York* 285 F. 295 (2nd Cir. 1922).

[13] *United States ex rel. Markarian et al. v. Tod* 290 F. 198 (2nd Cir. 1923).

[14] "Recent Court Decisions and the Quota," *Interpreter Releases* (4 March 1924), RACNS, FLIS, reel 1.

[15] Ibid.

warned, orders allowing the arrival of women as wives would be immediately withdrawn and the women would be excluded.[16]

While the INS had always sought to test women's claims to special status as wives through close interrogation of women immigrants, the courts insisted that derivative status had never been about the rights of alien wives but always about the rights of their citizen husbands. According to the federal courts, it was not her status as a wife that was decisive, but her husband's status as an immigrant—did he or did he not belong to one of the exempt classes? A wife was admitted not because of her right to derivative status under immigration law, but because of her husband's right to be accompanied by his wife.[17] As the federal district court of Rhode Island explained in the case of Emilie Dorto in 1924, the Cable Act had not been intended to separate husbands from their wives, and thus "deprive the American husband of the services of his lawful wife."[18] The term "alien," this court concluded, "does not include moral wife of American citizen."[19] While the Cable Act had separated marriage from citizenship, traditional ideas of marriage as a moral necessity and women's roles as wife and mother were slower to change.

In the conflict between civil law—which evaluated women immigrants on educational, physical, and race scales—and natural or moral law—which emphasized women immigrants as wives and mothers to future

[16] Ibid. By February 1924 the courts had expanded the category of wives to include women married by proxy marriage and thus women not accompanied by their husbands upon arrival. The case was *Nadal*; see ibid.

[17] Variano, who had returned to Italy to marry after living two years in the United States, was readmitted as a returning resident in 1920, but when his wife attempted to follow him in 1924 she was found in excess of quota and held for deportation. On appeal, the court refuted decades of bureau policy that had focused on the legality of marriage and the veracity of "alleged" wives. "Another Court Decision and the Quota Law," *Interpreter Releases* (7 March 1924), RACNS, FLIS, reel 1.

[18] Emilie Dorto landed in New York on 14 June 1922 and was excluded because the Italian quota was full. She was admitted on bail awaiting her appeal. Emilie Dorto's lawyers advised her that, if she could marry an American citizen, she could avoid deportation. Two months later she met Dorto who agreed to marry her. Witnesses testified that Dorto introduced her as his wife and that the two lived together in Dorto's tenement. The couple applied for a license in September, but were told to return two weeks later. As a result of this delay the Dortos were legally married 23 September 1922, one day after the Cable Act took effect. By April 1923, the Immigration Bureau had ruled on Emilie Dorto's appeal and confirmed her deportation to Italy. She sued for writ of habeas corpus. By June 1924, Dorto was pregnant. *Dorto v. Clark* 300 F. 568 (D.R.I. 1924).

[19] Finding in Dorto's favor, the court concluded that the law did not authorize the deportation of such women; "alien wives of American citizens" were not among the excluded classes which included prostitutes and convicts. *Dorto v. Clark* 300 F. 568 (D.R.I. 1924). On appeal, the circuit court confirmed the lower court's ruling, adding that a valid common-law marriage had existed between the Dortos before the Cable Act went into effect, *United States v. Dorto* 5 F.2d 596 (1st Cir. 1925); Bredbenner, *A Nationality of Her Own*, 123.

American citizens—was the crux of the matter. While Cable had signaled a move toward women's independent political status, older conceptions of citizenship that linked family, home, and motherhood to American nationalism were not easily displaced. In 1927, five years after the Cable Act passed, Congressman James O'Conner of Louisiana brought the case of Helene Stomas before the House Committee on Immigration and Naturalization. Stomas had been excluded upon arrival, but had married an American citizen and become pregnant while awaiting deportation. In pressing her case, O'Conner recycled older images of women as mothers and as the nation's caregivers, and drew a hierarchical distinction between "natural law" and the laws of man, "Long before we had constitutions women were mothers."[20]

Despite *Gottlieb* and *Markarian*, not all women found the doors open upon their arrival. Judgments that reinterpreted the exemptions provided in the 1921 law through a pre-Cable lens offered only a small window of possibility for some women. As in years past, domesticity proved a double-edged sword; entering as wives left women vulnerable and dependent on their husband's status.[21] Moreover, the *Gottlieb* and *Markarian* deci-

---

[20] As O'Conner explained, "In the face of the fact that her child is American-born the officials would deport the mother and forget that there is a higher law involved. That American-born child has inalienable rights which no law should violate—the care of its mother." James O'Conner, testimony, "Case of Helene Stomas," *Hearings before the Committee on Immigration and Naturalization*, 17 February 1927, House of Representatives, 69th Cong., 2nd sess., Washington, D.C., 4. Not everyone present supported O'Conner's emotional appeal on the grounds of women's traditional duties to home, family, and nation. Albert Johnson, chair of the House committee and co-sponsor of the 1924 National Origins Act, favored civic law over "natural" law. "This woman worked her way into the United States" Johnson retorted, and moreover she did so "in face of the fact that she had been told by immigration officials that she was inadmissible." Albert Johnson, "Case of Helene Stomas," *Hearings before the Committee on Immigration and Naturalization*, 5.

[21] Szejndla Gorelick and her two younger children, Berko and Anna, arrived at Ellis Island from Poland in January 1924. (Gorelick and her children arrived under the 1921 law; the Johnson Reed Act was passed in May 1924.) As the wife of a rabbi, Gorelick fell within one of the few nonquota slots available under the *Gottlieb* and *Markarian* interpretations of the 1921 law. However, unbeknownst to Gorelick, her husband had died in June, leaving her elder son to assume the duties of rabbi of his congregation in Vermont and leaving her a small estate of $1,000. Her elder son had postponed telling his mother of his father's death until she arrived over six months later. Gorelick and her two younger children were denied admission upon arrival; she was no longer the wife of a rabbi, and the quota for Poland was exhausted. In reviewing her case, the court ruled that the status of her admission was determined when she arrived, that of a widow, not when she left, that of a wife of a resident rabbi. While the court was sympathetic, the law left no room for leniency. *Ex parte Gorelick* 296 F. 572 (S.D.N.Y. 1924). In a similar case reported in the *New York Herald Tribune*, a husband died at sea en route to the United States with his new wife and she was denied admission as a widow. See *New York Herald Tribune*, 18 April 1929, as cited in Bredbenner, *A Nationality of Her Own*, 116.

sions totally ignored those women who fell outside the racial dyad of American citizenship.

While the courts, the immigration bureau, and immigrant families wrestled with the interpretations offered in the *Gottlieb* and *Markarian* decisions, the *Gottlieb* case had slowly been making its way to the Supreme Court. The lower court had found the wife of a minister admissible, incorporated within her husband's exempted immigration status, but in 1924 the Supreme Court disagreed. Henceforth, wives and children of resident aliens would be held subject to quota restrictions. The day after the Supreme Court's ruling in *Gottlieb*, the Bureau of Immigration rescinded its order allowing for the immigration of the families of resident aliens. While the families of citizens, the bureau assured the public, would still be allowed entrance and would be held exempt from numerical quota restrictions, they would be subject to all other requirements of the immigration law, accountable to race, educational, physical, and mental exclusions along with all other arriving immigrants.[22]

Despite the legal impediments, for women who could meet the race, educational, and medical requirements of immigration and naturalization law, entering as a wife still provided an important point of access.[23] The continued significance of marriage in the law and in the minds of many court and immigration officials, however, meant that women as wives came under rigorous scrutiny as they applied for nonquota visas, preference status, or exemption from deportation. In congressional debate over what would become the 1924 National Origins Act, apprehension over the hardship the law would create by separating immigrant families was tempered by anxieties that special exceptions for families would only lead to fraud. Senator Reed, sponsor of the Senate bill, warned that compassion must not blind Congress to the real possibility of abuse: "the moment we begin to make exceptions for relatives, we will find a tremendous amount

[22] Under *Gottlieb, Markarian,* and similar cases, eight thousand alien wives and children had been admitted. With the Supreme Court's reversal, these aliens were liable to arrest and deportation. To avoid mass deportation and separation of families, Congress passed a joint resolution to legalize the admission of these aliens and to permit them to remain. "Gottlieb Decision Reversed: But Admissions thereunder Legalized by Congress," *Interpreter Releases* (10 June 1924), RACNS, FLIS, reel 1.

[23] For example, Edith Zambernardi arrived with her mother and father from Italy in 1925. Her father was a returning citizen, having lived and worked in the United States for almost ten years. The family spent a month on Ellis Island awaiting resolution of their case. Zambernardi remembered, "They were saying something about that the law had changed, whatever it was, after we were in the middle of the ocean. I don't know what that meant. See, do you know how there's a quota and this, but he was an American citizen." Edith Zambernardi, interviewed by D. Gumb, 1985, in *Voices from Ellis Island,* reel 3, oral history no. 048.

of fraud in claims of relationship."[24] In hearing the case of Louisa Felipe Gomez, the Ninth Circuit Court of Appeals argued that naturalization law could not be used to distort immigration law. Gomez, who had married a citizen while awaiting deportation, argued that while she was not a legal citizen, neither was she an alien.[25] In finding for the right and need to exclude the wives of citizens, the appeals court drew as precedent on earlier cases of Chinese women excluded despite their marriage to citizens.[26]

The 1924 National Origins Act cleared up much of the legal wrangling about the status of wives that had swirled around the 1921 quota law and the 1922 Cable Act. Along with reducing the total annual quotas for many countries, the 1924 act offered nonquota status to the wives and minor children of citizens living in the United States, and to some ministers and professors along with their families.[27] The 1924 National Origins Act increased the numbers of relatives qualifying for nonquota status over the 1921 law, but it differentiated between residents and nonresidents—those who were living in the United States when they filed petitions for their families and those who were not.[28] In so doing, the 1924 law sought to prevent the arrival of new families while promoting the reunification of

[24] Senator Reed, 3 April 1924, as quoted in Frank L. Auerbach, "The Status of Women Under US Immigration Laws," *Interpreter Releases* 25, no. 1 (2 January 1948): 3, RACNS, reel 7. By 1937, Congress would pass legislation to provide for the immediate deportation of any one found to have obtained a visa through a fraudulent marriage. This included marriages that were subsequently annulled upon arrival in the United States. See Frank L. Auerback, "The Status of Women Under US Immigration Laws" *Interpreter Releases* 25, no. 1 (2 January 1948), RACNS, reel 7.

[25] This was the logic of the *Dorto* case. Gomez arrived in the United States from the Azore Islands in 1923. She moved to New Mexico and finally settled in Oakland, California. In 1924 Gomez came to the attention of the immigration authorities and was held for deportation. Officials charged her with being a person likely to become a public charge at the time of her entry; in addition, they determined she was a person of constitutional psychopathic inferiority.

[26] *Gomez v. Nagle, Commissioner of Immigration* 6 F.2d 520 (9th Cir. 1925). The court referenced *Low Wah Suey v. Backus* 225 U.S. 460 (1912), in which the court ruled a married woman might be as objectionable as a single one; and *Chung Fook v. White* 264 U.S. 443 (1924), in which the Supreme Court found to exclude a wife of a native-born citizen afflicted with a dangerous contagious disease. For a similar case, *Smith v. United States ex rel. Grisius* 58 F.2d 1 (7th Cir. 1932).

[27] Returning residents, natives of Western Hemisphere countries along with their wives and children, bona fide students at least fifteen years old, and white and black women who had lost their citizenship by marriage to an alien were also offered nonquota status. In 1928, the language of the act was changed from unmarried children under age eighteen to unmarried children under age twenty-one. The provisions were amended again in 1932 to include the husbands of citizens married prior to 1 June 1928. Hutchinson, *Legislative History of American Immigration Policy*, 190, 509.

[28] "American Citizens and their Alien Wives, Husbands, or Fiancees," *Interpreter Releases* (21 August 1924), RACNS, FLIS reel 1.

long-time European residents.[29] The wives and children of first-paper im-migrants, or husbands who had filed their declaration of intention, were given no preference under the new quota law. Wives and children of aliens living in the United States were subject to all restrictions and exclusions.

In even less subtle terms the law continued to differentiate between wives of citizens and husbands of citizens. Gender informed policy, and women citizens were viewed as homemakers rather than breadwinners, and thus incapable of offering financial support for arriving immigrant husbands. Wives of resident citizens were nonquota immigrants, but hus-bands of resident citizens were quota immigrants and received only prefer-ence. Finally, the Immigration Bureau insisted in its directive, "*In no case will a petition be entertained on behalf of a wife or husband by proxy or picture marriage.*"[30]

With the passage of ever more stringent immigration restrictions, the consequences of independent citizenship for foreign-born women became clear. The Cable Act had severed marriage and citizenship for white and black women, and in the process it had created an expanding class of immigrants—the alien wives of United States citizens. While marriage to a citizen could provide women with nonquota status, it did not exempt them from racial, geographic, educational, or physical exclusions. Jose-phine Roche, former director of the Foreign Language Information Ser-vice, made this point in her 1925 address to the National Conference on Social Work. "[I]n assuring her the right to independent citizenship," Roche insisted, "we have by no means equalized her chance with theirs, so that the gaining of the right seems to many mothers a doubtful blessing in comparison with the practical advantages they have lost."[31] The legal ground had shifted, as one court explained; a woman's role as a wife was no longer enough, and older arguments excusing the arrival of physically unworthy wives no longer held. Wives were subject to laws they had pre-viously circumvented.[32] Moreover, while marriage and citizenship, had

---

[29] U.S. Department of Labor Immigration Service, "Instructions for Executing Petitions for Issuance of Immigration Visas to Relatives," quoted in RACNS, FLIS, reel 1.

[30] Ibid., emphasis in original.

[31] Josephine Roche, "The Effect of the Cable Law on the Citizenship Status of Foreign Women," in *Proceedings of the National Conference of Social Work*, 52nd Annual Session, Denver, 1925 (Chicago: University of Chicago Press, 1925), 611–614.

[32] When Markin was found to be syphilitic and blind in one eye when she arrived in 1924 along with her son to join her husband, who had lived in the United States for eleven years, she was denied admission and held for deportation. The couple had been married before the Cable Act was passed, yet Markin's husband had been granted citizenship after 1922, six months before she and her son arrived. As a result, Markin did not automatically become a citizen when her husband was naturalized. In her defense before the court hearing her appeal, Markin drew on older arguments that justified alien women's arrival as wives of

been legally severed, race and marriage, and race and citizenship, remained tightly yoked.

ALIEN WIVES: ASIAN WOMEN AND THE 1924 NATIONAL ORIGINS ACT

Asian women, who in the past had used marriage as a strategy to avoid race-based exclusion laws, now confronted a dual threat. The 1922 Cable Act had separated marriage from citizenship status and the 1924 National Origins Act excluded all aliens ineligible for naturalization. Before 1922, marriage had offered immigrant women politico-familial status and thus race exemption, providing Chinese women an opportunity to immigrate as the wives of merchants or citizens despite radical race exclusion laws. Post-Cable, the ability of women to circumvent race-based immigration exclusion laws through arguments about marital exception was increasingly difficult.

Women who had left the United States as admissible wives found themselves excluded as racially ineligible aliens upon return.[33] For example, Ying Shee tried to return to Honolulu in July 1924 with her husband, a citizen, and her daughter and son. When the family had left for China, established principles within citizenship law—derivative status for the wives of citizens and the singular civic unity of the family—had allowed Asian wives to circumvent prohibitions against arrival of immigrants from the Asian Barred Zone. Before 1922, Ying Shee had needed no other proof of her legal status than evidence of her legal marriage to a citizen. However, when the family returned in July 1924, the Cable Act had replaced previous laws granting married women derivative citizenship and the National Origins Act prohibited the arrival of all racially ineligible aliens. In her hearing, Ying Shee insisted that she knew nothing of the new requirements:

> Q: Do you have now, or have you ever been in possession of an immigration visa, as required by the Immigration Act of 1924?
> A: I don't think so. That is the only document I secured [referring to affidavit

---

naturalized citizens despite medical exclusions. She also insisted that were she allowed to land she would quickly fulfill the race requirements for citizenship and thus become a citizen in her own right. The court, however, disagreed. *United States ex rel. Markin v. Curran, Commissioner of Immigration* 9 F.2d 900 (2nd Cir. 1925).

[33] Ching Low was unaware she needed any additional visas in addition to her status as a wife to return to the United States. She had left for China one month before the 1924 National Origins Act was passed. Husband and wife had followed all the legal requirements under the old immigration law prior to their departure and had obtained reentry permits, which were nullified with the new 1922 and 1924 laws. Ching Low [pseud.], INS file 4384/

executed by her husband testifying to their marriage and his United States citizenship].

Q: Had you heard that a new immigration law had been passed by the United States prior to the time that you left China for this country?

A: No.

While her children were admitted as the children of a citizen, Ying Shee was excluded and deported in September 1924.[34]

Asian women like Ying Shee, who had traveled to China and were attempting to return after 1924, could avoid race exclusion and be admitted under only two conditions: first, the time they spent out of the country could be considered a "temporary visit," and, second, they had received a nonquota visa from an American consul abroad. Consuls stationed abroad therefore ultimately decided whether a woman's absence consisted of a "temporary visit" or not. In general, immigration officials interpreted "temporary visit" as not more than six-months.[35] Given the high cost and long duration of travel between Asia and the United States, many women were unable to meet the six-month stipulation.[36]

The status of Asian women married to residents or citizens was a legal and procedural mess. Immigration officials and court officials tried with mixed success to weave married women's independent citizenship through conflicting policies of racial exclusion and a historic commitment to family reunification. As a designated racial group, Asian and Southeast Asian women were subject to severe immigration restrictions. Yet historically, even the most blanket exclusions offered amnesty to the wives of citizens and resident merchants, and some courts continued to find moral worth and legal weight in this historical argument. For example, in the case of Chiu Shee, wife of a citizen, a Massachusetts federal district court emphasized that the demands for racial purity expressed in the 1924 National Origins Act were bested by the needs of the nation's citizens and

88 (1924); Chinese Wives of Native-Born American Citizens, box 2; INS, HDO, RG85; NA-PSR.

[34] The family attempted to file writ of habeas corpus but were informed they lacked any grounds to contest the Board's findings. Ying Shee [pseud.], INS file 4384/316 (1924); Chinese Wives of Native-Born American Citizens, box 5; INS, HDO, RG85; NA-PSR.

[35] Ching Low [pseud.], INS file 4384/88 (1924); Chinese Wives of Native-Born American Citizens, box 2; INS, HDO, RG85; NA-PSR.

[36] Kan Wai Ching had been absent from Hawaii for nearly five years when she attempted to secure a visa in 1925, and it was unlikely the American Consul in China would find her time abroad a temporary trip. Kan Wai Ching [pseud.], INS file 4384/59 (1925); Chinese Wives of Native-Born American Citizens, box 2; INS, HDO, RG85; NA-PSR. By 1925, Honolulu immigration authorities began issuing return entry permits to Chinese women who were alien wives of American citizens to allow their reentry after a temporary trip abroad. INS file 4384/320 (1925); Chinese Wives of Native-Born American Citizens, box 5; INS, HDO, RG85; NA-PSR.

the dictates of moral law which tied families together. In finding in favor of Chiu Shee, the Massachusetts court differentiated between exclusion of unassimilable immigrants (the purpose of the law) and family reunification, which presumably aided assimilation. It also drew on older arguments about the rights of citizen men to the company of their wives; "it would deprive him of the society of his wife, to which he is entitled by law."[37]

Independent citizenship destabilized the precarious balance in the law between policies enforcing racial homogeneity and those encouraging family unity. When thirty-five Chinese women arrived in San Francisco in October 1924, expecting to enter the United States as the wives of merchants or citizens, the tensions within the law exploded.[38] The Supreme Court would eventually hear the appeals of Cheung Sun Shee, the wife of a Chinese merchant, and Ng Yeut Seung, the wife of a citizen. Ruling in favor of Cheung Sun Shee, the Court found the treaty governing relations with Chinese merchants still in effect. As had been true in the past, the Court ruled that specific guarantees that a merchant had rights to his "body and household servants" by implication included his wife.[39] Limited in scope, the decision to permit the arrival of wives of Chinese merchants would not be extended to Japanese or Korean women.[40]

In the case of Ng Yeut Seung, the wife of a Chinese American citizen, the Supreme Court ruled that these women possessed no such legal guarantee as was afforded Chinese wives of merchants, and they were there-

[37] The court explained, "It is well known that the evil aimed at by this act was the presence in the United States of a large number of aliens, who were not desirous of adopting our customs, but preferred to follow their old ways, and were thus not likely to be assimilated with the rest of the population and become desirable citizens." However, the court insisted, "The result desired by passage of the act, would not be furthered by prohibiting a wife from joining her husband, who is a citizen of the U.S. by virtue of his birth." *Ex parte Chiu Shee* 1 F.2d 798 (D.Mass. 1924) This case is also discussed in "Recent Court Decisions on Immigration and Naturalization," *Interpreter Releases* (27 December 1924), RACNS, FLIS, reel 1.

[38] Bredbenner, *A Nationality of Her Own*, 125–128; Chan, "The Exclusion of Chinese Women," 125–127. All thirty-five women were denied admission by the commissioner of immigration. The women appealed, but the secretary of labor upheld the decision and the women were held for deportation. Subsequently, the women filed habeas corpus proceedings.

[39] *Cheung Sum Shee et al. v. Nagle, Commissioner of Immigration* 268 U.S. 336 (1925). In a similar case, the judge ruled that the 1924 act was not intended to supersede previous treaty rights; see *Ex parte Goon Dip* 1 F.2d 811 (W.D.Wash. 1924).

[40] Youn Chuk Kim arrived in 1924 with her husband, a Korean merchant working in the United States. Kim was held for deportation on the grounds of race and medical inadmissibility (she was diagnosed with uncinariasis/hookworm). The court ruled, "The Japanese treaty contains no provision bringing the applicant within exception" as did the Chinese treaty which included merchants "together with their body and household servants," which was interpreted to include wives. *Ex parte So Hap Yon* 1 F.2d 814 (W.D.Wash. 1924).

fore inadmissible. Counsel representing the wives before the Court argued for the sanctity of the family: "To hold that these women are debarred from admission to the United States under the Immigration Act of 1924 means that their husbands are to be permanently separated from them unless they abandon the country of their birth and citizenship, and take up their residence in some other land which permits their wives to reside with them." The Court, drawing on Cable and the concept of women's independent citizenship, disagreed.[41] At the final gavel, the Chinese wives of merchants were admissible, while Chinese wives of citizens were not.

In hearings in 1928, Congress discussed the strange result of the Supreme Courts rulings in *Cheung Sum Shee* and *Chang Chan*.[42] Testifying before a House committee, Y. C. Hong, president of the Los Angeles Chapter of the Native Sons of the Golden State and the Chinese American Citizens Alliance of Los Angeles, emphasized that prior immigration restriction legislation and current miscegenation statutes left Asian men with little other alternative than to "seek wives of his [*sic*] own race" from home and then attempt to have them immigrate to the United States as their wives. Hong sought to reassure the committee that new legislation would not result in an influx of Chinese wives. According to Hong, from 1906 to 1924, the period in which the alien Chinese wife of an American citizen was allowed to emigrate, only 2,800 women were admitted as wives, not more than twenty wives each year. Similarly, Hong attempted to calm fears that legislation to allow the immigration of racially ineligible wives would result in an influx more generally of Asian women of questionable moral or matrimonial status, as had been rumored during the Japanese picture bride period ten years earlier.[43]

In the questioning that followed, Congressman John Box of Texas, an avid restrictionist, raised the ghost that haunted debates over immigration and naturalization. Any change to existing legislation that undermined strict racial eligibility protocols, he warned, would open the doors to the immigration of endless numbers of nondesirable racial minorities. Should exemptions to racial exclusions be approved, "Indians born north or south of the Rio Grande," Box suggested, might become admissible as immigrants.[44]

[41] *Chang Chan v. Nagle* 268 U.S. 346 (1925).

[42] *Wives of American Citizens of Oriental Race: Hearings Before the Committee on Immigration and Naturalization*, 1928, HR 6974; House of Representatives, 77th Cong., 1st sess., Washington, D.C.

[43] Y. C. Hong, president of the Los Angeles Chapter of the Native Sons of the Golden State, Chinese American Citizens Alliance, Los Angeles, Calif., *Wives of American Citizens of Oriental Race*, 1928, 3–7.

[44] Ibid., 12–13.

Two years later, in 1930, the Congressional committee reconvened to revisit the problem and to debate legislation to allow the immigration of Chinese wives of American citizens. Yet the ensuing discussion tied together the issues of immigration, race, and marriage in ways that revealed a significant tension between the desire to control the arrival of racially different immigrants and a similar desire to prevent miscegenation within the United States. Witnesses countered charges of racial mixing with claims to the right of a citizen husband to the companionship of a wife. For example, when Florence P. Kahn, representative from San Francisco, fielded questions from the committee, she argued that allowing the arrival of additional Chinese women immigrants would eliminate the need for interracial marriages:

> A (KAHN): We want to bring in these Chinese girls that these Chinese-Americans citizens marry. These men want to bring in their wives.
> Q (SAMUEL DICKSTEIN, NY): Do you believe that these Chinese should marry white women?
> A (KAHN): They want to marry girls of their own race. Miscegenation is not permitted in California. In other words, these American citizens who are of the Chinese race could not marry women of other races in California.
> Q (DICKSTEIN): You say that marriage between Chinese and people of the white race is prohibited in California?[45]

Kenneth Y. Fung, executive secretary of the Chinese American Citizens' Alliance of San Francisco, also testified before the committee. Fung played to race-based anxieties among committee members by arguing that race exclusions in immigration law forced conditions of miscegenation, creating what many members may have viewed as an even greater threat to moral or even biological law than that posed by immigration. "It is not good for man to practice celibacy," Fung emphasized, "Marriage and the association of a man with his wife constitute the greatest safeguard of public morals." As Y. C. Hong had in 1928, Fung maintained that allowing for the admission of women ineligible to citizenship would protect the nation's racial caste system rather than undermine it:

> Q (GEORGE SCHNEIDER, WI): What is the relationship between the Chinese and the Filipinos?
> A (FUNG): There is no relation between them at all. Recently there have been racial frictions in the State of California. I have read in the paper that it is because of the relations of Filipinos with white girls. Why? Because there is such a large body of men there without families. That is why we should

---

[45] Hon. Florence P. Kahn, representative from Calif., *Wives of American Citizens of the Oriental Race: Hearings before the Committee on Immigration and Naturalization*, 1930, 543–544.

allow these American citizens to have their wives with them. They want home association with their wives, which is the safest promoter of morality.

Q (SCHNEIDER): What about the Filipino bringing in his wife?

A (FUNG): It is said that they should stop them from coming or encourage them to bring their wives here.

Q (ROBERT GREEN, FL): A white citizen of the U.S. may go to Haiti and marry one of those black women and bring her here. Who is there to say that a Chinese or Japanese is not a better citizen than the blacks of Haiti?[46]

Perhaps moved by these arguments, by 1930, Congress removed restrictions in immigration law against Chinese wives of American citizens.[47] Women once excluded as racially ineligible were now admissible as wives. For example, Jin Shee, wife of a native-born citizen, attempted to enter the United States twice, once in 1924 and once in 1936. In her first attempt in 1924, she was excluded as an alien (under the Cable law divorcing marriage and citizenship) and as ineligible to citizenship (under the 1924 Immigration Act). Jin Shee returned to the United States a second time in 1936 and was granted nonquota status as the wife of a citizen.[48]

---

[46] Kenneth Y. Fung, executive secretary of the Chinese American Citizens' Alliance, San Francisco, Calif., *Wives of American Citizens of the Oriental Race*, 1930, 554.

[47] Congress amended the Immigration Act of 1924 to add Chinese wives of American citizens married before 1924 to the class of admittable aliens despite their racial ineligibility to citizenship. Also see Chan, "The Exclusion of Chinese Women," 126–127.

[48] After exhaustive questioning immigration authorities concluded Jin Shee was indeed legally married to a citizen, but it took them only moments to observe that Jin Shee could not satisfy racial requirements for naturalization. Jin Shee [pseud.], INS file 4384/318 (1936); Chinese Wives of Native-Born American Citizens, box 5; INS, HDO, RG85; NA-PSR; also, Fong Shee [pseud.], INS file 4384/111 (1934); Chinese Wives of Native-Born American Citizens, box 2; INS, HDO, RG85; NA-PSR.

CHAPTER EIGHT

When Citizens Are Not White

The Cable Act of 1922 challenged the idea that a woman's political status was determined by her husband's, but it reaffirmed race as a product of marriage and family. A period that saw the expansion of suffrage and citizenship rights for some women was marked as firmly by the increased exclusion and restriction of others. After 1922, only women who had married men racially eligible for citizenship were granted independent citizenship. While political status had been separated out from marriage for some women, race status remained in many ways a quality of marriage, mired in complicated webs of sexual intimacy, reproduction, and phenotype. In a letter to the Immigrants' Protective League in Chicago, a woman explained the consequences of race restrictions for her family,

> I was born in Czechoslovakia. My ten-year-old son whom I left with his uncle was also born there. His father was the rich man of the village. He did not marry me. So I came to the United States, hoping to save money and send for my boy. Several years later, I married a Japanese restaurant keeper here in Chicago. We are very happy. He would love to have my son come. But when I took my naturalization examination on my second papers, they told me I could not have them because my husband was born in Japan. My boy is waiting in the regular quota, but it is a long time.[1]

In stark and direct language, the Cable Act drew a firm and concrete race line through married women's independent citizenship. No woman, foreign or domestic, who married a man ineligible for citizenship could be naturalized "during the continuance of the marital status." Moreover, while the Cable Act had provided that white or black women who married men ineligible for citizenship could regain their citizenship upon termination of their marriage, it did not include women who themselves were racially ineligible to citizenship. These women could never regain their citizenship. A Japanese American woman, born in Hawaii, who had

---

[1] Quoted in Mrs. Kenneth F. Rich, "Citizenship—A Pivot in Family Relationships," speech delivered 15 June 1933 at the joint meeting arranged by the National Council of Citizenship and Naturalization and Division X—The Immigrant—at the National Conference of Social Work in Detroit, reprinted in Marian Schibsby, *Interpreter Release Clip Sheet*, 10, no 15 (6 September 1933), RACNS, reel 3.

married a Japanese subject prior to the Cable Act, secured a divorce from her husband and sought to reestablish her citizenship. Did such a woman, Honolulu officials queried, not only lose "her citizenship during the continuance of the marital relationship" as the Cable Act stipulated, but because of her race status could never again "become a citizen of the U.S.?"[2] Correct. Naturalization, the central bureau affirmed, was limited to white persons and persons of African nativity and African descent. A Japanese woman, married or not, was neither of these.[3] In a memo to district offices, Department of Labor officials notified their officers that the Cable Act would have clear racial restrictions: "the Department believes it to be accurate in stating that it was the legislative intention by use of the words 'ineligible to citizenship' as used in the [Cable Act] to debar from citizenship a woman citizen marrying an alien who is racially disqualified from naturalization, for example, a Chinese or Japanese."[4]

INTERRACIAL MARRIAGE: RACE AND THE CABLE ACT

Under the Cable Act, white women married to racially ineligible men acquired their husband's racial status. Interracial marriages placed both husband and wife beyond the pale of citizenship. Thus, while the Cable Act separated marriage from citizenship, it reinscribed the significance of race to both. Mary Ann Montoya, the Austrian immigrant who had married a Filipino man in 1926, wrote directly to Washington to inquire about her political status. Although she had been married four years after the Cable Act provided for independent citizenship, Montoya could not apply for naturalization. Married to a man racially ineligible for citizenship, Montoya became for the duration of her marriage, in effect, racially ineligible for citizenship.[5] Mrs. George S. Chinn, a white woman who had married a Chinese man, also wrote to Washington officials and asked whether she could apply for naturalization under the Cable Act. Immigration officials told Chinn that she had lost her citizenship by her marriage, and because

---

[2] Hawaii immigration officials to INS central offices, 19 July 1923; INS file 20/2 (1922–); RCO: Naturalization, entry 26, box 399; INS, DC, RG85; NA, DC. Both of the women discussed in this file were schoolteachers, and local statute in Hawaii required that they be citizens.

[3] Reply 28 August 1923, INS file 20/2; RCO: Naturalization, entry 26, box 399; INS, DC, RG85; NA, DC.

[4] Letter 2 July 1923 in reply to request for information, INS file 20/2; RCO: Naturalization, entry 26, box 399; INS, DC, RG85; NA, DC.

[5] Mary Ann Montoya to INS, Washington, DC, 18 June 1930; INS file 20/2; RCO: Naturalization, entry 26, box 399; INS, DC, RG85; NA, DC.

she was married to a man racially ineligible for citizenship she herself was not eligible to apply for naturalization under the Cable Act.[6]

For American-born women who married men ineligible for citizenship and were returning from abroad, marital-racial status left them vulnerable to laws excluding aliens. The Cable Act affected not only women's naturalization but, in conjunction with the 1924 National Origins Act, women's immigration as well. Recall Fung Sing, who was born in the United States in 1898, traveled to China in 1903, married a Chinese subject in 1920, and was widowed soon thereafter in 1924. In 1925, three years after Cable and one year after the National Origins Act, Fung tried to return to the United States to resume her American citizenship. The Cable Act applied only to women who had lost their citizenship because of their marriage to an alien "eligible for citizenship." Although she was no longer married, Fung remained an alien. The immigration law of 1924 prohibited the immigration of people "ineligible for citizenship"; Chinese immigrants were "ineligible for citizenship." In hearing her case, the court confirmed the decision of immigration authorities that race and marriage had trumped birth: "Racially the petitioner is a Chinese (yellow race); politically she was born a member of the citizenry of the United States." Fung was not allowed to reenter the United States.[7] Similarly, Sara Lydia Hing returned to the United States in 1925 after having lived a number of years in China and was denied admission as having married a man ineligible to citizenship. Hing was born in Vermont to a Chinese father and an English mother. Educated in the United States, she lived for some time in China and married a medical student named Rumjahn. Under questioning from immigration officials, Hing was asked about her husband's race designation:

Q: Where were you married?
A: In Canton, China.
Q: Where was your husband born?
A: Hong Kong.
Q: Of what race of people is he?
A: Indian. I mean Mohammedan, but he has never been out of Hong Kong.
   I think his ancestors were from India.
Q: Is he full-blooded Indian?
A: No; he is half Chinese.[8]

---

[6] As a single white woman she fulfilled racial requirements, however, and only after her marriage was ended and she complied with additional residency and education stipulations could she be naturalized. INS, Washington D.C., to Mrs. George S. Chinn, 27 August 1924 ; INS file 20/2; RCO: Naturalization; entry 26, box 399; INS, DC, RG85; NA, DC.

[7] *Ex parte Fung Sing* 6 F.2d 670 (W.D.Wash. 1925).

[8] Hing appealed her case to the secretary of labor but was denied and held for deportation. On appeal, however, the court ruled that her marriage, consummated by a "Moham-

Details mattered. Race status was determined through "blood" content, and race difference was calculated in fractions. A woman's status under the Cable Act depended entirely on the intricacies of her genealogy and that of her husband. More than fifty percent of nonwhite or nonblack "blood" provided grounds for exclusion from naturalization, and thus the guarantees offered by the Cable Act. This more lax definition of racial otherness contrasts sharply with miscegenation laws of the period (which generally held to a one-eighth standard) and school segregation laws (which tended to be "one-drop" laws).[9] As immigration authorities attempted to see race at the border, they employed gross, generalized categories of visible difference and family genealogy rather than the intricacies of the scientific debates that mar early twentieth-century thinking on race.[10]

Seattle officials inquired whether a native-born woman who was half Chinese and half Spanish could apply to be renaturalized after having married a Mexican man in 1917. Her father, the Seattle report detailed, "was a full blooded Chinaman, born in China," while her mother "was of pure Spanish blood." As a "foreign born," "half-cast-Chinese," the Seattle officials noted, "she could hardly expect to be naturalized." However, the problem lay in the fact that this woman applied for United States citizenship as a Mexican citizen, by virtue of her marriage, rather than as an expatriated American woman of partial Chinese ancestry, by virtue of her birth.[11] In response, Washington officials informed the Seattle officers that she was not eligible to become a citizen. Whether she was a Mexican political citizen as a result of her marriage was not the important question. Racially she remained Chinese: "She is a Chinese half-blood and, therefore, within the 1882 [Chinese Exclusion] Act. She voluntarily relinquished her birthright, and now, seeking to regain American citizenship, must comply with the terms of the naturalization statues. This she cannot do by reason of her race."[12]

Immigration officials routinely attempted to ascertain the racial composition of arriving immigrants and citizens through both close physical ob-

---

medan ceremony," was not a legal marriage in China and therefore Hing had not expatriated herself through her marriage to a man ineligible to citizenship. *Ex parte Hing* 22 F. 554 (W.D.Wash. 1927).

[9] My thanks to Peggy Pascoe for bring this contrasting treatment of race in the law to my attention. Also see Mae Ngai, "The Architecture of Race in American Immigration Law," *Journal of American History* 86, No. 1 (June 1999): 79.

[10] Peggy Pascoe, "Miscegenation Law, Court Cases, and Ideologies of 'Race' in Twentieth-Century America," *Journal of American History* 83, No. 1 (1996).

[11] Seattle to Washington, D.C., 13 September 1923; INS file 20/2; RCO: Naturalization, entry 26, box 399; INS, DC, RG85; NA, DC.

[12] Reply 11 October 1923; INS file 20/2; RCO: Naturalization, entry 26, box 399; INS, DC, RG85; NA, DC.

servation and genealogical histories. The American consul in Shanghai went to great pains to specify that Lilly Zecha was half Chinese and half Dutch, while her son was also one-half Chinese as both his mother and father were half Chinese.[13] Officials in Honolulu were less certain of Louise Abel's racial makeup, noting only that they believed her mother was "Caucasian-Hawaiian" and her father was "Chinese-Hawaiian-Caucasian."[14] When Marie Fawcett, a member of the Huron tribe, crossed the northern border from Quebec in 1937, officials noted that "her mother was born in Quebec City and has no Indian blood," while her grandfather was "part Indian," "part French," and married to "a person of the Irish race." Moreover, the report concluded, "because of the apparent preponderance of white blood of the subject, she may later be held to be racially eligible to naturalization as a citizen of the United States."[15]

Race status was a product of evidence, and women were often asked to supply corroborating witness testimony or photographs to substantiate their race-based claims. San Francisco officials surmised that Henrika W. Loveriks was half Dutch and some mixture of Malay blood and asked her to produce evidence of her father's race status.[16] Honolulu officials attempted to determine whether Lilly Aki was full-blooded Hawaiian— "Was he [her father] a Chinaman?" "Can you speak Chinese?" "Can you speak Hawaiian?" "Is your mother full-blooded Hawaiian?"—and concluded from "her characteristic Hawaiian features" that indeed she was.[17] Ten years later, in 1934, officials relied on witness testimony to verify her husband's racial identity. Aki, now Lilly Peterson, testified that

[13] The consul also noted that Zecha's nephew was three-quarters Chinese, "being born to a father who is full Chinese blood and a mother who is one-half Chinese," while her niece was also three-quarters Chinese, "being born to a father who is one-half Chinese and a mother who is full Chinese." Lily Zecha, INS file 18582/11–9 (1919); AICF, box 1383; INS, SFD, RG85; NA-PSR.

[14] Louse Abel [pseud.], INS file 4500/4740 (1943); U.S. Citizens of Chinese Race Applying for Certificates of Citizenship, box 123; INS, HDO, RG85; NA-PSR.

[15] Marie Fawcett [pseud.] INS file 55939/967 (1937); DJA-INS acc. 58 A 734, box 1110; INS, DC, RG85; NA, DC.

[16] Loveriks was born in Java and was traveling with her employer as a child's nurse. Henrika W. Loveriks, INS file 18431/1–6 (1919); AICF, box 1365; INS, SFD, RG85; NA-PSR.

[17] Aki was born in Hawaii in 1904, and by 1929 she was married to James Petterson, a white man who worked as a barber with the army. Aki appeared before immigration officials twice, once in 1925 and once in 1936, both times in an effort to secure permission to travel to the mainland. During her first hearing in 1925, immigration officials questioned Aki about her racial status in an effort to determine whether she was indeed Hawaiian and thus entitled to travel to the mainland. By 1925, Congress had passed strict laws regulating immigration between Hawaii and the continental United States in an effort to restrict further the arrival of Asian immigrants.

her husband was white and therefore her citizenship had not been affected by her marriage. Immigration officials, however, presumed a marriage that was racially homogenous and thus assumed her husband was not white:

Q: Were you ever married before you married James Peterson?
A: No.
Q: How old is he and where was he born?
A: 36 years old; born in Texas, U.S.A., January 13, 1898.
Q: Was he ever married before he married you?
A: I don't know.
Q: To what race does he belong?
A: Dutch-Irish. He served three enlistments in the U.S. army.

Immigration officials concluded in Aki Petterson's favor, finding that her husband was white and therefore she had not lost her citizenship through marriage.[18]

Immigrants of multiracial ancestry frustrated efforts to link race difference to appearance, as they challenged the idea of racial purity that was at the root of legal exclusion. Blackness and whiteness, or even Chineseness, were insufficient categories. Moreover, women arriving from regions like Hong Kong, Hawaii, or Malaysia, where dense intersections of national groups created multiethnic states, troubled any easy relationship between geography, national identity, and race.

In 1930 and 1931, the House Committee on Immigration and Naturalization discussed the possibility of allowing native-born women to retain their citizenship despite their marriage to men ineligible for citizenship. In these discussions of native-born women's citizenship, anxieties about miscegenation and reproduction were woven throughout.[19] Committee members linked nonwhite women's roles as possible citizens to their role in reproducing citizens. Undesirable citizen women marrying equally racially undesirable alien men, committee members argued, expedited the immigration of racial minorities and the creation of minority families in the United States. "If a white American citizen marries a Chinese," Representative Vincent queried, "why do you want her to be able to get her citizenship back while she is married to him?" "[A]s I understand it,"

---

[18] Aki lacked any documentary evidence of her husband's race status. Fortunately, Aki's cousin corroborated her story, confirming that James Peterson [pseud.] was indeed white. Lilly Aki [pseud.], INS file 4500/75 (1934); U.S. Citizens of Chinese Race Applying for Certificates of Citizenship, box 2; INS, HDO, RG85; NA-PSR.

[19] See, for example, Dorothy Straus, attorney at law, New York City, *Amendment to the Women's Citizenship Act of 1922: Hearings before the Committee on Immigration and Naturalization*, 1930, HR 10208; House of Representatives, 71st Cong., 2nd sess., Washington, D.C., 5.

Representative Esterly added, "the children become U.S. citizens," and moreover, "are spread into the U.S. without much ado."[20]

Emma Wold, representing the Women's Bar Association of the District of Columbia, dismissed the committee's concern over racial mixing. Wold noted that Asian American women often had little other choice than marriage to an ineligible immigrant. While miscegenation laws sought to discourage marriages between designated racialized groups, the Cable Act worked to discourage Asian American women from marrying other Asian men and penalized those who did. "It does not affect many white or Caucasian women. The provision in the law touches the large number of Chinese and Japanese girls born in the U.S. with the precious heritage of U.S. citizenship," Wold explained, "If, unfortunately but perfectly legitimately, such a girl falls in love with one of her own race who is an alien and marries him, she is the one who is penalized."[21]

Arguments marshaled on behalf of native-born women drew on ideals of gender equality and even class privilege in disputing charges of miscegenation. For example, Mrs. Burnita Matthews, chair of the lawyer's council of the National Woman's Party, long-time proponents of equal citizenship, defended the need for gender equity against the House committee's concerns for racial homogeneity. Matthews and the National Woman's Party called the committee's attention to gender inequity in the law— native-born, Asian-ancestry women lost their citizenship through marriage while native-born, Asian-ancestry men did not.[22]

Victor S. Houston, the delegate in Congress from the Territory of Hawaii, urged the committee to consider the fate of racially ineligible women living in his district. Houston depicted these women as middle-class, professional women worthy of citizenship. Over eight thousand women living in Hawaii, Houston argued, had been born in the Islands and had married racially ineligible men. These women were neither white nor black, and thus they were not eligible for citizenship under present naturalization laws. "I have in mind a very estimable part-Hawaiian girl, who married a half-Hindu," Houston explained, "Her husband is a resident of Hawaii, because he came there as a minor, whose father was a

---

[20] *Amendment to the Women's Citizenship Act of 1922, and for Other Purposes*, 1930–31, HR 14684, HR 14685, HR 16303; House of Representatives, 71st Cong., 3rd sess., Washington, DC, 9–10.

[21] Emma Wold, *Amendment to the Women's Citizenship Act of 1922, and for Other Purposess*, 1930–31, 27.

[22] Mrs. Burnita Matthews, chair of the lawyer's council of the National Woman's Party, *Amendment to the Women's Citizenship Act of 1922, and for Other Purposes*, 1930–31, 3. Candice Bredbenner notes that the NWP was aware that gender equity in naturalization law threatened to undermine the current system of immigration control. Bredbenner, *A Nationality of Her Own*, 229.

minister of religion. His father is a pure Caucasian, a Britisher who happens to be a Buddhist bishop." Houston suggested that the law had little to offer this "estimable" girl: "The department is not in favor of naturalizing people with less than 50% Caucasian or African blood, so we are absolutely without recourse." Similarly, Houston offered the example of a second woman, part Samoan and the daughter of an American father. Educated in France and Berlin, and married to a German citizen, she was an otherwise ideal citizen. "Then we have a young part-Tahitian girl who married a Caucasian, an American citizen, a scientific man connected with the Bishop Museum. And until she can prove that she was more than 50% Caucasian blood they would not accept her." Race restrictions, Houston maintained, prevented worthy women from becoming American citizens, "And further there are the cases of American women of various races who have married, as many marry Filipinos. What is their status now, and what will it be after the Philippines get their independence?"[23]

During the early 1930s, the Cable Act was amended to provide relief for nonwhite, nonblack American-born women but in ways that continued to make subtle distinctions by race. Importantly, the Cable Act and its amendments looked and acted more like immigration law then naturalization law. As was true in immigration law, women's appeals to citizenship were evaluated based on when they had been married and therefore which law had been in effect.[24]

With the act of March 3, 1931, Congress repealed the provision of the Cable Act declaring women ineligible for citizenship by virtue of their marriage to racially excluded men. All women who were citizens at birth had the right to regain their citizenship through repatriation.[25] However, enacting federal law was one thing, overcoming local resistance was another. In 1933, the Mexican consul at Calexico, California informed the attorney general that many Mexican women living in El Centro, California who had married "Hindus" were being denied naturalization rights by the local district attorney because of their marriage to ineligible aliens. As a result, these women were being prevented from purchasing or leasing

[23] Hon. Victor S. Houston, delegate in Congress from Territory of Hawaii; *Amendment to the Women's Citizenship Act of 1922, and for Other Purposes*, 1930–31, 18–20.

[24] Rather than reestablishing the citizenship of native-born American women who had been disenfranchised through marriage in a single piece of legislation as the Fourteenth Amendment had done, the Cable Act followed the piecemeal process of immigration law.

[25] By 1931 the process of repatriation involved filing a petition for naturalization at any time upon return; there was no residency requirement. Marian Schibsby, "Concerning Women Who Have Lost American Citizenship because of Marriage to an Alien," *Interpreter Releases*, 12, no. 10, series B, Naturalization no. 2 (12 March 1935), RACNS, reel 4.

land under California's Alien Land Law.[26] While immigration authorities agreed with the Mexican consul that, by law, these women could be naturalized if they met all other requirements, they left the task of implementing policy to local officials.[27]

Mexican women living in Arizona who had married South Asian immigrants met similar administrative resistance. For example, when Mercy Padilla and Isabel Cabinallis filed their petitions for naturalization in 1935, the Superior Court of Florence, Arizona raised questions about their qualifications for citizenship. Padilla was born at Altar, Sonora, Mexico, in 1907, and had entered the United States sometime during 1914 through Sasabe (also known as Mosquite), Arizona. In 1933, she married Amer Singh, an Indian immigrant and a man ineligible for citizenship. Isabel Cabinallis was born in Culiacan, Sinaloa, Mexico in 1906, and came to the United States in 1920 through Nogales, Arizona. In 1927 she married Diwan Singh, who was born in Punjab, India, and had entered the United States through San Francisco in 1906.[28] Important to the court's expressed hesitation was that both women had married men ineligible for citizenship, but in the background lay long-held questions about the acceptability of Mexican immigrants condemned as more Indian than Spanish.[29] Conditions of violent racial segregation and pernicious legal discrimination in the South and Southwest may help to explain why so few immigrant Mexican women pursued citizenship.[30]

---

[26] Harry W. Horton to Attorney General of the United States, 5 December 1933, INS file 20/113, 20/71; RCO: Naturalization, entry 26, box 404; INS, DC, RG85; NA, DC.

[27] Henry B. Hazard, Assistant to the Commissioner, to Harry W. Horton, 7 February 1934; INS file 20/113, 20/71; RCO: Naturalization, entry 26, box 404; INS, DC, RG85; NA, DC.

[28] In 1922, Cabinallis had married Jose Birli, who was born on a ranch near Tucson, Arizona. In 1926 the couple was divorced. She married Singh a year later. In Cabinallis' case, she had become a United States citizen though marriage in 1922 but then was denaturalized in 1927 when she married a man ineligible for citizenship.

[29] Court officials wrote to the INS for advice. INS officials responded that women who had married men ineligible for citizenship could now be naturalized, if, and only if, they had previously been citizens in their own right. Mercy Singh was never a citizen and Isable Singh had been a citizen only though marriage. Both women could apply for naturalization but only through compliance with general requirements. G. C. Wilmoth, District Director, El Paso, to Commissioner of Immigration and Naturalization, 28 March 1935, INS file 20/113, 20/71; RCO: Naturalization, entry 26, box 404; INS, DC, RG85; NA, DC.

[30] In her analysis of nationality problems facing nonwhite immigrant populations, Annie Clo Watson, executive secretary of the International Institute of San Francisco, noted that while Mexican immigrants were not expressly excluded from naturalization, examiners expressed doubts about their racial acceptability for citizenship. Watson suggested, "For the Mexican the uncertainty of naturalization, if Indian blood predominates, should be removed." Watson, "Special Nationality Problems of the Pacific Coast," paper presented at

SOME ARE BORN AND OTHERS ARE NATURALIZED:
"NATIONALS," RACE, AND CABLE

The process of legislating and adjudicating married women's independent citizenship found close parallels in the efforts to determine the citizenship status of Native Americans, Hawaiians, Filipino/as, and Puerto Ricans. The presence of "nationals," incorporated through U.S. imperialism at home and abroad, like that of Asian American women, created an ethnic multiplicity that frustrated the American legal tradition of biracialism. The 1931 law removing racial bars to women's repatriation after marriage specified that its provisions applied to citizens "at birth." As a result women who had been naturalized through marriage or through congressional fiat were excluded from the act's provision for racial equality.

The "at birth" clause had the most severe implications for Hawaiian, Puerto Rican, Philippine, and Native American women who had been naturalized through acts of Congress rather than through their birth in the United States. These groups of women were perceived as belonging to peoples that had been naturalized en masse, a status decidedly different from that of birthright citizens. Moreover, Hawaiian, Philippine, and Native American women did not meet racial eligibility clauses demanding that applicants to citizenship be either white or black. Honolulu officials inquired whether a Hawaiian woman, who prior to her marriage was a citizen of the United States, lost her citizenship when she married a Filipino resident of the Territory of Hawaii. Filipinos were not "citizens" under the law, Honolulu officials explained, but they had been granted a unique status as "subjects."[31] Authorities in Washington responded that the important question was not whether her husband was a citizen or not, but whether he was white or not.[32]

Native American women faced a confusing web of laws in navigating their citizenship claims, and women who married non-Indian men found both their "Indianness" and their "Americanness" in legal doubt. The

---

the National Conference of Social Work, Kansas City, Miss., 22 May 1934 and reproduced in *Interpreter Release Clip Sheet* 11, no. 18 (25 August 1934), RACNS, reel 4.

[31] The couple had married before the passage of the Cable Act and were still living together as man and wife. While her husband had never been naturalized, neither was he an alien. Honolulu officials suggested that because her husband was not an alien (though also not a citizen) she had not lost her citizenship when she married him. The bureau responded that this woman's citizenship status was less than clear. Hawaii to Washington, D.C. 19 July 1923, INS file 20/2; RCO: Naturalization, entry 26, box 399; INS, DC, RG85; NA, DC.

[32] The problem of race in this case, the bureau concluded, remained an open question. Washington, D.C. officials explained, "The courts are divided on the proposition of whether a Filipino is eligible for naturalization as an American citizen." Reply 28 August 1923, INS file 20/2; RCO: Naturalization, entry 26, box 399; INS, DC, RG85; NA, DC.

1924 immigration act tightened immigration restrictions by prohibiting the arrival of racially ineligible aliens, including Native Americans living in either Canada or Mexico. North and South American Indian communities living along the nation's borders found this to be a particularly onerous piece of legislation, one that limited their ability to travel back and forth to visit family and tribal members living on either side of the border. In 1924 Congress conferred citizenship on all Native Americans living in the United States, although the law did not address those born after the effective date of the act and offered no relief for relatives living across the border and stymied by immigration regulations.[33]

In 1927 hearings before the House Committee on Immigration and Naturalization, fears of racial hybridity dogged efforts to allow Native American communities to travel freely across the Canadian border. Robert Codd, a Buffalo attorney representing tribes living on the Tuscarora and Grand River Reservations, attempted to deflect the committee's concerns about the racial composition of Native American communities:

JOHN BOX (Rep, TX): Are many of them a mixed breed?

CODD: Not many. I should say not to exceed one-fifth of them.

BOX: You recognize, of course, that there are thousands of pure-blood and mixed-breed Indians on the Mexican border, and that this bill would apply to them also.

CODD: I presume it might do so. I did not have that in mind when I went into this matter.

ROBERT BACON (Rep, NY): Is it not true that 90 percent of all the people of Mexico are of Indian blood?

BOX: That is the major element in Mexico.

BACON: [This bill][34] would permit the free entry of practically all Mexicans.

"Surely you do not concede," Bird Vincent, Representative of Missouri demanded, "that this committee could possibly pass this bill for approval of the Congress in the form it is now, when it would have the effect of opening the gates to everybody of Indian blood in Mexico as well as in Canada, and in Central America as well as in Mexico."[35] By 1928, Con-

[33] In a letter to the commissioner-general, the British Embassy expressed its concern that "the United States Immigration Commissioner at Seattle has ruled that North American Indians shall be considered in the same category as Japanese and Chinese and other races ineligible for citizenship." British Embassy, Washington to commissioner-general, 10 June 1925, INS file 55466/182 (1925–); RCO, entry 9, box 384, 55466/51–55466/444; INS, DC, RG85; NA, DC.

[34] HR 16864, sec. 33: "North American Indians, of any and all classes, are hereby excluded from any and all provisions of this act" amending the 1924 immigration act.

[35] *Admission of Canadian Indians: Hearings before the Committee on Immigration and Naturalization*, Robert M. Codd, Jr., 1927, HR 16864; House of Representatives, 69th Cong., 2nd sess., Washington, D.C., 12.

gress had taken specific and narrow steps to amend the problem of Native American travel across the northern border while constraining that across the southern. The act of April 2, 1928 provided that the 1924 immigration law was not to be interpreted to limit the right of American Indians born in Canada to cross the border into the United States.[36]

For Native American women attempting to travel across the border, issues of marital status, race difference, and political identity converged. Dorothy Winnifred Goodwin was arrested by immigration authorities in 1946, found to be without an immigration visa or a passport, and held for deportation to Canada. Born on the Six Nations Reservation, Brantford, Ontario, Canada, in 1928, Goodwin claimed that her status as a full-blooded Northern American Indian under the 1928 law exempted her from the regulations of immigration law.[37] According to immigration authorities, however, as a result of her marriage to a white man and native of Canada in 1934, Goodwin was no longer an Indian. In essence, immigration authorities maintained that "Indian" was a political category subject to change with marriage. Goodwin, in defense, argued that "Indian" was a racial category, immutable and fundamentally individual. The district court agreed with Goodwin and ruled that "Indian" must be given a racial understanding since the history of legislation directed at Indians used blood quantum in defining Indian-ness. The court ruled that Goodwin had not lost her status as an "Indian" by her marriage to a white man in 1934 and she was released from custody.[38]

Transborder communities along the southern border, like Native American communities along the northern, left INS officials bewildered about the citizenship status of many a Mexican American woman who, as a Nogales official explained, "returns to the United States as do many other aliens, simply to pass the summer at the coast, or to make a temporary visit to relatives."[39] Naturalization officials in the Southwest were reluctant to extend citizenship rights to a community they viewed as part Indian, and thus nonwhite and racially suspect.[40] Nogales officials inquired about an American-born woman who had married a Mexican national after 1922. The couple had lived in Mexico for most of their marriage. The wife had returned to Nogales in 1936 with the intention of establishing her citizen-

---

[36] Amnesty was limited and the right of free travel did not extend to "adopted" members of Indian tribes. Hutchinson, *Legislative History of American Immigration Policy*, 204.

[37] Goodwin was a member of the Upper Cayuga tribe of the Six Nations.

[38] *United States ex rel. Goodwin v. Karnuth* 74 F.Supp. 660 (W.D.N.Y. 1947).

[39] Inspector in charge, Nogales, Arizona to district director, El Paso, 3 September 1936, INS file 20/154; RCO: Naturalization, entry 26, box 408; INS, DC, RG85; NA, DC.

[40] Annie Clo Watson, "Special Nationality Problems of the Pacific Coast," 105.

ship.[41] El Paso officials wrote to ask of the status of a women who had married a Mexican man before 1922. She was born in Mexico, her mother was a citizen of Mexico, but her father was an American citizen.[42]

Throughout the early 1930s, Hawaiian-born women continued to face the combined weight of marital and racial exclusion in naturalization and immigration law.[43] American annexation complicated citizenship. The 1931 amendment to the Cable Act guaranteeing that women who were born citizens of the United States could not be denied their citizenship on account of their race was limited to women who were citizens "at birth." Hawaiian women were citizens by Congressional decree, and thus by collective naturalization, not by birth.[44] Immigration officials did not believe Hawaiian women were covered under the 1931 amendment to the Cable Act, and thus any Hawaiian woman married to a man racially ineligible for naturalization remained stripped of her citizenship rights.[45]

The significance for Hawaiian women lay in the difference between the two types of citizenship status—birth and naturalization. Naturalization

[41] Nogales officials assumed that such a woman had lost her citizenship through prolonged absence abroad. Inspector in Charge, Nogales, Arizona to District Director, El Paso, 3 September 1936, INS file 20/154; RCO: Naturalization, entry 26, box 408; INS, DC, RG85; NA, DC.

[42] As a result, she was considered a citizen through naturalization and thus, El Paso officials believed, she could not be repatriated. El Paso to Washington, D.C., 13 January 1937, INS file 20/154; RCO: Naturalization, entry 26, box 408; INS, DC, RG85; NA, DC.

[43] Life and law were similarly complicated for nonwhite women who had immigrated to Hawaii. One Chinese woman applied for a certificate of citizenship for the Hawaiian Islands in 1937. She first arrived in Hawaii in 1884 or 1885 when she was fifteen years old. She married a naturalized citizen of Hawaii who had since died. Reviewing her case, the attorney general ruled that the statutory law of the Republic of Hawaii was silent on the question of marriage and citizenship. Armed with this silence, immigration authorities ruled to deny her application for naturalization. She received instead a return certificate for a lawfully domiciled Chinese laborer, INS file 4393/13 (1937); Chinese Wives of Native-Born American Citizens, box 1; INS, HDO, RG85; NA-PSR.

[44] This problem was raised by the governor of Hawaii in a letter to the secretary of the interior. The governor's query was forwarded on to the secretary of labor. Governor of Hawaii to Secretary of the Interior, 14 October 1931; INS file 20/113, 20/71; RCO: Naturalization, entry 26, box 404; INS, DC, RG85; NA, DC. See also Solicitor of Labor to INS Commissioner, memorandum, 10 August 1936, INS file 20/154; RCO: Naturalization, entry 26, box 408; INS, DC, RG85; NA, DC.

[45] The problem of marriage aside, courts in Hawaii disagreed on the question of Hawaiian women's citizenship. The federal court at Honolulu ruled that Hawaiian women were citizens at birth while the territorial court at Lihue, Kauai found Hawaiian women to be citizens by naturalization. The Department of Labor instructed Honolulu immigration officials to appeal the decision of the federal court in order to bring judicial interpretation in line with administrative policy. Senior Attorney, "Memorandum for the Correspondence Division," 27 November 1931; NS file 20/113, 20/71; RCO: Naturalization, entry 26, box 404; INS, DC, RG85; NA, DC.

required Hawaiian women to meet psychological, educational, and be-havioral tests proscribed by law. Naturalized citizens, unlike native-born citizens, could be divested of their citizenship for prolonged absences abroad, and naturalized women could be stripped of their citizenship if found guilty of immoral behavior. Moreover, naturalization required that the applicant fit within the biracial definition of a citizen. Many Hawaiian women could not. And as William B. Lymer, a district court judge in Hawaii, pointed out, many women living in Hawaii could not speak English, and thus could not pass the entrance requirements. "We have here many of such women who were citizens of the United States prior to marriage, who were of limited education and who could not speak English," Lymer explained, "people born in Puerto Rico, people of Hawaiian blood and others of the Japanese, Chinese, or Korean races. Especially are there women of Hawaiian blood, born here and who have always lived in the Hawaiian Islands, who are married to aliens but who are unable to speak English."[46]

In Congressional debate over legislation to allow Hawaiian women to retain their citizenship rights after marriage, concerns for the rights of native-born Hawaiian women intersected with demands that the government restrict immigration of racial others to the mainland. Immigration officials assured Congress that the new law would not provide a window through which racially ineligible aliens would flood the continental United States. Previous legislation addressing the plight of Hawaiian women had been rejected by Congress as "being without limit in the number who might claim birth in Hawaii and might be residing in various parts of the world outside of American jurisdiction." By restricting the application of the law in time and space, immigration officials sought to prevent fraudulent claims and minimize the inclusion of racially different citizens.[47] Albert Johnson, the representative from Washington, and Victor Houston, the Governor of Hawaii, sought to reassure their legislative peers that the inclusion of some would not mean inundation by many:

STAFFORD (Rep, WI): Where are these women living?

HOUSTON (Gov. of Hawaii): They are all living in Hawaii at the present time.

STAFFORD: And the gentleman is certain that this applies to only 12 women?

HOUSTON: These are the only ones whose cases have been brought to my attention.

JOHNSON (Rep, WA): The law was rewritten so that it does not apply to any

---

[46] William B. Lymer, Judge U.S. District Court, Territory of Hawaii, to Attorney General, 19 February 1934, INS file 20/113, 20/71; RCO: Naturalization, entry 26, box 404; INS, DC, RG85; NA, DC.

[47] Commissioner of Naturalization to Assistant Secretary, memorandum, INS file 20/137; RCO: Naturalization, entry 26, box 406; INS, DC, RG85; NA, DC.

person outside of the islands. . . .

STAFFORD: Is it the purpose also that their husbands may seek to have special privileges granted to them if this act is passed?

JOHNSON: No. The scope is limited.[48]

As immigration and judicial officials attempted to legislate Hawaiian women's citizenship, native-born Hawaiian women who had married men ineligible for citizenship attempted to disguise their marriage so as not to alert immigration officials to the possibility that they were no longer American citizens.[49] Law Nung arrived in Honolulu in 1936, and offered proof that she had been born in the Hawaiian Islands. Immigration officials, however, suspected that she was married, and, through that marriage, lost her citizenship:

Q: Have you ever had a married name?
A: No.
Q: Have you ever been married?
A: No.
Q: Have you ever lived with any man?
A: No.
Q: Have you ever given birth to a child?
A: No.
Q: Have you ever had sexual intercourse with any man?
A: No.

Under subsequent interrogation, Law admitted she had lied to conceal her marriage, explaining that "Friends in China advised me to state that I am not married, but I was married, but my husband disappeared over 10 years ago."[50]

Having confessed that she married a man ineligible for citizenship, Law was questioned on what grounds she thought she could enter Honolulu. In the resulting interchange, the limitations of citizenship, the implications of marriage, and the relevance of race make it all too clear that Law's marriage placed her outside the citizenry:

[48] Excerpts from the discussion in the House on 2 May when HR 10829 was passed; as cited in Marian Schibsby, "Legislative Bulletin No. VII," *Interpreter Releases* 9, no. 14 (6 July 1932), RACNS, reel 3.

[49] For example, Ho Yee [pseud.], INS file 4393/96 (1948); Chinese Wives and/or Children of Naturalized Chinese under HK, box 5; INS, HDO, RG85; NA-PSR.

[50] Upon arrival in Hawaii, many of Law's family members had testified that she had been married in China, a fact Law adamantly denied. Under reinvestigation, her mother refuted her former testimony, and corroborated her daughter's story that she had never married. Immigration officials suspected the family of lying to protect Law, and armed with the mother's original testimony from 1921 they confronted Law again.

Q: What causes you to think you are a citizen of the United States, other than that you were born here?

A: None other than my birth here.

Q: Do you understand that by reason of your marriage to a citizen of China you lost your American citizenship.

A: Yes.

Q: Is that the reason you gave false testimony about being married?

A: No, it was on the advice of my friend who bought the ticket, and he told me that if I stated I was married I can not enter the United States.

Law was denied admission. Still married to an ineligible alien, Law could not repatriate herself until her marriage was terminated, a task made more difficult by her husband's disappearance.[51]

By 1932, Congress took one more step toward eliminating racial barriers to women's independent citizenship with an additional amendment to the Cable Act which made "a woman born in Hawaii prior to June 14, 1900," a citizen at birth.[52] In the tradition of piecemeal legislation, the new amendment narrowed the window of opportunity to include only those Hawaiian-born women residing in the United States on 2 July 1932.[53] Dang Mew Wan Lum, arriving in Honolulu in 1937 to reestablish her citizenship, was five years too late. Dang was born in Hawaii in 1894, married a Chinese immigrant in 1910, and consequently lost her status as a naturalized citizen. The 1932 law which declared some Hawaiian women to be citizens at birth did not include Dang; she was not residing in the United States in 1932. Dang was found to be ineligible for citizenship and her naturalization was canceled.[54]

---

[51] She was found not to be a citizen of the United States by reason of her marriage to a Chinese man, and she was also found likely to become a public charge as the board was suspicious of her abilities to support herself on the money she might make as a seamstress. Finally, Law was excluded on a third charge of moral turpitude (perjury). Included in Law's file is a 1949 letter from Honolulu immigration office to the American consul in Canton, China. The letter provides a brief summary of Law's effort to enter the United States in 1936. It is apparent from this letter that Law attempted to secure a visa in 1949. There is no record indicating whether she was successful. Law Nung [pseud.], INS file 4382/5205 (1936); Chinese Applicants for Form 430, box 192; INS, HDO, RG85; NA-PSR.

[52] The 2 July 1932 amendment to the Cable Act.

[53] Hawaiian women born before 1900 were citizens of the Kingdom of Hawaii or the Republic of Hawaii, and had become naturalized United States citizens under the Organic Act in 1900. Women born in Hawaii after 1900, according to immigration officials, should be considered United States citizens at birth. The 1932 amendment altered the status of those born before 1900 to native-born citizens, and sought to place all Hawaiian women on similar constitutional footing. Those not in the Islands on 2 July 1932, however, were not included within the law's provisions. See INS file 20/137; RCO: Naturalization, entry 26, box 406; INS, DC, RG85; NA, DC.

[54] United States v. Dang Mew Wan Lum 88 F.2d 88 (9th Cir. 1937).

The general provisions of the 1922 Cable Act restored women to citizenship, but it reinstated them as naturalized citizens, not native-born citizens. Thus women who had lost their citizenship by marriage to a non-American were not repatriated under Cable but renaturalized, and thus were subject to expatriation. By 1936, Congress addressed this inequity and passed legislation allowing women to regain their native-born privileges in full.[55] As had been true in the original Cable Act, the 1936 amendment drew subtle but significant distinctions between women. The 1936 law referred only to "native-born" women, and as had been true for Hawaiian women in the past, this small phrase would make all the difference for women living in lands that had been annexed by the United States. Similarly, a 1936 letter from San Juan to Washington, D.C., asked the commissioner of immigration to clarify the position of Puerto Rican women under the new law—were Puerto Rican women naturalized citizens or citizens at birth?[56]

In 1900, Congress had made all Spanish subjects who were residents of Puerto Rico, and their children citizens of Puerto Rico.[57] A 1903 Supreme Court case had determined that Puerto Ricans were not aliens, but it had not ruled that they were citizens.[58] Fifteen years later, citizens of Puerto Rico were made citizens of the United States by Congressional fiat.[59] As had been true of Hawaiian women, Washington officials informed San Juan that Puerto Rican women were not citizens by birth. "The Supreme Court of the U.S. has said that citizenship is acquired by two means only, namely birth and naturalization," the bureau explained, and "Any process therefore by which an alien secures U.S. citizenship other than by

[55] The 1936 legislation specified that native-born American women whose marriage to an alien had ended could restore their citizenship by merely taking an oath of allegiance before any naturalization court or American consular officials. Once they had taken the oath of allegiance, these women would be considered native-born citizens, as if their marriage had taken place after 1922. Letters from immigration officials and women alike testify to the confusing state of married women's citizenship following the 1936 legislation. New Jersey to Washington, D.C., 15 July 1936; INS file 20/154; RCO: Naturalization, entry 26, box 408; INS, DC, RG85; NA, DC; Chicago to Washington, D.C., 8 August 1936, INS file 20/154; RCO: Naturalization, entry 26, box 408; INS, DC, RG85; NA, DC; Reply to Chicago, New Jersey, and Puerto Rico, 22 August 1936, INS file 20/154; RCO: Naturalization, entry 26, box 408; INS, DC, RG85; NA, DC.

[56] San Juan to Washington, D.C., memorandum, 10 July 1936, INS file 20/154; RCO: Naturalization, entry 26, box 408; INS, DC, RG85; NA, DC.

[57] Act of 12 April 1900.

[58] Isabella Gonzales, born in Puerto Rico, arrived at the Port of New York in 1902. Immigration officials detained Gonzales as an alien likely to become a public charge. Gonzales claimed she was not alien and therefore she was not subject to immigration laws. The Supreme Court agreed, finding Gonzales not to be an "alien immigrant." *Gonzales v. Williams* 192 U.S. 1 (1904).

[59] Act of 2 March 1917.

birth is considered to be by naturalization."[60] Fourteen years after independent citizenship had been established for women, Puerto Rican women who married men racially ineligible for citizenship were still outside the Cable Act and beyond the bounds of citizenship.[61]

From the beginning the law's intent was to limit the scope and effect of women's citizenship, and while the Cable Act had been reformed over the 1930s it had not been rewritten. Despite moves toward gender equity in citizenship, dramatic and unyielding race exclusions remained embedded in both immigration and naturalization law.[62] A sense of halting and grudging inclusion remained at the heart of the series of laws governing women's citizenship, and race continued to provide the sinew that sustained the corpus of legal exclusions and inclusions.

At various times over the course of the twentieth century, native-born American women have been considered noncitizens. Racial designation and colonized status proved the great divides separating women whose claims to membership in the nation were recognized and those whose claims were not. The process by which women were granted independent citizenship resembled the halting and conditional legislation that extended citizenship by treaty or by fiat to people living in American imperial possessions. Historically, wives belonged with husbands, husbands belonged to the nation. Race difference intersected with gender traditionalism to map clear boarders around the nation's families. While the 1922 Cable Act separated national identity from marriage, it simultaneously reinscribed the significance of racial identity in both.

---

[60] Reply Washington to San Juan, 22 August 1936, INS casefile 20/154; RCO: Naturalization, entry 26, box 408; INS, DC, RG85; NA, DC.

[61] For example, see INS casefile 55892/631 (1935); DJA-INS, acc. 58 A 734, box 767; INS, DC, RG85; NA, DC.

[62] In 1934, the Cable Act was extended to allow alien husbands to take advantage of the expeditious naturalization process that had been available to white and black alien women marring United States citizens since 1922. The Equal Nationality Act stipulated "there shall be no distinction based on sex in the law and practice relating to nationality." The 1934 law also allowed women to pass their American citizenship on to their children, a privilege previously limited only to fathers. As quoted in Bredbenner, *A Nationality of Her Own*, 218.

CHAPTER NINE

Reproducing the Nation

The Cable Act and its various amendments of the 1930s expanded the citizenship rights of some while insisting on the significance of race to the nation. This strange brew of ideas of equality and those of race simmered in a climate of conflict and fear; conflict between a legal tradition rooted in the Fourteenth Amendment that offered birthright citizenship to non-white children on the one hand and fears of immigrant women's reproduction of ever more nonwhite children on the other. The threat of immigrant women's reproduction became a clarion call to those seeking to shore up the nation's defenses against the unassimilable and the unwanted. Debates over granting immigrant women access to the United States revealed deep anxieties about the sweeping implications of citizenship.

Americans are either citizens of the soil or citizens of the law; they are either born in the United States or they are naturalized within it. Yet, in important ways, children can also be citizens by blood.[1] Citizen children are not only born or naturalized, they are also made citizens through the naturalization of their parents.[2] Citizenship was a family affair. Without having been born or naturalized in the United States, the children of citizens acquired derivative citizenship and the right to enter the country outside the reach of immigration restriction.[3] Concerns over place, sovereignty, race, and nation converged in the question of children's status.

---

[1] Historically, *jus soli* (law of soil) and *jus sanguinis* (law of blood) provided alternative conceptions of membership, the first rooted in place and the second routed through parentage. Following English common law, American legal traditions employed both, offering citizenship to those born in the United States, as well as to the children of American citizens traveling abroad and noncitizen parents naturalized in the United States. Neither path to citizenship, whether through roots or through routes, however, remained uncontested.

[2] Legally children derived citizenship from their father, and, before 1934, assumed their mother's citizenship only in the case of illegitimacy. Beginning in 1907, minor children were required to travel to the United States within five years of obtaining their majority in order to preserve their *jus sanguinis,* citizenship rights. Charles Hartshorn Maxson, *Citizenship* (New York: Oxford University Press, 1930), 80; general discussion 74–85.

[3] Children of naturalized or first-paper immigrants could be held for medical treatment rather than deportation if they were found to have a treatable medical condition; unmarried or widowed daughters were not required to pass a literacy test; and, the children of citizens were considered nonquota immigrants while the children of naturalized immigrants were

Before the Cable Act and its amendments, the citizenship status of minor children and wives was folded within that of fathers and husbands, uniting the family under a single civic identity. While both naturalization and immigration policies privileged family unity, they also defined the legal parameters of "family" and regulated the implications of inherited status. In the decades before 1922, legitimacy and authenticity became watch words in efforts to distinguish legally valid families, to verify the geography of birth, or to substantiate paternity. The civic status of native-born children of parents who could not themselves meet naturalization or immigration requirements challenged the ideal of a nation of families. Asian American children born on U.S. soil and children born in immigration stations to mothers awaiting deportation threatened the exclusionary intent of immigration and naturalization law.

By 1934, with the Equal Nationality Act, mothers as well as fathers could pass citizenship to their children. Debates over the legislation and the resulting citizenship status of immigrant women's children testify to the ways in which women's immigration and women's citizenship remained tied to worries over the reproduction of difference—cultural, religious, ethnic, racial—in twentieth-century American society. Arriving at the nation's borders, women immigrants were not only potential wives, workers, or even citizens, they were also potential mothers of citizens. When, where, and under what conditions did a woman give birth to an American citizen and when did she not?

ON THE EDGE OF THE NATION:
THE RACE AND PLACE OF CITIZENSHIP BY BIRTH BEFORE 1934

American-born children of noncitizen parents or of illegal resident immigrants or even of nonresident women awaiting deportation, brought Fourteenth Amendment ideas of place and belonging into direct conflict with those of racial homogeneity, family unity, and national selectivity. Place of birth confounded those parts of immigration and citizenship law that sought to limit membership to applicants deemed worthy of inclusion. Any child, born on United States soil, was an American citizen, regardless of her parents' legal claims on the nation.[4] In 1898 the Supreme Court interpreted the Fourteenth Amendment to provide citizenship to

---

offered preference status. Hutchinson, *Legislative History of American Immigration Law*, 506–507, 509–511.

[4] The only exception was the children of foreign dignitaries or foreign visitors living temporarily in the United States, who were not subject to the jurisdiction of the United States and thus were not "dwelling" on its soil.

all children born in the United States. Although their parents were racially ineligible for citizenship, Asian American children were citizens at birth.[5] In practice this meant that women who remained on the fringes of American civic society could give birth to children who would make up its center. Once in the United States, Asian women ineligible for citizenship and subject to restrictive immigration covenants became mothers of American citizens. Women held in immigration stations awaiting deportation might also give birth to citizens. The children of parents who were racially, morally, mentally, physically, or economically excluded from the nation could in their own right become citizens through the accident of birth.

Although American-born, Chinese-ancestry children were citizens by law, in practice race constantly placed their civic status in question. They did not look as if they belonged. Many Chinese American children had left as young children to be educated or visit family in China and were unable upon their return to provide adequate details of neighborhood streets, buildings, or family members to satisfy the demands of immigration and court authorities.[6] Immigration officials accused the Chinese American and immigrant communities of using citizenship to circumvent Asian exclusion laws, claiming that a large percentage of returning Chinese citizens were not who they claimed to be. According to officials, arriving Chinese-ancestry women were immigrants until proven citizens. When Chun Chung and Chun Tack arrived in San Francisco in 1897 to join their father, immigration officials insinuated that Chun Chung's life history was more memorization than memory. "You need have no fear to look over your written instructions," officials prodded, "if you have forgotten anything." Her sister, Chun Tack, faired little better. "Who told you that you were born in San Francisco?" officials queried. "I know it myself," Chun Tack replied.[7] Attempting to expose Leong Quai Ho as a fraud, San Francisco inspectors asked "In what part of China were you born?" "I was not born in China," Leong explained for the second time,

---

[5] *United States v. Wong Kim Ark* 169 U.S. 649 (1898). As Charles J. McClain and Laurene Wu McClain argue, in finding for Wong Kim Ark the Court drew on earlier decisions establishing Chinese Americans' rights to the protections afforded by the Fourteenth Amendment, particularly *Yick Wo v. Hopkins* 118 U.S. 356 (1886) and *State v. Ah Chew* 16 Nev. 50 (1881). McClain and McClain, "The Chinese Contribution to the Development of American Law," in *Entry Denied*, ed. Sucheng Chan (Philadelphia: Temple University Press, 1991), 20–21.

[6] Women were often nervous during their interviews, behavior immigration officials viewed as evidence of guilt. Fung Yuet You and Fung Yuet Ying, INS files 9565/739 and 740 (1897); AICF, box 35; INS, SFD, RG85; NA-PSR.

[7] Chun Chung was asked to describe her father, a man she had not seen since she was a child. Chun Chung and Chun Tack, INS file 9573/682–683 (1897); AICF, box 36; INS, SFD, RG85; NA-PSR. Eventually, the Chun sisters were landed. Chun Chung and Chun Tack, INS file 9573/682–683 (1897); AICF, box 36; INS, SFD, RG85; NA-PSR.

"I was born in California." "Well go on," frustrated inspectors prodded, "give us the rest of you story, let us have it."[8]

Facing the racially restrictive covenants of American immigration law, many Chinese immigrants did in fact assume the native-born status of a family member or friend to gain admission.[9] In his 1902 annual report, F. P. Sargent, commissioner-general of immigration, alerted Congress to fraud practiced by Chinese immigrants to secure admission as native-born citizens. While the immigration service remained vigilant, Sargent explained, the federal courts recognized many of the claims of these would-be-citizens, resulting in a "record of their right," which posed a grave threat to racial restrictions in immigration and naturalization law.[10] Only rigorous and systematic interrogation at the border, not in a court of law, Sargent insisted, could provide adequate proof of citizenship.

Chinese American women returning from abroad often lacked birth records, school documents, or other written evidence of their native birth and were forced to rely on witness testimony. Chinese American births often went unrecorded by state agencies. While midwives and other immigrant medical practitioners provided necessary services for their communities, they could not offer them legal validity.[11] Inspectors gave little weight to the testimony of the women applicants or the families and friends who appeared on their behalf. When Tan Fong Yuen returned to San Francisco in 1896 after having lived in China with her mother for fourteen years, she had little other than her word as evidence of her native-born status. "My mother told me I was born in San Francisco," Tan insisted. From the ship, Tan watched as her sister, father, and friends testified as witnesses on her behalf. None, however, had more than their word to provide as evidence. With only Chinese and Chinese American witnesses and without any legal record of birth in San Francisco, immigration officials doubted Tan was an American citizen and she was returned to China

---

[8] Her sister's (Leong Kum Ho) interview was equally confrontational. When asked how old she was, Leong responded, "Twenty-three years old. Yes I am sure, if I were not twenty-three years old why should I say so? Nobody said so—there is no reason why I should not know I am twenty-three years old." "You were born in China were you not?" inspectors continued. "Well if I was born in China," Leong retorted, "why should I say I was born in San Francisco?" Both were eventually admitted. Leong Quai Ho and Leong Kum Ho, INS file 9570/676–677 (1897); AICF, box 36; INS, SFD, RG85; NA-PSR.

[9] Xiaojian Zhao, *Remaking Chinese America: Immigration, Family, and Community, 1940–1965* (New Brunswick, N.J.: Rutgers University Press, 2002).

[10] Sargent noted that of 799 alleged Chinese Americans arrested and tried for unlawful entry in 1902, 540 were released by federal courts. Contrary to Sargent's protests, some courts did support the efforts of immigration authorities to scrutinize the claims of returning Chinese American citizens. For example, *U.S. v. Chung Fung Sun* 63 F. 261 (N.D.N.Y. 1894); *Gee Fook Sing v. U.S.* 49 F. 146 (9th Cir. 1892); *Lem Hing Dun v. Same* 49 F. 148 (9th Cir. 1892). *Annual Report of the Commissioner-General of Immigration* (1902), 77.

[11] Judy Yung, *Unbound Feet*, 81.

as an inadmissible immigrant.[12] In hearing the case of Lee Sing Far, who returned to San Francisco after seventeen years in China, the Ninth Circuit Court of Appeals argued Lee had failed the "crucial test" of credibility. The court argued that the burden of proof lay with Lee to prove her citizenship to the satisfaction of court authorities. Although four witnesses had testified on her behalf, all were Chinese, and enforcement of the Chinese exclusion laws, the court argued, necessitated that the testimony of Chinese witnesses be held in some doubt.[13]

Lacking documentary evidence of their birth, returning Chinese American women brought photographs of themselves as children in the United States to corroborate the testimony of long-time friends and neighbors. Visual evidence took on a scientific cast as immigration authorities scrutinized the visages of applicants and their photographs. When Yee Lin returned to San Francisco in 1903, nine years after she had left, she offered a photograph of herself taken as a child in San Francisco. Officials, however, did not believe that child in the picture was Yee Lin, and she was returned to China.[14] Drawing on visual cues, a white woman from the Chinese Mission School, who had known Wong Nie High as a child, suspected that the woman who had arrived in San Francisco in 1903 was a fraud. Comparing her memory of a little girl with a "full round face," a slight "droop in one of her eyelids," and prominent teeth when she smiled with Wong Nie High, the witness concluded the applicant was not who she claimed to be. "Seems to me there is something about the mouth and chin that does not compare with this girl," the witness confirmed, something about "the eyes" was not the same. On reviewing her petition for habeas corpus, the district judge disagreed, finding that the picture and the woman were indeed the same person and admitting Wong Nie High as a citizen.[15]

Immigration officials suspected oral testimony but believed the body could not lie. Anthropometry, or the careful measurement of the body,

[12] Tan Fong Yeun, INS file 9540/38 (1896); AICF, box 33; INS, SFD, RG85; NA-PSR. In a similar case, a woman's story is corroborated by her father and neighbors who remember her birth: Chan Yoke, INS file 9540/40 (1896); AICF, box 33; INS, SFD, RG85; NA-PSR. Also, Lum Ah Ging and Lam Ah Kue, INS file 9555/590 and 591 (1896); AICF, box 33; INS, SFD, RG85; NA-PSR.

[13] If the testimony of Chinese witnesses was too easily accepted, the court argued, "there would be no more Chinese remanded in such cases." *Lee Sing Far v. United States* 94 F. 834 (9th Cir. 1899).

[14] Under questioning, Yee Lin was asked to provide additional details about the photograph, "Q: Is that your photograph? A: Yes Q: Do you remember when you had that photograph taken? A: No, it is so long ago. Q: You have no recollection of having this picture taken, have you? A: No; I was quite small when it was taken." Yee Lin, INS file 9961/3145 (1903); AICF, box 88; INS, SFD, RG85; NA-PSR.

[15] Wong Nie High, INS file 9945 (1903); AICF, box 86; INS, SFD, RG85; NA-PSR.

provided immigration officials with an identification system they believed could discern fact from fiction. Evidence from INS files indicate that anthropometry was in use up until the 1950s.[16] Developed in 1882 by Alphonse Bertillon, a chief of criminal identification with the Paris police department, anthropometry (or the Bertillon system) used meticulous body measurements, physical description, and photographs as a means of identification.[17] In keeping with the Bertillon system, Asian immigrants and Asian American citizens were photographed by immigration authorities at arrival and departure. These photographs were then used to verify or invalidate applicants' identities upon readmission. Lee Sin returned to the United States in 1911 six years after she had left as an infant. Immigration officials scrutinized her photograph. Despite "apparent facial resemblance" close comparison of the ears, "which organ no less an authority than Bertillon has said constitutes the most important means of identification of the human visage, remaining as it does practically unaltered in shape from birth until death," officials argued, revealed the young girl to be a fraud.[18]

Ironically, while the shared physicality of race promoted the exclusion of Chinese American citizens, the individuating visual details of personal appearance could provide the needed proof to secure admission. The use of photographic and visual evidence by border authorities reveals a subtle working understanding of the relationship between race, difference, and identity. Race located Chinese Americans beyond the assumed perimeter of American citizenship. Birth gave them rights to membership that appearance belied. Immigration officials assumed fraud was possible only because Chinese immigrants and Chinese American citizens shared common physiognomy. Yet despite the homogenizing effect of racialized categories, by relying on careful physical descriptions, authorities suggested that difference and individuation were visible in the details.

---

[16] For an example of a later case, Ellen Kam Chew Young, INS file 1302/1645 (1938–1947); GICF; INS, SFD, RG85; NA-PSR.

[17] During the same period, Sir Edward R. Henry, chief commissioner with the London metropolitan police, working off the observations and experiments of Sir Francis Galton, developed fingerprinting as an alternative identification tool. The process of fingerprinting was simultaneously developed by Juan Vucetich, a police employee in Buenos Aires. The Henry system, or fingerprinting, was adopted by Scotland Yard in 1911 and would become the world standard. "Bertillon, Alphonse," *Encyclopedia Britannica Online* <http://www.eb.com:180/bol/topic?eu–81031&sctn=1&pm=1> (accessed May 7, 1999); "fingerprint," *Encyclopedia Britannica Online* <http://www.eb.com:180/bol/topic?eu=34906&sctn=1> (Accessed May 7, 1999). Also see H.T.F. Rhodes, *Alphonse Bertillon: Father of Scientific Detection* (New York: Abelard-Schuman, 1956).

[18] Officials noted that the photograph of the baby revealed a "protruding lobule" that the photo of the current applicant did not. This evidence alone, inspectors concluded, "offers

Meticulous physical descriptions were recorded for arriving and departing immigrants. The location of moles and scars were noted as "marks of identification," like the "brown mole right cheek, pit mark 1" "outer corner left side of mouth" noted on Lew Hong Tan's INS record.[19] When Ching Git Sim arrived in Honolulu with her mother in 1923, inspectors drew on physical evidence to substantiate Ching's status as the daughter of a native-born Hawaiian citizen. Her father was born in Hawaii and her mother in China; Ching's "bi-racial" appearance, "which clearly shows that she is not pure Chinese" according to immigration officials, provided satisfactory evidence of her lawful identity.[20]

As laws excluding immigrants began to be applied with greater rigor through the 1910s and 1920s, troubling questions also arose about the status of children born in immigration stations to mothers awaiting deportation. Children born on the border, like Chinese American children, occupied a small but significant space between immigration and citizenship law. Chinese Americans lived outside the assumed visual parameters of American citizenship, and their ability to move freely across the nation's borders was frustrated as a result. Children born in border hospitals were born on the edge of citizenship, both inside and outside the space of the nation. Sara Prazmowska gave birth to her child in 1906 awaiting deportation from Ellis Island. Nobu Uang gave birth to her child on board ship somewhere between Japan and Seattle. Elena Marakovic gave birth in 1910 on Ellis Island as she waited anxiously for relatives to locate her missing husband. All three women were denied entry as likely public charges. The status of their "American-born" children, however, was more complicated.[21]

Immigration officials often attempted to circumvent questions of citizenship through an emphasis on maternal responsibilities. Young children belonged with their mothers, officials argued, and what they lost in civic

substantial disproof the claim." Lee Sin, INS file 10447/6444 (1911); AICF, box 491; INS, SFD, RG85; NA-PSR. Also see *Ex parte Wong Suey Sem* 20 F.2d 148 (W.D.Wash. 1927).

[19] Lew Hong Tan [pseud.], INS file 4393/79 (1930); Chinese Wives and/or Children of Naturalized Chinese under HK, box 4; INS, HDO, RG85; NA-PSR.

[20] Ching Git Sim, INS file 4384/237 (1923); Chinese Wives of Native-Born American Citizens, box 4; INS, HDO, RG85; NA-PSR. Grace and Lillian Chiu corroborated their testimony upon returning to Honolulu in 1939 with photographs of themselves and their father. Noting that the Chiu sisters were "prepossessing in appearance, attractive, clean and neat, and speak English better than the average Chinese girl of the same age," "are direct and forward in their answers and appear to have full confidence and control in themselves," the "strong resemblance" between family members provided more than enough proof of the girls' Hawaiian birth. Grace and Lillian Chiu [pseuds.], INS file 4382/5545-6 (1939); Chinese Applicants for Form 430, box 203; INS, HDO, RG85; NA-PSR.

[21] Sara Prazmowska [pseud.], Nobu Uang [pseud.], and Elena Marakovic [pseud.], INS file 53438/11 (1906); DJA-INS, acc. 60 A 600, box 443; INS, DC, RG85; NA, DC.

rights by deportation they gained in maternal care. Maria Ricci had not seen her husband in three years, and he refused to receive her when she arrived in 1911 pregnant. Charged with adultery and excluded as a likely public charge, Ricci gave birth in the Philadelphia Hospital as immigration officials made arrangements for her deportation. "The troublesome feature," according to authorities was not Ricci's immigration status, but that of her American-born child. By not ruling on the issue of the new child's citizenship, officials sought to avoid the whole question. "The mother must, of course, be deported," immigration officials argued, and they could only hope she would "take the babe with her."[22]

By the later 1910s and 1920s, immigration officials insisted that points of arrival were thresholds just outside the territorial jurisdiction and political sovereignty of the United States. Thus children born on these thresholds were immigrants, not citizens, and they were without legal claims on the nation. Others disagreed, arguing instead that the mother's status was irrelevant and the distinction between points of entry and the United States proper was spurious. The solicitor general's office, for example, argued that any child, born within the physical boundaries of the United States, was, without question, a citizen.[23]

Pregnant when she arrived in 1918, Gina Missana hoped to gain admittance for herself and her child by testifying that she had been propositioned by immigration inspectors in Boston who offered to arrange for her admittance in exchange for sex. Missana believed conception and birth on U.S. soil would guarantee her child American citizenship. When she gave birth eight months after arriving, Missana confessed that she had been assaulted while on board ship. According to immigration officials, whether Missana had given birth on board ship or in the immigration station was irrelevant—neither space was included within the geographic or legal limits of the nation. "While this child was physically born in the United States," officials concluded, "it was not born to a Mother who was lawfully domiciled in this country."[24] The solicitor general disagreed and argued that Missana's status as an inadmissible immigrant was irrele-

[22] Maria Ricci [pseud.], INS file 53438/11 (1906); DJA-INS, acc. 60 A 600, box 443; INS, DC, RG85; NA, DC. In a similar case, Renee Martin was detained at Philadelphia Hospital and gave birth to an illegitimate child in 1911. The department recommended that Martin be admitted under bond, accompanied by her newborn child, and did not offer any ruling on the status of her child. Renee Martin [pseud.], INS file 53438/11 (1906); DJA-INS, acc. 60 A 600, box 443; INS, DC, RG85; NA, DC.

[23] Gina Missana [pseud.], INS file 54331/50 (1918–); DJA-INS, acc. 60 A 600, box 1026; INS, DC, RG85; NA, DC.

[24] In their final report, immigration officials also focused on Missana's conduct and the child's illegitimacy.

vant and incidental to the fact of birth. Mother and daughter, however, were returned to Italy.[25]

The status of children born on the border reinscribed the legal topography of citizenship. In finding these children not to be citizens of the United States, officials blended theories of citizenship by birth into those of citizenship by blood. Missana's daughter was not a citizen because her mother was not admissible. In evaluating the claims of these border children, the status of their mothers mattered. In essence, inadmissible women immigrants could not give birth to admissible citizen children.

Under the Fourteenth Amendment, every child born in the United States was a citizen. The civic status of two groups of children, however, revealed significant practical limitations to the law's universal embrace. Children born outside the black and white limits of naturalization law and those born in the space between arrival and admittance were beyond the race and place assumptions of citizenship.

THE MULTIPLIER EFFECT: REGULATING MOTHERS OF CITIZENS

If the Fourteenth Amendment threatened to create a porous border, than immigrant mothers were to blame. Early arguments linking biology, race, and reproduction contrasted immigrant women's fecundity with the declining birth rate of native-born women. In 1891, Francis Walker, economist and superintendent of the federal census, charged that foreign immigration created economic and reproductive competition where none had existed before. Confronted with the squalor of immigrant communities, "houses that were mere shells for human habitations, the gate unhung, the shutters flapping for falling, green pools in the yard, babes and young children rolling about half naked or worse, neglected, dirty, unkempt," Americans "shrank from the industrial competition thus thrust upon him," Walker explained.[26] Americans had fewer children to preserve their standard of living, he argued. The tragic result, however, was their retreat from the field of national culture, leaving Anglo-America to the non-Americans. Immigration was the cause, competition the process, and displacement and degradation the inevitable outcome.[27]

[25] Gina Missana [pseud.], INS file 54331/50 (1918–); DJA-INS, acc. 60 A 600, box 1026; INS, DC, RG85; NA, DC.

[26] General Francis Walker, "Immigration and Degradation," Forum 11 (March/August, 1891). Mae Ngai discusses the significance of the Census Bureau in the development of racial categories and immigration exclusion laws: Ngai, "Illegal Aliens and Alien Citizens: United States Immigration Policy and Racial Formation, 1924–1945," (Ph.D. diss., Columbia University, New York, 1998).

[27] Census figures seemed to suggest that native-born women were having fewer children than foreign born women. The federal censuses for 1890, 1900, and 1910 revealed high

This reproductive race model apportioned blame to both fertile immigrant women and less fertile native-born women alike. Immigrant women's reproduction became the focus of careful study by the Dillingham Commission, which included an analysis of the fecundity of immigrant women in its 1911 multivolume report to Congress.[28] Immigration restrictionists argued that reproduction created an unchecked and insatiable engine of difference. George B. Benham, member of the San Francisco Asiatic Exclusion League, for example, decried the "inexhaustible fountain of human life now confined beyond the Asiatic shores of the Pacific."[29] Theodore Roosevelt charged native-born white Protestant women with race suicide for their failure to reproduce at rates that would maintain the ascendancy of Anglo-Saxon culture and fortify the dominance of the Caucasian race.

The science of biological engineering gained force over the first decades of the twentieth century and reached the peak of its power and popularity in the 1920s.[30] Ideas of race and reproduction became central to arguments evaluating the impact of immigration on American society. In addition to an explanatory model based in economic competition, newer biologistic arguments emphasizing inheritance and sexual selection influenced how policy makers understood the relationship between reproduction, immigration, and citizenship. Informed by Mendelian gene theory and Darwinian natural selection, concern about immigrant women's fecundity was nuanced by anxieties about the impact of "cross breeding" on

---

birth rates among the foreign-born. The data also revealed, however, that second-generation daughters of immigrant women had fewer children than their mothers. Moreover, long-term projections revealed that American birth rates had been declining steadily, a pattern mirrored in the more recent experiences of immigrant women and second-generation native-born women. Fueled by nativism and anti-immigrant sentiment, few noted the long-term trends and most assumed instead a causal factor between native-born women's falling birth rate and the presence of increasing numbers of immigrants. By the 1920s and 1930s, scholars began to revise Walker's reproductive competition thesis: Joseph J. Spengler, "The Decline in Birth-Rate of the Foreign Born," *Scientific Monthly* 32 (January–June, 1931): 54–59; Maurice R. Davie, "Immigration and the Declining Birthrate," *Scientific Monthly* 19 (July–December 1924): 68–76.

[28] *Fecundity of Immigrant Women, Reports of the Immigration Commission Presented by Mr. Dillingham*, 1911, vol. 65; United States Senate, 61st Cong., 2nd sess., Washington, D.C.

[29] Geo. B. Benham, *The Asiatic Problem and American Opinions* (San Francisco: Asiatic Exclusion League, 1908), 6, in Japanese Immigration Pamphlets, Green Library, Stanford University.

[30] The eugenicist movement and the fear of race suicide have been treated in greater depth in Jacobson, *Whiteness of a Different Color*: Elaine Tyler May, *Barren in the Promised Land: Childless Americans and the Pursuit of Happiness* (New York: Basic Books, 1995); Linda Gordon, *Woman's Body, Woman's Right: Birth Control in America* (New York: Penguin Books, 1990); Higham, *Strangers in the Land*.

efforts to preserve "racial hygiene" and the Ango-American genetic "stock." Whereas earlier arguments had emphasized the reproduction of whole communities defined as racially other, by the 1920s eugenicists warned that the foreign menace could be neither maintained nor isolated within a separate community. Once inside genetic difference would, through interethnic and interracial unions, irrevocably degrade the nation as a biological whole.

Immigrant women from southern and eastern Europe, Asia, Latin America, and Mexico reproduced unwanted difference. Eugenicists argued that immigration laws that allowed these morally wanting, physically defective, or racially inferior women immigrants to enter the United States posed a grave threat to the nation's homogenous gene pool and thus its ultimate survival. In *The Passing of the Great Race* (1916), Madison Grant alerted the nation to the permeability of its borders, its families, and its biological unity to new genetic types. Immigrant women, Grant suggested, were the racial and genetic Other. According to Grant, "Whether we like to admit it or not, the result of the mixture of two races, in the long run, gives us a race reverting to the more ancient, generalized and lower type. The cross between a white man and an Indian is an Indian; the cross between a white man and a negro is a negro; the cross between a white man and a Hindu is a Hindu; and the cross between any of the three European races and a Jew is Jew."[31]

Nonassimilable women immigrants, eugenicists warned, gave birth to citizen children who remained culturally and racially other despite their civic status. In 1921 testimony before Congress, H. H. Laughlin of the Eugenics Research Association in Cold Spring Harbor, Long Island, put congressional committee members on notice: "In the last report that I read from the schools for delinquents at Whittier, Calif., and at Gainesville, Tex., about half of the names were American and the other half were Mexican or foreign sounding—names of delinquents of foreign stock who, in the case of Texas, has penetrated almost up to the Oklahoma border line."[32] One year earlier, the governor of Hawaii emphasized that

[31] Madison Grant, *Passing of the Great Race; or, The Racial Basis of European History* (New York: Charles Scribner's Sons, 1916), as quoted in Jacobson, *Whiteness of a Different Color*, 81. Compare Grant's approach with Earnest K. Coulter, deputy clerk of the New York Children's Court. Coulter concluded that the "lower order, morally and intellectually" of immigrants to the United States created separate settlements in the nation's cities isolated from "American ideas of wellbeing and citizenship." The threat for Coulter was not in the intermingling of immigrant and native but in their cultural and spatial division. "In these colonies," Coulter warned, "they are peoples unto themselves." Coulter, "Alien Colonies and the Children's Court," *North American Review* 179 (November 1904): 731–740; quotes appear on 731–732.

[32] Mr. H. H. Laughlin, *Biological Aspects of Immigration: Hearings before the Committee on Immigration and Naturalization*, 1921, Washington, D.C.

arrival of Japanese women led to ever greater numbers of nonwhite babies born in Hawaii. "And I am inclined to think," the governor concluded, "that another reason for the wives of these orientals to have these Hawaiian birth certificates is that later on they can prove their eligibility to draw our lands as American citizens."[33]

California Senator James Phelan responded to the growing presence of Japanese immigrants in Hawaii by proposing a constitutional amendment to limit birthright citizenship to those included within the biracial limits of naturalization law. Denying U.S. citizenship to native-born children of Asian ancestry, Phelan insisted, would work "to discourage their coming here and to render them innocuous when they do come."[34] In Phelan's scheme, ideas of race difference were fused onto those of national distinction to preserve a "cultural essence" unique to the Anglo-Saxon society of the United States by enforcing separate cultural, civic, historical, and biological development for the world's varied races.

Robert Foerster, a professor of economics at Princeton and an eager proponent of eugenics-based policies, used his 1925 report to the secretary of labor as an opportunity to link fears of miscegenation to those of foreign immigration. While cultural difference could act as a "barrier" to "prevent intermarriage," "absorption into the general population" was "only a question of time." Even color, Foerster concluded, "the most powerful of all barriers," was "far from insuperable; and there seems no reason to suppose that in the course of long time negroes and whites in the United States will not be indistinguishably blended."[35] The children who resulted from these blended unions were citizens by birth and their increasing presence would work to recolor American society.

Despite a dramatic shift in women's legal position with the 1920 voting rights amendment and the 1922 Cable Act, immigrant women continued to be perceived as a threat to the nation primarily because of their roles as mothers. With independent citizenship, home, marriage, and family remained central to how women's claims to political equality were assessed.[36] Domesticity took on a new political valence as immigrant women's reproductive roles were tied to their newly acquired political responsibilities.

---

[33] Governor McCarthy, *Japanese in Hawaii: Hearing before a Subcommittee of the Committee on Immigration,* 1920, S 3206; United States Senate, 66th Cong., 2nd sess., Washington, D.C., 20–21.

[34] Ibid.

[35] Robert F. Foerster, "The Racial Problems Involved in Immigration from Latin America and the West Indies to the United States," *Report Submitted to the Secretary of Labor, James J. Davis* (Washington, D.C.: Government Printing Office, 1925), 56.

[36] A 1930 amendment to the Cable Act listed women who could be excluded from its provisions as those women with diseases, polygamists, prostitutes, criminals, those previously deported, and contract laborers.

GOOD MORAL CHARACTER: SEX AND THE WOMAN CITIZEN

If women gave birth to citizens, then sex mattered. And if the Cable Act signaled a gradual shift in citizenship law toward gender neutrality, then older efforts to regulate women's private and public sexuality became intimately linked to newer efforts to apportion women's citizenship. Marriage and marital fidelity remained central concerns in evaluating women's applications for independent citizenship. Prostitutes who offered sex for hire outside the home were placed beyond the pale of American motherhood and American citizenship.[37] Women who had sexual liaisons beyond the bounds of legal marriage were judged as lacking in the moral qualities necessary for a citizen.[38] "Good moral character" had been a statutory requirement since the earliest naturalization laws, and all applicants were required to demonstrate good moral character for the five years proceeding their application to citizenship.[39] What exactly constituted "good moral character," however, was left unspecified until 1952.[40]

In its 1934 report to Congress, the Ellis Island Committee criticized a set of laws that demanded immigrant women remain chaste for life while excluding them from membership in the nation: "If, for instance, a girl who was brought to the U.S. as a baby in arms and who has lived here continuously until she is twenty-five or more, should then become a prostitute, she would, if still an alien, be liable to deportation to the country of which she is a citizen."[41] Sex was often taken as evidence of prostitution.[42] Orsola Sabino had lived in the United States since she was eighteen

---

[37] Neither could immigrant women charged with prostitution take advantage of expeditious naturalization procedures offered to any person marrying a United States citizen after 1934.

[38] Kathleen Adams, a twenty-six-year-old Jamaican dressmaker, was arrested for solicitation in 1939. Immigration authorities noted that Adams was married, but separated from her husband, and living "out of wedlock" with another man. "Reports to Central Authorities for Calendar Year 1939," INS file 55965/8 (1939); DJA-INS, acc. 58 A 734, box 1288; INS, DC, RG85; NA, DC.

[39] Prostitution, bigamy, adultery, and conducting a disorderly house, were placed alongside manslaughter or second-degree murder as offenses that negated good moral character. Milton R. Konvitz, *Civil Rights in Immigration* (Ithaca, N.Y.: Cornell University Press, 1953), 152.

[40] The Immigration and Naturalization Act of 1952 specified in the list excludable behaviors habitual drunkard, adultery, crimes involving moral turpitude, prostitution, a gambler or committed gambler, a convicted murder, and "the fact that any person is not within any of the foregoing classes shall not preclude a finding that for other reasons such person is or was not of good moral character." This final clause continued the infamous tradition of judicial interpretation and confusion.

[41] *Report of the Ellis Island Committee* (New York, 1934), 75.

[42] See *In the Matter of M———*, 2 I&N December 530 (BIA 1946).

months old. Married at twenty, she separated from her husband after three years and began living with Giovanni Balleiri, or John Blair, and calling herself Alice Blair. In 1924 she was arrested and convicted for vagrancy and prostitution. While in prison, Sabino was diagnosed with venereal disease and treated at the hospital. During her convalescence, she was sent to the Home of the Good Shepherd, where she resided when deportation proceedings were begun.[43]

In contrast to INS officials, by the mid-1930s the courts held to a decidedly modern interpretation of "prostitution." Women who occasionally had sex outside of marriage, or women who frequented places where prostitution was practiced did not fall within the court's definition of prostitution as sex work, work that was semipermanent and provided a woman with the bulk of her income.[44] "Unchastity," as one court explained, "is not proof of prostitution."[45] Yet the emphasis on conduct rather than conviction meant that immigration officials had license to inquire into immigrant women's personal, private sexual lives for evidence of immoral prostitute-like behavior.[46] Immigration officials argued forcefully for the links between prostitution and sex as they investigated immigrant women's sexual experiences. Immigrant women who had sex outside of marriage denied that they were professional prostitutes, and in their hearings with immigration officials, they attempted to differentiate single, isolated immoral acts from prostitution.[47]

With so much subject to bureaucratic and judicial interpretation, and with so much at stake, women immigrants faced a minefield of social custom and community inhibitions in their applications to citizenship. Demonstration of "moral character" could prove an exacting standard. Beginning in the 1930s and continuing into the post–World War II period, for example, women living in nonmarital or extramarital relationships were viewed as lacking in the "good moral character" necessary for citi-

---

[43] While she admitted to having solicited a policeman for five dollars, the crime she was convicted for, Sabino denied any history of prostitution. The court agreed, ruling, "The proof is at best (or worst) of an isolated act, and there is no evidence at all of pursuing the habit as a vocation. *United States ex rel. Mittler v. Curran, Commission of Immigration* 8 F.2d 355 (2nd Cir. 1925).

[44] By 1934, the Supreme Court sought to distinguish between prostitution and other lesser offenses against marriage and morality. Writing for the court, Justice Roberts argued that extramarital relations, short of concubinage, were not included under the statute as they were not of a like character with prostitution. *Hansen v. Haff, Acting Commissioner of Immigration* 291 U.S. 559 (1934). Also see *United States ex re Mantler v. Commissioner of Immigration* 3 F.2d 234 (2nd Cir. 1924).

[45] *Hansen v. Haff* 291 U.S. 559 (1934).

[46] Roberts, "Sex and the Immigration Law," 12.

[47] See for example, *In the Matter of U———*, 6 I&N December 743 (BIA 1955).

zenship.[48] In a 1937 handwritten letter addressed to "My Dear Mrs. Roosevelt," Theresa More asked the First Lady to help her become a citizen:

> I would like to become an American citizen although I am not married I have two children born here in Brooklyn, a boy seventeen a girl fifteen. I came here nineteen years ago from Canada, although not a bad woman. I am known here as Mrs. Howard More. His common law wife. I feel this is going to interfere with my becoming an American citizen. I feel I am going to be deported as I understand there will be a new law this January. I do so want to become a citizen. Won't you please give your consent? I will be waiting patiently for your answer.
>
> Sincerely yours,
Theresa More[49]

More's fears that her common law marriage would be judged as evidence of immoral conduct, and thus grounds for a denial, were well founded. Before 1947, even long-term, monogamous relationships between non-married couples could provide grounds for denial.[50] Women found guilty of adultery were often denied their applications to citizenship.[51]

MOTHER CITIZENS: THE EQUAL NATIONALITY ACT

The links between women's sexuality, racial exclusion, and the reproduction of difference surfaced in debates over women's equal nationality rights during the early 1930s. As had been true in decades past, anxieties about race, reproduction, and gender difference were tightly yoked. Proposals to allow women to pass their American citizenship onto their children raised the specter of morally, ethnically, or racially undesirable women reproducing citizens. The threat of this multiplier effect provided

---

[48] Edith Lowenstein, *The Alien and the Immigration Law: A Study of 1446 Cases Arising Under the Immigration and Naturalization Laws of the United States* (New York: Common Council for American Unity, 1957), 293–297.

[49] More had originally emigrated in 1918; INS file 23/32771 (1938); RCO, entry 26, box 819, 23/32651–23/32837; INS, DC, RG85; NA, DC.

[50] Beginning in 1947, Judge Learned Hand, writing for the Second Circuit Court of Appeals, offered some flexibility in the moral standard to reevaluate adultery. Heterosexual couples recognized as man and wife in their communities and by their long-term committed relationships, who would legalize their relationship if they could, Hand argued, were not technically adulterous and thus not lacking in good moral character. *Petitions of Rudder, et al.* 159 F.2d 695 (2nd Cir. 1947).

[51] Emma Wold, "Alien Women vs. the Immigration Bureau," 217–219. Wold argued that women immigrants were treated more fairly by the courts than they were by immigration officials.

a powerful emotional weapon for immigration restrictionists, eugenicists, and social conservatives seeking to limit access to American citizenship.[52]

Historically, citizenship followed paternity. Before the 1920s, mothers could not pass citizenship status onto their children because as wives they had no nationality of their own. The 1922 Cable Act and its 1930s amendments separating marriage and citizenship provided wives with naturalization but did not offer mothers the ability to pass their citizenship onto their children.[53] Derivative citizenship remained a male prerogative, linking whole families within a single civic identity routed through fathers. Only in the case of illegitimacy would the citizenship of a child follow that of her mother; an illegitimate child was her mother's sole responsibility.

The debate over extending to mothers the right of derivative citizenship for their children reveals the significance of race and reproduction to women's equal nationality rights. In 1933 testimony before the House Committee on Immigration and Naturalization, the extension of full and equal citizenship privileges to women was perceived by many as a direct threat to efforts to prohibit the arrival of racially ineligible and economically undesirable immigrants. Andrew Furuseth, president of the International Seamen's Union of America, warned the committee that the proposed extension of equal citizenship rights to mothers threatened the nation's ability to protect itself from the proliferation of unwanted Asian laborers. According to Furuseth, "The proposition that a man who was born here may transmit his citizenship through a woman that is not born here leaves the door open so that you can largely destroy your Chinese exclusion act, that is all." Furuseth's comments suggest that he misunderstood the effect of the legislation being discussed. His fear that race would be reproduced through Asian women, however, speaks to persistent anxieties about immigrant women, particularly those labeled racially undesirable.[54] Fred Ryons, legislative chair of the Military Order of the World War, linked racial undesirability to gender difference and economic dependency. "The skimmed milk of the problem is that a large number of the

---

[52] As Candice Bredbenner suggests, not everyone opposed to legislation allowing women to pass citizenship onto their children employed racialized arguments. The State Department feared that the legislation would both increase the number of Americans living abroad who had little connection to the United States, and lead to a growing number of children with dual citizenship. Bredbenner, *A Nationality of Her Own*, 226–242.

[53] *In re Citizenship Status of Minor Children where Mother Alone Becomes Citizen through Naturalization* 25 F.2d 210 (D.N.J. 1928).

[54] Statement of Andrew Furuseth, *Relating to Naturalization and Citizenship Status of Children whose Mothers are Citizens of the United States, and Relating to the Removal of Certain Inequalities in Matters of Nationality*, 1933, HR 3673, HR 77; Committee on Immigration and Naturalization House of Representatives, 73 Cong., 1st sess., Washington, D.C., 23.

mothers are poor," Ryons suggested, "and their children from one to twenty-one years of age would become public charges."[55]

This 1933 congressional discussion of women's ability to pass their American citizenship onto their children provided a forum to express more general anxieties about nonwhite citizens. The distinction between those rights gained through parentage and those acquired through place of birth blurred in critiques fearful of the reproduction of racialized citizens. Charles Kramer, a representative from California, argued that the extension of derivative citizenship to mothers would only increase the number of racially undesirable children entitled to state services as citizens. "We have Japs and Hawaiian boys and girls attending the public schools," Kramer explained, "sitting at the same benches with American children." "We are obliged to educate these Japs," Kramer continued, "because they are born here and they become American citizens."[56] In the midst of an economic disaster of global proportions, the distinction between Americans and non-Americans took on heightened significance. Representative William Traeger, also from California, suggested that the combined rights of citizenship by birth and those by blood menaced California's efforts to rid itself of Mexican nationals and their Mexican American citizen-children during the mass deportation drives of the early 1930s:

Those nationals remained in Los Angeles County long enough to produce children. Those children naturally, being born on the soil of the U.S. or under its jurisdiction, became citizens of the U.S. We have sent as many as 12,000 back to Mexico in one month. Those children, born in LA County, will remain in Mexico until there is some way of getting them back into the U.S. Suppose the female of the family remains in Mexico long enough to raise her own family. Then she is entitled to bring all of those back to the U.S. when they return.[57]

Women reproduced difference, critics insisted, and they should not be provided the reins of law with which to harness their folly. Martin Dies, representative from Texas, echoed Traeger's concerns. Rights by blood would only confound the racial havoc that rights by birth had created for California and Texas. "The States that are on the border," Dies explained, "are faced with the danger of having to let in every child that is born of aliens, because that child becomes an American citizen and is entitled to

[55] Statement of Fred Ryons, *Relating to Naturalization and Citizenship Status of Children*, 31.

[56] Statement of Charles Kramer, *Relating to Naturalization and Citizenship Status of Children*, 25–26.

[57] Traeger noted that Hawaii faced a similar threat from Japanese immigrants. Statement of William Traeger, *Relating to Naturalization and Citizenship Status of Children*, 41.

vote," creating a problem without end as "his children may go back and marry Mexicans." Mexicans who married across the border, Dies insisted, were unworthy citizens, "ignorant," "subject to boss control, " and "very difficult to deal with."[58] The American Federation of Labor decried the current state of law that created "the spectacle of Chinese, Japanese, or Hindus domiciled in the United States or Hawaii who are married either to women of their own race or some other race, begetting children and such children become, under the fourteenth amendment, citizens of the United States." To allow racially other mothers to pass citizenship to their children "simply doubles the number and the evil" practiced on white American communities.[59]

Even proponents of the legislation drew race into their lexicon. In their demands for equality, some women activists linked the rights of citizenship to privileges of race. Ruth Taunton, representing the Business Women's Legislative Council of California, reminded the House committee that a native-born white woman who married a non-American abroad could not offer citizenship to her children. A Chinese American man, however, could, and did, arriving at California's ports with "a half dozen little Chinese children, none of whom have ever seen this country and none of whom speak the English language." Racial equality in *jus soli* citizenship mocked the gender inequalities of *jus sanguinis*. "You are turning away a white child," Taunton scolded, "and letting in a yellow."[60]

In 1934 Congress passed, and President Roosevelt approved, the Equal Nationality Act, providing American mothers the opportunity to pass their citizenship on to their children at birth. The act also required that a child born to a native or naturalized American parent had to live in the United States at least five years before assuming citizenship rights. This prevented the reproduction of foreign-born American families by requiring citizens to return and reside within the United States before assuming citizenship.

As had been true during earlier arguments over tighter immigration restrictions, gender, race, and reproduction were woven through 1930s debates over women's equal nationality rights. Through a multiplier effect, critics insisted, women immigrants bred difference within the nation—a difference legalized through citizenship, and one creating children who were entitled to social services, legal representation, and permanent

---

[58] Statement of Martin Dies, *Relating to Naturalization and Citizenship Status of Children*, 40.

[59] William C. Hushing, legislative representative, American Federation of Labor, "Brief for the American Federation of Labor," *Relating to Naturalization and Citizenship Status of Children*, 46.

[60] Statement of Ruth Taunton, *Relating to Naturalization and Citizenship Status of Children*, 49.

membership. Reproduction was hard to control and undermined a careful system of legal inclusion and exclusion built on categories of race, physical, mental, educational, and economic difference. Reproduction mattered because children mattered, not only as sites of difference but as members of families entitled and encouraged by immigration law to remain with their parents.

CHAPTER TEN

Women in Need

If the presence of women and their children raised fears about racial difference, they also provoked anxieties about poverty and dependency. During the height of the Great Depression, few immigrants could claim to be free of the shadow of poverty. "Likely to become a public charge" (LPC) provided a malleable language of possibility that allowed the law to respond to changes in labor markets, social welfare, and women's role in the economy over the course of the twentieth century. By the mid-1930s, LPC was applied with greater frequency and greater vigor by immigration authorities, contributing to drastic reductions in the number of immigrants arriving into the United States through the 1930s and early 1940s. As the number of new arrivals dropped precipitously, the focus of social reform and administrative policy shifted inward and away from the nation's borders. Concerns about race and gender were increasingly expressed through the issue of economic self-sufficiency.

The depression unleashed calls for a relief program that distinguished between immigrant residents and American citizens. As the circle of national membership contracted during the economic pain of the 1930s, long-term residents were perceived as immediate economic liabilities rather than future American citizens. Just as many Americans demanded that federal jobs be reserved exclusively for citizens, local and federal authorities applied LPC liberally seeking to contain burgeoning welfare roles. "Voluntary deportation" policies, once a little used administrative tool, expanded through the 1930s, as federal immigration authorities and state government officials repatriated immigrants who had become dependent on public funds.

Older understandings of need rooted in an individual's failings were thrown into crisis by a global economic collapse that was structural in cause and indiscriminate in effect. Because civic identity was yoked to both work and welfare, citizenship took on a new valence. The implementation of federal and state relief policies to alleviate the effects of poverty distinguished between citizens and noncitizens in ways that raised central questions about the rights of each. For whom was the nation responsible? What was the relationship between work, residency, relief, and the privileges of citizenship?

A NATION IN NEED: POVERTY AND THE RIGHTS OF CITIZENSHIP

The collapse of the stock market in 1929 threw the economy into turmoil and also disrupted traditional understandings of the relationship between skill, effort, and work, on the one hand, and race, deficiency, and want, on the other. Skilled, well-paid jobs traditionally held by men and protected by unions went into steep decline. Where the railroads, coal mines, and steel plants of the industrial economy led, the nation soon followed. Ironically, the newly emerging service sector staffed by women, both native and foreign, would be the first to recover as it molded itself into the new fiscal constraints and market demands of the later twentieth century.[1]

Without the promise of ready work at a significant wage, European men elected to remain in their home countries rather than risk the expense of a transatlantic trip for uncertain gain. Beginning in 1930, women comprised the majority of immigrants arriving in the United States. Male migration had been declining since the implementation of severe restrictions in 1917, 1921, and 1924; it reached historic lows by 1930.[2] For the first time since the Civil War, immigration fell below 100,000 and the number of departures exceeded the number of arrivals.[3]

In his 1930 address to Congress, President Hoover informed Congress that administrative efforts would be made to limit any new immigration: "Under conditions of current unemployment it is obvious that persons coming to the United States seeking work would likely become either direct or indirect public charges." Acting under directives from Hoover, laws against immigrants "likely to become a public charge" were applied with greater strictness by consuls abroad, reducing the total number of applicants awarded visas throughout the 1930s.[4]

---

[1] Ruth Milkman, "Women's Work and the Economic Crisis: Some Lessons from the Great Depression," in *A Heritage of Her Own: Toward a New Social History of American Women*, eds. Nancy Cott and Elizabeth Pleck (New York: Simon and Schuster, 1979), 507–541.

[2] *Annual Report of the Commissioner-General of Immigration* (1925), 44–45, 154–155; *Annual Report of the Commissioner-General of Immigration* (1930), 142–143, 160–161.

[3] Harry E. Hull, "Information on Immigration," *Excerpts from the Annual Report of the Commissioner General of Immigration* (1931), United States Department of Labor, 3.

[4] Ibid., 5–6; Hutchinson, *Legislative History of American Immigration Policy*, 219. The number of visas issued monthly dropped precipitously from 24,000 to 7,000. 183,540 immigrants were admitted in 1930; 97,139 were nonquota aliens (wives or children of American citizens, professors and ministers with their families). Robert Divine has calculated that within five months of adopting the rigorous LPC policy, the State Department was able to cut European immigration by ninety percent. Divine also argues that Hoover's administrative restriction policy was a response to immigration restrictionists' calls to legislate a drastic reduction in immigration quotas. Divine, *American Immigration Policy, 1924–1952* (New Haven, Conn.: Yale University Press, 1957), 78–80. There is some disagreement among

The State Department issued general instructions to consul officials that LPC be interpreted not only in light of an applicant's financial wherewithal, but also with careful attention to whether any new immigrant might indirectly cause another citizen or resident to become a public charge. The consul in Berlin, for example, required evidence that a would-be immigrant could support himself "for a long time (perhaps several years) without having to earn his living," while the consul in Geneva insisted that immigrants be able to support themselves "independent" of work, "for an undetermined period."[5] This creative application of the law was particularly effective in drastically reducing the arrival of immigrants from countries unregulated by quotas, especially Mexican laborers.[6] Even immigrants who had family living in the United States were denied visas as likely to become public charges or as likely to cause others to become public charges.[7]

Women living in the United States had a difficult time providing the necessary financial affidavits to assure consuls that their husbands and children abroad would not become public charges after arrival. White American women who married European men in the years between 1924 and 1930 had returned to the United States with the expectation that their husbands would soon follow, preference visa in hand.[8] With the onset of global economic depression and the resulting refusal on the part of U.S. officials to admit either direct or indirect public charges, husbands and wives remained separated indefinitely. A group of predominately Jewish American women, the Citizens Wives Organization (CWO), testified before the House Committee on Immigration and Naturalization in 1932, blaming overzealous application of an indiscriminate law for separating

---

historians as to Franklin Roosevelt's use of the LPC restriction. Divine argues that Roosevelt initiated no change in Hoover's administrative restriction. While the State Department issued instructions in 1937 that consuls be less rigorous in their application of LPC, there was no reversal on fundamental policy. Roger Daniels argues that the 1930 presidential policy was rescinded by Franklin Roosevelt in 1936. However, Daniels continues, many consular officials continued to use the "indirect public charge" policy. Divine, *American Immigration Policy*, 88–89; Daniels, *Coming to America: A History of Immigration and Ethnicity in American Life* (New York: Harper Collins Publishers, 1990), 295.

[5] As quoted in Florina Lasker, "Likely to Become," *Survey*, 65, no. 8 (15 January 1931): 433.

[6] The number of visas issued to Mexico dropped from 4,000 to 250 per month, Hutchinson, *Legislative History of American Immigration Policy*, 219. Marian Schibsby, "The New Plan for Reducing Immigration to the United States," *Interpreter Releases* 7, no. 37 (27 October 1930), RACNS, reel 2.

[7] Lasker, "Likely to Become," 433–434; Bredbenner, *A Nationality of Her Own*, 175–176.

[8] The 1924 National Origins Act had offered nonquota status to the wives of citizens, while offering only preferential status for the husbands of U.S. citizens.

families.[9] The State Department expressed concerns that these women were using marriage as a vehicle to ease the arrival of Polish Jews, but the women of the CWO responded that as naturalized citizens, gainfully employed, and free of public assistance they were entitled and capable of supporting their immigrant husbands.[10]

At the House committee hearings, arguments pointing to women's diminished earning capacity, especially during a time of growing economic uncertainty, were countered with more universal claims to family unity and the rights of citizens. "Can a girl living here, a citizen," Albert Johnson queried, "support a husband and bring him here when she is making $30 a week?"[11] Through bank statements, employment records, and wage histories, the women of the Citizen's Wives Organization sought to assure the committee that indeed they could.[12] Ruth Bell Bielski testified that she had "all intentions" to support her husband on the "thirty dollars average" she earned weekly sewing underwear. Sarah Shiffman Rosenberg insisted that she planned on supporting her husband and their seven-month-old child on the thirty-six dollars monthly income.

Arthur Free, a Republican representative from California and staunch opponent of immigration, questioned the women about the sincerity of their marriages, the wisdom of their plans to support their husbands financially, and the economic consequences of any additional immigration during a period of economic contraction. When Miriam Zeli Flaschenberg testified that while her husband was unemployed, she earned twenty-eight dollars a week as a fringing operator, Free retorted, "And you expect to support your husband out of that?" When pushed by Free about her suggestion that she could support herself and her husband on twenty dollars a week, Gussie Rosenkranz Bradfeld responded, "Well, surely; why not; why can't I support him on that amount; and I make a very nice salary?"[13]

[9] To Exempt from the Quota Husbands of American Citizen Wives and to Limit the Presumption that Certain Alien Relatives May Become Public Charges: Hearings before the Committee on Immigration and Naturalization 1932, HR 5869, HR 7614, S 2656; House of Representatives, 72nd Cong., 1st sess., Washington, D.C. One hundred and sixty-five women belonged to the Citizen's Wives Organization. Most of the women had immigrated to the United States in the early 1920s from Poland. Most had been naturalized five years later, and 133 had married Polish men in 1930.

[10] Bredbenner details the multiyear struggle between the visa office and the CWO, Bredbenner, A Nationality of One's Own, 174–182.

[11] To Exempt from the Quota Husbands of American Citizen Wives, 2.

[12] The vast majority of women identified themselves as needle workers or factory operatives earning under forty dollars a week (sixty-eight earned between eighteen and thirty dollars a week, seventy earned between thirty-one and forty dollars a week). Eighty women had saved between one thousand and two thousand dollars.

[13] To Exempt from the Quota Husbands of American Citizen Wives, 2–8, 39–41, 44–47.

In the end, Congress proved receptive to the concerns of the CWO women and their supporters that charges of LPC were being applied by European consuls with unwarranted severity.[14] One year after the women testified before Congress, one hundred and nineteen of their husbands had received visas, and Congress passed legislation to allow those husbands married before 1932 to enter as nonquota immigrants.[15]

As the federal government acted both to restrict new arrivals and to create a social welfare system, citizenship took on increasing importance. Technically, five years separated immigrants from citizens. In practice, however, time proved discretionary. Immigrants found to be dependent on public or private assistance could be deported at any time if immigration officials suspected that the root of their poverty lay in physical, mental, or moral defects that predated their arrival. Despite long term residencies in the United States, non-naturalized immigrants who left for a brief visit abroad to see relatives or retrieve children could find themselves excluded as LPC upon return. Carmela Iovine, a seventy-year-old widow who had entered the United States twenty-one years earlier, was excluded as LPC in 1936 when she returned from a brief trip to visit her children in Italy. Her niece, whom she had raised, declined to support her and requested that her aunt be returned to Italy. Without familial or financial support, Iovine was a likely public charge. Despite legal appeals, Iovine was deported as LPC.[16]

In the face of diminishing relief resources, laws against immigrants becoming public charges penalized those who took advantage of direct relief, jobs programs, and financial services. As financial collapse became a protracted crisis, local relief services were stretched thin.[17] By 1932,

---

[14] Robert Divine notes that under criticism from Samuel Dickstein, chair of the House Committee on Immigration, and other proimmigrant groups, the State Department ordered American consuls to review the applications of those relatives of citizens and resident aliens who had been denied visas. As a result, Divine concludes, by 1934 fewer than two percent of relatives who applied for visas were denied. Divine, *American Immigration Policy*, 88.

[15] Bredbenner, *A Nationality of Her Own*, 182–183. The legislation recognizing marriages solemnized before 1932 was an uneasy compromise between restrictionists and advocates for greater compassion in immigration law. Those men married to citizen wives after the effective date of the act remained preference immigrants.

[16] *United States ex rel. Minuto v. Reimer, Com'r of Immigration and Naturalization* 83 F.2d 166 (2nd Cir. 1936). Iovine testified in court that her niece owed her money, which may account for her niece's insistence that her aunt be deported. A friend expressed willingness to support Iovine, but could not furnish adequate bond.

[17] In his discussion of WPA policy, Donald S. Howard, assistant director for the Charity Organization Department of the Russell Sage Foundation, notes that by 1939 employment on public works projects was restricted by law to U.S. citizens, Native Americans, and others owing allegiance to the United States (Filipinos). The 1939 law, Howard suggests, was the culmination of steady efforts on the part of federal policy makers to limit the number of noncitizens employed by the WPA. As a result, noncitizens were forced to turn to state

applications for relief had increased by forty percent, and many relief agencies collapsed. By 1933, one-third of the American workforce was out of work.[18]

The expanding role of federal and state governments in people's everyday lives meant greater scrutiny and greater risks for immigrants. Concetta Matterazza married an American citizen in 1932 and moved to Rochester from Italy a year later. Though her husband was briefly employed by a civilian works program, the family needed additional assistance. The Matterazza's application for relief, however, was denied in 1933 and again 1934. While on a return trip to Italy to retrieve her son, Matterazza's husband was committed to the Rochester State Hospital for the Insane. Upon her return, Matterazza applied for citizenship and attempted to take advantage of federal mortgage programs to gain necessary funds for herself and her son. Her successful application for relief, however, brought her to the attention of immigration authorities, who deported her and her son as LPC.[19]

Economic crisis divided long-term residents, like Matterazza, from citizens. As long as a woman remained a noncitizen, she remained subject to immigration law. Naturalized immigrants, like native-born citizens, had the right to ask for and receive relief. Immigrants who had last entered the U.S. more than five years before could also request relief without consequence providing that they had entered legally and that they did not belong to any excludable class (defined most commonly by disease, mental defect, race, literacy, moral character, criminal record, and poverty). Immigrants whose last entry was less than five years before, however, risked deportation if they asked for or received assistance from state or private charities. State-sponsored services automatically provided the names of immigrants to INS authorities; private charities or hospitals could at their own discretion report recipients to immigration officials. Immigrants were held for deportation either on charges that they became public charges for reasons previous to their entry (e.g., physical or mental disability) or that they belonged to one of the excluded classes and should never have been allowed to enter (e.g., prostitution, LPC, disease).[20]

In a climate of scarcity, immigrant women's status was precarious. Women who applied for relief or who received public health services risked being deported as public charges. Alice Love Woodhead arrived in

---

and private assistance, much to the frustration of local welfare officials. Howard, *The WPA and Federal Relief Policy* (New York: Russell Sage Foundation, 1943), 303–315.

[18] Frances Fox Piven and Richard A. Cloward, *Regulating the Poor: The Functions of Public Welfare* (New York: Vintage Books, 1971), 49, 55.

[19] *United States ex rel. Matterazza v. Fogarty* 13 F.Supp. 403 (W.D.N.Y. 1936).

[20] Marian Schibsby, "Deportation on the Ground of Being a Public Charge," *Interpreter Releases* 7, no. 42 (11 December 1930), RACNS, reel 2.

the United States from Scotland in 1924 and since then had been employed as a bookkeeper without a "blot on her character." Woodhead contracted tuberculosis in 1934 and was committed to a public hospital for treatment, "her own savings and those of her family having been swept away by the long period of depression." Woodhead had made a brief trip to Canada to do some shopping with several girl friends but upon return she was excluded as LPC. The appeals court recognized that Woodhead had contracted tuberculosis while living in the United States and that she had accepted government assistance during a period of extreme national hardship. She was not, however, a citizen and as the court noted, the "hazard of her failure to do so had never been brought home to her." However, "the law is clear," the Appeals Court argued, "and however cruel the result" Woodhead was deportable as a public charge.[21]

Deportation within five years presented a particular problem for women living on either border who regularly returned to Canada or Mexico for brief visits. As in the case of Woodhead, these women may not have understood that each time they left and returned to the United States their residency status began again at day one of five years of continuous residency in the United State required to move beyond the purview of deportation law for LPC.[22] Katie Dorn and her three young daughters returned from a brief visit to her grandmother in Canada in 1937 and were excluded as LPC.[23] The family had received relief and groceries from the Chippewa County Poor Commission in 1936 after her husband lost his job at the Northern Motor Company. In his report to the commissioner-general, the Michigan inspector concluded the family "will never be entirely self-supporting" and would remain a "relief problem" for the local community.[24]

---

[21] *Zurbrick, District Director of Immigration, v. Woodhead* 90 F.2d 991 (6th Cir. 1937). Woodward was married to an American citizen: however, after the 1922 Cable Act marriage offered immigrant women neither citizenship nor relief from immigration law. See also Dora Carney [pseud.], INS file 55941/13 (1936); DJA-INS, acc. 58 A 734, box 1112; INS, DC, RG85; NA, DC.

[22] Alice W. O'Connor, a social worker with the division of Immigration and Americanization in Boston, detailed the cases of a number of Canadian woman who, despite their long residency in the United States, faced deportation after returning from a brief trip home. O'Connor, "Citizen and Domicile Versus Social Considerations in Problems of Migrated Families," *Proceedings of the National Conference of Social Work*, 62nd Annual Session, Montreal (Chicago: University of Chicago Press, 1935); 671.

[23] Dorn had first crossed the border in 1932 without any visa to visit her husband who was living and working in the United States. She testified that she had meant to legalize her status but lacked the necessary funds. Dorn was also questioned extensively about incidents of domestic violence. On two occasions the police were called to their home to restrain Dorn's husband. Immigration officials were more concerned that the couple may separate, thus leaving the wife without financial support, than they were about Dorn's safety and well-being.

[24] The commissioner-general was more tolerant in his final decision and allowed Dorn voluntary departure to Canada so that she could obtain a visa. However, it was unlikely

Dolores Lopez Nunez originally entered the United States from Mexico when she was twelve. Sixteen years later in 1937, a widow with three children and weakened by tuberculosis, Lopez Nunez faced deportation charges as LPC, a result of her brief visit to Tijuana in 1934.[25] Off and on since 1931, the family had received groceries and clothing from public charities, while government welfare offices provided ten dollars a month each for her three small American-born children. Lopez Nunez could not work and lived with her mother, sister, and her nephew, all of whom were supported by her sister's weekly wages of fifteen dollars. On hearing her appeal, the district court acknowledged that under the law, Lopez Nunez was deportable as a public charge. However, her status as the mother of three American-born children mitigated against the austerity of the law. The court reasoned that the children were the primary beneficiaries of state aid and thus the deportation of their mother would accomplish little in the law's effort to rid the nation of foreign paupers.[26] Good news was fleeting, however, for the ninth circuit court of appeals disagreed, criticizing the lower court for exceeding its jurisdiction. While the ninth circuit noted "the hardship and injustice that befalls these innocent child citizens through the execution of the law," they ruled, "the law, as it stands, leaves no room for the exercise of discretion."[27] Lopez Nunez and her three American-born children were deported and could never legally return to the United States. Once deported as LPC, an immigrant forever remained inadmissible as a likely public charge.

REMOVAL: "VOLUNTARY" DEPORTATIONS AND THE NEW NON-AMERICANS

In addition to applying laws forcefully against immigrants likely to become public charges, depression-era immigration politics also resuscitated a little used law, originally passed in 1917, which provided for the voluntary repatriation of destitute immigrants.[28] In 1933, Federal Emer-

---

that Dorn could provide the necessary evidence of financial independence to procure a visa. Katie Dorn [pseud.], INS file 55941/59 (1937); DJA-INS, acc. 58 A 734, box 1112; INS, DC, RG85; NA, DC.

[25] She has used her identification card several times for temporary visits to Tijuana since her first entry in 1922. The last time she left the United States on one of these trips was 3 August 1934, returning within a few days.

[26] *In re Nunez* 18 F.Supp. 1007 (S.D.Cal. 1937).

[27] In immigration cases the courts were limited to an evaluation of whether the warrant was properly issued and whether the hearing had been fair. *Ex parte Nunez* 93 F.2d 41 (2nd Cir. 1937).

[28] The Immigration Act of 5 February 1917 authorized the immigration service to fund the repatriation of any immigration who within three years of their last entry fell "into distress" or needed public aid for reasons that occurred subsequent to their arrival and who

gency Relief Administrator Harry L. Hopkins notified his officers that the government would fund the travel of those families of deported aliens who wished to accompany them. Immigration inspectors were instructed to ascertain whether aliens held for deportation had needy dependents who wished to accompany them. The accompanying family's departure was voluntary. However immigration officers strongly encouraged, if not pressured, dependent immigrants to accompany their deported family member.[29]

In intent, the law was based on consent and confined to the three years following an immigrant's last entry; in practice, however, the law authorizing voluntary deportation wagered the needy would readily acquiesce to repatriation if it promised any relief. Many communities compelled impoverished immigrants to take relief in the form of repatriation.[30] Elizabeth Wienke emigrated to San Francisco from the Philippines with her German-born husband and their six children in 1932. With little prospect of work and even less of a regular wage sufficient to support a family of seven, Wienke sought public aid and learned she could secure free transportation back to the Philippines. In 1936, Wienke, her husband, and their six children were voluntarily repatriated to the Islands. Three years later the family attempted to return to the United States, but having accepted public assistance to finance their voluntary departure to the Philippines they were officially and terminally LPC.[31]

Evidence suggests that like Wienke, many immigrants misunderstood the implications of voluntary repatriation. Hopeful that mobility would provide relief, families may have left with the intention of returning when the

---

asked to be sent home. On 16 February 1931, the commissioner-general revived the policy by announcing government plans to fund the repatriation of destitute aliens. In the past, the department had lacked the funding to institute the provision. Marian Schibsby, "Repatriation by the United States Government of Aliens Who Are in Need of Public Aid," *Interpreter Releases* 8, no. 8 (3 March 1931), RACNS, reel 2; Marian Schibsby, "The Repatriation of Destitute Aliens," *Interpreter Releases* 12, no. 24, series E, Interpreter Report no. 4 (23 May 1935): 203, RACNS, reel 4.

[29] Marian Schibsby, "Concerning the Removal at Government Expense of the Families of Deported Aliens," *Interpreter Releases* 10, no. 34 (9 October 1933), RACNS, reel 3; "The 1932 Session of the Permanent Conference for the Protection of Migrants," *Interpreter Releases* 9, no. 20 (17 November 1932), RACNS, reel 3. The repatriation of immigrants in families reflected resolutions passed by the Permanent Conference of the Protection of Migrants in 1932. The group encouraged participating governments to implement deportation plans that relocated families rather than individuals.

[30] Marian Schibsby, "The Repatriation of Destitute Aliens," *Interpreter Releases* 12, no. 24, series E, Interpreter Report no. 4 (23 May 1935): 208, RACNS, reel 4.

[31] *Ex parte Wienke et al.* 31 F.Supp. 733 (N.D.Cal. 1940). Mae Ngai points out that voluntary repatriation programs for Filipino residents were implemented following Philippine independence in 1934. With Philippine independence, Filipinos no longer enjoyed special status as nationals but became immigrants and aliens subject to exclusion. Ngai, "Illegal Aliens and Alien Citizens," especially 298–312; Divine, *American Immigration Policy*, 69–76.

economic darkness had lifted.[32] Once they accepted aid in the form of transportation and once their American-born children were repatriated elsewhere, however, they were permanently outside the national community. American-born Ellen Vassilakis and her family were on relief for three years in Toledo when they approached the YMCA's International Institute in 1934 for help. The family wished to be repatriated to Greece, where Vassilakis's husband came from and where they believed they could support themselves on his father's farm. With the institute's help, the family was returned to Greece at government expense. Soon after arriving, however, Vassilakis wrote to the Institute staff in desperation, anxious to return: "we havnt [sic] got anything to eat except free figs and pears and grapes i [sic] dont know what we will do this winter we havnt [sic] as much as one potato for the winter time." Vassilakis pleaded for immediate help, fearing that "we will lose our children here." In breathless prose, Vassilakis wrote directly to First Lady Eleanor Roosevelt with the hope that one of the most powerful women in the world could act to help the family:

> please write and let me know if there is any chance for us to return to America for my family cant live with this conditions here we have no home here either the lord only knows how much we are sufering there isnt any charity or welfare here the people dont care if you dye [sic] from hunger they wont give you one crumb please write at once and let me know if we can get some help please dont wait too long yours truly Mrs Ellen Vassilakis.[33]

"Voluntary" repatriation policies tied relief to removal and sought an uncomfortable alliance between immigrant aid societies, local state relief services, and the federal immigration service.[34] Roosevelt forwarded the letter to officials with the Toledo Institute, who responded to Vassilakis' letter but offered little more than a polite rebuke and distant encouragement. Their effort to remind the family that repatriation had been voluntary raises significant questions about the nature of informed consent. The Institute was "sincerely sorry" for the way "matters have developed," but responsibility, they suggested, lay with the Vassilakis's themselves. "You

<hr/>

[32] Drawing from the case files of the New York Travelers Aid Society, Marian Schibsby described the tragic experiences of four women who returned to Europe in the early 1930s. Schibsby, "The Repatriation of Destitute Aliens," *Interpreter Releases* 12, no. 24, series E, Interpreter Report no 4 (23 May 1935): 211–213, RACNS, reel 4.

[33] Ellen Vassilakis [pseud.] (1934), Unprocessed, casefiles, D-Dramond—V-Vardinakis, box 5; International Institutes of Toeldo. The letter is from Mrs. Vassilakis (although it is signed Mr. it is written in the same handwriting as the letter to Roosevelt and the institute's response is addressed to Mrs.) and is addressed to the institute worker who assisted her 20 August 1934. There is no punctuation or capitalization. The Vassilakis letter to Mrs. Roosevelt, forwarded to the Toledo office, had no punctuation and no distinct capitalization pattern.

[34] Marian Schibsby, "Deportation on the Ground of Being a Public Charge," *Interpreter Releases* 7, no. 42 (11 December 1930), RACNS, reel 2.

remember there was no urging nor compulsion," the letter hastened to add, "The State offered to pay the fare of those who *wanted* to return." "As a resourceful American bred–woman," the letter offered, "I am sure you will help your husband to work out the problems." Despite this rebuke, internal institute correspondence reveals a growing unease with the policy of repatriation. Immigrant aid societies, like the institute, were aware that local relief agencies saw "voluntary" repatriation as a way to unburden their roles. As a memo from the Institute of Immigrant Welfare explained, "we knew a family or an individual would have very little chance of a comeback once they left the U.S. with a record of local dependence and having been sent abroad on public funds."[35]

Given their limited earning potential and domestic responsibilities, women without their husbands were perceived by immigration officials and social service providers at greater risk for poverty and thus good candidates for voluntary deportation. The story of Juana Cardenas, a Mexican immigrant and a legal resident, illustrates the increasing importance of economic self-sufficiency to the process of evaluating immigrants. Cardenas's efforts to remain in the United States with her three American-born daughters despite her husband's deportation to Cuba in 1934 reveal the ways in which need and work increasingly defined the boundaries of national membership.

Immigration authorities arued that Cardenas's rightful place was with the father of her children, and they encouraged her to accompany him to Cuba.[36] Cardenas, however, was unwilling to go, wary of leaving a home she knew for one she did not. If work was scarce and life was hard in the United States, Cardenas argued, it could only be worse in Cuba. Officials of the INS prevailed and Cardenas was returned to Cuba with her husband.[37] Her husband was deported, and Cardenas was "voluntarily" repatriated, but the result was the same.

[35] In this case, Ellen Vassilakis had been encouraged to sign a letter testifying that she did not seek repatriation under the Cable Act in order to allow her to be repatriated to Greece along with her husband at government expense. Similarly, their five children had traveled under their parents' Greek passports and thus had ceased to be U.S. citizens. There was no hope of repatriation. Reports from Greece confirmed conditions of extreme poverty and notified Toledo caseworkers that Mrs. Vassilakis was hospitalized and the family was being supported by the village. The Social Service Federation of Toledo began sending money to support the American-born children. Ellen Vassilakis [pseud.] (1934), Unprocessed, casefiles, D-Dramond—V-Vardinakis, box 5; International Institutes of Toledo.

[36] The INS also assured her she could reenter the United States at any time. Later, however, they would insist Cardenas lacked any legal grounds for a return visa.

[37] On relating her story to volunteers with the International Institute in Buffalo, Cardenas confessed that she knew conditions were very bad in Cuba and she had been unwilling to return with her husband. She had been living in the United States since the age of fifteen. According to Institute staffers, however, "her wifely duty overcame her objections." Other

Cardenas returned to the United States a few months later only to face deportation when local relief providers reported her to INS authorities. Cardenas's sister was ill and her brother-in-law out of work, so neither were in any position to support Cardenas and her children. With few options, Cardenas had applied for relief. Women like Cardenas often represented their family's needs to social service providers who brought their cases to the attention of the federal authorities. Although Cardenas had immigrated to the United States from Mexico when she was a girl, she was not a citizen, and she remained subject to immigration laws excluding likely public charges.[38] Cardenas appealed her deportation, explaining to a caseworker that she had not lived in Mexico since she was a girl, that she knew few people and had no relatives living south of the border, and that she would have no way to support herself and her young American-born daughters.[39] Unable to secure her own naturalization and unable to pursuade her new husband to seek his citizenship, Cardneas could not move beyond the arms of immigration law.[40]

Mexican immigrants were at particular risk for deportation as LPC or for "voluntary" departure if they applied for public or private assistance from their local communities. The proximity of the border lowered the administrative cost of repatriation, and limited regulation allowed many immigrants to make brief visits to Mexico to visit family. Each time they returned, however, the clock began anew, beginning its slow count toward the five years necessary to avoid deportation as a public charge. Stratified labor markets and racialist understandings of work and poverty meant many Mexican immigrant families lived on the fine edge of need with few reserves to withstand prolonged economic crisis. Finally, lower rates of naturalization left Mexican immigrants subject to immigration law, of

---

than this cryptic reference, there is no explanation in the records to suggest why Cardenas changed her mind. By law, Cardenas would have to volunteer to be "returned" to Cuba. However, faced with officials from both the INS and the International Institute, Cardenas may have felt she had no choice but to consent.

[38] Held for deportation, immigration authorities argued not only that Cardenas was a public charge, but also that she had not been entitled to return from Cuba and would be deported to Mexico.

[39] Cardenas's case was referred to the Buffalo International Institute. Deportation, she maintained, would unfairly penalize her American-born daughters who would face either poverty in Cuba or Mexico with their mother or indefinite separation from their mother if they remained in the United States. On a second visit by a caseworker with the Institute, Cardenas acknowledged that she feared that the immigrant aid society was allied with immigration authorities in trying to send her out of the country.

[40] Juana Cardenas [pseud.] (1936); Unprocessed, casefiles, box 30; International Institutes of Buffalo. Wanting to maintain ties to Mexico, her new husband refused to pursue naturalization. Within a few years, however, her second husband had deserted her, and Cardenas filed for divorce.

which LPC was a significant component, even after decades of residency in the United States.[41]

Individual states such as New York, Michigan, Massachusetts, Arizona, and California proved the most proficient and enthusiastic proponents of voluntary repatriation policies.[42] Colonel D. W. MacCormak, commissioner of immigration and naturalization, attributed growing numbers of departures throughout the early 1930s to, among other things, "the action of individual State governments in assisting aliens to return to their own countries," particularly in California, "which repatriated large numbers to Mexico." Officially, the federal government affected the repatriation of approximately 5,000 immigrants between 1930 and 1934. Several counties in Southern California alone removed almost 7,000 immigrants to Mexico between 1933 and 1935.[43]

Along with those "voluntarily" deported as LPC from southern California, Los Angeles immigration and police officials raided Mexican immigrant communities searching for those who lacked proper authorization to live in the United States. In a 1931 memo to the assistant secretary of labor, the Los Angeles supervisor reported that police, sheriff, and im-

[41] Despite long residences, the number of Mexican immigrants who had been naturalized or filed their declaration of intention by 1935 varied from four percent in California to eleven percent in New Mexico. Agnes K. Hanna, "Social Services on the Mexican Border," *Proceedings of the National Conference of Social Work*, 62nd Annual Session, Montreal (Chicago: University of Chicago Press, 1935), 693. George Sánchez suggests that until the late 1930s and early 1940s Mexican immigrants were hesitant to sever their civic connections to Mexico and thus did not pursue naturalization. See Sánchez, *Becoming Mexican American*, 251–252. Abraham Hoffman argues that naturalization offered Mexican immigrants few real benefits in a society organized around racial hierarchies. See Hoffman, *Unwanted Mexican Americans in the Great Depression: Repatriation Pressures, 1929–1939* (Tucson: University of Arizona Press, 1979, 1974), 19–20.

[42] Many states passed legislation, subsequently overturned in the federal courts, authorizing the deportation of any noncitizen accepting relief. New York instituted its deportation policy in 1933. For a number of years the state had authorized funds for the voluntary repatriation of immigrants no longer deportable under federal law. The 1933 legislation expanded that policy to included the forced deportation of all inmates of public institutions or those who were deemed a charge on public funds. Similar legislation developed in Michigan was declared unconstitutional in 1931 by the U.S. District Court for the Eastern District of Michigan (*Arrowsmith v. Voorhies* 55 F.2d 310). In 1933, the Massachusetts legislature considered prohibiting public relief to noncitizens or those who remained noncitizens after ten years of residency. Likewise, Arizona considered legislation to fine corporations or companies who employed noncitizens, $300,000 for each noncitizen hired. Pennsylvania considered legislation to make it unlawful to give public aid to any immigrant unable to prove lawful entrance. Marian Schibsby, "Certain State Legislation Affecting Aliens," *Interpreter Releases* 10, no. 20 (2 May 1933), RACNS, reel 3.

[43] Testimony before the House Committee on Appropriations, January 1934, as quoted in Marian Schibsby, "The Repatriation of Destitute Aliens," *Interpreter Releases* 12, no. 24, series E, Interpreter Report no. 4 (23 May 1935): 205, RACNS, reel 4.

migration authorities worked together to canvass "the various gathering places and 'hangouts' where aliens congregate and to detain temporarily such aliens as our inspectors find upon examination to be deportable." Word traveled fast, and Mexican immigrants prepared themselves for the onslaught. "Aliens questioned within the past few days on the street and in public gathering places," the Los Angeles supervisor complained, "apparently anticipating examination, have had in their possession head tax receipts or other documents or proof of entry ready for presentation to our officers."[44] In its effort to purge Mexican and even Mexican Americans, California was not alone, for Texas and Ohio also reported active programs to voluntarily repatriate scores of Mexican immigrants who were identified as public charges. Michigan officials detailed that they repatriated almost 1,500 immigrants to Mexico who had become public charges, and Des Moines, Iowa repatriated nearly 100, including many children who had been born in the United States.[45]

As local communities patrolled their welfare roles or, as in Los Angeles, their streets and neighborhoods for deportable Mexican immigrants, many other immigrants were caught in the dragnet. While the majority of those deported were Mexican or of Mexican ancestry, Chinese, Japanese, and various European immigrants were also subject to warrant, arrest, and deportation. Los Angeles officials reported that fear of deportation spread throughout the county, with whole immigrant communities disappearing in the night. "After two or three evenings of investigations through the alien settlements along East First Street," Los Angeles inspectors reported, "the district became deserted." Japanese immigrants, officials surmised, were "warned to refuse to answer questions of Immigration officers during their investigations."[46] Officials noted it was "extremely difficult

[44] F. W. Watkins, Los Angeles Supervisor to Assistant Secretary of Labor, 8 February 1931, INS file 55739/674 (1931–); RCO, entry 9, box 505, 55739/491A–55739/930; INS, DC, RG85; NA, DC. Abraham Hoffman argues that the deportations of Mexican immigrants in 1931 were a significant component of Secretary of Labor William N. Doak's plan for increasing employment. Hoffman, *Unwanted Mexican Americans in the Great Depression*, 38–66.

[45] Testimony before the House Committee on Appropriations, January 1934, as quoted in Marian Schibsby, "The Repatriation of Destitute Aliens," *Interpreter Releases* 12, no. 24, series E, Interpreter Report no. 4 (23 May 1935), RACNS, reel 4.

[46] F. W. Watkins, Los Angeles Supervisor to Assistant Secretary of Labor, 21 February 1931, INS file 55739/674 (1931–); RCO, entry 9, box 505, 55739/491A–55739/930; INS, DC, RG85; NA, DC. This February deportation campaign was the brainchild of Charles P. Visel, head of the Los Angeles Citizens Committee on Coordination of Unemployment Relief. In cooperation with Secretary of Labor William Doak and Colonel Arthur Woods, national coordinator of the President's Emergency Committee for Emplyment, Visel hoped to scare local immigrants into returning to their native countries. Sánchez, *Becoming Mexican American*, 214; Hoffman, *Unwanted Mexican Americans in the Great Depression*, 43–63.

to break down Chinese and Japanese aliens," especially Asian prostitutes who by "retaining counsel and placing every obstacle in the way of deportation" hampered the work of immigration officials.[47]

Official tallies vastly underestimated the number of Mexican immigrants and Mexican American citizens who were summarily deposited on the southern side of the Rio Grande. Historians have estimated that close to a million Mexican American citizens and Mexican immigrant noncitizens, adults and children, were repatriated during the early 1930s. Deportation was particularly hard on women traveling alone or with their children. Mexican women faced the difficult decision of leaving family members in Los Angeles, or, alternatively, refusing to accompany husbands to Mexico.[48] There is no way of knowing how many Asian and European immigrants were deported along with them. In January 1932, for example, Juana Lopez and Dionicio Aguilar, along with their three-year-old twins, were taken by train from Los Angeles to Nogales, Arizona, and finally to Culiacan, Mexico. Thousands followed. Adolfo and Leonides Camacho and with their six children Eleuteria, Lucio, Rosario, Silvestre, Isabel, and Graciano were also deported as public charges that month. Over five hundred Mexicans and Mexican Americans were shipped out along with Lopez, Aguilar, and the Camacho family by Los Angles county authorities in January 1932, the vast majority were families with young children.[49] Those whose names were officially recorded by immigration authorities would never be able to legally reenter the United States. According to INS policy, once a public charge, always likely to become a public charge.[50] Repatriated to Mexico in 1931, Carmela Gomez and her husband secured false papers and returned to the

---

[47] F. W. Watkins, Los Angeles Supervisor to Assistant Secretary of Labor, 2 March 1931, INS file 55739/674 (1931–); RCO, entry 9, box 505, 55739/491A–55739/930; INS, DC, RG85; NA, DC.

[48] Francisco E. Balderrama and Raymond Rodríquez, *Decade of Betrayal: Mexican Repatriation in the 1930s* (Albuquerque: University of New Mexico Press, 1995).

[49] Thirty three percent were men, twenty-two percent were women, and forty-four percent were children eighteen years or younger. Ages ranged from a six-month-old girl to a ninety-eight-year-old man and his seventy-year-old wife. List of Mexican Transits, Mexicali to Nogales, Arizona, 8 January 1932 and 27 January 1932, INS file 55739/674 (1931–); RCO, entry 9, box 505, 55739/491A–55739/930; INS, DC, RG85; NA, DC. Drawing on State Department records, Balderrama and Rodríquez record that between October and November of 1930, 8,250 repatriates moved through Nuevo Laredo. Between July 1 and December 31, 1930, Nuevo Laredo officials reported 21,700 returned to Mexico. Balderrama and Rodríquez, *Decade of Betrayal*, 120–122. According to George Sánchez, approxminately one-third of the Mexican communicty living in Los Angeles was repatriated during the 1930s; see Sánchez, *Becoming Mexican American*, 210.

[50] Hanna, "Social Services on the Mexican Border," 699.

United States after eight or nine months. They were arrested four years later and returned to Mexico.[51]

Private citizens and public officials alike complained bitterly about the presence of Mexican immigrants and exaggerated the financial burden these immigrants presented, contributing to an atmosphere of racialized nativism in which color reinforced the distinction between citizen and resident.[52] In a 1933 letter to President Franklin Roosevelt, J. F. Russel, a resident of Hollywood, California, linked race and blood to poverty and worth in his strident call for massive deportations: "Tens of thousands of our charitable cases are MEXICANS, or people of Mexican blood, (mixture of Indian, Spanish, half breeds, untracable, ect. [sic], and just worthless persons) and over half our Los Angeles County funds are being spend [sic] upon people of Mexican blood."[53] J. C. Brodie, chair of the Superior, Arizona, Democrat Committee, wrote to anyone who would listen, including the commissioner-general of immigration, the secretary of labor, and the president of the United States, condemning "Alien Mass Poverty" which forced millions of white citizens of the Southwest into "Bread Lines."[54] Brodie's racist attacks were not limited to Mexican and Mexican Americans but included "fresh hordes of Filipinos," "Hindus," "Japs and coolies" and "an influx of low grade European peasants not much removed from the ignorance and squalor of the off-colors from Mexico and the Orient."[55] Along with diatribes against nonwhite immigrants who threatened the moral and physical well-being of the Southwest, Brodie sent lists of names of immigrants he suspected of working for WPA projects or accepting relief services.[56]

[51] Over the next few years, each applied for a visa and was repeatedly denied. They were allowed temporary admission for a few days to shop and visit family in 1935, 1937, and 1938. Carmela Gomez [pseud.], INS file 56136–952, Board Decisions, 56136–952 (1941); DJA-INS, acc. 58 A 734, box 2531; INS, DC, RG85; NA, DC.

[52] George Sánchez notes that in 1931 California's Alien Labor Act made it illegal for any company doing business with the government to employ "aliens" on public jobs. Sánchez, *Becoming Mexican American*.

[53] J. F. Russel to Franklin D. Roosevelt, 3 April 1933, INS file 55739/674 (1931–); RCO, entry 9, box 505, 55739/491A–55739/930; INS, DC, RG85; NA, DC.

[54] Brodie to Mr. President, 4 April 1933, INS file 55739/674A (1933–); RCO, entry 9, box 505, 55739/491A–55739/930; INS, DC, RG85; NA, DC. This correspondence was so extensive that the INS maintained a separate file.

[55] Brodie to Jas. B. Buchanan, 5 February 1936; Agenda Letter to the President 30 October 1934; INS file 55739/674A (1933–); RCO, entry 9, box 505, 55739/491A–55739/930; INS, DC, RG85; NA, DC.

[56] Brodie even charged that Mexican children were infecting white children with gonorrhea through informal contact while at school. Immigration officials in Tucson, Arizona, were instructed to investigate some of the people Brodie fingered in his reports to Washington. Not surprisingly, the service found that Brodie exaggerated for effect. While immigra-

With good reason, immigrant families feared accepting relief from either public or private welfare services. Those who had entered the United States illegally or who had frequently traveled outside the United States accepted aid at their peril and risked drawing official attention to their immigration status. In a 1927 study conducted by United Charities into how their regional offices were assisting immigrants in need, agencies located in the west and along the southern border acknowledged that they actively reported families seeking relief to immigration officials for deportation. United Charities of El Paso explained that immigrants who "would not make citizens of the United States" or who had "smuggled themselves into the United States" were returned to Mexico along with their "entire family." El Paso officials insisted that it was not a matter of compassion but rather a matter of law. Of thirty-seven immigrants deported from Los Angeles in the spring of 1925, United Charities of Los Angeles reported twenty-nine cases to immigration authorities.[57] In a 1931 report to the assistant secretary of labor, Los Angeles immigration authorities explained that deportation remained central to city efforts to streamline financially and homogenize racially its welfare and employment roles. "Local officials hope to rid this locality of a great financial burden through the voluntary return of such aliens," the immigration supervisor explained; "They anticipate not only that the departure of many deportable aliens as well as undeportable aliens will be accomplished in this way, but also that many who are not aliens but who are of Mexican extraction whom the Mexican government is willing to receive, will take advantage of the opportunity to enter Mexico under the conditions outlined, it being borne in mind that all of these classes are now receiving charity in this community."[58]

---

tion officials recognized that Brodie was an "extremist," they also were careful to note in internal service documents that he spoke for many white Americans eager to be rid of racial others. G. C. Wilmoth, district director El Paso to Commissioner of Immigration and Naturalization, 24 April 1934, INS file 55739/674A (1933–); RCO, entry 9, box 505, 55739/491A–55739/930; INS, DC, RG85; NA, DC.

[57] During this period, an immigration official was installed in the offices of the County Charities. Mrs. Gudrum Rom, United Charities, Chicago, "Family Problems Resulting from the Present Deportation System," *Proceedings of the National Conference of Social Work*, 54th Annual Session, 1927 (Chicago: University of Chicago Press), 1927: 569–570.

[58] F. W. Watkins, Los Angeles Supervisor to Assistant Secretary of Labor, 8 February 1931, INS file 55739/674 (1931–); RCO, entry 9, box 505, 55739/491A–55739/930; INS, DC, RG85; NA, DC. George Sánchez notes that new policies under Roosevelt's administration offered some relief to Mexican immigrants by prohibiting service providers from allocating relief on the basis of legal status. However, immigrants could still be found deportable by the INS if found to be public charges within five years of their last entry. See Sánchez, *Becoming Mexican American*, 221–224.

Given the risk of deportation, immigrants avoided outside relief whenever possible and turned instead to their own communities for help. As early as 1930, Marian Schibsby, editor of the Foreign Language Information Service's *Interpreter Releases*, advised, "foreign groups—their fraternal organizations, their churches, their emergency relief committees . . . to take care of their countrymen as have been in the U.S. for less than five years."[59] Many immigrants did just that. Agnes K. Hanna, director of the social service division of the Children's Bureau, reported in 1935 that Mexican mothers refused to attend prenatal clinics, refused to give birth in hospitals, and refused to have their children seen by medical personnel for fear of being reported to immigration authorities as public charges.[60]

Faced with bitter attacks by white restrictionists, most notably Brodie, the Mexican and Mexican American community in Superior, Arizona, organized its own community chest to assist women and children in need of food or clothing without regard to their citizenship or immigration status. Along with contributions from local ethnic businesses, the community chest deducted one dollar from the pay of all Mexican and Mexican Americans employed by the Magma Copper Company. By prohibiting its members from soliciting aid from other outside sources, it sought to avoid the deportation of community members. With just over fifteen hundred dollars, the organization aided 131 families. When the local bank collapsed, however, so too did the community's efforts to help itself.[61]

"Voluntary" departures, less than voluntary deportations, and increasingly rigorous interpretations of LPC drew dark and fearsome divisions between the rights of citizens and the limitations of residency. Citizenship and race placed Mexican immigrants between the proverbial rock and hard place of American nationalism. Mexican immigrants and other racial and ethnic immigrant communities were criticized for their failure to pursue naturalization or, in the case of Asian immigrants, for their persistence on the fringes of American civil law. Race separated the worthy from the unworthy, distinguishing those folded within the nation from those incorporated within the law. Legally, immigrants of Mexican ances-

---

[59] Schibsby, "Deportation on the Ground of Being a Public Charge," *Interpreter Releases* 7, no. 42 (11 December 1930), RACNS, reel 2.

[60] Hanna, "Social Services on the Mexican Border," 700–701.

[61] Samuel T. Wright, immigrant inspector, to Inspector in Charge, Tucson, Arizona, 9 April 1934, INS file 55739/674A (1933–); RCO, entry 9, box 505, 55739/491A–55739/930; INS, DC, RG85; NA, DC. The Superior, Arizona, community chest provides an important example of what David Gutiérrez has termed ethnopolitical organizing by working-class Mexicans and Mexican Americans across citizenship divides. Gutiérrez, *Walls and Mirrors: Mexican Americans, Mexican Immigrants, and the Politics of Ethnicity* (Berkeley: University of California Press, 1995).

try fit within the racial dyad of American citizenship law; culturally and socially, however, they remained beyond the pale. As if fulfilling an unknown prophecy, few Mexican immigrants sought naturalization. In the face of virulent employment and welfare discrimination, housing segregation, and even political violence, many may have believed citizenship offered few real benefits.

THE RIGHT TO WORK: CITIZENSHIP AND THE NEW DEAL

The national experience of scarcity begot a new understanding of the rights of citizenship and the privileges of association within the nation. As the financial crisis turned into a lengthy depression, and the arrival of new immigrants all but came to a halt, long-term resident immigrants living and laboring in the United States became the focus for debate over the responsibilities of government and the rights of citizenship. Amidst scarcity, some challenged, work and welfare were exclusive privileges of citizenship. The American Legion, for example, advocated exclusive employment of citizens on federal relief projects and the exclusion of aliens from the Home Owners' Loan program.[62] Historically, work entitled one to entry but not to citizenship, which remained structured within a racial dyad of black and white. The advent of government-sponsored relief efforts for the working poor, however, was rooted in a shared experience of work, and raised questions about the relationship between the rights of citizens and those of residents.

Congress was at a loss to understand why immigrants remained in the legal limbo of "residency" and passed resolutions to deny noncitizens access to relief jobs or financial support.[63] In 1934 hearings before the House Committee on Immigration and Naturalization, and through thinly veiled references to Mexican immigrants, California Republican representative, and one-time sheriff of Los Angles county, William Traeger suggested that citizenship, once the symbol of political inclusion, had become tarnished through its association with economic benefits. "The thing that comes to me so forcibly at this time," the Los Angeles politician explained, "is the fact that so many people in my neighborhood

---

[62] Marion Schibsby, "Is there an Undue Proportion of Aliens on Relief?" *Interpreter Releases* 13, no. 48, series B, Naturalization no. 9 (19 October 1936): 289, RACNS, reel 5.

[63] Roger Daniels maintains that while Franklin Roosevelt "did not indulge in nativist rhetoric," neither did he offer a new deal for immigrants. The immigration system of the 1920s went largely unchallenged and unchanged during the 1930s. As a result, ships bearing European refugees were turned away from American shores and resident immigrants living in the United States were provided with little public assistance. See Daniels, *Coming to America*, 296–300.

had no desire to become an American citizen until the N.R.A. or the W.P.A., or some other 'A' or something offered them jobs, and they could not take them because they were not American citizens."[64] Citizenship for many immigrants, Traeger's comments suggested, no longer simply represented the right to vote but included the right to work and the right to be free from want. In conjunction with appropriating money to fund relief efforts in 1936, the House passed a resolution to forbid Works Progress Administration officials from employing noncitizens.[65] The amendment was not without its critics. Gerald Boileau, a Wisconsin Republican turned Progressive, called into question the very idea that years of work and years of residency left immigrants with no claim on the nation: "So long as we have permitted them to come here and permit them to remain here, we should not deprive them of the only opportunity they have to keep body and soul together."[66]

Despite public perception to the contrary, immigrants did not make up a disproportionate percentage of relief recipients. In part, this may have been a result of immigrants' reluctance to risk coming to the attention of immigration authorities. The Emergency Relief Bureau of New York reported that noncitizen immigrants represented just over fifteen percent

[64] Mr. Traeger, *Amendments to the Immigration Laws as Recommended by the Department of Labor and by the Secretary's Ellis Island Committee*, 1934, H.R. 9518, H.R. 9364, H.R. 9365, H.R. 9366, H.R. 9367 (the Five Bill Program); Public Hearings before the Committee on Immigration and Naturalization House of Representatives, 73rd Cong., 2nd sess., Washington, D.C., 62. Traeger was certainly not alone in his sentiments. Many other members of the committee and those who came to testify echoed Traeger's sense that citizenship had been joined in an unsavory union with welfare. Testifying a year later before the same House committee, James H. Patten, a representative of the Immigration Restriction League of New York, criticized those immigrants who failed to become citizens after five years of residency and called for their deportation. Statement of James H. Patten, representing Immigration Restriction League of N.Y., Inc.; State Council, Junior Order United American Mechanics of the State of N.Y., Inc.; commandery general, Patriotic Order Sons of America; ex. board, Fraternal Patriotic Americans; Patriotic American Civic Alliance, *Deportation of Aliens: Hearings before the Committee on Immigration and Naturalization*, 1935, HR 6795; House of Representatives, 74th Cong., 1st sess., Washington, D.C., 82. Benjamin Focht, a Republican representative from Pennsylvania, seconded Patten's critique and implied that immigrants who failed to seek naturalization brought deportation and potential separation from their families upon themselves. See Focht, *Deportation of Aliens: Hearings before the Committee on Immigration and Naturalization*, 1935, 156–157.

[65] The amendment was proposed by Congressman Woodward of Virginia to HR 12624. The Senate altered the wording of the amendment to read, "any alien who is illegally within the limits of the United States or who has not filed a declaration of intention to become a citizen of the United States and wherever such a person has been employed he shall be dismissed." Marian Schibsby, "Legislative Bulletin, no. V.," *Interpreter Releases* 13, no. 26, series D (6 June 1936): 165–166, RACNS, reel 5.

[66] Marian Schibsby, "Legislative Bulletin, no. V.," *Interpreter Releases*, vol. 13, no. 26, series D (6 June 1936): 172–173, RACNS, reel 5.

of the population of New York City in 1930 but made up less than thirteen percent of all relief cases in 1936 and less than eight percent of those transferred to the WPA in 1935. The Emergency Relief Bureau was also quick to note that among the 55,508 immigrant families who received home relief and WPA assistance were 86,944 American-born children.[67]

Growing popular distrust and Congressional ill will led many immigrants to the federal courts to declare their intention to become citizens. The number of people filing declarations of intention rose steadily between 1930 and 1932 and again from 1933 to 1936. The number of people petitioning for citizenship peaked in 1932 and 1936 at just over 145,000 and 167,000, respectively. By 1936, one-quarter of all immigrants living in the United States had filed their declarations of intention.[68] One year later, the 1937 Relief Act prohibited the employment of all immigrants who had not filed their declarations of intention. The Works Progress Administration for New York City quickly followed suit and announced that all foreign-born employees must provide evidence of citizenship or be dismissed from their positions. Subsequently, the Foreign Language Information Service published information on where naturalized citizens could procure proof of citizenship.[69]

Of particular concern were immigrants whose citizenship was derived from another rather than having been naturalized themselves. Women who had acquired citizenship through marriage or children who had become citizens as a result of their father's naturalization would lack proof of their status and would thus be unable to find work with government relief organizations. Nina Dunn approached the International Institute in Minneapolis for help with her citizenship status in 1938. She had immigrated thirty-three years before from Denmark and had since been married twice, both times to American citizens. Her second marriage took

[67] Marian Schibsby, "Is there an Undue Proportion of Aliens on Relief?" *Interpreter Releases* 13, no. 48, series B, Naturalization no. 9 (19 October 1936): 292–294, RACNS, reel 5.

[68] Marian Schibsby, "Naturalization in 1936," *Interpreter Releases* 13, no. 54, series B, Naturalization no. 12 (30 November 1936): 318–319; RACNS, reel 5.

[69] The 1937 law ranked applicants in preference order (akin to immigration law) with veterans of World War I and those of other wars given first preference, American citizens and American nationals in need second preference, and aliens in need who had their first papers third. Despite this system, the act remained vague and left unclear what distinguished nationals from resident immigrants. For example, the attorney general found that Filipinos were neither citizens nor first-paper immigrants and were thus not entitled to any preference in WPA employment. A year later, Congress introduced legislation (H.J. Res. 679) to alter the language of the second preference to include "American citizens, Indians, and other persons owing allegiance to the United States who are in need." Marian Schibsby, "Aliens on Relief, Legislative Bulletin No VI," *Interpreter Releases* 15, no. 22, series D, (17 May 1938): 200–201, RACNS, reel 5.

place after the Cable Act had been passed granting some married women independent citizenship. Institute personnel urged Dunn to secure a copy of her marriage license, her steamer ticket, and her birth certificate to prove she had become a citizen through her first marriage.[70] In general, the Foreign Language Information Service encouraged all women who were widowed, divorced, or deserted without evidence of their husbands' birth or naturalization to solicit affidavits from two American citizens who could attest to their husbands' citizenship status or to request election or census records from federal offices.[71] It was not easy, but it could be done with time; many immigrants, however, could not afford time without relief.

While federal relief legislation did not exclude immigrants, the application of state and federal policy often did. The federal statute enacted in 1935 did not specify that those receiving old-age pensions must be citizens, for example, but by 1937, only fifteen states authorized pensions for noncitizens; none of these were states with large immigrant populations.[72] Naturalization courts, particularly those on the Pacific Coast, routinely denied the applications of long-term residents who sought to formalize their status in order to become eligible for old-age assistance programs. "Applications for naturalization," a Washington District Court argued in 1935, "have largely increased since pension legislation agitation. Love of country and attachment to the principles of the Constitution are incidental." In denying the application of a thirty-year resident, the court dismissed new claims to individual assistance with older Republican arguments about general welfare: "Citizenship is a grave affair," one of "conscious dedication" by those "inspired to a common goal" and not one "inspired by expected largesse from a state or the nation."[73] Adelheid

[70] Nina Dunn [pseud.] (1938), major casefiles Dab–Fla, box 26; International Institute of Minnesota.

[71] Marian Schibsby, "Proof of American Citizenship: How and Where It May be Secured," *Interpreter Releases* 14, no. 35, series B, Naturalization no. 7 (8 July 1937): 234–235, RACNS, reel 5.

[72] While in 1934, only twenty-three states paid old-age pensions, by 1937 that number had almost doubled to include every state except Virginia (including Hawaii and the District of Columbia). Among those states *not* requiring citizenship were Arkansas, Connecticut, Delaware, Georgia, Louisiana, Mississippi, Nebraska, New Mexico, Tennessee, Utah, and Wyoming. Minnesota and Montana required twenty-five years of residence in lieu of citizenship, Rhode Island required twenty, and Wyoming fifteen. South Dakota required citizenship or a declaration of intention (first paper). New York introduced legislation in 1937 authorizing old-age pensions to alien residents who had filed a declaration of intention and had at least twenty years of residency immediately preceding their application. Marian Schibsby, "Aliens and Old Age Pensions," *Interpreter Releases*, 14, no. 19, series B, Naturalization no. 5 (27 April 1937): 108, RACNS, reel 5.

[73] *In re McIntosh* 12 F.Supp. 177 (W.D.Wash. 1935).

Hoffman appeared before the District Court of California in 1936 as an applicant for citizenship. She had been naturalized once before in 1908, but upon marriage to an alien she lost her citizenship. Her husband had died in 1931, and at age sixty-five she sought to become a citizen once more. In hearing her case, the court noted that Hoffman had become a public charge soon after her husband's death and was confined to a wheel chair. Citizenship, the court argued, was reciprocal; if Hoffman could not give in the form of service to her country then neither could she receive.[74]

The social welfare policies of the New Deal expanded the points of contact between citizens and the state from the traditional roles of voting and holding political office to include daily, ongoing efforts to obtain food and work, maintain home and family, and survive in old age. The protracted economic crisis of the 1930s was indiscriminate, devastating to new immigrants, long-term residents, and citizens alike. Federal policies that emphasized work, whether through government-sponsored work projects for those who were able or old-age assistance for those had worked for most of their lives, linked those who were members of the nation with those who were not.

The concept of citizenship that emerged from the wreckage of the Great Depression and the legislative energy of the New Deal was different from that of the early twentieth century. The right to work and the alleviation of poverty were part of a new understanding of American rights and responsibilities. Noncitizens would, in the years to come, make claims on the nation through a language and a history of work, and, in the process, they would raise important questions about the right to work and the right to be free from want.

[74] *In re Hoffmann*, 13 F.Supp. 907 (S.D.Cal. 1936).

CHAPTER ELEVEN

At Work in the Nation

World War II wrought new political allies and new economic realities. It also initiated a new phase in American immigration and naturalization policy. The slow dismantling of race-based exclusion policies between 1940 and 1965 constituted a radical departure from a legal tradition that insisted on the significance of race for citizenship and immigration status. New preference systems replaced older national origins schemes, and race finally ceased to be an independent category of exclusion, a century after its introduction. Yet economic status, race, and gender continued to play a significant role in determining arrival and access to citizenship well into the post–World War II period. Work and poverty remained signifiers of worthiness, folding within them later twentieth-century anxieties about the import of race difference, the significance of gender, the possibility of self-sufficiency, and the limits of citizenship.

War not only shifted the legal demarcations of citizenship but also impacted the experience of citizenship by placing a premium on membership. Noncitizen immigrants living in the United States faced increased scrutiny as the nation sought to insulate itself from further attack. Whether through the bureaucratic supervision of alien registration procedures, or through the physical isolation of internment policies, many noncitizens (and some citizens) living in the United States found themselves transformed from immigrants into enemy aliens.

Two programs in the 1940s and 1950s illustrate well the continuities in race and gender limitations on citizenship: the displaced persons program, implemented from 1948 to 1950; and the bracero program, operated from 1949 to 1964. The contracting of large numbers of Mexicans to work in the agricultural fields of the United States in the 1940s and 1950s through the bracero program created a class of male immigrants who were temporary employees rather than eventual citizens. The displaced persons program, instituted in the years following World War II, tied relief to political identity rather than to economic need. The result was a two-tier system of membership and quasimembership that separated immigrants whose claim on the nation was rooted in ideology from those whose claim on the nation was routed through the marketplace.

Policies like the bracero and displaced persons programs brought the central symbol of non-Americanism into the late twentieth century. Like the alien wives and non-American nationals that had proceeded them, braceros were in the nation but not of the nation. The creation of a large and permanent population of noncitizen residents would expand only with the dramatic growth and expanded reach of postwar American military and corporate global power.

Finally, significant reworkings of the immigration code in 1952 and 1965 reflected, in part, a renewed interest in evaluating immigrants' work skills and their contribution to an expanding American economy. Debate over the 1952 and 1965 reforms, however, also revealed deep ambivalence about the place of women's work in immigration law. Despite twenty additional years of severe restrictions on immigration and a protracted economic crisis that ended only as a war-related economy emerged, women entering as domestic servants continued to enjoy a privileged place in the law that singled out women's paid work in the home as valuable. While in many ways work functioned as a replacement for the discredited and overtly race-based national origins system, the continued privileged status enjoyed by domestic servants ironically eased the arrival of non-European women during a period of tight labor market regulation and immigration restriction between 1945 and 1965.

WARTIME CITIZENSHIP: RACE AND NATURALIZATION LAW

Between 1934 and 1952, U.S. citizenship law underwent historic transformations, creating gender and race equity under the law. Even as the nation's naturalization laws moved toward greater inclusivity, however, group identity and group categorization continued to provide the grounds on which individuals were incorporated into the civic polity. The long history of delineating exclusion through gender or race categories created a legacy of piecemeal inclusion. When a woman was married, what racial group she appeared to belong to, and what geographic area she was from continued to determine her rights to citizenship.

As immigration to the United States fell far below the heights reached during the 1920s, the focus of administrative policy shifted to address the loyalty and legality of immigrant minorities living in the United States.[1]

---

[1] Restrictive immigration covenants, global economic depression, and war combined to bring immigration to the United States to a virtual halt during the 1930s and early 1940s. *Annual Report of the Commissioner General of Immigration* (1931), 2, 45; Frank Auerback, "Immigration Statistics for 1946," *Interpreter Releases* 24, no. 13 (17 March 1947): 77, RACNS, reel 7.

The domestic economy retooled itself for wartime production, and work in war industries was reserved for American citizens. Many American-born women struggled to leave their low-paying clerical and service jobs for the munitions factories and defense plants of the industrialized homefront.

Demand for ready labor brought a temporary halt to the voluntary deportation policies of the 1930s but not to the argument that the opportunity to work and the promise to be free from want were privileges of citizenship. Juana Cardenas, a Mexican immigrant and long-time resident of the United States, was held for deportation in 1936 when she was unable to find work to support herself and her two American-born daughters.[2] By 1942, however, immigration authorities dropped deportation charges against Cardenas as she and her girls readied themselves to resettle in California, where Cardenas hoped to find work in the defense plants of Los Angeles. She had been offered work as a domestic, but it paid less than relief and was insufficient to support her family. Wartime production fueled the domestic economy and revalued Cardenas's potential contribution to the homefront in the shipyards of California. Cardenas applied for naturalization and in 1943 moved her family to Los Angeles.[3]

The confused and piecemeal legacy of legislation governing women's citizenship, however, meant many immigrant and native-born women remained beyond the borders of membership and thus employment. Violet Carson, for example, wanted to find more lucrative work in a local Buffalo defense plant and approached the International Institute in 1943 for help in securing her citizenship. Carson, an immigrant, hoped that her prior marriage to an American citizen before the Cable Act was passed might have provided her with derivative citizenship, and she offered her wedding band inscribed with a date of 1922 as evidence. Unfortunately, officers with the International Institute wrote to a local library and found that the date of her marriage was in fact 1923, one year after the Cable Act provided some women with independent citizenship. Carson would have to seek naturalization on her own.[4]

The 1922 Cable Act was finally amended in 1940 to allow women living in the United States who had married noncitizens to be repatriated during their marriage. Up until this point, women married before the 1922 Cable Act had to wait until their marriage had ended, through annulment, divorce, or death.[5] Demand was so great among women seeking

---

[2] Cardenas's story was related in greater detail in the previous chapter.

[3] Juana Cardenas [pseud.] (1936), Unprocessed, casefiles, box 30; International Institutes of Buffalo.

[4] Violet Carson [pseud.] (1943), Unprocessed, casefiles, box 15; International Institutes of Buffalo.

[5] However, the 1940 amendment required that these women had lived in the United States for the duration of their marriage. A letter from the YWCA offices in Akron, Ohio,

their citizenship that naturalization courts ran out of forms.[6] With each new addition to the legislation governing women's citizenship, however, court officials, naturalization examiners, and the women themselves found themselves lost in a sea of qualifications, exemptions, and exclusions.[7] Immigration authorities expressed concerns that new repatriation procedures authorized under the 1940 amendment allowed women to circumvent immigration procedures. A 1940 memo from El Paso officials questioned whether women repatriating themselves would need to speak English.[8] Authorities maintained that women applying for repatriation should be investigated, along with other immigrant applicants, before they were restored to native-born status.[9]

---

asked after the status of a American woman who had been taken to Czechoslovakia when she was two years old, and had married a Czech man in 1919. She returned to the United States in 1938 with her sixteen-year-old son. While still legally married, her husband had deserted her. Having lived outside the United States during her marriage, she did not fall within the confines of the 1940 amendment. YWCA in Akron, Ohio, to INS, 24 September 1940, INS file 56173–496 (1934–); DJA-INS acc. 58 A 734, box 2749; INS, DC, RG85; NA, DC; *Immigration and Nationality Laws and Regulations as of March 1, 1944* (Washington, D.C.: United States Government Printing Office, 1944), 556.

[6] Sixty-nine women from Michigan submitted a petition in 1940 demanding more forms be made available for those interested in repatriation. INS file 56173–496 (1934–); DJA-INS acc. 58 A 734, box 2749; INS, DC, RG85; NA, DC.

[7] Letters from women soliciting advice from the INS testify to the confusing state of married women's citizenship in the years leading up to World War II. Mrs. John Dipoma wrote one such letter in July, 1936. "Will you kindly answer this letter, and let me know if I've got to take out citizen-papers or not," she asked, "I am a native of America, Born in Convent, Louisiana, in 1898. Married to an Italian-foreigner in October 9th, 1921. Is it true I've lost my naturalization rights?" "Being he is deceased," she continued, "have I lost all right of voting." Mrs. John Dipoma to Naturalization Service, 3 July 1936, INS file 20/154; RCO: Naturalization, entry 26, box 408; INS, DC, RG85; NA, DC. Libbie Rudolf also wrote the Bureau of Naturalization for advice. "I was born in 1894 in Portland, Oregon but no record has been kept for my birth," she explained, "I was married in 1910 to an alien who died recently. My belief was all these years that I was a citizen but inquiring at the local office, I was refused citizen papers. Will appreciate if you can tell me the legal steps I need to take in order to become a citizen." Libbie Rudolf to Department of Labor, Bureau of Naturalization, from Libbie Rudolf, 22 June 1936, INS file 20/154; RCO: Naturalization, entry 26, box 408; INS, DC, RG85; NA, DC.

[8] INS file 20/2 (1922–); RCO: Naturalization, entry 26, box 399; INS, DC RG85; NA, DC. For debate over naturalization procedure see INS file 56173–496 (1934–); DJA-INS acc. 58 A 734, box 2749; INS, DC, RG85; NA, DC.

[9] Women repatriated under the act included women who were restored to citizenship and thus had never been considered an alien by the INS. However, the acquisition of this citizenship could be regarded as naturalization within the meaning of the 1940 Nationality Act because women took an oath of allegiance. The 1936 act gave naturalization courts jurisdiction over women's repatriation. Consequently, INS officials asked that the naturalization courts recognize the long-standing practice of having all repatriation cases investigated by the INS. INS file 56173–496 (1934–); DJA-INS acc. 58 A 734, box 2749; INS, DC, RG85; NA, DC.

The passage of the Alien Registration Act in 1940, requiring all aliens to be registered and fingerprinted with the federal government, brought urgency to the question of citizenship and vast numbers of women into the court system to have their citizenship status determined.[10] Legislative and administrative limits on citizenship that continued through the 1940s were most glaring in the United States' refusal to allow some racial minorities to become citizens. As evident in the 1940 case of Lelia M. Dodd, blood quantum defined by racial categories continued to divide citizens from noncitizens. Those whose appearance or ancestry could be traced to South Asia, Southeast Asia, or the Pacific Rim remained beyond the pale.

Dodd was born in French Indo-China in 1898 to a Thai mother and a French father. An American missionary and his wife adopted her as an infant. Raised in the United States, Dodd was unaware of her adoption or her Thai ancestry. Upon her adopted mother's death, Dodd learned of her tenuous civic status and attempted to apply for naturalization.

Q: Do you recall ever seeing your mother?
A: No.
Q: Were your adoptive parents acquainted with your mother?
A: Not that I know of.
Q: Then you do not know whether your blood mother is living or dead?
A: I don't know. I understood that she had died before I was adopted, but I could not say for sure.
Q: Do you know the blood race of your blood mother?
A: Siamese, from Northern Siam. Their race is also referred to as Thai and the country is now known as Thailand.

Dodd's petition for naturalization was denied. "I couldn't get citizenship on account of my mother's race," Dodd protested, "and yet I am not even sure of her race."[11] According to naturalization officials, Dodd was unable to meet the strict racial requirements of the law, "Being of the half-prohibited blood for naturalization purposes she can never acquire citizenship except by way of private bill."[12]

The fight to end both fascism and racial genocide abroad rang hollow in the face of continued racial segregation at home. By 1940, the national-

[10] The act made aliens deportable if they did not comply with the law. Some districts wondered whether native-born women expatriated through marriage, repatriated through legislation, should comply with the alien registration act, or if they could be removed from the alien rolls. INS files 56173–496 and 51934–(1934); DJA-INS acc. 58 A 734, box 2749; INS, DC, RG85; NA, DC.

[11] Lilia M. Dodd, INS file 20/180 (1940–); RCO: Naturalization, entry 26, box 410; INS, DC, RG85; NA, DC.

[12] Edward J. Shaughnessy, Deputy Commissioner, to Mr. Scholfield, memorandum, 8 March 1941, INS file 20/180 (1940–); RCO: Naturalization, entry 26, box 410; INS, DC, RG85; NA, DC.

ity laws were extended to include all those born in the United States "to a member of an Indian, Eskimo, Aleutian, or other aboriginal tribe," and naturalization was opened to "descendants of races indigenous to the Western Hemisphere." In addition, foreign policy concerns made it all but impossible to maintain an alliance with China or India while excluding their foreign nationals from citizenship. New enemies and new allies during World War II led to the extension of naturalization to "Chinese persons or persons of Chinese descent," in 1943, and by 1946 to "persons of races indigenous to India" and "Filipino persons or persons of Filipino descent." By 1950, Guamanians were added to the list of eligible racial candidates. Yet by expanding the number of races eligible for citizenship, new naturalization legislation served to reinscribe the significance of race to membership. Finally, in 1952, all racial bars to naturalization were removed. The piecemeal process of women's repatriation under the Cable Act, along with the incremental tangle of race-based naturalization legislation, meant that courts continued to hear women's appeals well into the next decades.[13]

WAR, WORK, AND REFUGEES: THE DISPLACED
PERSONS AND BRACERO PROGRAMS

Immigration policies implemented during the 1940s and 1950s also raised difficult questions about whether those who worked for the nation earned the privilege of becoming citizens. Two programs in particular—the effort to resettle European refugees in the United States, and the policy of allowing temporary workers from the Western Hemisphere to enter as contract laborers—structured the arrival of large groups of immigrants, many of whom were not considered candidates for citizenship. The former fostered a migration of families from Europe, and the latter of men from Mexico. Each illustrates how race, gender, and ethnic difference strained the ties between work and citizenship through the 1940s and 1950s.

---

[13] For example, Lee Hay was born in San Francisco in 1899. She returned to China as a young women to be married. Her husband died in 1941, never having come to the United States, and leaving her with three sons and one daughter. Hay attempted to return to the United States in 1950 as a native-born citizen. Fifty-one years after her birth, Hay had to provide evidence of her American birth. Fortunately, a letter from the Presbyterian Mission Home corroborated Hay's story, and she was admitted as a citizen. Lee Hay [pseud.], INS file 1300/108821–C (1950); Unprocessed, box 336187; INS, SFD, RG85; NA-PSR. See also Peggy Blake [pseud.], INS file 56175–570 (1945); DJA-INS acc. 58 A 734, box 2756; INS, DC, RG85; NA, DC; Mary Lind [pseud.], INS file 56, 233–892 (1948); DJA-INS acc. 58 A 734, box 3011; INS, DC, RG85; NA, DC.

After the war, the significance of economic status to national membership resumed center stage as the nation debated its responsibility to those
non-Americans displaced and bloodied by World War II. The cessation of
hostilities in Europe and Asia, coupled with the real fear that the end of
war would bring the reemergence of economic depression, resulted in new
immigration policies designed to control the influx of war-weary immigrants from abroad. The 1948 Displaced Persons Act authorized the admission of 205,000 displaced persons, or DPs, over two years.[14] Relief
was tempered, however, by now familiar anxieties about race, poverty,
and unchecked immigration. Opponents of the legislation suggested that
any chink in the armor of U.S. immigration law weakened the nation's
ability to prevent the arrival of non-European refugees from war-torn
regions of the world, such as China, Pakistan, or Palestine.[15] Despite these
objections, but sharing many of the same concerns, legislation was passed
limiting humanitarian relief to Europe, ignoring those in Asia and the
Middle East who also had been displaced by the war.[16] In what must have
struck those Jews in Europe who had survived the Holocaust as a final
irony, the act favored immigrants from the Baltic States and eastern Poland at the expense of Jews from other parts of eastern Europe.[17]

Alert to anxieties that economic depression would return with peace,
fearful of new urban ethnic immigrant enclaves, and aware of current
housing shortages, the act favored families who came to work on American farms by legislating that thirty percent of all refugees be agricultural-

[14] The Displaced Persons Commission placed the original number at 205,000; *Memo to
America: The DP Story, the Final Report of the United States Displaced Persons Commission* (Washington, D.C.: 1952), 7; Hutchinson puts the total number at 202,000, (Hutchinson, *Legislative History of American Immigration Policy*, 280–281). Neither source offers
a breakdown of their totals. The discrepancy may be a result of various amendments passed
after 1948 allowing for the admission of additional refugees. By 1952, some 395,000 refugees had been resettled in the United States; *Memo to America*, 65.

[15] *Congressional Record*, 28 February 1950, 2476, as cited in David M. Reimers, *Still
the Golden Door: The Third World Comes to America* (New York: Columbia University
Press, 1985, 1992), 23–24; Divine, *American Immigration Policy*, 113–114.

[16] Following two years of rancorous debate and thwarted reform, the act was finally
amended in 1950. Visa selection was to be made without regard to race, religion, or national
origin. *Memo to America*, 38. For a discussion of congressional debate leading up to the
1950 legislation, see Divine, *American Immigration Policy*, 130–145; the earlier legislation
is also discussed 110–129.

[17] In addition, the legislation allowed only those who had entered the displaced persons
camps before December 22, 1945 to be registered for American visas. As opponents were
quick to point out, recent refugees, particularly Jews fleeing eastern European, would be
ineligible. The legislation also discriminated against Catholics in that the geographic areas
favored were predominantly Protestant. *Memo to America*, 25–26; Frank L. Auerbach,
"The Displaced Persons Act—Its Interpretation and Administration (II)," *Interpreter Releases* 26, no. 3 (12 January 1949), RACNS, reel 8.

ists. In addition, displaced persons had to be sponsored by American citizens who could provide access to work and housing along with guaranties that the DPs would not become public charges after arrival.[18] Both as a result of legislation but also as a consequence of sponsor demand, over thirty percent of DPs arrived as farm workers, many sponsored by southern planters. Within a few years, however, the vast majority of DPs worked in skilled and semiskilled industrial trades in the urban Northeast.[19]

As has been true historically, large numbers of women refugees from Europe were sponsored to work as domestics. Women made up nearly half of all arriving DPs, most of whom were married.[20] Leveraging gender bias in the law, women DPs claimed official status as domestic service workers in order to be sponsored for one of the limited number of visas available. Over fourteen percent of all DPs were contracted to work as private household workers, but within a few years of living in the United States that number dropped by almost half.[21] One exsponsor wrote the Displaced Persons Committee to inform them that the woman they had sponsored as a domestic servant left after six weeks to seek work in a local hamburger shop.[22] Another sponsor wrote disdainfully of how higher wages in the city had lured an immigrant woman and her son to Chicago and away from domestic service.[23] Erika Eibl's casefile was referred to the International Institute of Buffalo in 1949 when both she and her employer were unhappy with her placement as a domestic servant.[24]

While these women were not required as a condition of their visas to remain in the employ of their sponsors, many sponsors and many women

---

[18] *Memo to America*, 23, 25; Frank L. Auerbach, "The Displaced Persons Act—Its Interpretation and Administration (II)," *Interpreter Releases* 26, no. 3 (12 January 1949), RACNS, reel 8.

[19] Just under twenty percent of all arrivals were transported to the southern states. However, over half of those contracted to work in the south had left by 1951. The north central states saw a net increase of over twenty-one percent as many DPs traveled a historically significant route out of the south to Chicago. Approximately sixty percent of all DPs listed the northeastern states as their residence in 1951. *Memo to America*, 249–251, 255.

[20] 45.6 percent of DPs were women; for those fourteen years and older, 62.6 percent were married. *Memo to America*, 245–247; Frank L. Auerbach, "Age and Sex Distribution of Displaced Persons," *Interpreter Releases* 25, no. 10 (24 February 1948), RACNS, reel 7.

[21] Unfortunately, no gender breakdown is available. Of the 14.2 percent sponsored as domestic laborers, most were likely to be women. The percentage was slightly higher among German expellees (20.8 percent). By December 1950, however, only 6.4 percent of DPs reported that they were working in domestic service. *Memo to America*, 368, 372.

[22] *Memo to America*, 227.

[23] Ibid., 229. The mother and son joined distant relatives living in Chicago.

[24] Erika Eibl [pseud.] (1949), Unprocessed, box 1; International Institutes of Buffalo. Also see, Sonia Ahlering [pseud.] (1956), Unprocessed, casefiles, M-Miller–P-Pappas, box 10; International Institutes of Toledo.

believed that immigration came with this price. Displaced persons were not contract laborers, for they maintained legal rights to leave the employ of their sponsors. Like contract laborers, however, DPs were vulnerable to exploitation. A neighbor wrote to the Displaced Persons Committee on behalf of a young immigrant girl employed as a domestic servant in Massachusetts who was badly mistreated by her employers. According to the informant, the girl was threatened with deportation by her sponsor if she complained about her wages or her working conditions. Moreover, the girl believed that her visa application had contracted her to work for the family for a year.[25] A second woman employed with her husband and sons on a farm in New York had worked as a cook for fourteen men for three months without being paid. The woman was afraid to report her employer for fear of deportation.[26] For some sponsors, long-term commitments were necessary as a route to citizenship. Domestic service provided valuable training in "Americanness," some sponsors argued, out of which worthy citizens would emerge. Writing to the Displaced Persons Committee, one employer noted that the girl they sponsored a year before as a domestic servant was still in their employ and "was willing to learn the American way." The girl, the letter concluded, "was going to make a good American citizen."[27]

The seasonal migration of male contract laborers primarily from Mexico into U.S. agricultural fields during the years of the bracero program provides a useful foil for the experiences of European refugees who immigrated primarily with their families at the behest of willing sponsors. Both the DP and bracero programs invited laborers to the United States but with different intentions toward their potential citizenship. The immigration of hundreds of thousands of destitute Eastern Europeans through the DP program rankled those who feared that their arrival signaled a return to the white ethnic heterogeneity of the early twentieth century. New European immigrants might contribute to a reemergence of the economic and political stains of the 1920s and 1930s. Despite these concerns, however, displaced persons fitted well into a mythic understanding of American cultural elasticity which promoted tolerance for European newcomers and humanitarian aid to foreign victims. Displaced persons came to work, often on American farms or in American kitchens, and through that work they would prove their worthiness for citizenship. By contrast, no matter how long braceros worked, they could never become citizens.

The domestic economy churned at unprecedented growth rates, bringing new demands for ready, available, and, whenever possible, cheap

---

[25] *Memo to America*, 233.
[26] Ibid., 233.
[27] Ibid., 215.

labor. The Western Hemisphere emerged as the primary source for America's labor needs. Congress officially authorized the importation of contract labor for agriculture in 1949, legalizing a bracero program that had been in operation since the war, and one that would continue until 1964. Between 1942 and 1952, over 800,000 braceros were contracted to work in American fields; millions more entered illegally outside the official program and were welcomed by American farmers seeking cheap sources of farm labor.[28] Like DPs, braceros arrived as employees, but, unlike DPs, braceros were confined to the temporal, spatial, and wage limits of their contracts.[29]

Historically, the proximity and permeability of the border had made labor migrations in and out of Mexico possible, but it had also made citizenship problematic. The Dillingham Commission's 1911 report to Congress recognized the value of Mexican labor but warned against the civic implications of settlement: "In the case of the Mexican, he is less desirable as a citizen than as a laborer."[30] In his 1925 report to the secretary of labor, Robert Foerster, a professor of economics at Princeton and an avid eugenicist, warned that the contributions Mexican immigrants made to the economy should not blind policy makers to the danger they posed as citizens. "No man is a worker alone," Foerster cautioned, "he is also a citizen and must further be viewed as the father of more citizens also. The years of his service as a wage earner are limited; not so the span of time in which those of his blood will play their parts in the country."[31] American

[28] In 1949, Congress added Title V to the Agriculture Act of 1949, which explicitly legalized the importation of agricultural workers and thus exempted these immigrants and their employers from the provisions of the contract labor law. The program had begun earlier in 1942 under a bilateral agreement to provide Mexican workers for American farms. The program, implemented by the Department of Agriculture from 1942 to 1947, provided about 219,500 Mexican nationals for American employers. Despite the war's end and the return of soldiers into the American labor force, agricultural employers in the South and Southwest convinced Congress that they remained dependent on large numbers of foreign laborers. The program was finally terminated in 1964. Kitty Calavita, *Inside the State: The Bracero Program, Immigration, and the INS* (New York: Routledge, 1992), 31–32.

[29] On the development and implementation of the Bracero program, as well as its effects on Mexican immigrants, see Ernesto Galarza, *Merchants of Labor: The Mexican Bracero Story: An Account of the Managed Migration of Mexican Farm Workers in California, 1942–1960* (Santa Barbara: McNally & Loftin, West, 1978); Mae M. Nai, "Braceros, 'Wetbacks,' and the National Boundaries of Class, 1942–1964, paper prepared for the Newberry Library Labor History Seminar, Chicago, 30 November 2001.

[30] Immigration Commission, *Reports of the Immigration Commission: Abstracts of the Reports of the Immigration Commission with Conclusions and Recommendations and Views of the Minority*, vol. 1, 1911, Senate document 747; United States Senate 61st Cong., 3d sess., Washington, D.C., 690–691.

[31] Robert F. Foerster, "The Racial Problems Involved in Immigration from Latin American and the West Indies to the United States," 55.

employers in the South and Southwest applied similar racial views to their understanding of work, poverty, and citizenship when they argued for a contract labor program in the decades following World War II.

Braceros fitted within a second, parallel understanding of the American immigrant past, one in which immigrants were primarily necessary laborers rather than potential citizens. Because they immigrated without their wives and families, Mexican braceros were unable to make the kinds of claims to citizenship which historically had proven powerful for other immigrant groups. Neither husbands nor fathers, Mexican immigrants were strictly laborers; they lacked, in the eyes of their employers, permanent, emotional, or legal ties to the nation.

Despite official policy, both contracted and noncontracted (illegal) braceros were often accompanied by family. According to a report issued by the President's Commission on Migratory Labor, "Many social complications are intensified by the presence of families. It must be noted moreover, that a child born in the U.S., though of Mexican illegal alien parents, is a citizen of the U.S."[32] The place of these children in American society troubled traditional insistence on the singular unity of family on the one hand and the rights of citizens on the other. In 1952, the INS defended itself against allegations that it routinely deported the American-born children of noncontracted Mexican laborers. In what must have seemed a cruel irony to those families who witnessed the deportation of their children, the INS insisted on the moral significance and thus the geographic and political displacement of Mexican families. The service argued that parents often elected to have their children accompany them to Mexico. According to the commissioner of immigration, "These children, of course, have dual nationality. As small children, they are much better off with their parents whom they have every legal and natural right to accompany to their homes in Mexico."[33]

Mexican nationals contracted to work under the bracero program were men, and little has been recovered of Mexican women's historical experiences with the contract labor program as wives or family members.[34] Those women who stayed behind in Mexico faced the daunting

[32] Frank L. Auerbach, "The Wetback Invasion—Illegal Alien Labor in American Agriculture," *Interpreter Releases* 28, no. 21 (3 May 1951), RACNS, CCAU, reel 8.

[33] The Southern Texas Association, chartered by a former INS patrol inspector, charged that INS deported nearly 500 American-born children of these nonregistered immigrants in 1952. INS file 56, 339–765, "Gen. File: Allegation that the Immigration and Naturalization Service is Deporting United States Citizen. Children to Mexico" (1952); DJA-INS acc. 58 A 734, box 3340; INS, DC, RG85; NA, DC.

[34] Pierrette Hondagneu-Sotelo notes that the bracero program created a network of relatives that provided systems of assistance and receptivity for Mexican women migrating in the 1960s and 1970s. Hondagneu-Sotelo, *Gendered Transitions: Mexican Experiences of Immigration* (Berkeley: University of California Press, 1994), 92.

challenge of supporting their families while they awaited remittances from El Norte. In her study of women's immigration experiences, Pierrette Hondagneu-Sotelo argues that scant remittances and long absences created by the bracero program pushed Mexican women into the labor force and into occupations traditionally dominated by men.[35] Women whose husbands never sent money or never returned often remarried or formed new households.[36]

Other women crossed the border unofficially to find work as domestic servants, creating an underground "bracera" program of informal female laborers. Immigration records indicate high demand for Mexican immigrant women's household labor.[37] A 1949 letter from an attorney in El Paso to Texas Senator Tom Commally queried why "the El Paso housewife cannot have and use the services of Mexican maids if the big farmers can get Mexicans to gather and harvest their crops." The attorney suggested that the government establish a "bracero program for maids," one that would provide Mexican women with visas that required them to work as domestic servants and have their immigration status renewed annually.[38]

A memo to the deputy commissioner from El Paso officials confirmed that Mexican women were in high demand in American cities along the Mexican border but that consular officials in Mexico were reluctant to issue visas that would entitle women to legal residence.[39] Moreover, according to El Paso officials, American consuls believed that Mexican women should be allowed to work as domestic servants in the United States without visas, therefore encouraging women to enter outside offi-

---

[35] Ibid., 12.

[36] As Dona Rosaura Barragan de Perez explained, "It's still very hard on the young women who have their husbands in the north. Not very long ago, a young woman from here fell. I could see it was going to happen. Her husband went up there, but he never sent her money. She had little children to feed. Well, what could she do? She went to Zacoalco to work, and of course she met someone else, and now she's pregnant." Marilyn P. Davis, ed., *Mexican Voices/American Dreams: An Oral History of Mexican Immigration to the United States* (New York: Henry Holt and Company, 1990), 21–22. See also testimony of María de Jesús Medina and Leonara Ruiz Carrilla in *Mexican Voices/American Dreams*, 23–26.

[37] For example, see INS file 56231/543 (1948); DJA-INS acc. 58 A 734, box 3002; INS, DC, RG85; NA, DC.

[38] Attorney in El Paso to Senator Tom Connally, 29 July 1949, INS file 56, 281–320 (1949); DJA-INS acc. 58 A 734, box 3148; INS, DC, RG85; NA, DC. The attorney wrote a similar letter to then Senator Lyndon B. Johnson, attorney in El Paso, to Senator Lyndon B. Johnson 29 July 1949, INS file 56, 281–320 (1949); DJA-INS acc. 58 A 734, box 3148; INS, DC, RG85; NA, DC.

[39] El Paso office to Deputy Commissioner, 1 April 1944, INS file 56, 281–320 (1949); DJA-INS acc. 58 A 734, box 3148; INS, DC, RG85; NA, DC.

cial channels.[40] El Paso officials informed Washington authorities that they conducted occasional raids on undocumented Mexican maids, confiscating border crossing permits and deporting offenders who would be unable to return through legal channels.[41] The INS records suggest that Mexican women also crossed the northern border into California, where they also risked deportation as undocumented immigrants. Monica Baez crossed the border "one block west of the port of entry at Calexico, California" in 1949 and found work as a domestic servant for a family in Holtville, California. Fearing she would be deported before her son had an opportunity to finish school, Baez wrote to the president to ask him to intercede on her behalf. Sadly, her letter for help was forwarded to immigration authorities, who held Baez for deportation.[42] By 1965, official certification as a domestic servant was one of the few ways women like Monica Baez could obtain a visa to work in the United States.

Both the bracero and displaced persons programs reveal postwar anxieties about the relationship between need, work, and potential citizenship in immigration law. Fearful of a return to the high levels of unemployment of the 1930s and wary of any influx of immigrants marked as racially or ethnically "different," Congress sought to limit the economic and cultural impact of European refugees. By narrowly defining those included as "refugees," Congress struck a compromise between policies restricting immigration and those offering humanitarian relief. Ideals of domesticity played a pivotal role in the evaluation of women refugees. As a result, most women DPs were admitted as wives and domestic servants. Similarly, Congress acquiesced to the vocal demands of organized agriculture for a ready supply of low-wage labor by allowing the importation of braceros, but it was cautious to limit the new labor program to working men. As potential mothers of citizens, Mexican women threatened to destabilize the precarious legal distinction policy makers hoped to achieve between migrants who came only to work and immigrants who might become citizens. The result was to stymie the development of immigrant families and slow the overall growth of Mexican American communities.

[40] Wilmoth, El Paso District Director to Commissioner Miller, 16 August 1949, INS casefile 56, 281–320 (1949); DJA-INS acc. 58 A 734, box 3148; INS, DC, RG85; NA, DC.

[41] This memo noted that the El Paso attorney's own Mexican domestic servant had been deported during such a raid. Wilmoth, El Paso District Director to Commissioner Miller, 16 August 1949, INS casefile 56, 281–320 (1949); DJA-INS acc. 58 A 734, box 3148; INS, DC, RG85; NA, DC.

[42] Baez was born in Mexico in 1914, and first immigrated to the United States in 1944, one year after her common-law husband died. She briefly returned to Mexico in 1947 for surgery, reentering through Calexico. Her son, thirteen years old, was born in Mexico. The family was given ten days to sell their things before they were deported 10 June 1949. Monica Baez [pseud.], INS file 56, 276–949 (1949); DJA-INS acc. 58 A 734, box 3137; INS, DC, RG85; NA, DC.

THE LIVE-IN MAID PROBLEM:
WOMEN'S WORK AND THE WORK VISA SYSTEM

Gender and race continued to mold immigration policy after 1940, but in ways that reflected the dramatic shift from conditions of scarcity to those of labor demand and emerging abundance. Following the depression era, much of the responsibility and power to implement economic provisions in immigration law was shifted out from the border to the consuls abroad.[43] At this distant, procedural border, gender and race remained important tools in the effort to distinguish skilled work from unskilled, worthy worker from unworthy. Both the 1952 McCarren-Walter Act and the 1965 Immigration Act emphasized immigrants' potential contributions as skilled workers and their likely cost as unskilled or surplus laborers.

The advent of a work visa system instituted after World War II, authorized by the Department of Labor and administered by the foreign consuls, necessitated a reevaluation of over half a century of contract labor laws. However, there was no such reevaluation of how women's work was understood and valued under the law. In codifying work in terms of its value to the nation, post–World War II policy recognized immigrant women, particularly those from Mexico and the Caribbean, for their labor in American homes and hospitals, providing visas to those willing to work as domestic servants, live-in maids, and nurses.[44]

The 1952 McCarren-Walter Act revised the quota structure that had been established thirty years earlier by giving first preference to immigrants whose work skills were in high demand. Half of all visas awarded under the 1952 law were awarded for skilled work.[45] In a nod to immigration restrictionists and labor unions, the act authorized the secretary of labor to exclude any laborers deemed not to be in short supply and whose arrival therefore posed a threat to domestic wages and working conditions. This passive restriction, however, was layered onto concurrent policies authorizing the temporary admission of agricultural laborers predominantly from Mexico. Thus, the 1952 act mindfully exempted immigrants from the Western Hemisphere and left intact the official bracero program and the less official "illegal" immigration it had engendered in its wake.

[43] Hutchinson, *Legislative History of American Immigration Policy*, 414.

[44] Edith Lowenstein, "Occupations and Groups of Occupations for which Nationally the Supply of Available Workers is Inadequate to Meet All Demands," *Interpreter Releases* 30, no. 25, appendix I (27 May 1953), RACNS, reel 9. Fung-Yea Huang notes that labor certificates as live-in maids were easy to obtain. Huang, *Asian and Hispanic Immigrant Women in the Work Force: Implications of the United States Immigration Policies since 1965* (New York: Garland Publishing, 1997), 57.

[45] Hutchinson, *Legislative History of American Immigration Policy*, 306–310.

Most categories of women's work were classified as unskilled under the 1952 law, making it very difficult for women to secure any visa to the United States. For example, the Board of Immigration Appeals denied the appeal of an Italian woman, ruling that her work as a beauty operator was not skilled work worthy of a preference visa, but granting the petition of a man who worked as a ladies' hair stylist, arguing that he fitted prevailing definitions of skilled work.[46] In determining an immigrant's potential work status, immigration authorities consulted the *Dictionary of Occupational Titles*, which distinguished among "hand-sewers," "seamstresses," and "tailors," or between "professional nurses" and "registered nurses." The specifics of work determined its value under the law. When a Mrs. Leo attempted to help her seventeen-year-old sister Rose Crespino secure a visa in 1954, the International Institute of Buffalo explained to her that the wait for Italian visas was several years, so there was little hope that her sister could join her in the United States, Leo tried again in 1959. This time she asked if her sister might enter under the preference for skilled immigrants. However, the International Institute informed Leo that, as a tailoress, her sister did not fall within one of the privileged categories of skilled work. By 1963, Leo's sister had married and move to Canada, but was still awaiting a visa.[47] Similarly, a woman who worked as a sample stitcher, sewing sample garments together by following sketches and patterns, was denied a skilled work visa. The Board of Immigration Appeals did, however, authorize the admission of a flight stewardess whose language abilities, appearance, weight, height, and moral character uniquely qualified her for employment.[48]

According to immigration authorities, domestic service, historically a source of easier access for immigrant women, was unskilled work. In hearing the case of four Italian women intending to work in a Catholic orphanage outside Philadelphia, the Board of Immigration Appeals denied that domestic service required skills above that of a housewife. Thus it fell well short of the professional standard necessary for first-preference visas under the 1952 law. "Nowhere," the board concluded, "does it ap-

[46] *Matter of A—— P——*, 7 I & N 640 (BIA 1958); *Matter of Bozdogan*, Int. Dec. 1804, file A-1434968, 19 October 1967, as cited in Edith Lowenstein "Administrative Decisions under the Immigration and Nationality Laws of the United States," *Interpreter Releases* 45, no. 4 (25 January 1968), RACNS, reel 15. Also see *Matter of Ko*, 10 I & N 626 (BIA 1964).

[47] Rose Crespino [pseud.] (1954), Unprocessed, box 1; International Institutes of Buffalo. For a similar case see Martha Fleck [pseud.] (1965), Unprocessed, box 1; International Institutes of Buffalo.

[48] *In the Matter of Pan American World Airways, Inc.*, Int. Dec. 906, file VP-3 I-117018, 24 December 1957, as cited in Edith Lowenstein, "Administrative Decisions under the Immigration and Nationality Laws of the United States," *Interpreter Releases* 35, no. 18 (26 May 1958), RACNS, reel 11.

pear that these beneficiaries have any special education, experience, technical training or exceptional ability. Pure and simple, they are and will be domestic servants."[49]

Some domestic servants were permitted to travel to the United States with their employers, including chauffeurs, valets, lady's maids, nursemaids, and private social secretaries, but excluding butlers, cooks, general maids, charwomen, and gardeners. Some women were able to enter within these narrow parameters.[50] In 1950, ten percent of all foreign-born white women and 16.5 percent of all Mexican immigrant women in the workforce found employment as private household workers.[51]

The 1965 Immigration Act eliminated the national origins system that had been in place since the 1920s and shifted the emphasis between family connections and work skills established in the McCarren-Walter legislation. The act gave first preference and the largest number of visas to the children, spouses, brothers, and sisters of U.S. citizens. Immigration from the Western Hemisphere was folded into the preference system, placing a total cap on annual arrivals for the first time in history.[52] The labor certification program expanded under the 1965 law, which now required immigrants to demonstrate available employment as a condition of their visa.[53]

In his analysis of postwar immigration policy, David Reimers suggests that a growing tolerance for racial, ethnic, and religious diversity created a general climate for legal reform. By 1965 a Democratic majority in Congress, backing from the AFL-CIO, and the deaths of both McCarran and Walter opened the door to long-awaited reform legislation.[54] Despite this

---

[49] *Matter of I—— et al.* 7 I & N 292 (BIA 1956).

[50] Regulations issued 19 December 1952, as cited in Edith Lowenstein, "Amendments to Regulations Under the Immigration and Nationality Act, Part II: Amendments to Regulations Issued by the Visa Office of the Department of State," *Interpreter Releases* 30, no. 42 (27 October 1953), RACNS, reel 9.

[51] The census calculation underestimates the vast numbers of women who crossed the border extralegally to obtain employment in American homes, but it does indicate that household labor provided ready means for legal employment for many Mexican women. Overall, Mexican women constitute six percent of the total domestic service labor force in 1950. E. P. Hutchinson, *Immigrants and Their Children 1850–1950* (New York: John Wiley & Sons, 1956), 350–364.

[52] However, the Western Hemisphere had neither a family preference system nor a per nation limit.

[53] Hutchinson, *Legislative History of American Immigration Policy*, 377–378.

[54] Presidents Truman, Eisenhower, and Kennedy, along with liberal, proimmigration advocates, had attempted without success since 1952 to eliminate the national origins quota system and the Asia-Pacific triangle allocations from immigration law. Calls to eliminate race and ethnic discrimination were met with steady resistance from a restrictionist lobby backed by patriotic societies and many southern politicians. David Reimers notes that the Johnson administration had favored granting the majority of visas to immigrants with desirable work skills, but compromised with Representative Michael Feighan, chair of the House

reform effort, however, family reunification policies embedded in the 1965 legislation promised to maintain current immigration patterns and thus historical race and ethnic discriminations in the law. Categories of work and anxieties about immigrant workers remained integral to the 1965 reforms. Although the racist languages of the quota system and Asian barred zone were gone by 1965, the emphasis on family and skilled work created de facto racial and gender-based segregation in American immigration law.

Administrative discretion in determining work skills and valuable workers remained colored by race and conceptions of unassimilable difference. In hearings before Congress in 1964, Assistant Attorney General Schiei reminded House members that the proposed legislation "would make Jamaica, Trinidad and Tobago nonquota, like every other country in the Western Hemisphere." However, Schiei continued, "as you know, the real limitation on immigration from the Western Hemisphere is the power of the Secretary of Labor and the Immigration and Naturalization Service to confine immigrants to those who can find a place in our employment picture in the U.S."[55] Before 1965, immigrants from the Western Hemisphere needed only to reassure immigration officials that they would not become public charges. With the 1965 reforms these immigrants would have to meet a higher standard of economic self-sufficiency, one that assured immigration officials their work would neither displace American workers nor adversely affect American wages.[56]

The 1965 law made other subtle but significant distinctions between immigrants by requiring that adult relatives of immigrants from the Western Hemisphere obtain labor certifications, while their European counterparts did not face this additional burden. The law thus defined adult immigrants from the Caribbean, Central America, Latin American, Mexico, and Canada as workers, making subtle and consequential distinctions between European relatives, refugees, and future employees.[57]

Immigration Subcommittee, to give seventy-four percent of the total number of visas to those with close relatives in the United States. The administration also recognized AFL-CIO concerns over employment competition by providing the Labor Department with authority to issue visas for those entering as workers. Reimers, *Still the Golden Door*, 61–72.

[55] Edith Lowenstein, "House Hearings on Pending Immigration Legislation I," *Interpreter Releases* 41, no. 38 (21 October 1964), RACNS, reel 14.

[56] Edith Lowenstein, "The Act of October 3, 1965 to Amend the Immigration and Nationality Act; and for Other Purposes," *Interpreter Releases* 43, no. 6 (3 February 1966), RACNS, reel 14.

[57] Specifically, the law required work visas from sons and daughters of citizens or lawful residents who were either married or unmarried and over age 21, and the brothers and sisters of American citizens. Edith Lowenstein, "The Act of October 3, 1965 to Amend the Immigration and Nationality Act; and for Other Purposes," *Interpreter Releases*, 43, no. 6 (3 February 1966), RACNS, reel 14.

Beginning in 1965, the labor department began certifying live-in domestic servants as sixth-preference immigrants (skilled and unskilled workers in short supply). With American women entering the paid workforce in ever greater numbers, household laborers emerged as a new and increasingly necessary occupational category. Women willing to work in domestic service, especially those willing to live in their employers' homes, were in demand, and foreign women presented a ready supply.[58] By 1967 the number of immigrants approved for permanent employment in the United States as domestic service workers ballooned to thirty-seven percent of all visas issued. Fifty-nine percent of all visas approved for immigrants from the Western Hemisphere went to those certified in service occupations; eighty-eight percent of all service employees were destined for live-in domestic service.[59] Immigrant women, especially those from the Western Hemisphere, clearly strategized to take advantage of limited opportunities for women workers to enter within an increasingly rigid and restricted work visa system, so much so that immigration and labor department officials struggled with what they perceived as a "live-in maid problem."[60]

For women in the Western Hemisphere, domestic service created a small space of entry that many quickly fitted to their own devices.[61] The American labor force remained highly sexually segregated, and women found employment most readily in the pink collar ghettos of the low-paying service sector. While barriers to women's employment in traditionally "male" occupations were about to be challenged, with no legal provisions to ensure equal opportunity, cultural stereotypes about women and work remained virulent. Women immigrants entered as domestic servants in large numbers, particularly after 1965, because it was so difficult to obtain labor certification as anything else.[62] As had been true under the 1952 legislation, most of women's work remained outside the occupational visa structure. A thirty-four-year-old woman from the Dominican Republic obtained certification as a live-in domestic in 1966 but sought

---

[58] Edith Lowenstein, "Labor Department Struggles with Live-in Maid Problem," *Interpreter Releases* 46, no. 45 (20 November 1969), RACNS, reel 16.

[59] In 1968 hearings before the House Committee on the Judiciary, Stanley Ruttenbery, assistant secretary for the Department of Labor, estimated that ninety-five percent of all visas issued to service employees from the Western Hemisphere went to live-in maids. Lowenstein, "Review of the Operation of the Immigration and Nationality Act as Amended by the Act of October 3, 1965, Part III: Labor Department," *Interpreter Releases* 45, no. 50 (30 December 1968), RACNS, reel 15.

[60] Edith Lowenstein, "Labor Department Struggles with Live-in Maid Problem," *Interpreter Releases* 46, no. 45 (20 November 1969), RACNS, reel 16.

[61] This was also true for European women facing oversubscribed visas. *Matter of Izdebska*, 12 I & N 54 (BIA 1966); *Matter of Romano*, 12 I & N 731 (BIA 1968).

[62] Fung-Yea Huang, *Asian and Hispanic Immigrant Women in the Work Force*, 57.

work as a linking machine operator in a jewelry factory soon after her arrival in New York. The woman had been working in New York on a temporary visa in 1964 and had returned home in order to secure a domestic service certification after being unable to obtain a visa for factory work.[63]

In 1968 hearings before the House Committee on the Judiciary, Stanley Ruttenberg, assistant secretary for the Department of Labor, drew public attention to the maid crisis. "We have been deeply concerned about the number of live-in maids in relation to the number of immigrants in other occupations," Ruttenberg explained, "and about the attendant problems of fraud and misrepresentation involving live-in maid cases." In an investigation of foreign domestic workers in Chicago, the Department of Labor found that only two out of thirty immigrant women who had entered as maids were employed as domestic servants after two months. The department estimated that over a third of all immigrants approved for permanent employment worked in the service occupations, and between eighty-eight and ninety-five percent were live-in maids. Despite employer demand, according to the Department of Labor, these women were not valuable and skilled immigrants. "These low-skilled workers" Ruttenberg concluded, took "immigration opportunities from highly skilled individuals whose contribution to our society and economy would be greater."[64]

In response to the numbers of women using live-in certification to enter the United States, the Labor Department began requiring evidence of past experience in domestic service work, essentially calling for the formalization of household labor. The department insisted that employers supply written contracts specifying hours, wages, overtime, and responsibilities, in addition to accommodations if the employee was to live in.[65] Despite these regulations, the flow of women willing to work as domestic servants remained unabated. In 1969 the Department of Labor issued even more specific guidelines that sought to narrow and specifically define the quality and quantity of household labor.[66]

[63] She had left her children in the Dominican Republic. She was offered voluntary departure in 1969. *Matter of Santana*, 13 I & N 362 (BIA 1969). This case is also mentioned in Edith Lowenstein, "Recent Decisions under the Immigration Laws," *Interpreter Releases* 46, no. 24 (30 June 1969), RACNS, reel 15.

[64] Testimony before Subcommittee No. 1 of the Committee on the Judiciary of the House in charge of immigration legislation, 22 May and 13 June 1968 as cited in Edith Lowenstein, "Review of the Operation of the Immigration and Nationality Act as Amended by the Act of October 3, 1965, Part III: Labor Department," *Interpreter Releases* 45, no. 50 (30 December 1968), RACNS, reel 15.

[65] Edith Lowenstein, "More About Labor Certifications," *Interpreter Releases* 45, no. 38 (11 October 1968), RACNS, reel 15.

[66] U.S. Department of Labor, Manpower Administration Memo to All Regional Manpower Administrators 10 October 1969, as reproduced in Edith Lowenstein, "Labor De-

Immigration records suggest that possible fraud on the part of immigrant women was matched only by misrepresentation by potential employers. When women arrived, their status was tied to their employers, leaving them vulnerable to exploitation.[67] Many immigrant women arrived only to find that the job they had been certified to do was no longer available. These women were left with little choice but to find other work. Should they find work outside of domestic service, however, they could be deported for fraud. A thirty-seven-year-old Jamaican woman left her family behind to seek work in Roxbury, Massachusetts, as a domestic servant. When she arrived in 1966 she found her employer had hired a Haitian woman.[68] She quickly found work as a sewing machine operator in Boston for seventy dollars a week. Ironically, she had originally tried to secure a visa as a stitcher or telephone operator but had been denied. She was held for deportation in 1967 and granted voluntary departure to Jamaica.[69] A second woman received her labor certification for domestic work only to see her employer withdraw the application. The woman left her children in the care of her mother in Honduras and entered the United States under her now defunct labor certification. The woman continued on to the United States despite her lack of employment and briefly found work as a domestic servant with another employer. The language barrier proved too difficult and she sought work in a factory that employed relatives from Honduras.[70] When she was brought up on charges by immigration authorities, she had again found work in domestic service. She was granted voluntary departure in 1969.[71] Threat of deportation placed do-

---

partment Struggles with Live-in Maid Problem," *Interpreter Releases* 46, no. 45 (20 November 1969), RACNS, reel 16.

[67] Edith Drake [pseud.] (1956), Unprocessed, casefiles, D-Dramond—V-Vardinakis, box 5; International Institutes of Toledo.

[68] This employer had filed employment certifications for five or six women, and testified that she had intended to help her friends find suitable maids.

[69] *Matter of Tucker*, 12 I & N 328 (BIA 1967). This case is also discussed in Edith Lowenstein, "Alien Ordered Deported because of Noncompliance with Labor Certification," *Interpreter Releases*, 44, no. 39 (22 September 1967), RACNS, reel 15.

[70] She was fired from her position as a domestic servant after she was unable to find her way back to her employer's house after her day off.

[71] *Matter of Welcome*, decided by the Board of Immigration Appeals, 6 August 1969, as cited in Edith Lowenstein, "Administrative Decisions under the Immigration and Nationality Laws of the United States," *Interpreter Releases* 46, no. 43 (3 November 1969), RACNS, reel 16. For related cases, see *Matter of Morgan*, decided by the Board of Immigration Appeals, 22 May 1969, in Edith Lowenstein, "Administrative Decisions under the Immigration and Nationality Laws of the United States," *Interpreter Releases* 46, no. 38 (29 September 1969), RACNS, reel 15; *Matter of Stevens*, decided by the Board of Immigration Appeals, 12 April 1968, in Edith Lowenstein, "Administrative Decisions under the Immigration and Nationality Laws of the United States," *Interpreter Releases* 46, no. 6 (25 February 1969), RACNS, reel 15.

mestic service workers in an extremely vulnerable position, risking deportation should they leave their employer. Lilly Dubois arrived from Trinidad in 1968 certified to work as a domestic servant in Buffalo. Dubois left her employer after three days and sought the assistance of Traveler's Aid. Dubois explained that her employer had called her various names and she was unable to continue working there.[72]

While postwar immigration reforms sought to address historic race and geographic inequities in immigration law, gender continued to structure how work was valued under the law. Domestic service offered immigrant women, especially those from the Western Hemisphere, one of the only means of securing a visa and, in the process, firmly located women's work in the home, if not her own then someone else's. Women's success in using domestic service visas to gain access became a problem for immigration and Congressional officials concerned with regulating the arrival of unskilled, third-world workers.

The experience of the Great Depression had raised troubling questions about the nation's responsibility to those who worked and lived within its borders. Congress, immigration officials, and the American public debated what separated residents from citizens and whether government-sponsored relief was a right of citizenship or an entitlement of workers. The displaced persons and bracero programs continued in the groove cut by prewar debates, suggesting that immigrants who came to work need not necessarily become citizens. Race and gender structured evaluations of work and need within both programs, determining how, where, and which women would be admitted. Finally, the 1952 and 1965 immigration reforms shifted the focus of law from exclusion of unwanted laborers to the inclusion of specific skills. Gender and race were central to the process of evaluating skilled labor, and few traditionally female professions were offered skill status.

Conceptions of want, scarcity, and need, like those of work and skill, structured women's relationship to the law. Immigrant women acted in dialogue with the law and entering as domestic servants whenever possible. Their success in using the law garnered accusations of fraud and misuse. Faced with limited employment opportunities rarely recognized as "skilled" laborers, however, working women's shrewd manipulation of the work visa system in the decades after World War II laid bare the deep roots of gender bias and race discrimination in immigration law.

---

[72] Lilly Dubois [pseud.] (1968), Unprocessed, box 25; International Institutes of Buffalo.

∞ Part III ∞

MARRIAGE, FAMILY, AND THE LAW

CHAPTER TWELVE

Families, Made in America

In 1953 and 1956, *Life Magazine* followed the efforts of two women to join their husbands living in the United States. Loyalty, commitment, patience, and love provided the emotional ground for these women's public appeal, while laws that prohibited families and separated husbands and wives were condemned as un-American. "Love or the Law?," which appeared in 1953, related the story of Anne Craps, a Belgian bride, and Ray Urabazo, her American airman husband.[1] In a final picture in the photo essay, Craps is shown sitting on 700 sheets of paper, a year of love letters from her husband, carefully lined up in rows as far as the eye can see.[2] Three years later, Grace Li's story appeared in *Life*. "The Agonizing Odyssey of Two People in Love" told the story of Li's marriage to Pei-Chao Li, and their seven-year ordeal to be reunited in the United States.[3] Illustrated with photographs from her wedding, and somber pictures of Li, alone leaning over the telephone during a brief call to her husband, the article heaped scorn on arbitrary regulations and unyielding officials standing in the way of a happy marriage.[4]

Both "Love or the Law?" and "The Agonizing Odyssey of Two People in Love" invoked many of the themes that had historically served as the

---

[1] The two had been married in 1952, but Craps was unable to obtain a visa because of a criminal record. While working in a German factory in 1942, Craps had torn down a portrait of Hitler and used a ration card to obtain food for French prisoners. A German court sentenced her to three years of hard labor. American immigration officials insisted that their decisions could not be ruled "by compassion" but must "adhere strictly to the law."

[2] "Love or the Law? One Draws Belgian Bride to GI Husband; Other Keeps Them Apart," *Life*, 23 February 1953, 61. Five months later, *Life* reported and photographed the happy reunion of Craps and Urabazo. "The Sergeant Gets His Belgian Bride," *Life*, 22 July 1953, 111.

[3] The two had met in 1944 and married in 1946 when Grace Li was twenty years old. After two years of happy marriage, her husband left for the United States to attend Columbia University while Li found work as a secretary in Shanghai. In 1949, following the Communist takeover, Li fled to Hong Kong where she began the process of securing a visa to join her husband in the United States. Pei-Chao Li was a Chinese citizen and could not return to join his wife in Hong Kong. Unable to obtain a visa as a wife, Li attempted to immigrate as a student and traveled to Great Britain and to France where she hoped to find a more sympathetic audience.

[4] William Brinkley, "The Agonizing Odyssey of Two People in Love," *Life*, 5 March 1956, 160. Four months later, *Life* photographed the happy ending, "Happy Outcome for Grace Li," *Life*, 2 July 1956, 94.

justification for maintaining a unique and privileged place for wives in immigration law. Families divided by legal and geographic borders could not stand; a nation of divided families would certainly fall. While ideas of family and home had always been central to American nationalism, the new political realities of a Cold War world tied national survival ever more forcefully to domestic tranquility. Craps and Li were not only legal wives, they were also loyal wives. Yet these two stories also highlight issues unique to the post–World War II period. Domesticity retained a powerful hold on immigration law in defining the limits of legal marriage and the qualities of a loyal wife. Yet gender, race, and nation intersected in new ways in the years surrounding the war, creating new opportunities for Asian immigrant women.

Paradoxically, war both fractured and created families. Children lost parents and created new homes with relatives, neighbors, or other local adults. Many women lost fiancées or husbands during the war, others married soldiers stationed in their towns and villages, and some even became pregnant awaiting disarmament. With peace came the daunting task of reuniting those who had been separated, incorporating those who had been left alone, and evaluating those who would be admitted to the United States. In regulating the arrival of foreign-born women and their children in the decades after World War II, immigration and naturalization law delineated the boundaries of the modern American family. The status of adopted children and those born of common-law marriages, adulterous relationships, or illicit sexual unions had to be debated at the bar. By the 1940s and 1950s, families increasingly became products of evidence, substantiated and verified through biological testing and legal argument.

Historically, policies encouraging family reunification had come into direct conflict with those insisting on race exclusion. Ironically, each had at its root a similar goal—racially homogenous American families. Family reunification policies that followed World War II, like those that came before, favored women whose primary work lay in their reproductive and productive responsibilities in the immigrant home. However, the sympathetic portrayal of a Chinese woman's efforts to join her husband in the United States would have been impossible amidst the loud and long attacks on Chinese immigration that sounded over the first half of the twentieth century.

LOYAL WIVES, LEGAL WIVES: DOMESTICITY AFTER WORLD WAR II

When oversubscribed quotas for most countries could mean years of waiting for intended immigrants, wives maintained their privileged position in the law.[5] Yet as had been true in decades past, domesticity proved the price of admission. The arrival of women in the second half of the twentieth century continued to be thought of in terms of immigrant women as wives and mothers, rather than as independent immigrants, workers, or refugees. For immigration officials stationed at the nation's borders, the appearance of domesticity was colored by race. Although legal barriers against the arrival of Asian women were steadily dismantled, race difference remained central to how these women were evaluated as wives when they arrived at the border.[6]

In the decades following World War II, women arrived in ever greater numbers, many of them as wives and many under the provisions of the War Brides and GI Fiancées Acts.[7] Both acts rewarded the sacrifices of soldiers by reuniting them with their foreign-born wives.[8] The 1945 War Brides Act allowed for the admission of alien spouses and minor children of citizen members of the armed forces.[9] One year later, the GI Fiancées Act granted women engaged to be married to citizen members of the armed forces temporary admission for three months conditional upon their immediate marriage. In 1946, seventy-five percent of all arriving immigrants were women; of these women forty-one percent were wives of United States servicemen arriving under the GI Fiancées Act. Most of these women were from Great Britain, with smaller numbers from Australia, France, Italy, and Canada.[10]

[5] The Immigration Acts of 1952 and 1965 both admitted wives as nonquota or quota-free immigrants.

[6] Chinese wives of American citizens who had been married before 1924 were given nonquota immigration status in 1946.

[7] Throughout the 1930s and 1940s women comprised between fifty-five and sixty percent of arriving immigrants; in the postwar period women have continued to arrive in sizable numbers, over half (fifty-three to fifty-five percent) of immigrants are women. See Marion F. Houstoun et al., "Female Predominance of Immigration to the United States since 1930: A First Look," *International Migration Review* 28 (winter 1984): 908–963; Gabaccia, *From the Other Side*, 28.

[8] Service in the armed forces traditionally had offered immigrant men an expeditious route to citizenship, thus offering increased benefits to their wives and daughters. For example, illiterate immigrant women arriving as fiancées of men who had served in World War I were given special status, and allowed an additional sixty days after arrival to learn to read and demonstrate their ability to pass the literacy test. E.S.P., "Women Immigrants and the Law," *Foreign Born* 1, no. 6 (May 1920): 4–5; published by the Committee on Work with Foreign-Born Women, National Board of the YWCA by the Woman's Press for the Committee, from microfilm provided by the New York Public Library.

[9] Hutchinson, *Legislative History of American Immigration Policy*, 269. For an account of the experiences of British women, see Jenel Virden, *Good-bye Piccadilly: British War Brides in America* (Urbana: University of Illinois Press, 1996).

[10] In 1946, 44,775 women arrived as fiancées; fifty-eight percent women were from Great Britain, nine percent were from Australia, eight percent were French, five percent were Italian, and four percent were Canadian. Frank Auerbach, "Immigration Statistics for 1946,"

Echoes of earlier debates over marriage hung in the air, for both acts defined the limits of legal marriage and of loyal wives. The War Brides Act included only "spouses" of members of the armed forces; thus neither a woman whose soldier husband had obtained a divorce without her knowledge, nor a widow of a serviceman, was admissible.[11] Proxy marriages or telephone marriages were not recognized as valid unless these marriages had been "consummated by subsequent cohabitation."[12] While the spouses and children of servicemen were admitted as nonquota immigrants and exempted from educational and physical requirements, they were still required to meet race-based eligibility laws which allowed only those eligible for naturalization access to immigration—those who were white or black, those who were of races indigenous to the Western Hemisphere, and those of Chinese descent.[13] The GI Fiancées Act expired a few years after it was passed, thus providing only a brief window of opportunity for would-be brides.[14] Moreover, in language that reverberated with the concerns of the picture bride era, the American citizen applicant was required to have "personally met his or her fiancé or fiancée," and any alien applicant who did not marry upon arrival was subject to deportation.[15]

Interpreter Releases 24, no. 13 (17 March 1947), RACNS, reel 7. Data taken from "Table 2. Aliens Admitted—Number and Percent by Classes under the Immigration Act of 1924 as Amended Years Ended June 30, 1941 to 1946."

[11] General Council to Commissioner, Memorandum Answering Questions about Application of War Bride Law, 13 November 1946, INS File 56013/373 (1946); DJA-INS acc. 58 A 734, box 1595; INS, DC, RG85; NA, DC.

[12] Frank L. Auerbach, " 'GI Brides Act': and 'GI Fiancees Act': Some Questions Concerning Their Interpretation and Administration," *Interpreter Releases* 24, no. 10 (24 February 1947).

[13] Those remaining outside the reach of the 1945 War Brides Act were all immigrants living in the Asian Barred Zone except for "persons of Chinese descent." Congress did make one exception, Philippine citizens "of the Philippine races" were allowed to enter as nonquota immigrants although they were not eligible for naturalization in 1945. INS, Washington, D.C. to INS, Detroit, 2 April 1946, INS file 56, 229–478 (1946); DJA-INS acc.. 58 A 734, box 2994; INS, DC, RG85; NA, DC.

[14] The first law expired 1 July 1947. It was extended to 31 December 1947, and finally to 31 December 1948. After the 1948 expiration date had passed, several hundred applications for fiancées were still pending. Congress allowed consular officials to finish processing these applications provided that the aliens arrived within five months. See Hutchinson, *Legislative History of American Immigration Policy*, 516.

[15] Section 2, act of June 29, 1946, see INS file 56, 230–853 (1946); DJA-INS acc. 58 A 734, box 3001; INS, DC, RG85; NA, DC; Hutchinson, *Legislative History of American Immigration Policy*, 517. When Louise Ann Jacobs arrived in San Francisco in 1947, she wanted to remain in the United States but she no longer wanted to marry her serviceman fiancé. Jacobs had married another American man, though not a soldier, while waiting in Australia for her first fiancé to send for her. Under questioning, Jacobs pressed her case, arguing in the end that she was still the wife of a citizen. Louise Ann Jacobs [pseud.], INS file

Marriage to a soldier was no guarantee of admission for any immigrant woman. As had been true in years past, entering as a wife came at a cost. Women remained subject to intense scrutiny about the logistics and legitimacy of their marriages.[16] Women arriving as war brides were asked to provide proof of their marriage or engagement to a United States veteran. When Ngo Shee arrived with her children in 1947, the only evidence she had of her marriage was a "three-generation paper" now lost in the war.[17] Ngo Shee had some letters that her husband had written her during the war, but on the advice of friends she had not brought these with her, "People in China said that those letters were of no use should not be brought along."[18]

A war bride's status was dependent on that of her husband; should he be found not to be a citizen, not to have been a soldier, not to have been honorably discharged, or not of a race eligible, then she too was inadmissible.[19] Many women fell outside the strict racial, moral, or temporal limits of wartime wifeness. For example, Helene Emilie Bouiss was prevented from joining her American soldier husband in the United States when immigration and court officials determined that Bouiss was of biracial ancestry, one-half white and one-half Japanese.[20] According to the federal

---

1300/46960 (1947); GICF, box 70; INS, SFD, RG85; NA-PSR. See also Katherine Dawson [pseud.], INS file 1300/46868 (1947); GICF, box 70; INS, SFD, RG85; NA-PSR.

[16] A Japanese woman who had been married in Japan by a religious ceremony but not by a civil ceremony was found not to have been legally married. *In the Matter of B———*, Int. Dec. 687, file VP 8–14341, Visa Petition Proceedings, Decided by the Board February 10, 1955, in Edith Lowenstein, "Decisions by the Board of Immigration Appeals," *Interpreter Releases* 32, no. 47 (1 December 1955), RACNS, reel 10.

[17] Ngo Shee asserted that she had received benefits from the United States government as the wife of a soldier, and that her husband had also provided some financial support while the family was in China.

[18] Unfortunately for Ngo Shee, like her marriage, her husband's status as a native-born United States citizen could not be verified. After consulting birth records, city registries, and local newspapers, immigration officials found no evidence corroborating her husband's biography. Moreover, immigration officials suspected that Ngo Shee's husband had served less than three years in the army and had not served overseas. Records in the file indicate that immigration officials were aware that Congress was contemplating offering immediate naturalization to all those who had served during World War II; such legislation would allow Ngo Shee to enter as a wife. Ngo Shee was advised to attempt to reimmigrate one year hence. Ngo Shee [pseud.], INS casefile 1300/46686 (1947); GICF, box 67; INS, SFD, RG85; NA-PSR.

[19] Husbands who had misrepresented themselves in the past to avoid the ubiquitous Chinese exclusion laws now found themselves having to correct their personal histories with the immigration authorities in order to apply for visas for family members. See, for example, Ming Shee [pseud.], INS file 1300/46842 (1947); GICF, box 71; INS, SFD, RG85; NA-PSR.

[20] Born and raised in Japan, Bouiss met and married an American soldier while Japan was occupied by United States troops in the years following World War II. When her husband was shipped out, Bouiss obtained passage on the ship and the two were married at

court, "Congress intended to let down only two bars—one as to physical and mental defects and the other as to documentary requirements."[21] Race difference remained a barrier to admission.

Increasing numbers of women arriving as wives in the decades following World War II also sparked general concerns about marital fraud. Officials were wary of significant legal privileges provided for wives under immigration law and the ease with which divorces could be obtained in Mexico. Officials suspected a Philippine woman who arrived in the United States with her two sons in 1955 and applied for a Mexican "mail order" divorce from her husband living in the Philippines. Neither she nor her husband ever traveled to Mexico. Two years later she married an American citizen and applied to have her immigration status changed from visitor to resident. Her application was denied.[22] Women were to be met by their husbands at port, and the failure to be met by her husband resulted in increased suspicion of fraud.[23] A growing emphasis was placed on whether couples actually lived together as man and wife. A Greek woman, who had arrived in 1950 as the spouse of an American citizen, refused to "assume the marital relationship" unless her husband would meet specific financial conditions he had agreed to before marriage. He refused, she secured a divorce, and immigration officials held her for deportation for fraud—"Failure to fulfill marital agreement."[24]

---

sea. When Bouiss arrived in Seattle in 1947 as the wife of a soldier, immigration authorities accused her of not being a virtuous wife, specifically of having "cohabited" with her husband before they were married as well as "openly engaged in immoral practices with other men."

[21] *Bonham v. Bouiss* 161 F.2d 678 (9th Cir. 1947).

[22] Mexican "mail order" divorces, a phrase coined by immigration officials, did not require either party to be present in Mexico when the divorce was issued. In general, the validity of both marriages and divorces was determined by the laws of the country in which either action was issued. Consequently, citizens of one nation who obtained a divorce in another could appeared to evade the dictates of religious and civil authorities. Immigration officials suspected the motives of a California woman who had taken up residence in Mexico in 1954 only to secure a divorce from her first husband. Soon thereafter she applied for a visa for her second husband living abroad. The Board of Immigration Appeals sustained her appeal, finding that the divorce was valid under Mexican law. *In the Matter of W———,* Decided by the Regional Commissioner February 18, 1958, in Edith Lowenstein, "Decisions by the Board of Immigration Appeals," *Interpreter Releases*, vol. 36, no. 13 (20 April 1959), RACNS, reel 11; *In the Matter of B———,* Int. Dec. 551, file VP 13–3521, Visa Petition Proceedings. Decisions by the Board February 1, 1954, in Edith Lowenstein, "Decisions by the Board of Immigration Appeals," *Interpreter Releases* 32, no. 10 (14 March 1955), RACNS, reel 10.

[23] This was especially true for Chinese women. Sun Shee [pseud.], INS file 1300/46641 (1947); GICF, box 69; INS, SFD, RG85; NA-PSR.

[24] On appeal, the Board of Immigration Appeals ruled that the court had granted her a divorce, not an annulment, thus she had been legally married upon arrival. *In the Matter of S———,* Int. Dec. 930, file A-7451818, Deportation Proceedings Decided by the Board

While in many respects both the War Brides Act and the Fiancées Act reflected decades-old concerns about the arrival of women as wives and their status as privileged, exempted immigrants, both allowed eligible Chinese wives and fiancées to immigrate on a nonquota basis—the first time in American history Chinese wives had been considered on equal terms with white wives. In addition, in 1946 Congress authorized the admission of the Chinese wives of American citizens as nonquota immigrants.[25] Xialoan Boa has argued that this legislation significantly impacted Chinese American communities, causing a shift from a primarily bachelor society to a more diverse and family-oriented community.[26] Importantly, even these more liberal provisions had their limitations. Chinese women entering as wives of citizens were required to have been married before May 26, 1924. Thus the law applied only to women who had been married for at least twenty-two years, rewarding long-time citizens for their loyalty while still controlling the growth of the Chinese American community.

Yet even during this period of greater inclusion, Chinese wives were still closely scrutinized upon arrival, and asked many of the same questions about family and village life that had been central to administering the Chinese Exclusion Acts in the first half of the twentieth century.[27] The truth, according to immigration officials, or the devil, as the women themselves may have felt, lay in the details. Arriving in 1947, Lee Hong Chen was asked to describe her wedding feast, pinpoint where her house was located in the village, and testify as to whether her mother-in-law had bound feet—stock-in-trade questions asked of Chinese women arriving in the late nineteenth century.[28] Sook Fong was asked to describe the de-

---

May 2, 1958, in Edith Lowenstein, "Administrative Decisions under the Immigration and Nationality Laws of the United States," *Interpreter Releases* 35, no. 42 (12 November 1958), RACNS, reel 11. Similarly, a woman who applied for a visa for her mentally ill husband was denied, not on grounds of mental illness but because the couple had not lived together during her husband's treatment. This case was overturned on appeal to the Board of Immigration Appeals: *In the Matter of E———.*, Int. Dec. 465, file VP 16–1667, Visa Petition Proceedings, Decisions by the Board June 23, 1953, *Interpreter Releases* 30, no. 44 (11 November 1953), RACNS, reel 9.

[25] The act of 9 August 1946 (60 Stat. 975) passed in close proximity to the GI Fiancées bill (29 June 1946); these were separate pieces of legislation. Hutchinson, *Legislative History of American Immigration Policy*, 510, 516.

[26] Xiaolan Bao, "When Women Arrived: The Transformation of New York's Chinatown," in *Not June Cleaver: Women and Gender in Postwar America, 1945–1960*, ed. Joanne Meyerowitz (Philadelphia: Temple University Press, 1994), 19–36; Zhao, *Remaking Chinese America*.

[27] See, for example, Hong Yen [pseud.], INS file 1300/46854 (1947); GICF, box 71; INS, SFD, RG85; NA-PSR; Zhao, *Remaking Chinese America*.

[28] Lee Hong Chen [pseud.], INS file 1300/46678 (1947); GICF, box 69; INS, SFD, RG85; NA-PSR.

tails of her marriage ceremony, tested on her knowledge of her husband's family, and questioned about her whereabouts during the recent war.[29]

Chinese war brides were asked to offer evidence of their "alleged relationship" and proof that their husband had contributed to their support.[30] Joon Shau Low arrived in San Francisco in 1951; she offered a photograph of her and her husband together as proof of their relationship.[31] Similarly, Yee Chang had only a wedding ring engraved with her husband's name to prove her marriage to an American soldier.[32] When Wong Wai arrived in 1947, all she had was a photo to substantiate her marriage. Under questioning, immigration officials grew suspicious of Wong, and noted that she did not know how much money her husband had sent her or where in Hong Kong she was married: "This applicant is a city girl, and quite intelligent, however, she testified in a manner tending to indicate she was trying to repeat a memorized story. She was confused frequently and I doubt she was truthful." Moreover, immigration officials doubted that Wong was thirty-four years old as she claimed, but believed she was in fact a much younger woman, "In my opinion she is about 22 years of age or less. Medical examination should be made."[33]

Despite the continuation of such vigorous interrogations, war forever changed the face of immigration and naturalization law. The import of race difference had been reshuffled by the war experience, and Chinese women were finally, and for the first time, included on a par with European immigrants. Yet in drawing the lines of a new legal map that would

[29] She arrived in San Francisco as the wife of a solider in 1947. Sook Fong [pseud.], INS file 1300/46621 (1947); GICF, box 68; INS, SFD, RG85; NA-PSR.

[30] These were standard questions on the form immigration officials used when interrogating Chinese immigrants who arrived as relatives. See, for example, May Yuk [pseud.], INS file 1300/46601 (1947); GICF, box 68; INS, SFD, RG85; NA-PSR; Myong Fung [pseud.], INS file 1300/46613 (1947); GICF, box 68; INS, SFD, RG85; NA-PSR; and, Young Bo [pseud.], INS file 1300/46586 (1947); GICF, box 67; INS, SFD, RG85; NA-PSR.

[31] Joon Shau Low [pseud.], SF file 1300/107311-C (1951); Unprocessed; INS, SFD, RG85; NA-PSR. Ngan Lee offered a picture of herself with her husband, taken in Army uniform. Ngan Lee [pseud.], INS file 1300/46612 (1947); GICF, box 68; INS, SFD, RG85; NA-PSR.

[32] Yee Chang [pseud.], INS file 1300/46836 (1947); GICF, box 71; INS, SFD, RG85; NA-PSR.

[33] On appeal, Wong was admitted on the strength of the photo alone. Wong Wai [pseud.], INS file 1300/46622 (1947); GICF, box 68; INS, SFD, RG85; NA-PSR. Similarly, Sing Hai arrived with her son in 1947. Sing last saw her husband seven years previously when he returned to the United States from China. Interviewed by immigration officials multiple times, Sing seemed more confused and flustered, even frightened, with each additional question. Immigration officials remarked that Sing's answers failed to correspond with those provided by her husband, that her answers changed under requestioning, and that she seemed less confident and less sure than a wife should be: Sing Hai [pseud.], INS file 1300/46861 (1947); GICF, box 69; INS, SFD, RG85; NA-PSR.

guide the process of inclusion and exclusion after 1945, immigration and naturalization law followed the fault lines of older debates over the significance of family unity, the contours of a legal marriage, the qualities of a loyal wife, and the value of race difference. On the surface, war had created opportunities for women, but restrictions over legality and loyalty persisted. Rather than awash in a sea of domesticity and national unity, immigration law fractured along familiar ambiguities and contradictions over race, gender, and marriage.

ILLEGITIMACY: LEGAL FAMILIES

In additional to the loyalty of wives and the legality of marriage, the legitimacy of children was subject to official scrutiny throughout the post–World War II period. As in decades past, wartime immigration law sought to foster family unity while regulating both its color and content. Concerns over legitimacy and illegitimacy structured the inclusion of children. Legal marriages produced admissible children, other sexual relationships did not. By the 1950s, children and families had become scientifically verifiable, products of medical evidence and a process of legitimation.

Before World War II, immigration and judicial officials understood "child" to include only those born within the narrow confines of marriage. The status of other children—those formally or informally adopted into a family, those born outside legal marriage, and those incorporated from previous marriages—was less clear.[34] The 1934 Equal Nationality Act provided American women who had previously lived in the United States with the ability to pass citizenship onto their children, legitimate and illegitimate.[35] While mothers could pass citizenship onto their illegitimate children, however, the same was not true of fathers. A child's status had to be legitimated by her father before she would be entitled to legal recognition and derivative citizenship.[36] In essence, a child was her moth-

---

[34] Children adopted before 1924 were expressly excluded from the definition of "child" outlined under the 1924 Quota Act. Hutchinson, *Legislative History of American Immigration Law*, 514.

[35] *In the Matter of M———*, 4 I & N 400 (BIA 1951); *Petition of Sadin* 100 F.Supp 14 (S.D.N.Y. 1951).

[36] State Department and immigration authorities disagreed on the status of illegitimate children born before 1934. Before 1934, the State Department, working under the assumption that in a case of illegitimacy the woman was both father and mother, issued American passports to the illegitimate children of American mothers. Immigration authorities, however, argued that before 1934 women were incapable of transmitting citizenship to their children, the marital status of the parents notwithstanding. In practice, however, these children were regularly admitted by immigration officials when they arrived at the border. Beginning in 1940, the State Department reversed itself, ruling that illegitimate children born

er's by birth but her father's only by law. Paternity outside of marriage, officials contended, could not be assumed. As the Court of Claims explained in 1948, "The purpose of statute bestowing citizenship on foreign-born 'child' of an American citizen was to insure that the child had in it the blood of an American citizen and that the fact would be evident without the uncertainties of a contested trial of paternity."[37] This link between blood and citizenship raised complicated questions of biological, social, and legal legitimacy.

The violence of world war, however, severed families, leaving many children without the legal shelter provided by married parents. The visible crisis of orphans, step-children, and adopted children forced a rethinking of how "child" would be understood by American immigration authorities. The newly acquired right of American mothers to pass their citizenship on to their children remained a flash point for controversy as unmarried American women arrived at the borders in the decades following World War II with their illegitimate, step, or adopted children. With few congressional guidelines, immigration and naturalization officials were left to weigh the significance of family unity against long-held suspicions that children arriving at the nation's borders were often not who they appeared to be.

Women and children left stranded in refugee camps or foreign cities waited for American husbands and fathers to send money that could reunite the family. According to the Economic and Social Council of the United Nations, these women and their children often waited in vain, abandoned by their husbands and fiancées. Far from home and family, they became a drain on local relief services.[38] The maintenance of these

---

abroad before 1934 to American mothers would not be issued American passports. "Administrative policy to be adopted in cases involving the question of citizenship status of illegitimate children born abroad to American mothers prior and subsequent to the Act of May 24, 1934," memorandum, 6 August 1940; Lemuel B. Schofield, Special Assistant to the Attorney General, to Robert H. Jackson, Attorney General, 4 September 1940; Newman A. Townsend, Acting Assistant Solicitor General, "Memorandum for the Attorney General," 14 September 1940, INS file 69155; DJA-INS, box 1065; INS, DC, RG85; NA, DC. For example, see *In the Matter of M——D——*, 3 I & N 485 (BIA 1949); Lowenstein, *The Alien and the Immigration Law*, 33–35.

[37] *Compagnie Generale Transtlantique v. United States* 78 F.Supp. 797 (Court of Claims 1948).

[38] Following World War I, the league of Nations had addressed the problem of abandoned families. Various and divergent legal systems made the prospect of suing for alimony and financial support difficult if not impossible. In 1929, the league initiated a study to propose workable solutions to the problem of overlapping legal jurisdictions, the primary result of which was to suggest that the court of the country of the plaintiff would have jurisdiction. Common-law countries, the United States among them, found this proposal unacceptable. By 1954, the United Nations' Committee of Experts (a group of specialists in international law) suggested that the emphasis should shift from enforcing the order of

families in Europe and Asia presented a significant economic burden to countries struggling to rebuild. With the demobilization of American troops, securing financial support from vanishing fathers for their illegitimate children presented a difficult and acute problem.[39] Yet, for many in the United States, the immigration of women and children, some legitimized by marriage and some not, posed a threat to efforts to regulate the arrival of unwanted foreigners.

Immigration law distinguished between children born within marriage and those born without. Only children who had been legally legitimated by their American GI fathers were eligible for nonquota status as a part of postwar efforts to reunite veterans and their foreign-born wives.[40] Moreover, while the 1952 McCarren-Walter Act included children and spouses of citizens as nonquota immigrants, the INS interpreted the act to limit the definition of "child" to those born within legal marriage.[41] Consuls in London, Naples, and Antwerp required that illegitimate children of American GIs have visas separate from their mothers.[42]

The possible arrival of five thousand biracial children fathered by African American soldiers who had been stationed in England was met with particular fear and indignation. The London office of the United Press reported that the Negro Welfare Society of London and Liverpool was attempting to find homes for the children in African American communities in the United States and that the society had received support from Eleanor Roosevelt in its efforts.[43] Abandoned by white English mothers fearful of the prospect of raising a biracial child on their own, unwanted by an American society which dehumanized those with black skin, housed in British orphanages with limited resources to provide for their care,

---

foreign courts to assisting plaintiffs in their efforts to seek legal redress in the defendant's country of residence. Edith Lowenstein, "Problems of Support of Abandoned Families of Migrants," *Interpreter Releases* 31, no. 14 (25 March 1954): 110–111, RACNS, reel 9.

[39] Edith Lowenstein, "Problems of Support of Abandoned Families of Migrants," *Interpreter Releases* 31, no. 14 (25 March 1954): 110, RACNS, reel 9.

[40] Edith Lowenstein, "Administrative Decisions under the Immigration and Nationality Laws of the United States: The Illegitimate Child, Adjustment of Status under Section 245," *Interpreter Releases* 38, no. 25 (14 July 1961), RACNS, reel 12.

[41] Before 1952, adoption was not recognized as a privileged relationship, unless the adoption took place before January 1, 1924. Lowenstein, *The Alien and the Immigration Law*, 29.

[42] Although once the parents were married in the United States, the child could become a stepchild, this new legitimated status garnered only first priority under the quota system. Frank L. Auerbach, " 'GI Brides Act' and 'GI Fiancees Act': Some Questions Concerning Their Interpretation and Administration" *Interpreter Releases* 24, no. 10 (24 February 1947): 50–51, RACNS, reel 7.

[43] Commissioner to Representative Bertrant Gearhart, 16 May 1947, INS file 55880/239 (1947); DJA-INS acc. 58 A 734, box 717; INS, DC, RG85; NA, DC. Jenel Virden cites a December 1945 British government report that estimated there were 550 or more mixed-race children living in Britain. Virden, *Good-bye Piccadilly*, 99.

these children were homeless.[44] In a letter to the INS, one American woman condemned the moral impropriety of the young English mothers and denied that these children had any claim on the nation. "Girls who cannot behave themselves should take care of their own babies," she explained, "or the British Government should do it for them."[45] Over the next decades, similar debates on the status of multiracial children would follow American soldiers and American military engagements abroad to Japan, Korea, Vietnam, and the Philippines. Ironically, the Cold War both insisted on the significance of family and created the context in which families ruptured the legal, racial, and geographic assumptions of the American home.

Women who applied for visas as quota immigrants or as nonquota wives of citizens in the years following World War II were unable to secure the admission of their illegitimate children.[46] Once a woman achieved citizenship she could request for her illegitimate child preference status as a "son" or "daughter." However, fourth-preference visas remained grossly oversubscribed and resulted in long separations for eager family members. For example, a Japanese woman who had married an American soldier stationed in Kobe in 1952 could not obtain nonquota status for her three-year-old child born out of wedlock. According to the Board of Immigration Appeals, "adoption" did not "confer the status of legitimacy for immigration purposes" when the adoptive parent was not the child's "natural parent."[47] An Austrian woman applied for visas for her son and herself in 1949. While waiting for approval, she was married in 1952 to a resident immigrant and her son was adopted by her new husband. As a result, she was entitled to third-preference status as the wife of a resident, but her child was not. She placed her son with friends and emigrated to the United States with her husband with the hope that her status as a resident immigrant would facilitate the quick admission of her son. Her petition on her son's behalf, however, was denied by immigration authorities; he was not, under the law, an admittable child.[48]

[44] Virden, Good-bye Piccadilly, 99–100.

[45] An article in the Chicago Tribune sparked letters from Chicagoans and their representative, Bertrant Gearhart. Whitney Dickinson [pseud.] to INS, 11 December 1947, INS file 55880/239 (1947); DJA-INS acc. 58 A 734, box 717; INS, DC, RG85; NA, DC.

[46] In the Matter of M——, 5 I & N 120 (BIA 1953); also, "In the Matter of M., Interim Decision No. 441 (1953)," Interpreter Releases 30, no. 32 (29 July 1953), RACNS, reel 9; Lowenstein, The Alien and the Immigration Law, 30.

[47] Matter of A, 5 I & N 272 (BIA 1953); In the Matter of S——, 5 I & N 289 (BIA 1953). Also see In the Matter of G——, 5 I & N 731 (BIA 1954); Matter of Young, 12 I & N 340 (BIA 1967).

[48] The couple sought the assistance of the Common Council for American Unity who secured a private bill on her son's behalf. The bill failed to pass. The mother sought to return to Austria to be with her child but risked losing her residence status though a long absence

Questions of illegitimacy structured the legal acceptance of children in the decades following World War II. Significantly, as American soldiers returned home, they left behind women and children who felt some claim on the United States. In an effort to provide the INS with a more precise definition of child under immigration law, Congress amended the legislation in 1957 to include within the definition of stepchildren those children "whether or not born out of wedlock," as well as "an illegitimate child" who sought inclusion by virtue of her relationship with her "natural mother."[49] The legislative change allowed children who were included within a marriage, although they had not been born within one, to remain with their families. The concept of blood ties remained significant, however, as the law continued to privilege the link between children and their biological mothers.[50]

LEGITIMACY: SCIENTIFIC FAMILIES

Debates over the significance of illegitimacy and legitimacy not only invoked questions of marital status but also raised concerns about authenticity. With the end of war and the resumption of safe travel, immigration to the United States increased, and with it INS suspicions that many of the children arriving at the nation's borders were not who they or their parents claimed them to be. Among the new arrivals after World War II were increasing numbers of Chinese children who claimed citizenship through an American-born parent. Many Chinese children arriving in the United States during the later 1940s and 1950s were the children of soldiers or citizens and thus citizens in their own right. Long-held suspicions that Chinese immigrants used derivative citizenship policies to create fictitious, paper families reemerged in the post–World War II period as immigration authorities sought proof of legitimacy in Chinese claims to entry.[51]

Children submitted letters from family members, records of financial support from American fathers, and the corroborating testimony of

---

abroad. The Council generated a second private bill, which was passed in 1955. Lowenstein, *The Alien and the Immigration Law*, 30–32, see also 32–34.

[49] *Nation v. Esperdy* 239 F.Supp. 531 (S.D.N.Y. 1965).

[50] Ibid.

[51] When Kim Jin Kang arrived with his mother in San Francisco in 1947, officials doubted he was the son of a citizen. Immigration officials queried Kim, his mother, and his father about details of the family's life in China during the war. Unsatisfied with the three sets of responses, officials demanded if Kim had "been instructed orally or in writing as to what you should, or should not, say at this examination?" Kim Jin Kang [pseud.], in Lau Wu Yao [pseud.], INS file 1300/46647 (1947); GICF, box 67; INS, SFD, RG85; NA-PSR. For similar cases, Goon Lu Lan [pseud.], in Sun Shee [pseud.], INS file 1300/46641 (1947); GICF, box

friends and family as evidence to incredulous immigration inspectors.[52] Fong He Lin submitted army receipts detailing how a percentage of his pay was sent directly to his wife in China, along with a letter from the American Red Cross in San Francisco to support the petitions of his wife, son, and daughter.[53] Carefully substantiated life histories could backfire, however, if immigration officials suspected that the applicants' testimonies mirrored each other too closely. Immigration officials believed that Kwock Mo Siu was not the daughter of a citizen and noted in their final report that her statements were "corroborated" by those of her brother and father "to the last detail in such a way that showed thorough memorization of the family data." Inspectors dismissed a family photograph taken in China as evidence of their relationship, noting that Kwock Ma Sau's photograph had been inserted by a photographer.[54]

In addition to documentary proof, immigration officials drew on physical evidence to substantiate the claims of arriving applicants. In the decades before World War II, the INS had relied on specific physical features, most often the ears, in their efforts to prove or disprove an applicant's identity. Kam Yung Quan was admitted in 1937 after the Board agreed that "what can be seen of the ears in the photograph they appear to be similar to those of the girl now before me; the mouth, nose, eyes and eyebrows bear a good resemblance to those of the present applicant."[55] Officials also made use of x-ray machines and developing medical knowledge about the growth and development of the bone and vascular systems in their interrogations of applicants. Officials did not believe that Lee Mu Sing was eighteen years old and had the epiphyseal lines of her bones x-rayed to establish her age scientifically. After careful observa-

---

69; INS, SFD, RG85; NA-PSR; Qi Mu Yip [pseud.], INS file 1300/47165 (1947); GICF, box 74; INS, SFD, RG85; NA-PSR.

[52] For example, a letter from Wong Jin [pseud.] to her "little sister" Shu Jin [pseud.] was used to prove that the two were indeed sisters, INS file 63; GICF, box 5 1076; INS, SFD, RG85; NA-PSR. Records of financial support were also submitted as evidence: Bo Lee To [pseud.], INS file 1300/46587 (1947); GICF, box 67; INS, SFD, RG85; NA-PSR.

[53] Fong He Lin [pseud.], INS files 1300/46819; GICF; INS, SFD, RG85; NA-PSR; Li Gee Park [pseud.], INS file 1300/47499, 47498, and 47497 (1947); Chinese Immigration Records; INS, HDO, RG85; NA-PSR.

[54] Inspectors noted that both children provided the father's four names in the exact same order, and that they both approximated that there were "about 700 houses" and "23 or 24 lanes" in their village. Kwock Ma Sau [pseud.], INS file 4393/72 (1948); Chinese Wives and/or Children of Naturalized Chinese under HK, box 4; INS, HDO, RG85; NA-PSR.

[55] Kam Yung Quan [pseud.], INS file 4384/132 (1937); Chinese Wives of Native-Born American Citizens, box 3; INS, HDO, RG85; NA-PSR. The case of Emily Chin gained public notoriety in Honolulu for over a year in 1938 and 1939 as newspapers reported that "Miss Chin's future hangs by her ears. If they are 11 o'clock ears she may stay in Hawaii; if they are 1 o'clock ears she must return to China." Emily Chin [pseud.], INS file 1302/1645 (1938–); GICF; INS, HDO, RG85; NA-PSR.

tion, inspectors concluded Lee was twenty years old, not eighteen, and she was deported,[56] although, according to the INS's own documents, epiphyseal evidence could only pinpoint age, at best, to within a four-year range.[57] Through older techniques of anthropometry and newer technological innovations like the x-ray, immigration officials created a science of legitimation.

While immigration authorities continued to include photographs of Asian applicants in official files, by the 1950s fingerprinting and blood testing supplemented x-rays and body measurements as legitimizing tools.[58] Ming Kai Ma submitted to a blood test in 1953 to prove her son was indeed her son.[59] Jai Wu Park and her husband were also asked to submit to blood tests to verify their sons' identities.[60] Immigration authorities hoped that blood typing could replace the exhaustive family histories and efforts to discern family resemblance in the battle against immigration fraud.[61] In general, however, immigration authorities seemed to em-

[56] In children, epiphyseal vessels serve as the only source of nutrition for growing cartilage. Once the growth plate closes in adults, the epiphyseal vessels are connected to two additional nutrient systems, nutrient arteries and periosteal vessels. Drawing on a chart that listed when different epiphyses appeared and when they fused to the bone, Public Health Service administrators made approximations of applicants' ages. Significantly, according to the PHS's own documents, the average age in which the nutrient systems of the bones under consideration in Lee Mu Sing's, case merged was between sixteen and twenty. "Bone" *Encyclopedia Britannica Online*: http://www.eb.com:180/bol/topic?eu–118814&sctn–5 (accessed 25 May 1999).

[57] Lee Mu Sing [pseud.], INS file 1700/1690 (1937); U.S. Citizens of Chinese Race Applying for Certificates of Citizenship; INS, HDO, RG85; NA-PSR. Evidence suggests that courts proved willing to accept epiphyseal evidence in deportation and citizenship hearings: *Lew Mun Way v. Acheson* 110 F.Supp. 64 (S.D.Cal. 1953).

[58] Blood evidence was submitted for Kai Ha Lee, Wu Je Moy, and Moo Wun Lee [pseuds.], nearly twenty years after they had arrived in Honolulu in 1938. INS file 4384/369 (1956); Chinese Wives of Native-Born American Citizens, box 6; INS, HDO, RG85; NA-PSR. I have found evidence that the service continued to order x-rays to verify applicants' ages, but doctors usually supplemented their findings with evidence from dental records. Yung Wa Lan [pseud.], INS file 1300/106428 (1950); Unprocessed, box 336182; INS, SFD, RG85; NA-PSR. Comparison of the ears also remained a favored tool. See, for example, Susie Lau [pseud.], INS file 1300/108174 (1950); Unprocessed, box 336186; INS, SFD, RG85; NA-PSR.

[59] Ming Kai Ma [pseud.], INS file 4384/349 (1953); Chinese Wives of Native-Born American Citizens, box 6; INS, HDO, RG85; NA-PSR.

[60] Jai's husband wrote to the INS informing them that Jai, who had a history of mental instability, refused to have her blood taken. Jai Wu Park [pseud], INS file 41235/14–29 (1953); AICF; INS, SFD, RG85; NA-PSR.

[61] *In the Matter of L—— F—— F——*, 5 I & N 149 (BIA 1953). For example, Yee Chin Shen [pseud.], INS file 1300/108336-C (1950); Unprocessed, box 336186; INS, SFD, RG85; NA-PSR; Tien Woo [pseud.], INS file 1300/108055-C (1950); Unprocessed, box 336185; INS, SFD, RG85; NA-PSR; "Exploratory Report on the Use of Blood-Grouping Tests for Chinese Claimants to U.S. Citizenship, Petitioners and Beneficiaries of Immi-

ploy the new evidence to prove what they already suspected. As the Bureau of Immigration Appeals noted in a 1953 case, although "It is not a biological impossibility, of course, for the alleged wife of W——— Y——— to have given birth to her seventh and eighth sons at the ages of 47 and 49. It does seem to us highly unlikely that she did so."[62]

A history of exclusion cast a long shadow over Chinese immigrants, giving rise to separate procedures intended to expose fraud among this targeted community. Blood testing was used almost exclusively in Chinese and Chinese American cases to verify family relationship or to prove paternity. Through their lawyers, Chinese ancestry applicants protested their unfair treatment under the law. Ruling in 1954, the Board of Immigration Appeals found that the use of blood testing in Chinese cases did not constitute race discrimination. According to the board it was a question of "identity" not of "race."[63] The Circuit Court of Appeals in New York likewise dismissed charges of racial discrimination in blood testing procedures. Even if it were true that the test was applied only to Chinese-ancestry applicants, the court argued, "it would not in itself show that the discrimination was based on race or color." Conditions in China that left marriage, birth, and death records inaccessible to American officials, the court concluded, necessitated scientific testing.[64] Drawing on these decisions, the Board of Immigration Appeals affirmed that blood tests were a practical necessity. "Applicants from all over China descend upon the Hong Kong consulate claiming to be sons of United States citizens," the BIA explained, "most of them inadequately documented."[65]

Some of the children who arrived from China and claimed citizenship through one of their parents were not, as immigration officials suspected, who they claimed to be. Paper families were long and complicated affairs built on careful duplicity and practiced fiction.[66] Some applicants, as offi-

grant Visas, and Applicants for Certificate of Citizenship," (1957?); American Federation of International Institutes, box 268, file 15; Immigration History Research Center.

[62] In the Matter of W——— K——— S——— and W——— P———S——— 5, I & N 232 (BIA 1953).

[63] In the Matter of D——— W——— O——— and D——— W——— H———, 5 I & N 351 (BIA 1954).

[64] Lue Chow Kon, et al. v. Brownell 220 F.2d 187 (2nd Cir. 1955); also United States ex rel. Dong Wing Ott and Dong Wing Han v. Shaughnessy 220 F.2d 537 (2nd Cir. 1955).

[65] In the Matter of L——— K——— H———, L——— K——— C———, and L——— M——— W———, 6 I & N 573 (BIA 1955); Lowenstein, "Judicial Decisions Construing Certain Provisions of the Immigration and Nationality Act," Interpreter Releases 41, no. 5 (7 February 1964): 30, RACNS, reel 13; Lowenstein, "Supreme Court Decisions on Immigration and Naturalization During the 1957–1958 Term, Part I," Interpreter Releases (24 January 1958), RACNS, reel 11.

[66] Files that disclosed paper daughters uncovered in the amnesty program include INS file 1300/47103 (1947); GICF, box 73; INS, SFD, RG85; NA-PSR; INS file 1300/46708

cials charged, memorized family histories and forged documentary evidence to obtain entry. Arriving in 1950 when she was fifteen, Jin Hon Ma drew suspicion when she was unable to remember her cousin's names under questioning by immigration authorities:

> Q: For how many weeks or months prior to your departure for the U.S., did your mother coach you on what to say?
>
> A: My mother did not coach me. Concerning the names of my uncles [sic] sons, she just never mentioned it to me. I possibly had forgotten some of them.
>
> Q: Did anyone give you the information you're supposed to know written on a piece of paper?
>
> A: No. Is there such a paper?[67]

Questions of authenticity, veracity, and genuineness structured the interaction between Chinese-ancestry children and the Immigration Bureau. By the 1950s and 1960s, families had become scientifically verifiable and legitimacy, a product of biological evidence. Over time, truth came to rest in biology as blood tests and fingerprinting complemented x-ray and physiognomy techniques in the project of proving identity.

For a nation emerging from the economic stagnation and global violence of the 1930s and 1940s, ideals of domesticity, family unity, and nation signaled a return to normalcy, economic prosperity, and social cohesion. Immigration laws passed in the wake of World War II united husbands with wives and children with parents as the nation sought to mend the fissures war had created. Yet while reinscribing the significance of family in postwar American society, World War II also rewrote the rules of race difference. Although experiences of the war eliminated race as a legal category of exclusion, race remained embedded in the practice of law. Race haunted questions of legitimacy as the biracial children of American soldiers and the Chinese children of Chinese American citizens met stiff resistance to their efforts to become part of the nation.

(1964); GICF, box 68; INS, SFD, RG85; NA-PSR; INS file 1300/106498 (1967); Unprocessed, box 336182; INS, SFD, RG85; NA-PSR. And for paper mothers, INS file 1300/106573 (1922–1951); Unprocessed, box 336182; INS, SFD, RG85; NA-PSR.

[67] Although she was admitted, fifteen years later, under an amnesty program, Jin's father confessed that she was not his daughter. He had brought Jin to the United States to marry a cousin and fellow restaurant worker. Immigration officials attempted to find Jay but could only ascertain that she had got married and moved to Chicago. Jin Hong Ma [pseud.], INS file 1300/107493-C (1950); Unprocessed, box 336184; INS, SFD, RG85; NA-PSR.

CHAPTER THIRTEEN

Marriage and Morality

If postwar America was a nation of families, then traditional ideas of marriage stood at the center of this idea of the nation as home. In contrast to those who came to work, but not to stay, those who sought only material advantage, not civic fidelity, those who seemed alone and adrift rather than contributing as members of strong families and productive communities, marriage symbolized belonging, permanence, loyalty, and commitment to the nation. As one court argued in 1952, "we must not forget that our civilization is built around a family relation which should be held as sacred as possible if we are not to become an amoral people."[1]

Historically, sex outside the boundaries of heterosexual marriage had been viewed as beyond the pale of a moral citizen. Naturalization laws requiring citizens to demonstrate good moral character and immigration laws punishing applicants who demonstrated immoral intent were constructed to protect the moral fabric of American society by guarding against those behaviors that were seen to pose a direct threat to marriage and family. Promiscuity became immorality when it violated the principles of home, marriage, and family.

In the post–World War II period, the boundary marking morality was shifting to allow private, discreet, noncommercial, extramarital relations. By the late 1940s and early 1950s, the courts demonstrated greater tolerance for most private heterosexual relationships between adults. Even adulterous relationships that did not threaten an existing marriage or mimic a marriage through cohabitation were adjudicated within a broad understanding of good moral character. Tolerance, however, had its limits. Homosexuality, whether freely given or for hire, public or private, remained a matter of official concern.[2] In the later half of the twentieth century, same-sex relationships provided the foil for traditional definitions of marriage.

Despite judicial review, in the years following World War II immigration authorities continued to bring women up on charges of prostitution

---

[1] *Petition of Anzalone* 107 F.Supp. 770 (N.J. 1952).

[2] For an early case of a gay man running afoul of local sex ordinances and being deported for conviction of an offense of moral turpitude, see *In the Matter of J———*, 2 I. & N. Dec. 533 (BIA 1946).

for sexual liaisons outside the purview of marriage. Significantly, sexual relationships that mimicked marriage remained suspect well into the 1950s.[3] While the courts denied such an easy and direct relationship between sex and immorality, women continued to be excluded and deported for having sex outside the confines of monogamous marriage and the privacy of home.

CONDUCT UNBECOMING A CITIZEN: SEX AND MARRIAGE IN LATER TWENTIETH-CENTURY IMMIGRATION LAW

In the decades prior to World War II, immigration and court officials had patrolled the borders of sexual order by regulating immigrant women's private experiences as well as their public behaviors. Yet the ties that bound sex to marriage had frayed over the twentieth century as women became a greater presence in the public workforce and the new public commercial leisure spaces that were becoming part of the social topography of American cities. Increasingly, women sought sexual pleasure before, within, and outside marriage.[4] Legal interpretations of sexual conduct, however, were slow to change, and as a result immigrant women could find themselves and their sexuality on trial. Prostitution, bigamy, adultery, and conducting a disorderly house, were placed alongside manslaughter or second-degree murder as offenses that negated good moral character.[5]

A thirty-three-year-old Mexican woman working as a waitress was charged with prostitution and held for deportation in 1944. She had originally emigrated through Laredo, Texas, in 1913. She married in 1920 and

---

[3] *In re C.*, 3 I. & N. Dec 790 (BIA, 1949); *In re M.*, 2 I. & N. Dec 530 (BIA 1946).

[4] Released in 1953, Alfred Kinsey's study of American women, *Sexual Behavior in the Human Female*, documented women's sexual experiences outside marriage. Kinsey reported that half of the women he surveyed during the 1930s and 1940s had engaged in premarital intercourse, and a quarter had extramarital relations. John D'Emilio and Estelle Freedman, *Intimate Matters: A History of Sexuality in America* (New York: Harper & Row, 1988), 285–286.

[5] Konvitz, *Civil Rights in Immigration*, 152. Emma Wold argued that the "moral turpitude" clause against adultery was administered unevenly and often gender specifically. Wold also argued that women immigrants were treated more fairly by the courts than they were by immigration officials. Emma Wold, "Alien Women vs. the Immigration Bureau," 217–219. The evidence suggests that the courts and the INS dismissed without much comment the appeals of both men and women accused of adultery. *United States v. Wexler* 8 F.2d 880 (E.D.N.Y. 1925); *United States v. Unger* 26 F.2d 114 (S.D.N.Y. 1928); *United States ex rel. Tourney v. Reimer* 8 F.Supp. 91 (S.D.N.Y. 1934); *Estrin v. United States*, 80 F.2d 105 (2nd Cir. 1935); *In re A.*, 3 I. & N. Dec. 163 (BIA 1948); *In re H.*, 7 I & N. Dec. 617 (BIA, 1957); Roberts, "Sex and the Immigration Law," 16–17.

the couple lived together for nine years, during which time they had three children. After separating from her husband, she lived with another man and had four children. After her lover deserted her in 1940, she received state aid until she found work as a waitress. Court documents noted that she had venereal disease. A police matron testifying at the hearing suggested that the cafe served more than food and drink. According to the officer, women employees were required to dance with men and encourage them to buy drinks. While the women may have made dates with male patrons, the police matron admitted that the cafe had never been raided for prostitution. In response, the defendant admitted that she had sex with three different men over a period of two weeks while she had been employed as a waitress. She explained that the cafe paid only five dollars a week and, while she made no demands for payment, the men had offered her additional money. One of the men had wanted to marry her and support her and her children. The court found her conduct tragic rather than criminal.[6] Yet even in the 1950s the INS held to a policy that any applicant who could be found guilty of prostitution in a civil action could not, by definition, demonstrate the good moral character necessary to citizenship.[7]

Following World War II, however, shifting understandings of marriage and sexuality led to new understandings of adultery and moral citizenship on the part of the judiciary. Beginning in 1947, Judge Learned Hand, writing for the Second Circuit Court of Appeals, offered some flexibility in the moral standard to reevaluate adultery. Heterosexual couples recognized as man and wife in their communities and by their long-term committed relationships, who would legalize their relationship if they could, Hand argued, were not technically adulterous and thus not lacking in good moral character.[8] The 1947 ruling did not usher in a period of tolerance for sexuality outside marriage; instead the emphasis on conduct and community standards rather than conviction and statute meant that good moral character remained more a product of interpretation than of legislation. Thus, precedent seemed to play little role as each candidate's moral character was evaluated individually.[9]

---

[6] *In the Matter of R———*, 2 I & N 50 (BIA 1944) By the 1940s, the courts had come to a more lenient reading of heterosexual sex between unmarried, single adults, finding that simple fornication was not a deportable or excludable offense. See *Lane ex rel. Cromin v. Tillinghast* 38 F.2d 231 (1st Cir. 1930); *In re D.*, 1 I. & N. Dec. 186 (BIA 1941); *In re R.*, 6 I. & N. Dec. 444 (BIA 1954).

[7] Lowenstein, *The Alien and the Immigration Law*, 296.

[8] *Petitions of Rudder, et al.* 159 F.2d 695 (2nd Cir. 1947); Lowenstein, *The Alien and Immigration Law*, 295.

[9] Milton Konvitz, in his analysis of moral character statues, wryly observed "That the test of 'good moral character' is a variable one, which may lead to opposite findings, de-

Throughout the 1940s, the courts and the Board of Immigration Appeals attempted to draw a fine distinction between marital misconduct, or technical adultery, and martial disruption, or adultery that resulted in the breakup of a family. Adultery could be forgiven, as the Board of Immigration Appeals commented in 1947, only when "no one was injured, no family was broken up, and the public was not offended."[10] Immigrants charged with adultery who demonstrated efforts to adjust their marital status or end their illicit affairs could be granted leniency by the courts if their affair had remained private and could be legitimated through eventual divorce and remarriage.[11] For example, Florence R. was awarded naturalization in 1944 despite the fact that her husband had never received a legal divorce from his first wife. While under Massachusetts law Florence R. had committed fornication, a criminal act, the court ruled that she had not "done anything which the community regards as reprehensible."[12]

However, not all relationships were adjudicated as long-term, loving relationships sanctioned by community understandings of moral decency and marital companionship. Jeanne Cloutier arrived in 1937 as a domestic servant hired to work in the home of Mr. and Mrs. Joseph Landre. Joseph Landre and Cloutier began an "infatuation" that ended when she left his employment in 1941. By 1943 Cloutier had found work elsewhere and her affair with Landre began in earnest. In her application for naturalization in 1949, Cloutier testified that she did not feel her affair with Landre demonstrated a lack of moral character. She felt her deep affection for Landre mitigated against her potentially immoral activity. The court disagreed and refused her naturalization, for hers was an "infatuation," not a long-term, committed relationship akin to marriage.[13]

With the passage of the 1952 Immigration Act, Congress attempted to rein in the liberal interpretations of the courts by precluding any finding of good moral character in the case of an immigrant who had committed adultery within five years of their application to citizenship. Immigration officials categorically insisted that adultery negated any finding of moral character worthy of a citizen. A couple who had begun living together as man and wife before she had received a final divorce decree from her first husband were found not to have demonstrated good moral character. The woman had lived in the United States since her arrival in 1908, and the couple had legally married two months after her divorce was finalized.

---

pending on what judge the alien petitioner is lucky or unlucky enough to face." Konvitz, *Civil Rights in Immigration*, 152.

[10] *In re O.*, 2 I. & N. Dec. 840 (BIA 1947).

[11] Roberts, "Sex and the Immigration Law," 30.

[12] *Petition of R——— 56 F.Supp. 969 (D.Mass. 1944).

[13] *United States v. Cloutier* 87 F.Supp. 848 (E.D.Mich. 1949).

Nevertheless, when she applied for citizenship in 1956 she was denied.[14] Similarly, in a 1956 decision by a district director, a woman was denied her application for permanent residency on grounds of adultery, despite the fact that she had eventually obtained an annulment. In confirming the decision, the regional commissioner wrote that "In considering her conduct and behavior during the five year period, it is concluded that it falls below that of the average person and she, therefore, has not established that she has been a person of good moral character."[15] Reviewing her case, the Second Circuit Court of Appeals recognized the difficulty in adjudicating moral character. "Values are incommensurables," the court observed; moreover, "the law is full of standards that admit of no qualitative measure." "The best we can do," the court suggested, "is to improvise the response that the 'ordinary' man or woman would make."[16] And the ordinary man or woman, the court determined in this 1956 case, would not condone adultery among its citizenry.

The interpretive space allowed by the "ordinary man or woman" standard placed the moral qualities of a citizen within a maze of state statues, congressional vagaries, and judicial and bureaucratic evaluations of sexual and martial misconduct.[17] Throughout the 1950s and 1960s, neither the courts, nor the Immigration Service, nor Congress could manage to agree. The service held firmly to its position that marital misconduct was a moral wrong, one that could not be remedied by legalizing the relationship of an adulterous couple though marriage.[18] A young woman sought the advice of the Common Council on American Unity before making her application for citizenship. She had borne two illegitimate children of two different fathers within the five years preceding her application. The CCAU advised the woman that her petition would be denied by the service, and that her status in the courts remained unclear. She decided to

---

[14] *Petitions for Naturalization of F—— G—— and E—— E—— G——* 137 F.Supp. 782 (S.D.N.Y. 1956).

[15] *In the Matter of S——*, Decided by the Regional Commissioner 18 June 1956, as reviewed in Edith Lowenstein, Administrative Decisions under the Immigration and Nationality Laws of the United States, *Interpreter Releases* 34, no. 4 (22 January 1957), RACNS, reel 11.

[16] *Marie Posusta v. United States of America* 285 F.2d 533 (2nd Cir. 1961), in Edith Lowenstein, "Administrative Decisions under the Immigration and Nationality Laws of the United States," *Interpreter Releases* 34 no. 4 (22 January 1957), RACNS, reel 11.

[17] Congress failed to specify in the 1952 legislation what it meant by "adultery" and failed to offer any guidance to how sexual relationships should be evaluated and judged in relation to the good moral character standard of the "ordinary" man or woman. Roberts, *Sex and the Immigration Law*, 31. For courts that attempted to differentiate between "technical" adultery and adulterous relationships, *Petition of Da Silva* 140 F.Supp. 596 (N.J. 1956); *Dickoff v. Shaughnessy* 142 F.Supp. 535 (S.D.N.Y. 1956).

[18] Roberts, *Sex and the Immigration Law*, 35–36.

wait an additional five years before filing a second application, and the CCAU concluded this was the "safer course."[19]

The courts, however, continued to attempt to distinguish those marriages that were harmed by adultery from those that were in disarray before the affair, and those couples that attempted to legalize their illicit relationship from those who did not.[20] Martha Marie Kielblock admitted that she had an affair with a man whose divorce had not been finalized. The court recognized the technicality of fornication and adultery, but emphasized mitigating circumstances in its ruling. According to the court, Kielblock's affair had been characterized by affection, discretion, and consent. "The woman loved the man and hoped that he would ultimately marry her," the court argued, "The acts occurred in the privacy of her home. . . . The parties are mature adults."[21]

The difference between a moral relationship of mutual affection and one that transgressed social mores lay in the distinction between private and public sexuality. While the court would allow that sex had moved out from the marriage bed, it continued to insist that sex be confined to the privacy of the bedroom. "The satisfaction of sexual appetite is a peculiarly private matter," the court argued, "ordinarily concerning only the participants in the sexual act." However, the court continued, sex became a matter of "official concern" when it became the subject of public law:

> Otherwise, it will be treated by courts as an act of immorality if it be commercialized, as in the case of prostitution, or if illegitimate children are begotten. Likewise, open flaunting publicly what should be a private matter of promiscuity might adversely affect a petitioner's standing as a moral person.[22]

Defined not by statute but by common understandings, "good moral character" and "other immoral purposes," and "adultery" had to be investigated, evaluated, tried, and judged at the border. Even women who had not been convicted of any illegal offense like prostitution, adultery, or fornication could still be found to be without good moral character. What resulted was a long, complicated, sometimes intractable, often inconsistent, debate over the content of morality and the confines of public and private sexuality. Hubertine Van Dessel, a divorced woman, testified that she had been having an affair with an unmarried man from 1959 to

[19] In her discussion of this case, Lowenstein notes that a similar case of a male applicant had been decided in his favor. *Schmidt v. United States* 177 F.2d 450 (2nd Cir. 1949), as quoted in Lowenstein, *The Alien and the Immigration Law*, 298.

[20] Roberts, *Sex and the Immigration Law*, 32. See, for example, *Posusta v. United States* 285 F.2d 533 (2nd Cir. 1961); *In re Mortyr* 320 F.Supp. 1222 (Or. 1970).

[21] *Petition of Martha Marie Kielblock* 163 F.Supp. 687 (S.D.Cal. 1958).

[22] *In re Kielblock* 163 F.Supp. 687 (S.D.Cal. 1958).

1962. He wanted to marry her, but she refused, citing religious differences. The INS recommended denial of Dessel's citizenship application. The court disagreed.[23]

MEDICALIZING IMMORALITY: DEFINING HOMOSEXUALITY

Laws prohibiting the arrival of immigrants labeled as homosexuals, like those regulating public and private heterosexuality, highlight the historical significance of traditional marriage to ideas of home and nation. Homosexuality remained an excludable and deportable offense until 1990. Gay men and women could avoid the perils of immigration law only by becoming citizens, yet charges of homosexuality often precluded "good moral character" and thus access to citizenship.[24]

Yet, as was true in the early-twentieth-century debate over prostitutes, seeing homosexuality at the border proved difficult. Immigration and court officials turned increasingly to science to delineate the boundaries of both racial and sexual categories, and by the later twentieth century the boundaries of marriage. Like the women immigrants labeled likely public charges, gay men and lesbians denied entry as homosexuals contested the assumption that they were a likely drain on American society, sapping its moral reserves as debt-ridden immigrants strained its financial capacities. Finally, the debate over homosexual immigrants reveals the ways in which immigrants arrived cognizant of the law and its exclusions as they worked to challenge laws that discriminated against them and their communities.

Historically in immigration law, homosexuality had not been grouped with prostitution, adultery, and fornication as a moral offense, but rather with epilepsy, feeblemindedness, and insanity as a medical exclusion.[25] The Immigration Act of 1917 first included the term "constitutional psychopathic inferiority" in an effort to accomplish full exclusion of all people deemed mentally defective. Drafted in the heyday of eugenics-inspired

---

[23] *In re Petition for Naturalization of Marcella Hubertine Van Dessel* 243 F.Supp. 328 (E.D.Pa. 1965).

[24] *In re Schmidt* 289 N.Y. 2d 89 (1963). Shannon Minter notes that by 1971 a series of landmark cases had held that homosexual activity that remained private and discreet did not bar a finding of good moral character. However, as Minter argues, the distinction between private permissibility and public exclusion offered only limited amnesty for many immigrants. Minter, "Sodomy and Public Morality Offenses under U.S. Immigration Law," 794–800. Also see Roberts, "Sex and the Immigration Laws."

[25] Robert J. Foss, "The Demise of the Homosexual Exclusion: New Possibilities for Gay and Lesbian Immigration," *Harvard Civil Rights–Civil Liberties Law Review* 29, no. 2 (summer 1994): 445–446.

efforts to preserve the mentally and physically superior breeding stock of the Anglo-Saxon "race," the 1917 act reflected public concerns that many immigrants were not only morally unworthy to be admitted but that large numbers of them were also mentally and physically unfit. The 1918 *Manual of the Mental Examination of Aliens*, issued by the United States Public Health Service, included under constitutional psychopathic inferiority "persons with abnormal sexual instincts."[26]

During the 1920s and 1930s, psychiatric and psychoanalytic concepts developed by Freud gained popular notoriety in America. Freud's work on human behavior and emotion offered a scientific, medicalized grammar of "abnormality" and "impulse" for sexuality, a language the public health service readily adopted. Subsequent 1930 revisions of the guidelines included "sexual perverts" and "persons who because of eccentric behavior, defective judgment, or abnormal impulses are in repeated conflict with social customs."[27] "Psychopathic inferiority" was a catchall category that could include a wide range of medicalized disorders, and thus we cannot know how many of those deported under its provisions were diagnosed as "persons with abnormal sexual instincts" or even "sexual perverts."[28] Moreover, sexual perversion could refer to child molestation as easily as it could to homosexuality.

The war experience of the 1940s dramatically altered American understandings of the responsibilities of science, the significance of deviance, and the consequences of sex. While the pseudoscience of eugenics had been under fire since the 1920s, the horrors of the Nazi "final solution" discredited government-sponsored policies that linked race to mental and physical defects. Medical exclusions, a historical staple of United States immigration policies, would have to be revamped. War also meant mas-

---

[26] United States Public Health Service, *Manual of the Mental Examination of Aliens*, (Washington Government Printing Office, Miscellaneous Publication No. 18, Treasury Department, United States Public Health Service, 1918); *Matter of LaRochelle*, 11 I. & N. Dec. 436 (BIA 1965).

[27] United States Public Health Service, *Regulations Governing the Medical Examination of Aliens, Revised* August, 1930, (Miscellaneous Publication No 5, United States Treasure Department, Public Health Service), 13; *Matter of LaRochelle*, 11 I. & N. Dec. 436 (BIA 1965).

[28] Psychopathic inferiority, along with idiocy, imbecility, feeble-mindedness, epilepsy, insanity, tuberculosis, and chronic alcoholism, was a "class A(1) defect" from which, in the eyes of health experts, there was slim chance of recovery, and from which, in the eyes of immigration authorities, there little hope of appeal. In 1920, 2.5 percent of immigrants referred to the Public Health Service were certified with psychopahtic inferiority, and virtually all of them were subsequently deported. By 1930, 17.5 percent of immigrants seen by the Public Health Service were certified with psychopathic inferiority, almost 90 percent were deported. *Annual Report to the Commissioner-General of Immigration* (1920), 252–253; *Annual Report of the Commissioner-General of Immigration* (1925), 166–167, 170–171; *Annual Report of the Commissioner-General of Immigration* (1930), 174–175.

sive mobilization of the American population, bringing young, single men and women out of their families and into the armed forces overseas or into urban war jobs on the home front. New social communities offered new sexual opportunities as men and women formed same-sex networks of mutual affection and support. Yet new possibilities also wrought new fears. Military psychiatrists probed for evidence of homosexual experiences and desire as they screened civilian draftees for induction.[29]

The publication of Alfred Kinsey's studies of male and female sexuality in 1948 and 1953 catapulted the issue of homosexuality into American popular consciousness. Kinsey's claim that homosexuality was not isolated to a small, discrete portion of American society, but rather that it was widespread, permeating class, race, generational, occupational, and geographic boundaries, created a sensation. With the advent of the Cold War, sensation became panic as concerns over homosexuality were woven through anxieties that American institutions were jeopardized by a subversive menace that threatened from both within and without the nation's borders. As Senator Joseph McCarthy lectured to an attentive nation about lists of known subversive elements working from within to destroy a traditional way of life, communism and homosexuality became dual enemies of a nation at risk.[30]

Rising concerns about homosexuality were evident in postwar debates over immigration legislation. In its 1947 study of immigration policy, the Judiciary Committee generally approved of current language restricting the arrival of "mentally and physically defective aliens" but recommended that "the classes of mentally defectives should be enlarged to include homosexuals and other sex perverts."[31] In legislative proposals that followed the Judiciary Committee's report, "homosexuals" and "sex perverts" were specifically listed as excludable aliens.

Like early-twentieth-century efforts to regulate the arrival of racial outsiders, later-twentieth-century attempts to exclude sexual outsiders relied on science to delineate the boundaries of sexual otherness. Yet in commenting on the proposed exclusions, the acting surgeon general cautioned Congress that the public health service would have a difficult time "substantiating a diagnosis of homosexuality or sexual perversion." As the surgeon general explained, "In other instances where the action and behavior of the person is more obvious, as might be noted in the manner of dress, the condition may be more easily substantiated." However, "Con-

---

[29] Allan Bérubé, *Coming Out Under Fire: The History of Gay Men and Women in World War II* (New York: Free Press, 1990).

[30] D'Emilio and Freedman, *Intimate Matters*, 288–295.

[31] Senate Report No. 151, 1947; United States Senate, 80th Cong., 1st sess. (Washington, D.C.), 345; Foss, "The Demise of the Homosexuality Exclusion," 451.

siderably more difficulty may be encountered in uncovering the homosexual person."[32]

In its final version, the Immigration Act of 1952 did not specifically provide for the exclusion of "homosexuals" or "sex perverts."[33] The 1952 law did, however, replace the term "constitutional psychopathic inferiority" with the term "psychopathic personality," and added "sex perversion" to the list of crimes involving moral turpitude. Despite the change in nomenclature, Congress made its intentions to continue to prevent the arrival of homosexuals under medical exclusions all too clear.[34] The Senate committee report on the 1952 legislation included the following: "This change of nomenclature is not to be construed in any way as modifying the intent to exclude all aliens who are sexual deviate."[35] A 1952 version of the *Manual* stated unequivocally how psychopathic personality was to be understood: "under this legal category will be classified those applicants who are diagnosed as sexual deviates."[36]

As had been true in laws regulating marriage and adultery, judicial and immigration officials were left to determine whether men and women who demonstrated homosexual behaviors were in fact "psychopathic personalities." Legal categories rarely fitted well on individual experience, and inquiry and inference were used to squeeze the interpretive space between law and its application. In their arrival hearings with immigration officials or in their appeals to the court, immigrants were forced to deny their sexuality outright or manipulate their testimony so as to conform to other, nonexcludable, psychiatric disorders. For example, S. testified that while he had "homosexual tendencies" since he was fifteen or sixteen, he had

[32] H.R. Report No. 1365, No. 1952; House of Representatives, 82nd Cong., 2nd sess. (Washington, D.C.) 47; Foss, "The Demise of the Homosexuality Exclusion," 451–452.

[33] Senate Committee Report, 29 January 1952, S. Doc. 1137; 82d Cong., 2nd sess. (Washington, D.C.); see also House Committee on the Judiciary, Report, 14 February 1952, H. Doc. 1365; 82d Cong., 2nd. sess., Washington, D.C. Senate and House committees drafting the law were assured by Public Health officials that the new terminology was sufficiently broad to be used to exclude gay and lesbian immigrants.

[34] Shannon Minter suggests that Congress followed the advise of the Public Health Service in adapting the new grammar of "psychopathic personality" rather than "homosexuality" in its final provisions for the 1952 law. Robert Foss agrees that the PHS played a major role in revamping the language of medical exclusion, but he emphasizes that PHS anticipated problems in enforcing explicit provisions against homosexuals and wanted to avoid charges of "soft on homosexuals." Minter, "Sodomy and Public Morality Offense Under U.S. Immigration Law: Penalizing Lesbian and Gay Identity" *Cornell Int'l Law Journal* 26 no. 3 (1993): 776–777; Foss, "The Demise of the Homosexual Exclusion," 451–453.

[35] Senate Committee Report, 29 January 1952, S. Doc. 1137; 82d Cong., 2nd sess.

[36] United States Department of Health, Education, and Welfare, Public Health, Service, *Manual for Medical Examination of Aliens*, chap. 6, Mental Diseases and Defects, sec. A, 6–5; see also *Matter of S———*, 8 I. & N. Dec. 409 (BIA 1959).

maintained the dominant role in all his encounters with other men. In response to questions asking whether he had engaged in sodomy, the defendant specified, "I have done that to somebody but I never let them do it to me." S. sought to defend himself against charges of deviance by drawing on traditional gender stereotypes; as the dominant partner in the sexual encounter, S. suggested he maintained a masculine role despite his homosexual desire. Psychiatrists testifying on his behalf corroborated his testimony, finding him to be suffering from "psychosexual infantilism" not homosexuality.[37] Similarly, Enrique Esteban Gandux y Marino, charged with psychopathic personality, offered an affidavit from a physician certifying that he was not homosexual.[38]

If charges of homosexuality or psychopathic personality proved insufficient, the same evidence of illicit sexual relationships could be used to prove charges of moral turpitude; either way deportation was the final result.[39] Immigrants who admitted to acts of sodomy were charged with moral turpitude and deported.[40] Yet an immigrant need not be charged with "sodomy" to be found deportable as a homosexual. For example, an immigrant who admitted that he had engaged in mutual masturbation was convicted of moral turpitude and deported. In commenting on his case, the Board of Immigration Appeals condemned mutual masturbation as "vile, base, depraved and contrary to the tenets of society."[41] Convictions for disorderly conduct were found to be deportable offenses by courts that emphasized that crimes involving loitering "about a public place soliciting men for the purposes of committing a crime against nature or other lewdness" were immoral.[42]

---

[37] *Matter of S———*, 8 I. & N. Dec. 409 (BIA 1959).

[38] *Engrique Esteban Ganduxe y Marino v. John L. Murff, District Director of the Immigration and Naturalization Service for the New York District* 183 F.Supp. 565 (S.D.N.Y. 1959).

[39] Minter has suggested that the crimes involving the moral turpitude provision and the medical exclusion of homosexuals were "mutually reinforcing." Minter, "Sodomy and Public Morality Offense Under U.S. Immigration Law," 189.

[40] *In re S.*, 8 I. & N. Dec. 409 (BIA 1959). Even heterosexual couples who engaged in sodomy could be charged with moral turpitude: *Velez-Lozano v. INS* 463 F.2d 1305 (D.C. Cir. 1972).

[41] *In re W.*, 5 I. & N. Dec. 576 (BIA 1953).

[42] *Hudson v. Esperdy* 290 F.2d. 879 (2nd Cir. 1961). This case was appealed to the Supreme Court but was denied: 368 U.S. 918 (1961). See also *Wyngaard v. Kennedy* 295 F.2d 184 (D.C. Cir. 1961), also denied at the Supreme Court level, 368 U.S. 926 (1961); *Babouris v. Esperdy* 269 F.2d 621 (2nd Cir. 1959), Supreme Court case 362 U.S. 913 (1959); *United States v. Flores-Rodreguez* 237 F.2d 405 (2nd Cir. 1956); *In re Alfonso-Bermudez*, 12 I. & N. Dec. 225 (BIA 1967); *In re G.*, 7 I. & N. Dec. 520 (BIA 1957); Foss, "Sex and the Immigration Law," 19, Minter, "Sodomy and Public Morality Offense Under U.S. Immigration Law," 788.

Immigration authorities and court officials read between the lines of police blotters to find evidence of sexual deviance or more general immorality and thus grounds for exclusion. In ruling to deport Flores-Rodriquez, an immigrant who had been convicted twice of soliciting sex with men in a public place, the court insisted "It cannot be supposed that Congress did not intend to include such undesirables within the excluded classes of immigrants."[43]

Like the women immigrants labeled as prostitutes, immoral women, likely public charges, fraudulent wives, or racial outsiders, gay men and lesbians denied entry contested the assumption that they were a threat to American society.[44] As immigrants charged with psychopathic personality took their case to court, they disputed a medicalized discourse that categorized sexuality as disease. Alternative medical expertise was marshaled to dispute or even dismiss charges of psychopathic personality. In response to these appeals, the courts moved to embrace what they believed was the more colloquial or common understanding of the law's intent to exclude "psychopathic personalities." This move from scientific evidence to common sense understandings reflects an earlier, parallel shift in legal arguments about race. During the heyday of scientific racism, the federal courts had drawn from scientific opinion in finding Japanese and Indian immigrants nonwhite and thus ineligible for citizenship. As the scientific community distanced itself from biological understandings of racial groups, the courts cited "common sense" understandings of whiteness to enforce federal prohibitions against the naturalization of nonwhite or nonblack applicants.

Over time, as psychiatry distanced itself from an understanding of homosexuality as a mental disease, the courts increasingly distanced themselves from psychiatry and medical nomenclature. While in 1965 an immigrant accused of psychopathic personality admitted to a dozen sexual experiences with other men over a period of three years, expert witnesses testified that psychopathic personality was an obsolete term, and even that homosexuality was no longer an appropriate medical term. The court, however, sided with public health and immigration officials, finding that the vague language of the 1952 law was intended to include just such men despite what new understandings in psychiatry might suggest:

We are not concerned with the niceties of semantic differences indulged in by psychiatrists. The words, "psychopathic personality" have become words of

---

[43] *United States v. Flores-Rodreguez* 237 F.2d 405 (2nd Cir. 1956).

[44] *Matter of S.*, 8 I. & N. Dec. 409 (BIA 1959); *Engrique Esteban Ganduxe y Marino v. John L. Murff, District Director of the Immigration and Naturalization Service for the New York District* 183 F.Supp. 565 (S.D.N.Y. 1959).

art which, whatever else they might mean, include homosexuality and sex perverts and the term is applied as it is commonly understood.[45]

The Supreme Court agreed, ruling in 1967 that the "legislative history of the Act indicate[d] beyond a shadow of a doubt that the Congress intended the phrase 'psychopathic personality' to include homosexuals." The Court concluded "that the Congress used the phrase 'psychopathic personality' not in the clinical sense, but to effectuate its purpose to exclude from entry all homosexuals and other sexual perverts."[46]

The INS policy implemented judicial interpretation. Consulates were advised in 1965 that applicants afflicted with "psychopathic personality," "sexual deviation," or other mental defects were ineligible to receive visas.[47] There is no way of knowing how many men and women were prevented from immigrating by the immigration law's first line of defense, the foreign consulate. While homosexuals could also be deported under moral turpitude laws, which classed homosexuality as illicit sexual deviance, "psychopathic personality," as interpreted by the courts, provided a broad exclusionary net.[48]

Gay men and lesbians could avoid the perils of immigration law only by becoming citizens, yet, as was the case with prostitution or adultery, charges of homosexuality precluded "good moral character" and thus citizenship. As late as 1973, the INS maintained that any applicant for naturalization "who is or has been a practicing sexual deviate, a homosexual," during the five years preceding their application, could not becoming a citizen.[49] For example, a woman who had lived and worked in the United States for fourteen years was denied her application to citizenship in 1963 when she testified to having sexual relationships with other women. Although she had broken no law, and, according to the court, "although her activities were confined to her home and with persons with whom she lived," the court ruled that such behavior made her unworthy of citizenship.[50] While by the late 1950s the courts had come to a more liberal interpretation of heterosexual relationships that lay outside marriage but were private and discreet, homosexuality, whether monogamous or not, whether private or not, continued to provide grounds for exclusion from citizenship.

---

[45] *Matter of Lovie*, 11 I. & N. Dec. 224 (BIA 1965).

[46] *Boutilier v. INS* 387 U.S. 118, 120 (1967).

[47] Interestingly, "sexual deviation" was added to the 1965 law, while "epilepsy" was removed. See Edith Lowenstein, "The Act of October 3, 1965 'To Amend the Immigration and Nationality Act; and for other purposes' Part II," *Interpreter Releases* (November 9, 1965), RACNS, reel 14.

[48] See *Wyngaard v. Rogers* 187 F.Supp. 527 (D.C. 1960).

[49] Roberts, "Sex and the Immigration Laws."

[50] *In re Schmidt* 289 N.Y. 2d 89 (1963).

The American Psychiatric Association finally removed homosexuality from its list of mental disorders in 1974, and by the 1970s "psychopathic personality" had become an increasingly difficult category to apply to incoming immigrants. Yet even those who avoided medical exclusion upon arrival faced the risk of later deportation under charges of moral turpitude, charges that relied on more nebulous and malleable interpretations of social mores rather than concrete medical diagnosis.[51] By 1979, the public heath service followed the lead of psychiatry more generally and revised its policy, stating that it no longer considered homosexuality to be a mental disease or defect. The surgeon general requested that immigration authorities no longer refer immigrants suspected of being homosexual to the public health service for certification.[52]

By the 1980s, enforcing laws against the arrival of gay men and lesbians relied on confession rather than disclosure. In the wake of this loss of medical approval, the Immigration and Naturalization Service issued new guidelines which instructed officers not to ask arriving immigrants questions about their sexual preference. Essentially, the new guidelines constituted a "don't ask, don't tell" policy. Only those immigrants who declared themselves as gay or lesbian would be held for secondary inspection. Immigrants, in essence, inhabited, articulated, and enacted the law. Yet in claiming a sexualized identity and asserting the legal legitimacy of homosexuality, gay and lesbian immigrants challenged the very idea that sexual difference constituted a difference of legal consequence to the qualities of a citizen. One thirty-four-year-old English immigrant provided just such an unsolicited statement when he arrived in San Francisco in 1980. At his exclusion hearing, the applicant argued that he did so as a matter of principle because he did not think he should be excluded from the United States for that reason.[53]

---

[51] Minter, "Sodomy and Public Morality Offenses Under U.S. Immigration Law," 794–800.

[52] See *Matter of Hill*, 18 I. & N. Dec. 81 (BIA 1981).

[53] Ibid.

∽ CONCLUSION ∾

Regulating Belonging

Elaine Archtans wanted to travel to the United States to see the World Cup soccer championships in 1994. When she appeared before U.S. consular officials in Sao Pāulo, Brazil, however, the twenty-three-year-old office worker was denied as "LP! ! ! !" by American officials who believed Archtans "looks poor." A second Brazilian woman was refused by consular officials in 1993 with the evaluation "No way. Poor, poor, poor." A third woman was denied her visa when consular officials in Sao Pāulo determined that she "L scary"—looks scary. Pointing to a history of "major fraud," U.S. officials in Brazil were instructed to give particular scrutiny to the visa applications of Chinese or Korean ethnic applicants. "Visas are rarely issued to these groups," the consular manual specified, "unless they have had previous visas and are older."[1]

The system of immigration laws and regulations Elaine Archtans confronted in the closing years of the twentieth century was no less daunting than that faced by immigrant women arriving during the end of the nineteenth. Yet, as ideas of who might belong to the nation shifted over the twentieth century, laws regulating arrival and membership were reshaped to incorporate those once denied access. Significantly, race and gender were no longer differences that legally mattered.

Yet although race and gender had been eliminated from the body of immigration and naturalization law, each lingered within the shadow of the law, shading how respectability, domesticity, economic viability, and moral character were visualized at the border. Like a prism, morality and immorality, self-sufficiency and dependency, legitimacy and illegitimacy, fractured race and gender into individuating hues, at once breaking exclusionary systems of their meaningful unity and multiplying their constituent parts across a wider field of vision. Race difference remained visible in evaluations of immigrant women's respectability, moral character, work skills, and economic dependency. Moreover, race difference merged with traditional understandings of women's roles in the home, resulting in gendered evaluations of work and wage that informed how immigrant

---

[1] Quoted in Philip Shenon, "Judge Denounces U.S. Visa Policies Based on Race or Looks," *New York Times*, 23 January 1998, sec. A.

women workers were seen at the border and how their potential contributions to the nation were weighed against their probable cost. Marital fraud, adultery, poverty, homosexuality, and unskilled labor colored a new system of exclusion, marking Elaine Archtans and others beyond the pale.

Immigration and naturalization law sought to regulate the borders of belonging by constructing the boundaries of the nation state around legal ideals of moral order, family unity, economic independence, and racial homogeneity. Anxieties over immigrant women's roles in racial intermarriage, reproduction, labor competition, and welfare costs are endemic to historical discussions of immigration and naturalization policies. During the later decades of the nineteenth century, Chinese women immigrants suspected of practicing prostitution became the focus of a moral and legal crisis concerned with reestablishing order and control. From the 1875 law forbidding the arrival of Chinese prostitutes, a system of federal restrictions premised on the necessity and possibility of excluding whole categories of people took shape.

The exclusionary project, whether rooted in sexuality, domesticity, work, reproduction, or race, proved difficult as immigrants contested the categories they were placed in and immigration officials struggled to see difference and deviance at the border. A crisis sparked in the permeability of the border became, over the course of the twentieth century, a crisis in the law and its application. Laws premised on the exclusion of difference foundered on the pliability of laws regulating belonging as women immigrants and government officials debated the significance of race, the contours of domesticity, the realities of work, and the qualities of a citizen.

A Brief Guide to Archival Sources

My research draws from the INS casefiles of 333 women immigrants arriving be-tween the 1880s and the 1970s. Files were selected in the following manner: every tenth woman arrival for those records that have been processed by the National Archives, every fifth carton for those records that have not been processed by the National Archives, and the first file in every carton for those records referenced in a card catalogue at one time maintained by INS authorities. Identifying informa-tion for women arriving after 1922 has been changed to protect the privacy of these individuals. The INS archival sources are identified in the notes as follows.

Records from the Immigration and Naturalization Service, San Francisco; San Bruno, California

Arrival Investigation Case Files, 1884–1944; Records of the Immigration and Nat-uralization Service, San Francisco District, Record Group 85; National Ar-chives–Pacific Sierra Region. (Abbreviated as AICF; INS, SFD, RG85; NA-PSR.)

Chinese Immigration Case Files, 1903–1915; Records of the Immigration and Naturalization Service, San Francisco District, Record Group 85; National Ar-chives–Pacific Sierra Region. (Abbreviated as CICF; INS, SFD, RG85; NA-PSR.)

General Immigration Case Files, 1944–1955; Records of the Immigration and Naturalization Service, San Francisco District, Record Group 85; National Ar-chives–Pacific Sierra Region. (These records are currently closed to the public without special permission from the National Archives. Abbreviated as GICF; INS, SFD, RG85; NA-PSR.)

Records of the Immigration and Naturalization Service, Unprocessed; San Fran-cisco District, Record Group 85; National Archives–Pacific Sierra Region. (These records had not been formally processed as of April 1997. They are currently closed to the public without special permission from the National Archives. Abbreviated as Unprocessed; INS, SFD, RG85; NA-PSR.)

Records from the Immigration and Naturalization Service, Honolulu District; San Bruno, California

Chinese Applicants for Admission as Wives and/or Children of Naturalized Chi-nese under Hawaiian Kingdom, 1919–1925; Records of the Immigration and Naturalization Service, Honolulu District Office, Record Group 85; National Archives–Pacific Sierra Region. (Abbreviated as Chinese Wives and/or Children of Naturalized Chinese under HK; INS, HDO, RG85; NA-PSR.)

Case Files of Chinese Applicants for Admission as Wives of Merchants, Teachers, and Ministers, 1916–1939; Records of the Immigration and Naturalization Ser-

vice, Honolulu District Office, Record Group 85; National Archives–Pacific
Sierra Region. (Abbreviated as Chinese Wives of Merchants; INS, HDO, RG85;
NA-PSR.)
Case Files of Chinese Applicants for Admission as Wives of Native-Born American
Citizens, 1916–1939; Records of the Immigration and Naturalization Service,
Honolulu District Office, Record Group 85; National Archives–Pacific Sierra
Region. (Abbreviated as Chinese Wives of Native-Born American Citizens; INS,
HDO, RG85; NA-PSR.)
Case Files of Chinese Applicants for Form 430—American Citizens of Chinese
Race for Preinvestigation of Status, and Chinese Applicants for Admission as
United States Citizens; Records of the Immigration and Naturalization Service,
Honolulu District Office, Record Group 85; National Archives–Pacific Sierra
Region. (Abbreviated as Chinese Applicants for Form 430; INS, HDO, RG85;
NA-PSR.)
Case Files of United States Citizens of Chinese Race Applying for Certificates of
Citizenship—Hawaiian Islands, Departing to the Continental United States or
Foreign Destinations, 1924–1942; Records of the Immigration and Naturaliza-
tion Service, Honolulu District Office, Record Group 85; National Archives–
Pacific Sierra Region. (Abbreviated as U.S. Citizens of Chinese Race Applying
for Certificates of Citizenship; INS, HDO, RG85; NA-PSR.)

Records from the Immigration and Naturalization Service, Washington, D.C.

Records of the Central Office: Subject Correspondence, 1906–1932, entry 9;
Records of the Immigration and Naturalization Service, Washington, D.C.,
Record Group 85; National Archives, Washington, D.C. (Abbreviated as RCO;
INS, DC, RG85; NA, DC.)
Records of the Central Office: Administrative Files Relating to Naturalization,
1906–1940, entry 26; Records of the Immigration and Naturalization Service,
Washington, D.C., Record Group 85; National Archives, Washington, D.C.
(Abbreviated as RCO: Naturalization; INS, DC, RG85; NA, DC.)
Department of Justice, Administrative—Immigration and Naturalization Service,
Records Administration and Information Branch; Unprocessed; Records of the
Immigration and Naturalization Service, Washington, D.C., Record Group 85;
National Archives, Washington, D.C. (These records had not been formally
processed as of April 1997. They are currently closed to the public without
special permission from the National Archives. Abbreviated as DJA-INS; INS,
DC, RG85; NA, DC.)

*My research also includes thirty-three casefiles from the YWCA International In-
stitutes of women immigrants and citizens seeking assistance, most in the years
between 1920 and 1960. These files are identified in the notes as follows.*

**Records from the Immigration History Research Center,
Minneapolis, Minnesota**

International Institutes of Buffalo; Immigration and Refugee Services of America;
Immigration History Research Center, University of Minnesota, Minneapolis,

Minnesota. (These records are closed without special permission from the Directors of the Buffalo International Institute. Abbreviated as International Institutes of Buffalo.)

International Institutes of Toledo; Immigration and Refugee Services of America; Immigration History Research Center, University of Minnesota, Minneapolis, Minnesota. (These records are closed without special permission from the Directors of the Toledo International Institute. Abbreviated as International Institutes of Toledo.)

International Institutes of St. Louis; Immigration and Refugee Services of America; Immigration History Research Center, University of Minnesota, Minneapolis, Minnesota. (These records are closed without special permission from the Directors of the St. Louis International Institute. Abbreviated as International Institutes of St. Louis.)

International Institutes of Minnesota; Immigration and Refugee Services of America; Immigration History Research Center, University of Minnesota, Minneapolis, Minnesota. (These records are closed without special permission from the Directors of the Minnesota International Institute. Abbreviated as International Institutes of Minnesota.)

International Institutes of Boston; Immigration and Refugee Services of America; Immigration History Research Center, Minneapolis, Minnesota. (These records are closed without special permission from the Directors of the Boston International Institute. Abbreviated as International Institutes of Boston.)

In addition, I made use of ninety-nine oral histories collected by the Statue of Liberty—Ellis Island Foundation of women immigrants who arrived in Ellis Island during the first half of the twentieth century. These oral histories are identified in the notes as follows.

Voices from Ellis Island: an Oral History of American Immigration: a project of the Statute of Liberty–Ellis Island Foundation: University Publications of America, 1985. (Abbreviated as *Voices from Ellis Island*.)

Microfilmed records of the Immigration and Naturalization Service and American Council for Nationalities Service are referenced as follows.

Records of the Immigration and Naturalization Service, Series A: Subject Correspondence Files, Part 2: Mexican Immigration, 1906–1930, ed. Rudolph Vecoli; Research Collections in American Immigration, ed. Rudolph Vecoli; Frederick, Maryland: University Publications of America, 1992. (Abbreviated as RINS, SCF, MI.)

Records of the Immigration and Naturalization Service, Series A: Subject Correspondence Files, Part 3: Ellis Island, 1900–1933, ed. Rudolph Vecoli; Research Collections in American Immigration, ed. Rudolph Vecoli; Frederick, Maryland: University Publications of America, 1992. (Abbreviated as RINS, SCF, EI.)

Records of the Immigration and Naturalization Service, Series A: Subject Corre-spondence Files, Part 5: Prostitution and "White Slavery," 1902–1933, ed. Ru-dolph Vecoli; Research Collections in American Immigration, ed. Rudolph Ve-coli; Frederick, Maryland: University Publications of America, 1992. (Abbrevi-ated as RINS, SCF, PWS.)

Interpreter Releases; Records of the American Council for Nationalities Service; Immigration History Research Center, University of Minnesota, Twin Cities; Research Collections in American Immigration, ed. Rudolph Vecoli; Frederick, Maryland: University Publications of America, 1989. (Abbreviated as RACNS.)

Finally, my research includes 222 cases adjudicated before the federal district and appeals courts, twenty-eight cases heard before the Supreme Court, and twenty-nine cases decided by the Board of Immigration Appeals. Complete citations ap-pear in the notes.

∞ Acknowledgments ∞

I have many to thank.

I owe a great debt and a hearty thanks to the archivists who allowed me to rummage through the records of countless immigrant women: Marian Smith at the Immigration and Naturalization Service, Waverly Lowell and Neil Thomsen at the National Archives in San Bruno, California, Robert Ellis at the National Archives in Washington, D.C., and Joel Wurl at the Immigration History Research Center at the University of Minnesota. I would also like to thank the current boards of directors of the Immigration and Refugee Services of America in Minnesota, Connecticut, Buffalo, New Jersey, and Toledo for allowing me to use to their records.

Grants from the Mellon Foundation and the Stanford University History department, along with a fellowship from the Institute for Research on Women and Gender, helped to defer some of the costs of travel. Sara Evans kindly offered me a place to stay in St. Paul. Julie Gardner gave me a home away from home in Washington, D.C.

Fellowships from the School of Humanities and Social Sciences at Stanford University, the Center for Comparative Studies in Race and Ethnicity at Stanford University, and the Ford Foundation Workshop on Inequalities and Identities at Stanford University offered me the opportunity to devote two years to research and writing. Additional funding from the DePaul University summer research program and the DePaul University Humanities Center Critical Race Theory Faculty Seminar supported by a Humanities Focus Grant from the National Endowment for the Humanities allowed me time to rethink and revise. Members of the Workshop on Inequalities and Identities at Stanford University and the Critical Race Theory Faculty Seminar at DePaul University contributed greatly to my thinking about the intersections between race, class, gender, and law.

To those who read, and read again, and listened, and listened again, my thanks. Your engaged discussion, insightful criticism, moral support, and general good humor sustained me. In particular, I would like to thank Estelle Freedman and Peggy Pascoe, who were generous with their time, with their creative energies, and with their friendship. Also my thanks to Leslie Berlin, Al Camarillo, Roberta Chávez, Jennifer Gee, Gina Marie Pitti, Emily Osborn, and Richard Roberts. Brigitta van Rheinberg, Alison Kalett, and Jennifer Slater ushered the book through the rigors of publication while tending to the anxieties of a first-time author. My colleagues in the DePaul University History Department never let me forget that great teachers make great historians. Lilia Martinez and Jill Rodriquez helped me find time to write and think.

For my family, who respected my passion for history but never allowed me to take myself too seriously: my parents, Jim and Kay Mabie, and my comrades, Anne, Brent, Sarah, David, Dave, and Amanda. They are my first, best, and toughest audience.

Thank you, Joby. You believed from the beginning, insisting in all my moments of doubt that there was a story worth telling. Finally, for Zoe, who arrived at the beginning, Senna, who came in the middle, and Mason, who made it just in time for the end.

Breinigsville, PA USA
10 February 2010
232292BV00003B/24/P